Knowledge Management for Process, Organizational and Marketing Innovation:

Tools and Methods

Emma O'Brien
University of Limerick, Ireland

Seamus Clifford
University of Limerick, Ireland

Mark Southern
University of Limerick, Ireland

A volume in the Advances in Knowledge
Acquisition, Transfer, and Management
(AKATM) Book Series

Director of Editorial Content:	Kristin Klinger
Director of Book Publications:	Julia Mosemann
Acquisitions Editor:	Lindsay Johnston
Development Editor:	Christine Bufton
Publishing Assistant:	Milan Vracharich, Jr.
Typesetter:	Michael Brehm
Production Editor:	Jamie Snavely
Cover Design:	Lisa Tosheff

Published in the United States of America by
Information Science Reference (an imprint of IGI Global)
701 E. Chocolate Avenue
Hershey PA 17033
Tel: 717-533-8845
Fax: 717-533-8661
E-mail: cust@igi-global.com
Web site: http://www.igi-global.com

Library of Congress Cataloging-in-Publication Data

Knowledge management for process, organizational and marketing innovation : tools and methods / Emma O'Brien, Seamus Clifford and Mark Southern, editors.
    p. cm.
  Includes bibliographical references and index.
  Summary: "This book outlines different tools and technologies that can be applied depending on the type of innovation an organization desires, providing concrete advice on the different types of innovation, situations in which innovation may be useful and the role of knowledge and different tools and technologies to support it"--Provided by publisher.
  ISBN 978-1-61520-829-6 (hbk.) -- ISBN 978-1-61520-830-2 (ebook) 1. Knowledge management. 2. Diffusion of innovations. 3. New products. I. O'Brien, Emma. II. Clifford, Seamus. III. Southern, Mark, 1967-
  HD30.2.K636886 2010
  658.4'038--dc22
                                          2010024437

This book is published in the IGI Global book series Advances in Knowledge Acquisition, Transfer, and Management (AKATM) Book Series (ISSN: 2326-7607; eISSN: 2326-7615)

British Cataloguing in Publication Data
A Cataloguing in Publication record for this book is available from the British Library.

All work contributed to this book is new, previously-unpublished material. The views expressed in this book are those of the authors, but not necessarily of the publisher.

Advances in Knowledge Acquisition, Transfer, and Management (AKATM) Book Series

Murray E. Jennex
San Diego State University, USA

ISSN: 2326-7607
EISSN: 2326-7615

MISSION

Organizations and businesses continue to utilize knowledge management practices in order to streamline processes and procedures. The emergence of web technologies has provided new methods of information usage and knowledge sharing. The **Advances in Knowledge Acquisition, Transfer, and Management (AKATM) Book Series** brings together research on emerging technologies and its effect on information systems and knowledge society.AKATM will provide researchers, students, practitioners, and industry leaders with highlights on the knowledge management discipline, including technology support issues and knowledge representation.

COVERAGE

- Cognitive Theories
- Cultural Impacts
- Information and Communication Systems
- Knowledge Acquisition and Transfer Processes
- Knowledge Management Strategy
- Knowledge Sharing
- Organizational Learning
- Organizational Memory
- Small and Medium Enterprises
- Virtual Communities

IGI Global is currently accepting manuscripts for publication within this series. To submit a proposal for a volume in this series, please contact our Acquisition Editors at Acquisitions@igi-global.com or visit: http://www.igi-global.com/publish/.

Titles in this Series

For a list of additional titles in this series, please visit: www.igi-global.com

Ontology-Based Applications for Enterprise Systems and Knowledge Management
Mohammad Nazir Ahmad (Universiti Teknologi Malaysia, Malaysia) Robert M. Colomb (University of Queensland, Australia) and Mohd Syazwan Abdullah (Universiti Utara Malaysia, Malaysia)
Information Science Reference • copyright 2013 • 423pp • H/C (ISBN: 9781466619937) • US $175.00 (our price)

Knowledge Management and Drivers of Innovation in Services Industries
Patricia Ordóñez de Pablos (Universidad de Oviedo, Spain) and Miltiadis D. Lytras (The American College of Greece, Greece)
Information Science Reference • copyright 2012 • 349pp • H/C (ISBN: 9781466609488) • US $175.00 (our price)

Customer-Centric Knowledge Management Concepts and Applications
Minwir Al-Shammari (University of Bahrain, Bahrain)
Information Science Reference • copyright 2012 • 315pp • H/C (ISBN: 9781613500897) • US $175.00 (our price)

Knowledge Management for Process, Organizational and Marketing Innovation Tools and Methods
Emma O'Brien (University of Limerick, Ireland) Seamus Clifford (University of Limerick, Ireland) and Mark Southern (University of Limerick, Ireland)
Information Science Reference • copyright 2011 • 308pp • H/C (ISBN: 9781615208296) • US $180.00 (our price)

Strategies for Knowledge Management Success Exploring Organizational Efficacy
Murray E. Jennex (San Diego State University, USA) and Stefan Smolnik (International University Schloss Reichartshausen, Germany)
Information Science Reference • copyright 2011 • 350pp • H/C (ISBN: 9781605667096) • US $180.00 (our price)

Intellectual Capital and Technological Innovation Knowledge-Based Theory and Practice
Pedro López Sáez (Universidad Complutense de Madrid, Spain) Gregorio Martín de Castro (Universidad Complutense de Madrid, Spain) José Emilio Navas López (Universidad Complutense de Madrid, Spain) and Miriam Delgado Verde (Universidad Complutense de Madrid, Spain)
Information Science Reference • copyright 2010 • 398pp • H/C (ISBN: 9781615208753) • US $180.00 (our price)

Cultural Implications of Knowledge Sharing, Management and Transfer Identifying Competitive Advantage
Deogratias Harorimana (Southampton Solent University, UK)
Information Science Reference • copyright 2010 • 464pp • H/C (ISBN: 9781605667904) • US $180.00 (our price)

www.igi-global.com

701 E. Chocolate Ave., Hershey, PA 17033
Order online at www.igi-global.com or call 717-533-8845 x100
To place a standing order for titles released in this series, contact: cust@igi-global.com
Mon-Fri 8:00 am - 5:00 pm (est) or fax 24 hours a day 717-533-8661

Editorial Advisory Board

Table of Contents

Section 1
Organisational Innovation

Section 2
Knowledge Management in NPD

Section 3
Process Innovation

Section 4
Marketing Innovation

Section 5
Maximising Intellectual Assets

Detailed Table of Contents

Section 1
Organisational Innovation

Chapter 1

    Ileana Hamburg, Institut Arbeit und Technik, FH Gelsenkirchen, Germany
    Timothy Hall, University of Limerick, Ireland

Nowadays many European small and medium-sized companies (SMEs) are not ready for significant required international social and economic changes. Some of them have focused on approaches of knowledge management (KM) as an enabler for their innovation capability, but these have failed. One of the most critical but important aspect to be considered when developing Knowledge Management Strategies in companies to support Process, Organizational and/or Marketing Innovation is an evaluation of KM readiness. The next step after conducting KM readiness assessment is to use the results of the KM readiness for the development of KM approaches supporting the innovation. This chapter puts forward a method of determining the readiness of SMEs for KM, discusses how to improve links between KM practices and innovation and gives examples of methods like the Innovation Biographies (IB). Finally, the authors present knowledge intensive Communities of Practice (CoPs) supported through Web 2.0 as suitable environments to foster innovation within SMEs.

Chapter 2

    Rivadávia Correa Drummond de Alvarenga Neto, Fundação Dom Cabral, Brazil
    Renato Rocha Souza, Fundação Getúlio Vargas, Brazil

The management of knowledge is a multifaceted organizational process that involves three parts. They are (i) a strategy, (ii) the creation of an organizational environment or space for knowledge - known as the "enabling context" or "Ba" and (iii) an operational/action toolbox consisting of IT tools and managerial practices to effectively put the strategy into action. The main objective of this chapter is to propose a conceptual integrative map for Knowledge Management that was built as the result of a longitudinal programme of research on knowledge management, conducted between the years of 2001 and 2009. As an outcome of this research, knowledge management concepts, motivation, practices, results and implementation processes will be highlighted. The qualitative research strategy used was the study of multiple cases with incorporated units of analysis and three criteria were observed for the judgment of the quality of the research project: validity of the construct, external validity and reliability. Multiple sources of evidence were used and data analysis consisted of three flows of activities: data reduction, data displays and conclusion drawing/verification. The results confirmed the presuppositions and the conclusions suggest that organizational knowledge cannot be managed; it is just promoted or stimulated through the creation of a favorable organizational context, namely "Ba".

Chapter 3

Federica Ricceri, University of Padua, Italy
James Guthrie, University of Bologna, Italy
Rodney Coyte, The University of Sydney, Australia

National economies have rapidly moved from their industrial economic base and shifted towards a knowledge base, in which wealth creation is associated with the ability to develop and manage knowledge resources (KR) (see, among others, MERITUM, 2002; EC, 2006). Several national and international institutions have produced various Intellectual Capital (IC) frameworks and guidelines (e.g. MERITUM, 2002; SKE, 2007; EC, 2006) to guide in the management, measurement and reporting of IC. However, there appear to be few studies of private company practices (Guthrie & Ricceri, 2009). The above informed the following two research questions of this study: (1) In what ways, did the private companies express their strategy and the role of KR within it? (2) What tools, including 'inscription devices', were used for understanding and managing KR within a specific organisation? This chapter answers these questions by providing illustrations of KR and their management in practice in a variety of private companies.

Chapter 4

Steve Russell, Siemens Corporate Research, USA

Project management can be improved using modern interfaces that more naturally show work situations. Employees have deep real world knowledge that can be exploited, and a sense of common purpose among team members that can be enhanced. But, project efforts are currently guided only with structured charts and diagrams that show participants the state of their team's work activities. These charting tools have become more colorful and visually clear over time to reduce any uncertainty regarding task assignments, interdependencies, and any important schedule delays. However, a three dimensional environment extends the range of vision dramatically. Any team member can see what is currently being developed, the status of the process, and any pertinent actions needing focus, all in persistent and prominent wall displays. Discussions among remote collaborators are facilitated, focused on common views of pressing circumstances. Knowledge retention and transfer is more robust, and is illustrated in more compelling contexts keyed to current work activities. The immediacy of three dimensional world immersion will allow even forgetful workers to see at a glance the state of their contribution as well as the completion progress of those upon whom they depend.

When analysing the transformation of the information society an industrialisation of knowledge work can be observed. The maturity, the quality, the process-orientation and the alignment of knowledge to personal or organisational requirements are industrialisation aspects covered by knowledge work. This chapter focuses on process-orientation, discusses the evolution of process-oriented knowledge management and sees the current industrialisation of knowledge work as a challenge that needs to be tackled not only on social and technical level but also on a conceptual level. Hence the so-called knowledge conveyer belt approach is introduced that is a realisation framework of process-oriented and service based knowledge management. This approach is seen as an answer for the requirements of industrialisation of knowledge work that keeps the "human in the loop" and enables the business and knowledge alignment. The realisation concepts and two implementation show cases are introduced.

In today's changing environment, the competitiveness and sustainability of a modern organisation, be they global large scale enterprises (LSE's) or local small to medium scale enterprises (SME's), depends on its ability to innovate. Innovation can be viewed as the combined activity of generating creative ideas and the subsequent successful exploitation of these concepts for benefit. Access to relevant and up to date information provides a critical competitive edge for organisations innovation efforts. Given that social relationships are key to enhancing the ability to gather knowledge and that creation of knowledge is primarily a social process among individuals, organisations' need to optimise the supporting mechanisms by which its people and processes accumulate, structure, and transfer knowledge effectively. Mechanisms such as social networks promote both organisational and collective learning and participation in these social networks are a significant source of knowledge, which subsequently leads to innovation. Consequently, this chapter will outline the innovation process with its knowledge management phases and extrapolate the role of social networks in this process. It will then outline the steps of the social network analysis tool and illustrate how it can be used to enhance knowledge management for innovation efforts.

Chapter 7

Besides being a basic way to understand the world and an appropriate behavior to survival and development of organizations, the knowledge – acquisition, updating, and use – must be managed to increase creativity, and should be taken as a force to drive the human being in the field of competitive innovation. In this chapter the potential contribution of knowledge workers is discussed. Considering an assets approach, these reflections may enable the organization to promote and use the creativity of their knowledge workers, which are seen as a specific set of assets in the organization. This specificity should be considered in the policies of human resources management and also in the formulation of competitive strategies. Some suggestions are made for improving the utilization of knowledge workers to increase the level of productive creativity.

Section 2
Knowledge Management in NPD

Chapter 8

The main purpose of this chapter is to conduct a theoretical analysis of how product innovation is influenced by the process of knowledge management, and to show that it is necessary to complete the entire process in order to develop incremental as well as radical innovations. Other studies have associated different knowledge development processes with different types of product innovation by specifically linking radical innovation with exploration processes, and incremental innovation with exploitation processes. The author of this chapter differ from this point of view, since they consider both processes as being necessary to the development of the two kinds of innovations.

Chapter 9

The aim of this chapter is to investigate if and to what extend the process of New Product Development, today, is based on Knowledge Creation and Technology Education. The value chain and the way it allows the company to achieve and sustain competitive advantage is used, in this chapter, in a way that facilitates the exploration of the relationship between technology and competitive advantage. This is done under the competence-based perspective of the organization, where knowledge is the point of departure and the individual – in this case the industrial employee– the relevant unit of analysis. With knowledge and knowledge creation being the reference point, their influence on new products and on the product life cycle has been investigated. The significance of the technology education background of each individual has also been examined in an effort to determine whether there is a need to strengthen

Technology Education in existing national curricula. Surveys collected from 486 employees, of 51 industrial companies in Spain, were analyzed in order to test the authors' hypothesis. The results of this study support their main hypothesis and allow them to draw conclusions on the significance of the relationship under investigation.

Section 3
Process Innovation

Chapter 10

Daniela Butan, University of Limerick, Ireland
Emma O'Brien, University of Limerick, Ireland
Mark Southern, University of Limerick, Ireland
Seamus Clifford, University of Limerick, Ireland

This chapter presents a novel Knowledge Management model - VDF (Variation Mode and Effect Analysis & Design of Experiments & Finite Element Analysis) for process innovation and efficient problem solving in enterprises.

Section 4
Marketing Innovation

Chapter 11

Saïda Habhab-Rave, ISTEC, France

Global economy is transforming the sources of the competitive advantages of firms, especially for firms embedded in local manufacturing systems. Based on the theoretical contributions to knowledge management and industrial districts, this chapter describes alternatives firm's strategies and upgrading options by exploring the relationships among innovation, marketing and network technologies. Starting from the analysis of the global competitiveness report and the European Innovation Scoreboard, this chapter focuses on the case of firms specializing in "furniture and textile" industries (fashion, mode, home products) to outline a framework explaining the new competitive opportunities for SMEs. Through a qualitative analysis, this chapter presents two case studies of French firms that promote successful strategies based on a coherent mix of R&D based innovation, experienced marketing and design, by leveraging on ICT.

Chapter 12

Steve Russell, Siemens Corporate Research, USA
Candemir Toklu, Siemens Corporate Research, USA

Personal profiles of the top managers in a corporation help marketers to position and promote large software products. Sales calls are more targeted and cordial, aligned with the needs and communication styles of the prospects. The methods applied in the archetype discovery are complemented by knowledge of corporate structures and influence networks. When the key customer concerns and constraints are clarified, the software vendor can craft informational programs, sales plans, and product improvement projects to outperform their competition. The added persona-model knowledge complements the vendor's existing knowledge of their software products, helping to build compelling marketing programs and to significantly improve software sales.

This chapter contributes to organizational innovation theory and provides a practical approach to promote companies and create relationships with their customers. This research study investigates the primary visual attention of customers in online flight booking and uses interviews, think-aloud protocols, and eye-tracking tools to collect data. Findings show that the visual structure of the webpage strongly influences the overall effectiveness of the booking process and that participants ignore peripheral information when it does not appear relevant or associated with the main task. It is also found that the effective segmentation of different elements of the webpage helps direct attention and guides participants to the relevant section. Implications from these findings are discussed, and a general framework to help practitioners to manage knowledge collected from their customers is presented.

Section 5
Maximising Intellectual Assets

The objective of this chapter is to develop a framework that depicts the antecedents of intellectual capital in an organization. In gist, the framework specifies three dimensions of intellectual capital, namely, human capital, structural capital and customer capital. Organizational conditions such as opportunities, values, motivation and capability influence human capital; Organizational conditions such as the infrastructure, existing knowledge and the knowledge sharing process influence structural capital; Organizational conditions such as products and services, relationships and brand value influence customer capital; and organizational conditions such as culture and leadership influence all three dimensions of intellectual capital. In addition, individual dimension of intellectual capital mutually influences each other, and in sum, leads to positive organizational outcomes such as branding, reputation, competitiveness and sustainability.

Chapter 15

Maria do Rosário Cabrita, Universidade Nova de Lisboa, Portugal
Virgílio Cruz Machado, Universidade Nova de Lisboa, Portugal
António Grilo, Universidade Nova de Lisboa, Portugal

With the rise of the "new economy", knowledge became a most valuable resource. Accepting knowledge as a resource suggests that knowledge can be acquired, transferred, combined and used, and it may be a potential source of sustainable competitive advantage. In this context, knowing how an organization creates value, based on its potential of knowledge, became a central question in management research. Under a strategic perspective, knowledge that creates value is defined as intellectual capital, the application of which will give organisations sustainable competitive advantage. Therefore, identifying, measuring and managing intellectual capital is crucial for corporate innovation and competitiveness. The purpose of this study is to examine the interrelationships and the effects of interaction between intellectual capital components and organisational performance, and defines how knowledge creates value. The study is developed in the context of Portuguese banks, an industry where differentiation of products and services almost exclusively hinges on the continuous rejuvenation of the underlying knowledge base. Empirical findings from this study support the propositions that intellectual capital is a key driver of organisational performance and that a knowledge-based perspective holds a more holistic model of organisations' value creation.

Foreword

ON KNOWLEDGE MANAGEMENT

As Robert Cole in his California Management Review article claims, "Knowledge, particularly as manifested in the creation of new products and services, has become the primary source of wealth creation and sustainable competitive advantage."[1] Knowledge represents a key to companies' ability to succeed at innovation because it is through knowledge that companies learn from mistakes, improve product development performance, augment marketing prowess, and achieve eventual success. This highlights the important relationship between innovation and knowledge management – the topic of the present book.

A basic understanding of knowledge management begins with distinguishing the elements called data, information, and knowledge. Data are defined as a collection of facts such as raw numbers corresponding to sales, invoices, returns. When unanalyzed, even if downloaded from the company computer system, sales numbers residing in a spreadsheet are just data. Information exists when data are organized, summarized, analyzed and evaluated to create an understanding of a focal question or phenomenon. Graphing the sales data in a spreadsheet to conduct a trend analysis would provide information about company performance. Knowledge is the combination of information with experience, context, and reflections to derive implications, tactics, and strategies on which to base decisions. Building on the trend analysis example, knowledge is created when inferences and implications are drawn from the results of the trend analysis helping to form an action plan based on intuition and experience. In sum, data can be systematically summarized and analyzed to become information; information can be evaluated, synthesized, and laden with intuition and experiences to bring about knowledge for guiding future endeavors.

Simply recognizing the distinction between data, information, and knowledge does not mean that a company has a knowledge management process in place. Nor does collecting data imply that information is generated in a real-time fashion or that the presence of information denotes knowledge as being generated. It also cannot be assumed that data leads to information, and that information leads to knowledge in every circumstance. In other words, recognizing and generating data, information, and knowledge does not complete the knowledge management process. The exchange of data, information, and/or knowledge between individuals and departments is crucial, which evidences the need for tools and methods to manifest knowledge management. This book's focus on tools and methods is therefore on target, with the presentation of case studies enlightening the contexts for knowledge management application.

Construing facts, insights, experiences, and lessons learned from previous innovation activities all comprise the knowledge management process, which corresponds to organizational learning and the company's ability to develop new products and services. Unfortunately, literature tends to equate data, information, and knowledge, with studies predominantly using meetings and documented information exchange as a metric of the knowledge process. Simply exchanging information by way of meetings and documented information exchange does not lead to better knowledge or resulting actions. And too much data and/or information can diminish the effectiveness of a company's ability to respond. The existence of data and information thus does not ensure that an organization is increasing its knowledge. Data and information are necessary but not sufficient condition for enhanced innovation performance or customer responsiveness[2].

Another critical consideration is to distinguish between methods of delivering data, information and/ or knowledge, which provide the infrastructure for knowledge management during product development. These are called "exchange networks" and serve the purpose to exchange data, information, and/ or knowledge. "Networks" mean different things to different organizations and in different streams of research. To some, networks are networks of people or social networks, where the exchanging of knowledge occurs through relationships developed among the participants. To others, networks are networks of computers, storing information and knowledge and making it broadly available to everyone in the firm on-line. This distinction has repercussions for how fast and how broadly intelligence is disseminated; for what kinds of intelligence are disseminated, and for how they are used. The explosion of computing capabilities allows for instant access to a wealth of data, information, and knowledge and has improved the ability for everyone within a firm to access all that has been documented. Consequently, there is a major effort going on in and among firms to improve the on-line collection, dissemination, and use of the firm's data, information, and knowledge. The potential, if not reality in many cases, is for this vehicle to largely replace face-to-face communication. Both relationship-based networks (social media) and computer-based networks are important, and must be managed to optimize the firm's knowledge. The present book addresses the issues of networks by discussing social networks, change management, and case examples reflecting these aspects.

Knowledge is indeed intellectual capital for the company. As stated by a Hewlett-Packard executive, "If HP knew what HP knows, then we would be three times as profitable"[3]. The last section of the book focuses on this issue, linking knowledge and value. Together the chapters of this book lead the reader from organizational readiness to understanding the nature of knowledge management to creating innovations though knowledge management, and evaluating the intellectual capital manifested by knowledge management. Product and marketing innovation remains a top priority for all companies and because of the strong link between knowledge management and innovation, this book is contemporary and timely.

Kenneth B. Kahn, Ph.D.
Director, da Vinci Center for Innovation
Virginia Commonwealth University, USA

ENDNOTES

[1]   Cole, Robert E. (1998), "Introduction," California Management Review, Spring, 40, 3, 15-21.
[2]   Kahn, Kenneth B. (1996), "Interdepartmental Integration: A Definition with Implications for Product Development Performance," Journal of Product Innovation Management, 13, 2, 137-151; Maltz, Elliot (2000), "Is All Communication Created Equal?: An Investigation into the Effects of

Communication Mode on Perceived Information Quality," Journal of Product Innovation Management, 17, 2, 110-127.

[3] Coats, Joseph F. (1999), "The Inevitability of Knowledge Management," Research and Technology Management, 42, 4 (July), 6-7.

Kenneth B. Kahn, *PhD is a Professor of Marketing and Director of the daVinci Center for Innovation at Virginia Commonwealth University in Richmond, Virginia. His teaching and research interests address product development, product management, and demand forecasting of current and new products. He has published in a variety of journals, including the Journal of Product Innovation Management, Journal of Business Research, Journal of Forecasting, Journal of Business Forecasting, Marketing Management, and R&D Management. He also has authored the books Product Planning Essentials (Sage Publications, 2000; 2nd Edition by ME Sharpe, 2011) and New Product Forecasting: An Applied Approach (M.E. Sharpe, 2006), and served as editor of the PDMA Handbook on New Product Development, 2nd Edition (Wiley & Sons, 2004). Prior to joining the faculty of VCU, Dr. Kahn was a professor in the College of Technology and the Avrum and Joyce Gray Director of the Burton D. Morgan Center for Entrepreneurship at Purdue University in West Lafayette, Indiana. His university experience also includes co-founding Director of the University of Tennessee's Sales Forecasting Management Forum, Director of Georgia Tech's Marketing Analysis Laboratory, and co-founder of Georgia Tech's Collaborative Product Development Laboratory – each of these initiatives keenly emphasized company collaborations to augment the education and research experience for students and faculty. Dr. Kahn's industrial experience includes serving as an industrial engineer and project engineer for the Weyerhaeuser Company and a manufacturing engineer for Respironics, Inc. He has consulted and conducted training sessions with numerous companies, including Accenture, Acco Brands, Coca-Cola, ConAgra, Enfasis, Harley-Davidson, Honeywell, John Deere, Lego, McNeil Nutritionals, Procter & Gamble, and the SAS Institute.*

Preface

The idea for this book first came into mind when working with organizations regarding problems with their products, processes and general enterprise issues. It was found that many companies particularly SMEs operate in a chaotic, disorganized manner and that when problems arose they simply did enough to plug a hole in it to temporarily fix the problem rather than solving the issue permanently. The reason being was that companies did not invest the time into creating and amalgamating the knowledge to innovate at an organizational, process or marketing level to develop a sustainable solution to the problem that was often symptomatic of other problems in the organization. Furthermore people issues such as inertia to change, cultural issues and historical knowledge developed by senior management were experienced by the editors. There is a lack of structured tools and technologies available to companies to assist them to develop sufficient knowledge to reinvent themselves in order to address problems within the organization resulting in a competitive sustainable enterprise. The ability of a firm to continuously reinvent and innovate is key to survival in today's economic climate.

The book focuses on the practical use of knowledge management as a tool for innovation. It determines the role of knowledge management to facilitate innovation in adding value to the organization. It focuses on the tools and technologies surrounding different types of innovation and how they can be used to maximize knowledge in order to encourage such outside thinking resulting in innovation. It discusses and identifies tools and technologies to foster product, process and marketing innovation in terms of their ability to add value to the organization. Furthermore it examines the role of organizational innovation and the management of intellectual assets in supporting these types of innovation and identifies practical applications of enabling such to take place.

OVERVIEW OF THE BOOK

It has long been recognised the role of innovation in increasing the competitiveness of a firm. Innovation provides a mechanism for a firm to respond to changes quickly and thus improve its lifecycle.

Innovation involves the utilisation of new knowledge or a new use or combination of existing knowledge. New knowledge may either be generated by the innovating firm in the course of its innovation activities (i.e. through intramural R&D) or acquired externally through various channels (e.g. purchase of new technology). The use of new knowledge or the combination of existing knowledge requires innovative efforts that can be distinguished from standardised routines (OECD, 2005).

Innovation is reliant on the use and reuse of existing knowledge to create new knowledge. Knowledge can be created or obtained internally within a firm or externally. Knowledge is viewed as an asset which is key to the organisations sustainability. Maximising the use of such an asset is crucial to the innovation process. The ability to access and develop relevant knowledge quickly affects the firm's capacity to respond to environmental changes and survive in todays fast pace business world. Traditionally innovation was viewed as the development of new products, however this view is changing and innovation is now considered "a new idea, method or device". Thus as well as at the product level innovation can occur at the organisational wide level, at a marketing level regarding the firms ability to maximise its promotion mechanisms and at a process level regarding the reinvention of methods of conducting key business activities.

Because innovation is largely dependant on the application of existing knowledge to create new knowledge it is imperative that it is effectively managed. Despite the importance of knowledge in the innovation process, little research has been conducted into how knowledge management can be applied to make the innovation process more effective.

Knowledge Management for Process, Organizational and Marketing Innovation: Tools and Methods provides a practical guide to those companies and academics involved in the area of innovation and knowledge management. The aim is to provide a book from which individuals can take the information and apply it to their own organizations.

This book outlines to companies different tools and technologies that can be applied depending on the type of innovation they wish to adopt in their organisation. It provides concrete advice on the different types of innovation, situations in which they may be useful, the role of knowledge and different tools, and technologies to support it.

The book is divided into five main sections corresponding to the different types of innovation that can take place and the knowledge needed to maximize success in this area. The aim of these sections is to provide measurable results to companies:

- **Section 1 on Organizational Innovation** is concerned with looking at assessing the firms readiness for knowledge management, knowledge resources and managing knowledge in project management, such chapters will aid companies to achieve increased organizational efficiency and decision making through organizational innovation.
- **Section 2 on Knowledge management in New Product Development** is concerned with the use of knowledge management to encourage NPD resulting **in** self-sustainable and increased innovation activity through product innovation from idea to launch and post launch follow up.
- **Section 3 on Process innovation** looks at the use of a model to maximize the knowledge within the firm to produce process innovations resulting in reduced cost and time to market, improved productivity and quality through process innovation
- **Section 4 on Marketing Innovation** is concerned with acquiring market knowledge and the integration of ICT to enhance marketing innovation resulting in increased market share and companies becoming adaptive to customer requirements through marketing innovation.
- **Section 5 on Maximising Intellectual Assets** is concerned with treating knowledge as an asset and maximizing this asset.

We suggest you use this book chapter by chapter at different stages your organisation might want to adopt different types of innovation. Rather than reading the entire book it is recommended that you read the relevant sections to your situation at the time.

Section 1
Organisational Innovation

Chapter 1
Readiness for Knowledge Management, Methods and Environments for Innovation

Ileana Hamburg
Institut Arbeit und Technik, FH Gelsenkirchen, Germany

Timothy Hall
University of Limerick, Ireland

ABSTRACT

Nowadays many European small and medium-sized companies (SMEs) are not ready for significant required international social and economic changes. Some of them have focused on approaches of knowledge management (KM) as an enabler for their innovation capability, but these have failed. One of the most critical but important aspect to be considered when developing Knowledge Management Strategies in companies to support Process, Organizational and/or Marketing Innovation is an evaluation of KM readiness. The next step after conducting KM readiness assessment is to use the results of the KM readiness for the development of KM approaches supporting the innovation. In this chapter we put forward a method of determining the readiness of SMEs for KM, discuss how to improve links between KM practices and innovation and give examples of methods like the Innovation Biographies (IB). Finally we present knowledge intensive Communities of Practice (CoPs) supported through Web 2.0 as suitable environments to foster innovation within SMEs.

INTRODUCTION

Knowledge is the key for all organisations and the success of many of them depends on the effective deployment and continual enhancement of their knowledge base so as to be innovative and to remain/become competitive (Hamburg & Widmaier, 2004). As great challenges loom

DOI: 10.4018/978-1-61520-829-6.ch001

large for the world economy the need to manage company knowledge becomes more acute.

Small and medium-sized enterprises (SMEs) are socially and economically important, since they represent 99% of all enterprises in the EU, provide around 65 million jobs and contribute to entrepreneurship and innovation. But many European SMEs are not ready for significant international social and economic changes (European Comission, 2003; Amtsblatt, 2003; Attwell et al., 2003;

Averill & Hall, 2005; Beer et al., 2006). Some have focused on knowledge management (KM) and used it as an enabler for innovation capability, but for many the accepted KM approaches, developed for larger organisations, have failed. It can be very difficult for an SME to manage and sustain business whilst engaging in KM and associated training (Doppler & Lauterburg, 1997). Their priority is survival, leading to just-in-time activities; the benefits of KM to the business have to be very clear and measurable (O´Brien et al., 2008). To be effective and acceptable to staff, knowledge management has to be directly related to activities on the job (Dede, 2005).

Results of studies, projects and discussions with SME experts and representatives show that one of the most critical but important aspect to be considered when developing Knowledge Management Strategies in companies to support Process, Organizational and/or Marketing Innovation is an evaluation of KM readiness. Many companies lack understanding of their knowledge needs - of what they want to accomplish with a KM effort (Hamburg et al., 2006).

They do not know if the organization, the management, the culture, the staff and infrastructures are "ready" for this or not. The aim of conducting KM readiness assessment is to measure the readiness of the company for KM implementation/ improvement. If possible, within this evaluation the innovation acceptance/responsiveness of the company should be also checked.

The next step is to use the results of the KM readiness for the development of KM approaches supporting the innovation.

Say (2006) described how researchers try to develop so-called "third generation" KM approaches that will be focused on enabling the sharing of tacit knowledge. Knowledge intensive, practice-oriented and strong interactive co-operations like Communities of Practice (CoPs) fulfil such requirements. This construct (Wenger et al., 2002) has been used in many different fields including company training. More recently CoPs

have been associated with KM and are seen as a way of developing social capital, through sharing existing tacit knowledge by the members (who are the practitioners), so stimulating innovation. CoPs offer new opportunities for KM and learning processes by using new forms of interaction within teams or looser contact networks. They can be considered as innovative tools for a social KM approach. The knowledge that is shared and learned in CoPs is social capital. People connect at different levels and across departments, both internally and externally of the company, without formal constraints. Benefits include problem solving, developing new capabilities, creating knowledge that can be applied for the job, time-saving, leveraging and standardizing practices.

It is assumed that CoPs will be an accepted part of organisational development of the companies.

An intelligent use of information and communication technologies (ICT), particularly Web 2.0 methods and applications, to support KM within SMEs can contribute to the efficiency of such approaches. These technologies are flexible; they support the combination of different forms of learning, collaboration and individualized working. Specifically, they can be used to support the work and interactions within CoPs that are particularly beneficial for SMEs.

In this chapter we put forward a method of determining the readiness of SMEs for KM, discuss how to improve links between KM practices and innovation giving examples. Finally we present knowledge intensive CoPs supported through Web 2.0 as suitable environments to foster innovation within SMEs.

KM READINESS OF SMES

A wide variety of approaches have been proposed in conducting assessments of KM readiness but there is a lack of systematic approach and the practice varies with different industries and companies. Here systematic KM readiness model is

Figure 1. Categories for modelling Knowledge Management Readiness (Source: IAT)

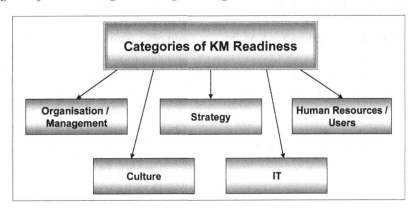

presented. Some proposed categories for the model are Organization, Strategy, Human resources/Users, Culture, IT used (Figure 1).

Research on KM readiness has matured, experience show that a suitable assessment of KM readiness in SMEs (because of their limited resources) can be realized in form of a simple questionnaire survey for managers and other key employees. Analysis, if possible conducted together with a company consultant, KM experts and representatives of the company management, leads to planned strategies for KM.

The following are suitable main and derive questions:

Organisation/Management: Is your enterprise organized to use its existing knowledge effectively, to acquire and create new?

- Is there adequate understanding that KM means much more that implementing an IT tool or solution?
- Is there a well structured knowledge base of the enterprise readily available to staff?
- Are informal and/or knowledge intensive networks like CoPs across different units of the enterprise encouraged?
- Are informal and/or knowledge intensive networks like CoPs across the enterprise encouraged?

- Are partners identified for developing of knowledge intensive networks like CoPs?
- Is the knowledge to be used across different units available in a standard format?
- Are the interaction facilities with the knowledge base and other knowledge sources user friendly and reliable?
- Is the dissemination of best practice supported in your enterprise?
- Is the enterprise connected with external networks and knowledge sources?

Strategy: Has your enterprise a sustainable program for improvement of KM?

- Is there a track record in the enterprise of successful implementation of innovative approaches?
- Has your enterprise a vision how KM can support the company business and work tasks?
- Is there a strategy for doing this over the next 3 years?
- Are the tasks and responsibilities for KM improvement clear?
- Are there some measures for improving KM over the next 3 years?
- Is there a strategy to protect the key information and shared knowledge in the enterprise?

- Is there a complete IT security procedure for information?
- Are key performance indicators for KM in place?
- Is there a regular measurement of the impact KM has on the ways the staff do business and work in the enterprise?

Human resources/Users: Do staff understand the concept of KM and are managers committed to support it?

- Do staffs understand the term KM and how to use existing knowledge for their business and work?
- Is the management of KM within the company someone's responsibility?
- Do senior managers support knowledge sharing (i.e. during meetings)?
- Are the interactions among staff within and across company units favorable for knowledge sharing?
- Is there a senior level systematical review of the effectiveness the staff use KM?
- Are staffs encouraged to contribute new ideas for creating new knowledge?

Culture: Do behaviours and interactions in the company enable effective KM?

- Is the recording and sharing of knowledge routine in the company?
- Is time allowed for creative thinking and reflections?
- Are best practices systematically selected and the corresponding knowledge used whenever staff needs it?
- Is everyone willing to give advice and to help on request to anyone else in the company?
- Are individuals rewarded for team work and knowledge sharing?
- Is there a strong belief that the work is done best only by sharing ideas?

Information technology -IT: Is there suitable IT support for KM in the enterprise and is this used efficiently to support KM?

- Is the available technology suitable for knowledge sharing and is this a main criteria when new IT acquisitions are discussed?
- Does the company IT unit/team check constantly if the existing IT platform for KM supports knowledge needs of the staff?
- Does the existing IT support effective communication across boundaries?
- Is it a normal working practice for staff to interact through IT?

For many small companies the next stage is the planning of the implementation steps for a KM approach. For middle sized companies a more detailed KM implementation strategy is needed.

IMPROVING LINKS BETWEEN KM PRACTICES AND INNOVATION

KM is frequently identified as an important antecedent of innovation but very little research has addressed both: the antecedents and consequences of effective KM in order to positively affect innovation (Grant, 1997). For example, when a company is trying to introduce new processes or products, gaps occur between existing knowledge and knowledge requirements for the innovation. The need to identify, manage and develop intangible assets such intellectual capital is necessary but the SMEs need also adequate directions how this can be achieved. In manufacturing industry for example effective KM can help to quickly find out the best process for producing products. It can help design engineers to generate new designs in shorter period of time, innovative products at lower production costs can be launched faster and this helps SMEs to be more competitive.

There is a significant difference in KM practices and innovation between academia and industry. In the academic context the new is often celebrated, whether it is useful or not. Innovation in industry will often draw on lessons from the past, particularly those that have been forgotten, or those that can be put together in combinations to achieve new results. In practice the "newness" of the knowledge is not important; what is important is that it works and can be immediately applied for the innovation.

The following scheme or framework can assist SMEs in examining existing knowledge as well as knowledge gaps so that they can be bridged when the company wants to introduce an innovation – a knowledge audit for innovation. If the company does not know what knowledge it has and what knowledge is important for the innovation, then it is not only difficult but also risky for the company to implement KM strategies. It is waste of time and other resources to develop tools and policies that the organization cannot use effectively, capital and resources will be expended for no return. The KM strategies for the innovation will fail and innovation is in jeopardy. A design or development brief should define the features and knowledge that are required in the new product or service before the audit takes place.

The concept of a knowledge audit is defined by National Electronic Library for Health (2005). The objectives of a such audit in an innovation context is to know what knowledge is necessary, what knowledge the company already has, what knowledge is missing, who needs this knowledge, how they will acquire it, and how they will use the knowledge to solve the problem. A knowledge inventory can be used to record the knowledge need for product or process design and development. It identifies knowledge resources for the innovation throughout the organisation (Cheung et al., 2005).

The audit for the innovation can be applied after a KM readiness assessment survey has conducted or before (or the two can be integrated) it and is based on knowledge and experience employees already have. People should be selected to par-ticipate in face-to-face interviews to discuss the knowledge they already have, understand the process of design of an innovative product and process cycle and their tasks within the innovation process.

Some recommended discussion topics to elicit explicit knowledge (Group 1) and implicit (Group 2) are listed below.

Group 1:

- What knowledge already exists in the company (types and categories of documents, data bases, intranets, web sites, links, access to external sources, etc)
- Location of the knowledge
- Access of the staff to this knowledge
- Relevance and appropriateness of the knowledge to the innovation
- Quality and reliability of the knowledge
- Who actually uses this knowledge

Group 2:

- Within the company are there existing experts on the innovation topic
- In which departments, project teams, etc do they work
- What are their work tasks now
- What do they know in connection with the innovation
- Do they make decisions
- What and how will they have to learn?
- Are external experts needed, if so, what expertise should they have

An example of a template of a knowledge repository is given in Table 1.

The results of the audit, including knowledge flows, should be analyzed looking at how knowledge moves around the company, where is it from, where is it going to. How staff will find and access the knowledge they need for the innovation, how they share the knowledge they have, how they can create new knowledge. The barriers and

Table 1. Template of knowledge inventory

Issue No.	Innovation Objective	Knowledge Item	Knowledge Source	E(explicit)/ I(implicit)	Document needed (if explicit)

policies in the company, the habits and behaviours that can affect flow, and the use of knowledge for the innovation should be discussed.

The analysis of knowledge flows also allows further identification of gaps in the organisational knowledge and fields for improvement. Examples of KM good practices within company or from other companies that can be used should be highlighted.

In Hall & Pierpaolo (2003) six strategic KM steps are proposed to help bridge gaps:

1. Externalisation, involving taking knowledge from a person and codifying it
2. Communication of explicit knowledge
3. Socialisation involving the communication and possibly enhancement of knowledge
4. Locating and acquiring external (to the group) explicit knowledge
5. Locating and acquiring external (to the group) implicit knowledge
6. Creating new (to the group) knowledge.

For each step actions or solutions should be recommended. Some assessments are needed to evaluate the key capabilities that are used in each recommended action or solution. This includes the technical infrastructure, ICT, content management, accessibility, easy of use and current level of use. In other words this assessment evaluates the "extent" which makes the KM more efficient and helps to connect people with the knowledge and with other people (Hall & Pierpaolo, 2003).

There are specific processes inside and outside of organisations, for example the "division of knowledge" (Brödner et al., 1999; Helmstädter, 2004, 2007; Butzin & Widmaier, 2007), which

are not sufficiently known when an innovation is done. This uncertainty is the starting point for an approach using Innovation Biographies (IB) that can improve the links between KM and innovation. An IB is an instrument of qualitative research that aims to explain the knowledge dynamics in innovation processes over its total life span. An IB allows detailed insights in companies' knowledge mechanisms and into interactions in the network of partners that contributed to an innovation.

Focusing on knowledge sharing the organisational aspect is decisive and shared knowledge needs a common context, a shared framework of its interpretation and qualification. The sources of innovation can be internal or external to the company, or both. Innovations are regarded in company centred approaches as the result of successful combination of internal resources, competences, processes and capabilities (Novikova, 2005). On the other hand, they could be the result of an interactive process with external collaborations and inter-company linkages. The IB approach considers these two points of view as complementary so enabling a comprehension of factors and knowledge processes relevant to a particular innovation in a company. Three aspects are considered: the time/space dimension, the nature of the generated and applied knowledge, and the interactions and networking of partners (Larsson et al., 2006).

Spatial aspects of knowledge and innovation have been often neglected (Oinas & Malecki, 2002). Amin & Cohendet, 2006 suggest that spatial aspects of knowledge creation should be understood as composed of many simultaneous processes. Both local-social community-interactions and trans-local transactions work at the same time to form the conditions at any particular place. IBs consider special aspects, for example in order to better understand of proximity for knowledge flows, the links between tacit knowledge and different aspects of proximity and if and how different spatial scales work simultaneously in the creation and communication of knowledge (Larsson et al., 2006).

Similarly, the time dimension plays an important role in IBs. Oinas & Malecki (2002) underline time and space constraint on innovation by the fact that physical actors can be only at one time at one place and that movement takes place. Innovation/ knowledge is dependent on other knowledge that is not "synchronized" in time. So being at the right place and at the right time could be essential in order to understand current situation from a historical perspective. So Innovation Biographies can be useful to understand the time factor in innovation and knowledge formation.

The starting point of an IB is the selection of a case of innovation in a company, university or research laboratory, i.e. any organisation considered a driver of innovation process. The preparation stage includes an analysis of available documents and a narrative interview with a person with a central role in the innovation development. This person is asked to tell "the story" of innovation from the beginning until the end of its implementation phase. So the time dimension is covered. The focus is also on the knowledge flows and the role of different actors. By extracting from the narration what sources of knowledge from where have been used the spatial dimension is considered. This biographical method with narrative interview enables an interactive exploration of flows inside the organisation (between persons, departments) and outside (external actors and institutions). Though originally developed in anthropology and psychology it has found useful application in the study of other social or economic processes. The "biography" is the "backbone" of the study from which the researcher derives further starting points for interviews on different levels. It is important

Figure 2. The pattern of innovation biographies in relation with their environment (Source: IAT)

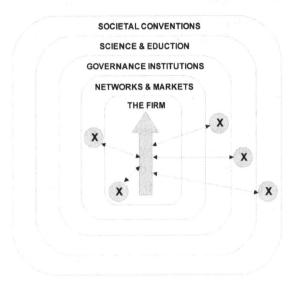

to identify persons, networks or institutions taking part in the KM and innovation process to be interviewed. Figure 2 shows the pattern of innovation biographies in relation with their environment.

Experience shows that the data collected in qualitative research studies does not always undergo systematic analysis, there are procedures to solve this problem (Wengraf, 2001) yet data often remains under analysed. When working with case studies each case is unique with respect to time, space, historical circumstances, actors involved and their interactions with knowledge flows. But it is important to compare and contrast multiple cases, develop topologies and make generalizations. This requires from the beginning defined rules for data analysis and for reporting of findings.

The grounded theory (Kelle & Kluge, 1999) including methodological rules and procedures to develop new insights inductively from a corpus of data can be used within IB. However, the research design should still be open for interpretations that arise from the material and during the interviews.

In the following, an example the research design for IBs conducted within the European project Eurodite (Larsson et al., 2006) is given. Eurodite (www.eurodite.bham.ac.uk) is a current European project that plans to conduct several IBs in European companies including SMEs: it seeks to enhance understanding of the nature and dynamics of the knowledge economy and its impact on the development of different European regions

The first stage of an IB involves case studies of specific company based innovations they can be product, process or organalisational innovation. Within these studies the development of a product/process is followed from the beginning to its successful introduction to the market/organisation (total life span of innovation or its "biography").

In the second stage regional and sector agents and agencies identified during the first stage are interviewed in order to find out in detail their role in the process of knowledge sharing within the innovation. In this way more details about the knowledge flows within regions that may support KM processes within the companies is obtained.

One important aspect for consideration within the project is how to compare and extract generalized extensions using data collected from seven different sectors and over 20 regions across Europe. The final results of Eurodite will not be available until 2010.

COMMUNITIES OF PRACTICE AND FUTURE KM DEVELOPMENTS BY USING WEB 2.0: VISIONS AND CHALLENGES FOR SMES

Some success factors and obstacles to effective KM have been presented, but based on new technological developments such as Web 2.0, methods and tools can be developed for improving KM strategies particularly for SMEs because of the possibilities to connect, in social networks like Communities of Practice (CoPs), and to interact across boundaries.

CoPs are groups of people working together at solving open-ended questions, learning in social and physical contexts about real-world problems and using collaboration and cognitive tools for KM and learning. Some main characteristics of CoPs are the following:

- a shared domain of interest of its members, their commitment to this domain and a shared competence,
- common ideas, joint activities. Members engage in pursuing their interest for the domain and build relationships that enable them to learn from each other,
- common practice, because members of a community are practitioners with different levels of expertise. They develop a shared repertoire of resources e.g. experiences, tools, ways to solve problems, a knowledge base of best practices.

CoPs are becoming the core knowledge strategy for global organisations. As groups of people who come together to share and learn from one another face-to-face and virtually, communities of practice are held together by a common interest in a body of knowledge and are driven by a desire and need to share problems, experiences, insights, templates, tools and best practices. (APQC, 2004).

Wenger et al. (2002) consider the acquisition of knowledge within CoPs as a social process where people can participate in communal learning at different levels. The process by which a newcomer learns from the group is important, a new member can move from peripheral to full participation as they gain experience through participation. Initially the activities of new members may be restricted, for example, to simple gathering of information, they may then become involved with gaining knowledge associated with specific work practices, and finally interpreting this into new activities.

CoPs address not only the acquisition of technical skills for a determined practice but also social and informal aspects of creating and sharing knowledge, and of development of innovative KM approaches. Interesting research on this aspect has been carried out in the field of organisational learning, in attempts to explain how personal knowledge and skills become shared in CoPs and organisations, and how new knowledge is developed. Nonaka & Konno (1998) have described a knowledge development cycle showing how tacit or implicit knowledge can be made explicit in learning processes. This work, and others, point out that knowledge developed in CoPs is important for understanding different types of knowledge and how knowledge develops in different contexts. These distinctions are important when processes of innovation and knowledge development in SMEs are analysed.

There are other beneficial characteristics associated with CoPs, one being time saving. Studies show that company staff spend a third of their time looking for information and they often prefer to turn to a colleague (expert) rather than to look into a book, manual or data base. So time is saved by discussing with members of the CoP who have more practical experience in the corresponding field. Members can discuss and mature new projects or innovations with peers before making formal proposals that can lead more quickly to new capabilities, processes or products. The type of information shared or learned in a CoP is not bounded (Dalkir, 2005).

The structure and design of a CoP is important, shared learning and interests are what keep CoPs together – they exist as long as participation has value to the members. Some principles of "designing for aliveness", which can guide organisations wishing to start CoPs are:

- Design for evolution e.g. design elements should be combined in a way that they may act as catalysts for a natural evolution to a life-long learning oriented CoP,
- Keep an open dialog between inside and outside perspectives of the CoP because

the latter can help community members to see new possibilities and act effectively,
- Consider different levels of participation for the members of the CoP (leadership roles, core active group, occasional participants, etc.),
- Develop public and private community spaces,
- Create a rhythm and rules for the community.

These issues are explored in the Encyclopaedia of Communities of Practice in Information and Knowledge Management (Coakes & Clarke, 2006), which also reveals that CoPs are less helpfully governed by internal, informal and unspoken rules dominated by specialized language development.

Vestal (2003) classifies the main types of communities as following:

- innovation communities that are cross-functional to work out new solutions utilizing existing knowledge,
- helping communities that solve problems,
- best-practice communities that attain, validate and disseminate information,
- knowledge-stewarding communities that collect and organise information and knowledge across the organisation.

Of course, there are CoPs that combine more than one of these functions.

The CoPs can be consider as powerful environments for understanding how innovation, KM, work and learning are interconnected. CoPs are often formed within a determined discipline, or work division, in order to focus the effort in sharing knowledge, solve concrete problems or innovative ventures. But taking into consideration the complex nature of new ICT, the global economical and financial problems and the profile of many enterprises, multidisciplinary participation CoPs can provide advantages. The keys are

Figure 3. Interpretation models for creating an enabling context within a CoP (Source: IAT)

<u>a) within a company</u>

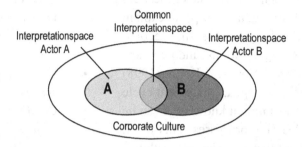

<u>b) cross-companies</u>

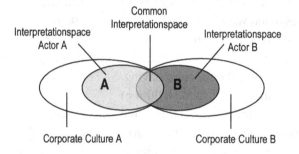

diversity of membership and interests. Such CoPs are nowadays much less common than single disciplinary ones but it is supposed that they will grow in importance in developing new scientific fields in which knowledge from one branch is not sufficient.

ICT support for CoPs should be as transparent as possible, anything that is complex to learn or use will have a negative and possibly a fatal impact. The best environments and tools are those with which the user community is most familiar, either from a work or social environment, and this is sufficient justification for adoption of Web 2.0. There are additional financial and technical advantages, also privacy and security concerns that must be addressed, but the most important consideration is usability.

Internet technologies (Diemers, 2001; Trier, 2007) extend the interactions within communities of practice beyond geographical limitations

and make possible the building of virtual CoPs (VCoP). These communities free their members from constraints of time and space. In comparison with technical solutions for knowledge management, VCoPs can mark a change from "managing knowledge" to "enabling knowledge".

Effective knowledge creation depends on an enabling context. What we mean by enabling context is a shared space that fosters emerging relationships. (Krogh et al., 2003).

Figure 3 shows the building of an enabling context for KM.

The current generation Web 2.0 (O´Reilly, 2005; Kerres 2006), has a vast potential to create prospering environments for emerging CoPs. It can easily support activities within a community, such as the staff of SMEs, to collaborate; content and services can be adapted and made responsive to specific needs and goals of SMEs. These communities are nurtured by the idea of connectivism developed by Siemens (2005) where information is constantly changing, learning takes place in distributed networks of people based on diversity of opinions. For example: writing in public blogs encourages the writer to think about the issues in question. In communities, an individual will receive help from a network of peers, so unnecessary searching activity and time can be saved. Castro (2006) underlines how the virtual environments help feedback mechanisms by reducing costs of communication and by storing and effectively retrieving informal feedback. When considering tacit knowledge, CoP actors interviewed in Germany indicate that for them one of the useful work related technique is by asking for and receiving opinions about their written work or decisions they have made. Thus the use of blogs or the interactive environment that online forums provide are clear means by which tacit knowledge can be shared. So knowledge intensive VCoP would have a positive impact on the sharing of tacit knowledge, i.e. tacit knowledge that is shared spontaneously in an office, about new technologies or about company news finds a natural home in a VCoP.

Often a transition takes place from a face-to-face to a virtual CoP, in order to reach more continuous levels of information sharing.

The lack of face-to-face contact within an ICT mediated CoP can often be an advantage, because it helps to suppress traditional group norm behaviour (Johnson, 2001). On the other hand, it remains open if a community of practice where face-to-face contact is entirely excluded can be sustained over a long period. Despite their great potential, there are also limitations of current technologies in relation to virtual CoPs: since a virtual community infrastructure is not bounded by geography, cultural and language differences can change the interactions and hinder the flux of activities in the CoP.

We applied the above ideas within the activities of the EU project SIMPEL (SME Improving Practice in eLearning) tracking the suitability and our usage of Web 2.0 and utilizing the CoP structure as an intensive KM environment (Beer et al., 2008). We developed strategies to enable SMEs to take full advantage of the eLearning in their training. We involved SMEs and eLearning experts in two communities of practice (one European and one German) (Hamburg et al., 2008) to share learning and knowledge and to develop continuous vocational education strategies based on Web 2.0 leading towards the creation of innovative and dynamic personalized learning environments. The European CoP was a loosely coupled (weakly framed) CoP, the German one strongly framed where the transmission of knowledge occurred closely between its members.

In the European CoP an "optimal vocational training model" based on eLearning in SMEs was developed. Best practice for capturing and sharing of knowledge and for using eLearning were collected and guidelines for using them produced. This CoP, multifunctional, attracted members engaged in support, training, design/development, use, in consulting and in policy formulation concerning eLearning in SMEs in the European Union.

The German CoP focused particularly on analysis and testing of how informal, workplace oriented, learning can be used efficiently in SMEs by working and acting in CoPs (Garrick, 1998; Hall, 2000). The topic was chosen because analysis showed that individual SME staff show more interest in achieving of competences based on intensive KM (Hamburg, 2007; Hamburg & Engert, 2007) for things they can do (competences), rather than for certification. The framework of the CoP is useful for informal learning and knowledge sharing; the social participation of the members is the key for informal learning to become embedded into practices and relationships of the workplace, such as, keeping up-to-date with administrative and technical changes necessary to solve daily tasks efficient, and strategies to help solve problems and communicate with colleagues and co-workers.

Both SIMPEL CoPs have permanent members who make regular contributions but also occasional members who use the information and knowledge needed for their work and business and sometimes contribute. Across each of the two CoPs SMEs whose representatives are active members show significantly more improvements in searching needed information and KM practices learned in CoPs then the less active counterparts. For the future it is intended to encourage more SME to participate actively and to use the CoPs knowledge and resources developed.

In looking for suitable software framework to support communities of practice and to facilitate the processes of knowledge sharing and learning, the SIMPEL consortium adopted Moodle (Dougiamas, 2007). This choice was first based on an analysis of some open source virtual learning environments (VLEs) taking account of sustainability and viability (that influence the costs for adoption and further developments of the system with personalized - PLE services) and of the pedagogical rationale of the environment (how the VLE fits the pedagogical aims of the organisations which uses it). Some of the key points for evaluating sustainability and viability refer to implementation, maintainability and further developments and are: activity of the community, level of usability, requirements in hardware and software, reliability of the system, support, modular system architecture, compatibility with existing systems within SMEs. Moodle was also chosen because some partners had previous user experience, this adoption of the familiar is an important human factor in supporting VCoPs. The platform for the German CoP offers sites around typical work tasks and roles particularly in a virtual enterprise; a familiar scenario structure was built showing how a knowledge intensive virtual enterprise model can support eLearning at work experience. The scenario was based on the idea that several organizations to which CoP mem-bers belong should share their knowledge bases, technologies, competences, practice experience of the members. A wide range of media (music, video, animation) was used to communicate the message of the scenario. Based on the scenario, knowledge-enabling services improved eLearning services, document sharing services and eCommerce services are in the development.

CONCLUSION

In order to maintain competitive advantage in today's difficult economic climate both the commercial and academic communities are showing increased interest in the linked areas of Innovation and Knowledge Management. Increased attention is also being paid to training and education in the techniques and tools of these areas. The associated literature suggests that competitive advantage results from the sharing, creation, protection and use of knowledge resources within the company and its partners.

This chapter has presented some aspects, methods and strategies in the context of innovation, KM and learning that can be considered to improve the innovative ability of companies, particularly of SMEs. Some important findings from both the literature and from projects are that all innovations require flexible organisations, motivated staff, sharing and dissemination of knowledge, collaboration and where appropriate the use of new technologies.

If managers seek to understand the benefits of KM they can employ the measures presented in this chapter starting with a KM readiness analysis and followed by a KM audit.

Though led by existing theoretical concepts, access to innovation processes via exemplar cases is relatively open, the narrative interview as a first building block has great value. By inviting people to speak freely about they experienced rather than pre-formulating questions an "undistorted" image of the innovation process can be obtained. There is then the possibility of making realistic comparisons between cases taking into account reliability problems as to what extent each interview actually presents "real" knowledge flows or more reflect the subjective story of the interviewee.

Nowadays knowledge is most often created by interdisciplinary activity and across organisations, features ideally suited to the CoP concept. CoPs also provide an environment where the connection of work, KM and learning can be realised. Through their explorative character they can promote innovation to a high degree and contribute to the improvement of the knowledge base of a company. To ensure that the effort made within a CoP is successful and meets objectives it is necessary to link the reported community benefits and impacts to the needs and wishes of the strategic management of the company.

The utilisation of Web 2.0 and familiar application such as Wikis and Blogs can improve the learning about, and interactions of, innovation and KM processes. But they need to be in regular use and kept up to date in order to be useful information sources for staff, customer and the media. Podcasts, Facebook, Widgests, Wikipedia entry, RSS etc can all be useful depending on the core business and needs of the company.

Training techniques and technologies in companies need to be re-engineered to combine approaches that enable individuals to develop to their full potential and to support collective knowledge development and creativity through individuals' engagement in their company and within networks. It is important to help companies, particularly SMEs, to have an open and adaptable spirit towards these tools and methods by initiating and supporting collaborative projects.

REFERENCES

American Productivity and Quality Center – APQC. (2004). Communities of practice. http://www.apqc.org

Amin, A., & Cohendet, P. (2006). Geographies of Knowledge Formation in Firms. *Industry and Innovation*, *12*(4), 465–486. doi:10.1080/13662710500381658

Amtsblatt der Europäischen Union. (2003). *Empfehlungen der Kommission vom 6. Mai 2003 betreffend die Definition der Kleinstunternehmen sowie der kleinen und mittleren Unternehmen.* Retrieved July 30, 2007 from http://europa.eu.int/eur-lex/pri/de/oj/dat/2003/l_124/l_12420030520de00360041.pdf

Attwell, G., Dirckinck-Holmfeld, D., Fabian, P., Kárpáti, A., & Littig, P. (2003). *E-learning in Europe – Results and Recommendations.* Thematic Monitoring under the LEONARDO DA VINCI Programme. Bonn, Germany. Report., Impuls 010.

Averill, S., & Hall, T. (2005). *An observatory of eLearning in Small Medium Enterprises (SMEs).* In G. Richards (Ed.), *Proceedings of World Conference on E-Learning in Corporate, Government, Healthcare and Higher Education* (pp. 220-225). Chesapeake: VA: AACE.

Beer, D., Berger, K., Busse, T., Engert, S., Hall, T., Hamburg, I., & ten Thij, H. (Eds.). (2008). *Strategies, models, guidelines to use eLearning in SMEs.* Duisburg: Univ.Verlag.

Beer, D., Busse, T., Hamburg, I., Mill, U., & Paul, H. (Eds.). (2006). *e-learning in European SMEs: observations, analyses & forecasting.* Münster: Waxmann.

Beer, D., Busse, T., Hamburg, I., & Oehler, C. (Eds.). (2008). Improving eLearning practices in SMEs. In *Proceedings of the SIMPEL final conference.* Universitas-Györ.

Brödner, P., Helmstädter, E., & Widmaier, B. (Eds.). (1999). *Wissensteilung. Zur Dynamik von Innovation und kollektivem Lernen* (*Vol. 13*). München: Hampp, Arbeit und Technik.

Butzin, A., & Widmaier, B. (2008). Innovations-biographien. In *Institut Arbeit und Technik: Jahrbuch 2007*. Gelsenkirchen, S. 44-51.

Castro M. C. (2006). *Revisiting Communities of Practice: from fishermen guilds to the global village*. Posted on 28 July 2006 by jrobes.

Cheung, C.F., Ko, K.C., Chu, K.F., & Lee, W.B. (2005). Systematic Knowledge Auditing With Applications. *Journal of Knowledge Management Practice*.

Coakes, E., & Clarke, S. (Eds.). (2006). *Encyclopedia of Communities of Practice in Information and Knowledge Management*. Hershey, PA: Idea Group Reference.

Dalkir, K. (2005). *Knowledge Management in Theory and Practice*. Butterworth Heinemann.

Dede, C. (2005). Planning for neomillennial learning styles. *Educause Quarterly, 28*(1). Retrieved on November, 2006, from http://www.educause.edu/pub/eq/eqm05/eqm0511.asp

Diemers, D. (2001). Virtual Knowledge Communities. *Erfolgreicher Umgang mit Wissen in digitalen Zeitalter*. Dissertation der Universität St. Gallen.

Doppler, K., & Lauterburg, C. (1997). *Change Management: den Unternehmenswandel gestalten*. Frankfurt am Main: Campus Verlag.

Dougiamas, M. (2004). *Moodle: Using Learning Communities to Create an Open Source Course Management System*. Perth, Australia.

European Commission (2003). *Observatory of European SMEs*.

Garrick, J. (1998). *Informal Learning in the Workplace: Unmasking Human Resource Development*. London: Routledge.

Grant, R. M. (1997). The knowledge-based view of the firm: implications for management practice. *Long Range Planning, 30*(3), 451. doi:10.1016/S0024-6301(97)00025-3

Hall, B. (2000). *Learning goes online: how companies can use networks to turn change into a competitive advantage* (Cisco Systems: Packet Magazine).

Hall, R., & Pierpaolo, A. (2003). Managing knowledge associated with innovation. *Journal of Business Research, 56*(2), 145–152. doi:10.1016/S0148-2963(01)00287-9

Hamburg, I. (2007). Shifting eLearning in SMEs to a Work-based and Business Oriented Topic. In *European Distance and ELearning Network: New learning 2.0? Emerging digital territories–developing continuities – new divides* (p. 4).

Hamburg, I., & Engert, S. (2007). Competency-based Training in SMEs: The Role of ELearning and E-Competence. In *Proceedings of the 6th IASTED International Conference "Web-based Education* (pp. 189-193). Anaheim: Acta Press.

Hamburg, I., Engert, S., Petschenka, A., & Marin, M. (2008). Improving e-learning 2.0-based training strategies on SMEs through communities of practice. In *The International Association of Science and Technology for Development* (pp. 200–205). IASTED.

Hamburg, I., Rehfeld, D., & Terstriep, J. (2006). Knowledge-based services for economic agencies. *The ICFAI Journal of Knowledge Management, 4*(4), 15–27.

Hamburg, I., & Widmaier, B. (2004). Wissensverarbeitung in der Wirtschaftsförderung. In B. Widmaier, D. Beer, St. Gärtner, I. Hamburg, & J. Terstriep (Eds.), Wege zu einer integrierten Wirtschaftsförderung. Baden-Baden: Nomos Verl.-Ges., S. 75-112.

Helmstädter, E. (2004). Arbeits- und Wissensteilung als Prozesse gesellschaftlicher Interaktion. In Held, M., Kubon-Gilke, G., & Sturn, R. (Eds.), *Jahrbuch Normative und institutionelle Grundfragen der Ökonomik. Marburg: Metropolis-Verl* (*Vol. 3*, pp. 97–125).

Helmstädter, E. (2007). The role of knowledge in the Schumpeterian economy. In Hanusch, H. (Ed.), *Elgar companion to neo-Schumpeterian economics* (pp. 296–315). Cheltenham: Elgar.

Johnson, C. (2001). A survey of current research on online communities of practice. *The Internet and Higher Education*, *4*, 45–60. doi:10.1016/S1096-7516(01)00047-1

Kelle, U., & Kluge, S. (1999). *Vom Einzelfall zum Typus. Leske+Budrich*. Opladen.

Kerres, M. (2006). Potenziale von Web 2.0 nutzen. In Hohenstein, A., & Wilbers, K. (Eds.), *Handbuch eLearning*. München.

Krogh, G., Ichijo, K., & Nonaka, I. (2000). *Enabling Knowledge Creation. How to Unlock the Mystery of Tacit Knowledge and Release the Power of Innovation*. New York: Oxford University Press.

Larsson, A., Rehfeld, D., Widmaier, B., & Öz, F. (2006). *A Firm Case-Study Methodology: Approaches to measure Knowledge Flows in Firms and their Environment*. Paper presented to 5th Proximity Congress, Bordeaux, June 28-30, 2006.

National Electronic Library for Health. (2005). Retrieved from http://www.nelh.nhs.uk/knowledge_management/km2/ audit_toolkit.asp

Nonaka, I., & Konno, N. (1998). The concept of 'ba': building a foundation for knowledge creation. *California Management Review*, *40*(3), 40–54.

Novikova, J. (2005). Firms or Networks: In Search of the Locus of Innovation. In *DRUID Academy's 2005 Winter Conference on Industrial Evolution and Dynamics, Aalborg, Denmark, January* (pp. 27-29).

O'Brien, E., Hall, T., & Johnson, K. (2008). The Importance of Training Needs Analysis in Authoring Technology Enhanced Learning for Companies. In Lyras, M. D., Gasevi, D., & Ordóñez de Pablos, P. (Eds.), *Technology Enhanced Learning: Best Practices* (pp. 107–134). Hershey, PA: IGI Global.

O'Reilly, T. (2005). What is Web 2.0. *Design patterns and Business models for the next generation of Software*. Retrieved from http://www.oreillynet.com/lp/a/6228

Oinas, P., & Malecki, E. (2002). The Evolution of Technologies in Time and Space: Form National and Regional Spatial Innovations Systems. *International Regional Science Review*, *25*(1), 102–131. doi:10.1177/016001702762039402

Say, M. (2006). *Government Computing Magazine*.

Siemens, G. (2005). Connectivism: A learning theory for the digital age. *International Journal of Instructional Technology and Distance Learning*. Retrieved from http://www.idtl.org/Journal/Jam_05/article01.htm.

Trier, M. (2007). *Virtual Knowledge Communities – IT-supported Visualization and Analysis*. VDM Saarbruecken.

Vestal (2003). Ten traits for a successful community of practice. *Knowledge Management Review, 5*(6), 6.

Wenger, E., McDermott, R., & Sydner, W. (2002). *Cultivating communities of practice: a guide to managing knowledge*. Boston: Harvard Business School Press.

Wengraf, T. (2001). *Qualitative Research Interviewing: Biographic Narrative and Semi-Structured Methods*. London: Sage Publications.

Chapter 2

Knowledge Management as an Organizational Process:
From a Theoretical Framework to Implementation Guidelines

Rivadávia Correa Drummond de Alvarenga Neto
Fundação Dom Cabral, Brazil

Renato Rocha Souza
Fundação Getúlio Vargas, Brazil

ABSTRACT

The management of knowledge is a multifaceted organizational process that involves three parts. They are (i) a strategy, (ii) the creation of an organizational environment or space for knowledge - known as the "enabling context" or "Ba" and (iii) an operational/action toolbox consisting of IT tools and managerial practices to effectively put the strategy into action. The main objective of this paper is to propose a conceptual integrative map for Knowledge Management that was built as the result of a longitudinal programme of research on knowledge management, conducted between the years of 2001 and 2009. As an outcome of this research, knowledge management concepts, motivation, practices, results and implementation processes will be highlighted. The qualitative research strategy used was the study of multiple cases with incorporated units of analysis and three criteria were observed for the judgment of the quality of the research project: validity of the construct, external validity and reliability. Multiple sources of evidence were used and data analysis consisted of three flows of activities: data reduction, data displays and conclusion drawing/verification. The results confirmed the presuppositions and the conclusions suggest that organizational knowledge cannot be managed; it is just promoted or stimulated through the creation of a favorable organizational context, namely "Ba".

INTRODUCTION

The current debate about Knowledge Management is not only divulged in recent publications and research works of mainstream authors from the field of business administration, but also from the library and information science, such as Davenport & Cronin (2000). They suggest that:

DOI: 10.4018/978-1-61520-829-6.ch002

(…) though considerable academic and professional attention has been focused on this area in the past decade, the concept is not yet stable: the term appears to be used differently across domains with each claiming that its partial understanding represents a definitive articulation of the concept. (Davenport & Cronin, 2000)

Therefore, contemporary organizations face new terms such as "knowledge management", "communities of practice", "strategic intellectual capital management", "competitive intelligence", "organizational learning" and many others. These different perspectives reflect different conceptions of organizational knowledge and organizations themselves, besides a growing need of meticulous analysis about the upcoming opportunities for gaining competitive advantages through strategic use of information and knowledge. In this particular arena, knowledge management arises both as an opportunity and an oxymoron, depending on how it is conceived, analyzed, practiced and measured for its results concerning the organizations' core-business and readiness to compete.

Alvarenga Neto (2002, 2005) and Marchand & Davenport (2004) suggest that most of what it is called "knowledge management" is actually information management. They also state that knowledge management is more than simply information management due to the fact that it includes and incorporates other concerns such as the creation, use and sharing of information and knowledge in the organizational context, not to mention the creation of the so called "enabling context" or "enabling conditions", among others. Hence, information management is just one of the components of knowledge management and a starting point for other related initiatives and approaches.

Debates like these, associated with the lack of a conceptual definition and all the controversy surrounding the term motivated a longitudinal re-search on organizational knowledge management conducted in between 2001 to 2009. The first set of studies involved 20 world cases related in the literature and served as basis for a theoretical framework entitled "Knowledge Management Integrative Conceptual Mapping Proposition". This theoretical proposal was then put into proof in a qualitative study with three large organizations within the Brazilian organizational context. Both studies concerned how organizations understand, define, implement, practice, measure and evaluate knowledge management, what motives led them to those initiatives and what they expect to achieve with it. The basic presuppositions were two, respectively: (i) most of what it's referred to or named "Knowledge Management" is actually "Information Management" and information management is just one of the components of knowledge management. Consequently, knowledge management is more than simply information management due to the fact that it includes and incorporates other aspects, themes, approaches and concerns such as the creation, use and sharing of information and knowledge in the organizational context, not to mention the creation of the so called "enabling context" or "enabling conditions", among others; (ii) a conceptual model or map can be formulated based on three basic conceptions: (a) a strategic conception of information and knowledge, factors of competitiveness for organizations and nations; (b) the creation of an organizational space for knowledge or the enabling context – the favorable conditions that should be provided by organizations in order for them to use the best information and knowledge available; (c) the introduction of such strategy in the tactical and operational levels through the several managerial approaches and information technology tools, which are susceptible to communication and orchestration. The results of such study will be presented in this paper.

Figure 1. KM: an integrative conceptual model proposition (Alvarenga Neto, 2005)

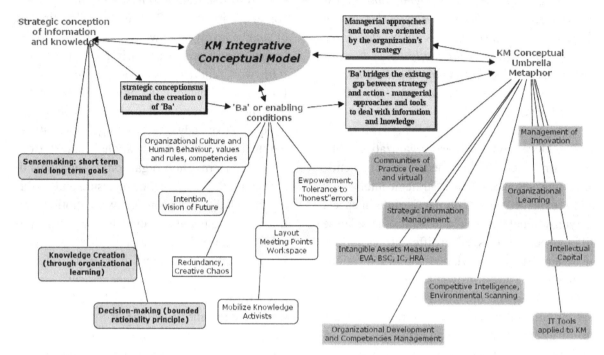

KNOWLEDGE MANAGEMENT: MODELS, MAPS AND CONCEPTUAL TRIALS

Alvarenga Neto (2005) presented a knowledge management integrative conceptual mapping proposition. His theoretical framework was based on three basic conceptions: 1. a strategic conception of information and knowledge - as proposed by Choo (1998) - factors of competitiveness for organizations and nations; 2. the creation of an organizational space (in the tactical level) for knowledge, the enabling context or "Ba": the favorable conditions that should be provided by organizations in order for them to use the best information and knowledge available - as suggested by Von Krogh, Ichijo & Nonaka (2001); 3. the introduction of such strategy in the operational level through several managerial approaches and information technology tools, which are susceptible to communication and orchestration, metaphorically named here as a "knowledge

management umbrella". Figure 1 represents and summarizes the original integrative conceptual map used both as a theoretical framework and a guide for field research and data collection.

These conceptions will be roughly discussed below.

1. A Strategic Conception for Information and Knowledge in Organizations

Choo (1998) asserts that the "knowing organizations" are those that use information strategically in the context of three arenas, namely, a. sense making, b. knowledge creation and c. decision making.

Concerning *a. sense making*, its immediate goal is to allow the organizations' members the construction of a mutual and shared understanding of what the organization is and what it does. Strategic reflections must be done concerning the organization's mission, vision, values and culture,

Table 1. The sense making process (adapted from Choo, 1998)

Information Needs	Information Seeking	Information Use
What are the new trends in our industry?	Environmental scanning	Reduction of uncertainty and management of ambiguity: collective interpretation
What are the core competences of our competitors?	Information systems	Shared knowledge construction
What do our clients value?	Researches	Decision Making

allowing its members to bring meaning to their lives and jobs. An ambitious and challenging vision or state of the future reveals the organization's intention and it is extremely valuable, contributing to communicate the types of knowledge that are welcomed and will be nurtured. Sense making's long term goal is the warranty that organizations will adapt and continue to prosper in a dynamic and complex environment through activities of prospect and interpretation of relevant information that allow them to understand changes, trends and scenarios about clients, suppliers, competitors and other external environment actors. Organizations face issues such as the reduction of uncertainty and the management of ambiguity. Competitive, competitor and social intelligences, environmental scanning, marketing research and activities alike are organizational initiatives that aim at constructing meaning about issues for which there are no clear answers. Table 1 presents the organizational sense making process through an information perspective:

b. Knowledge creation is a process that allows an organization to create or acquire, organize and process information in order to generate new knowledge through organizational learning. The new knowledge generated then allows the organization to develop new abilities and capabilities, create new products and new services, improve the existing ones and redesign its organizational processes. A direct connection in between knowledge creation and innovation can be established at this point, as knowledge is crystallized in the organization in any different combinations of a product, service or process. In this sense, innovation is co-created in different levels of interaction (individual, teams, organizations, networks), as a result of dynamic interactions between tacit, explicit and cultural knowledge, augmented by different groups of organizational enabling conditions. Nonaka et al. (2006) suggest that a central purpose of organizational knowledge creating theory is to identify conditions enabling knowledge creation in order to improve innovation and learning. In developing and promoting the sharing of knowledge assets, Nonaka et al. (2000) warn that successful experience leads to excessive exploitation (utilization) of the existing knowledge, and in turn hinders the exploration (creation) of new knowledge:

"Therefore, current capabilities may both impel and constrain future learning and actions taken by a firm. Core capabilities may turn into 'core rigidities' or a 'competence trap' which hinders innovation rather than promotes it." (Nonaka et al., 2000)

Table 2 outlines some differences and similarities in various knowledge creation models.

c. Decision-making is the third component of Choo's (1998) model. The enterprise must choose the best option among those that are plausible and presented and pursue it based on the organization's strategy. The decision making process in organizations is constrained by the bounded rationality principle, as advocated by March & Simon (1975). Many inferences can be made upon the decision theory, Choo (1998) and also March & Simon (1975) list a few of them: (i) the decision making

Table 2. Knowledge creation processes (Choo, 1998, p.130)

Knowledge Processes (Wikström & Normann, 1994)	Knowledge Creation Phases (Nonaka & Takeuchi, 1995)	Knowledge-Building Activities (Leonard-Barton, 1995)
Generative Processes: Generating new knowledge	Sharing tacit knowledge	Shared problem solving
	Creating concepts	Experimenting and prototyping
Productive Processes: operationalizing new knowledge	Justifying concepts Building an archetype	Implementing and integrating new processes and tools
Representative Processes: Diffusing and transferring new knowledge	Cross-leveling knowledge	Importing knowledge

process is driven by the search for alternatives that are satisfactory or good enough, rather than seeking for the optimal solution; (ii) the choice of one single alternative implies in giving up the remaining ones and concomitantly in the emergence of trade-offs or costs of opportunity; (iii) a completely rational decision would require information beyond the capability of the organization to collect, and information processing beyond the human capacity to execute.

2. The Creation of an Organizational Space for Knowledge, the Enabling Context or "Ba"

The creation of knowledge in the organization is, potentially, the collective creation of knowledge by the sum of the individuals, given that the environmental conditions are provided by the organization. This is what Von Krogh, Ichijo & Nonaka (2001) call "Ba", the enabling conditions or enabling context. "Ba" is needed in the tactical level in order to bridge the existing gap between strategy and action. In this context, the understanding of the word "management" when associated with the word "knowledge" should not mean control, but promotion of activities of knowledge creation and sharing in the organizational space. Hence, knowledge management assumes a new hermeneutic perspective – from knowledge as a resource to knowledge as a capability, from knowledge management to a management towards knowledge. Nonaka & Takeuchi (1995)

and Von Krogh, Ichijo & Nonaka (2001) list the many elements of "Ba", namely: creative chaos, redundancy, layout, organizational culture and human behavior, leadership, intention or vision of future and empowerment, not to mention organizational structure and layout, among others.

3. The "KM Umbrella" Metaphor

At last, the "KM Umbrella" metaphor assumes that below its boundaries, many themes, ideas, managerial approaches and IT tools concerning information and knowledge in the organizational context are addressed and susceptible to communication and orchestration. It's imperative to highlight a few of them, such as, 'strategic information management', 'intellectual capital', 'organizational learning', 'competitive intelligence' and 'communities of practice', among others. It's exactly the interrelation and permeability between those many themes that enable and delimitate the upbringing of a possible theoretical framework which can be entitled "knowledge management". Feedback is achieved by classifying the themes below the "KM umbrella" in the model proposed by Choo (1998). Competitive intelligence and environmental scanning are initiatives – managerial approaches and IT tools - that drive the strategic concept sense making into action. That is, sense making is a strategic conception and, e.g., competitive intelligence, an action-driven managerial approach - a way to turn strategy into action is by using the right managerial approach or IT tool that

Figure 2. Knowledge management: Multifaceted organizational process (Alvarenga Neto, 2008)

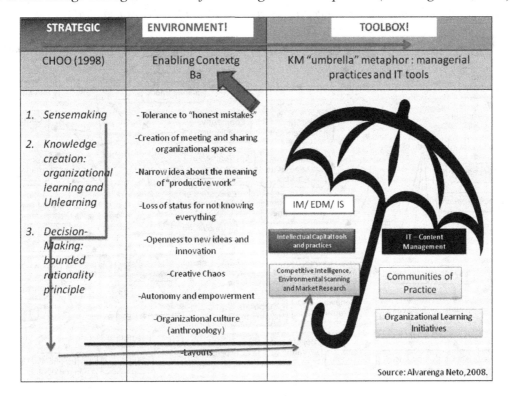

can be found in the "KM umbrella". Communities of practice, strategic information management and organizational learning fit into the thematic of knowledge creation and so on.

Figure 2 represents knowledge management as a multifaceted organizational process that involves (i) a strategy, (b) the creation of an organizational environment or space for knowledge - known as the "enabling context" or the Japanese concept of "Ba" - which in its turn is quintessential to bridge the gap between organizational strategy and organizational action and (iii) an operational/action toolbox consisting of IT tools and managerial practices to effectively put the strategy into action.

Figure 3 updates Alvarenga Neto's (2005) original integrative conceptual map. This map is an evolution of the studies of the authors (Souza & Alvarenga Neto, 2003; Alvarenga Neto, 2005, 2008) and was used both as a theoretical framework and a guide for field research and data collection, and shows the levels of strategy (knowl-

edge organization), environment ("BA", or the enabling context and the action level, comprising all the initiatives traditionally associated to knowledge management, along with the technology information tools and managerial methodologies, or "management tools".

Corroborating with the integrative conceptual map above, a conceptual basis towards a management model for knowledge based organizations or knowing organizations can also be proposed. The starting point is a quadripartite organizational architecture, as follows: (i) strategy: focus on the firm's knowledge and core competencies; (ii) structure: seeks flexibility for knowledge creation and dissemination; (iii) technology/ processes: includes the functions of identification, capture, selection and validation, organization and storage, sharing, access and distribution, application and creation of knowledge; (iv) people: skilled knowledge workers. This proposal is performed through practices such as organiza-

Figure 3. Knowledge management: Alvarenga Neto & Souza's update to Alvarenga Neto's original knowledge management integrative conceptual map (Alvarenga Neto & Souza, 2008)

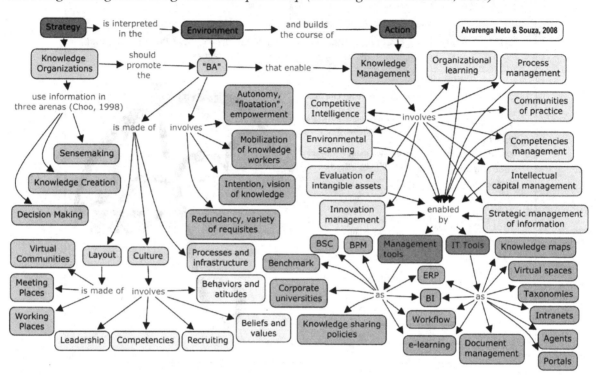

tional learning, intellectual capital management and competitive intelligence, among others. Figure 4 summarizes the quadripartite organizational architecture of the "Knowing Organization":

In the next section, before presenting the results, the research methodologies are explained.

THE METHOD

Two sets of studies will be presented in a longitudinal perspective (2001-2009) and its unique goal was to investigate and analyzed "Knowledge Management" processes effectively implemented in world class organizations. The main objective was to investigate and analyze the conceptions, motivations, implementation processes, practices, metrics and results of knowledge management processes effectively implemented in multiple industries.

The first set of studies involved 20 world cases related in the literature and served as basis for the theoretical framework entitled "KM Integrative Conceptual Mapping Proposition". This study involved both private and public organizations randomly selected from web sites, journals and specialized magazines in the information and knowledge management field.

This theoretical proposal was then put to proof in a second set of studies, namely a qualitative study with three world class large organizations within the Brazilian organizational context. A sine qua non condition in choosing the organizations was the fact that they should have already had knowledge management implemented and, for this matter, three organizations - each one belonging to one of economy's three sectors - were chosen, that is to say, Centro de Tecnologia Canavieira –CTC (Sugarcane Technology Center), Siemens Brazil and Pricewaterhouse & Coopers Brazil (PwC).

Figure 4. A quadripartite organizational architecture for the "knowing organization" (Alvarenga Neto & Souza, 2008)

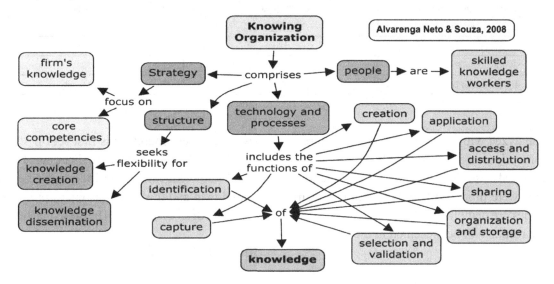

Figure 5. Components of data analysis: Interactive model (Miles & Huberman, 1984)

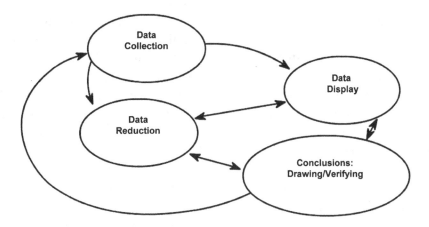

The qualitative research strategy used was the study of multiple cases with incorporated units of analysis and three criteria were observed for the judgment of the quality of the research project: validity of the construct, external validity and reliability. Multiple sources of evidence were used – semi-structured interviews, documental research and direct observation - and the proposal of Miles & Huberman (1984) was adopted in order to analyze the data collected in the field.

Their proposal consists of three flows of activities: data reduction, data displays and conclusion drawing/verification (Figure 5).

The field research was realized in the cities of (i) Piracicaba, SP, (ii) São Paulo, SP and (iii) Belo Horizonte, MG in the period of March, 19th, 2005 to April, 12th, 2005. A total of 17 interviews were conducted, which resulted in 35 hours of tape recording and 533 pages of transcriptions. As to documental research, approximately 1600 pages

Table 3. Data Reduction Processes–Data Analysis of Field Research (Alvarenga Neto, 2005)

Data Reduction Processes	From (pages)	To (pages)
1st Reduction Process	**2150**	180
2nd Reduction Process	180	100
3rd Reduction Process	100	52
4th Reduction Process	52	**Final work**

were analyzed with a loss of 12%. Four data reduction cycles were necessary until data could be incorporated to the final work and eight reduction displays were produced based on the analytical categories created (Table 3).

The results will be presented in the lines bellow.

RESULTS ANALYSIS

First Set of Studies

As mentioned before, the first set of studies was conducted by Alvarenga Neto (2002) and involved 20 world class organizations committed to knowledge management, both from the public and private sector. The sources for his study involved magazines (such as CIO and Darwin magazines), public databases available on the World Wide Web (such as Webcom) and universities' databases (such as Texas University's). Table 4 brings a comprehensive list of the organizations studied:

His analysis' model involved multiple variables but the main one revolved around Choo's (1998) proposal for the three arenas of strategic use of information in organizations: sensemaking, knowledge creation and decision making. The results revealed that the main emphasis of the 20 cases resided in the arena of knowledge creation, with a strong commitment to information management. Among the list of practices delimited in his research, practices such as competitive intelligence, communities of practice, organizational learning, intellectual capital management and a

few others were found. This first set off studies served as a cornerstone for Alvarenga Neto's (2005) knowledge management integrative conceptual map and this map was put to proof on a second set of studies that will be presented bellow.

Second Set of Studies

The analytical model was divided in five analytical categories as guidelines to field research, namely: i. reasons or motives that lead the organization to knowledge management initiatives; ii. the firm's definition or understanding of knowledge management or/and knowledge management's concepts; iii. the knowledge management implementation process' main steps, iv. aspects, managerial approaches and tools considered under the aegis of the firm's knowledge management area, program or project ("KM Conceptual Umbrella"); v. main results related to or generated by knowledge management initiatives.

Main Reason or Motives for the Adoption of Knowledge Management Initiatives

The main reasons or motives for the adoption of knowledge management in the organizations of this study concerned the following aspects:

1. Lack of practices of protection and sharing of information and knowledge, leading the organization to a constant reinvention of the wheel and continuous duplication of efforts;

Table 4. Firms comprehended in the first set of studies x references x knowledge management emphasis

Firm	References	Knowledge Management Emphasis
British Telecom	Compton, J. **Dial K For Knowledge,** CIO Magazine, 2001. From: < http://www.cio.com/archive/061501/dial.html>	Competitive intelligence
Frito Lay-	Schein, E. **The Knowledge Crunch,** CIO Magazine, 2001. From: < http://www.cio.com/archive/050101/crunch.html	Information management
JP Morgan Partners	Berkman, E. **Project Win,** CIO Magazine, 2001. From: <http://www.cio.com/archive/090101/win.html>	Information management
Ketchum	Santosus, M. **KM Works Magic For Ketchum,** CIO Magazine, 2001. From: < http://www.cio.com/research/knowledge/edit/ketchum.html>	Information management and Intellectual Capital management
Microsoft	Davenport, T. H. **Knowledge Management At Microsoft,** 1997. From: < http://www.bus.utexas.edu/kman/microsoft.htm	Intellectual Capital management and Competencies management
Northrop Grumman	Santosus, M. **Thanks For The Memories,** CIO Magazine, 2001. From: <http://www.cio.com/archive/090101/thanks.htm	Intellectual Capital management
Teltech	Davenport, T. H. **Teltech: The Business Of Knowledge Management Case Study,** 1998. From: < http://www.bus.utexas.edu/kman/telcase.htm>	Information management
Xerox	Mitchell, M. **Share….And Share Alike,** Darwin Magazine, Feb., 2001. From: < http://www.darwinmag.com/read/020101/share.html>	Communities of Practice
CNA	Santosus, M. **Underwritng Knowledge,** CIO Magazine, 2002. From: < http://www.cio.com/archive/090102/underwriting.html>	Information management and Intellectual Capital management
Sevin Rosen Funds	Santosus, M. **Tricle Up Theory,** CIO Magazine, 2002. From: <http://www.cio.com/research/knowledge/edit/k041902_crm.html>	Information management and CRM
CIA – Central Intelligence Agency	Varon, E. **The Langley Files**, CIO Magazine, 2000. From: <http://www.cio.com/archive/080100/langley.html>	Information management
TVA – Tennessee Valley Authority	Hildebrand, C. **Knowledge Fusion**, CIO Magazine, 2000. From: < http://www.cio.com/archive/060100/fusion.html>	Information management
H&K – Hill & Knowlton	Berkman, E. **Don't Lose Your Mind Share,** CIO Magazine, 2000. From: < http://www.cio.com/archive/100100/mindshare.html>	Information management
Dow Chemical	Manasco, B. **Dow Chemical Capitalizes On Intellectual Assests, Knowledge** Inc., 1997. From: < http://webcom.com/quantera/Dow.html> e < http://www.knowledgeinc.com/ICAP.html>	Intellectual Capital management
Novartis	Abramson, G. **Wiring The Corporate Brain**, CIO Magazine, 1999. From: < http://www.cio.com/archive/enterprise/031599_nova.html>	Intellectual Capital management
Chevron	Allee, V. **Chevron Maps Key Processes And Transfers Best Practices,** Knowledge Inc., 1997. From: <http://webcom.com/quantera/Chevron.html> e http://www.knowledgeinc.com/ICAP.html	Knowledge Transfer
WSIB Canada - Workplace Safety & Insurance Board	Genusa, A. **Chaos Theory**, CIO Magazine, 2000. From: <http://www.cio.com/archive/120100/chaos.html	Information management
Ernst & Young	Davenport, T. H. **Knowledge Management At Ernst & Young,** 1997. From: < http://www.bus.utexas.edu/kman/e_y.htm>	Information management
Departament of Defense (USA)	Glasser, P. **Armed With Intelligence**, CIO Magazine, 1997. From: < http://www.cio.com/archive/080197_learn.html>	Organizational Learning
3M - Minnesota Mining & Manufacturing Co.	Edwards, J. **What's Your Problem?**, CIO Magazine, 2000. From: < http://www.cio.com/archive/090100/problem.html>	Information management and CRM

Source: Alvarenga Neto, 2002.

2. Problems with data/information collection, treatment, organization and dissemination, indicating lack of strategic information management;
3. Recognition that both information and knowledge are the mains factors of competitiveness of modern times;
4. Need for the creation of an organizational space for knowledge, also knows as "Ba" or "enabling conditions", vis-à-vis the need to address cultural and behavioral issues.

Evidences and testimonies collected in field interviews confirm the statements above:

[...] each part, area or department of our firm had idiosyncratic methods for storing and managing knowledge... [...] nowadays the firm is concerned with knowledge because knowledge is the main factor of competitiveness. [...] there were problems with information retrieval. (CTC's Coordinator of Technology Transfer)

[...] I think it was a threat: the entrance of new competitors in the market, mainly in the external market. []... and the need to do faster researches and face the new competitors: Australia, India and South Africa. [...] we had a huge knowledge loss with downsizing and retirements. (CTC's Knowledge Manager)

[...] both critical information and vital knowledge were lost and not shared. (PwC's Auditing Manager)

[...] PwC's greatest asset is the knowledge of its people... to make the knowledge of those professionals sharable. (PwC's Director of the Auditing Department and Human Resources Department)

[...] a transformation in the management model: from a very hierarchical model, stamp here, stamp there (sic), which is a slow model, to a much

more network organic model. [...] that's the idea of knowledge management, to break all kinds of barriers: geographical, hierarchical, linguistic, temporal, and personal, among others. (Siemens' Knowledge and Information Manager)

[...] quick access to organizational knowledge is a competitive differential. (Siemens' Sales Manager)

[...] someone, somewhere in the world, has already solved this problem. (Siemens' Human Resources Manager)

[...] if Siemens knew what it knows... [...] knowledge management is one of the processes that support strategy through innovation, customer satisfaction and global competitiveness. (Siemens' Regional Director)

Organizational Definitions for Knowledge Management

There was a lack of consensus concerning a definition for knowledge management in the organizations of this study. Nevertheless, a few terms were common in the answers of interviewees (content analysis), namely, process, information, knowledge, innovation, tacit-explicit knowledge conversion, registration, sharing, organizational culture, access and use, among others. Here are a few testimonies of interviewees that confirm this assertion:

[...] there is no consensus of what knowledge management is or should be in the organization – it's a challenge. [...] there's a delimitation of performance areas: information treatment, tacit knowledge, enabling of sharing... [...] knowledge management is a process; it has phases but no end. [...] process that aims to enable information and knowledge sharing, intangible assets protection, (sic) where knowledge is focused. (CTC's Knowledge Manager)

[...] it's not very clear, but it's all that is managed for obtaining knowledge, innovation. (CTC's Chief Executive Officer)

[...] it's a process that contributes to place the workers' knowledge in a network. (Siemens' Regional Director)

[...] it's not a miracle, it's not a 'knowledge unlocker plus' (sic). It's a great change in the philosophy of the organization's strategic management. [...] tools for collaboration and the creation of channels. (Siemens' Knowledge and Information Manager)

[...] knowledge management is sustaining an environment that enables the coexistence of creation, development, sharing and dissemination of strategic knowledge to the organization – it's creating the context, it's a process that should permeate all the business processes of the organization. (PwC's knowledge management Coordinator for South and Central America)

[...] knowledge management is not a project, it's a process that involves the organization as a whole: to make knowledge available to the right people at the right time, being a key factor for maintaining an organizational culture of shared values, styles and behaviours. (Documental Research, PwC, 2005)

The Knowledge Management Implementation Process' Main Steps

The analysis of the processes of knowledge management implementation revealed a cycle made of 6 basic steps as shown in Figure 6.

Managerial Approaches and Tools Considered Under the "KM Conceptual Umbrella"

The next step was to investigate the theoretical proposal entitled "KM conceptual umbrella".

Henceforth, the interviewees were asked to answer which aspects, managerial approaches and tools were considered under the aegis of the knowledge management area, program or project in their respective organizations. Here's a comprehensive summary of the answers: (a) environmental scanning, competitive intelligence, market research, (b) strategic information management, electronic document management, process mapping, (c) intellectual capital management, competencies and people management, intangible assets, (d) communities of practice – both real and virtual, (e) organizational learning, including e-learning, (f) decision making support and (f) creation of the enabling conditions or "Ba".

[...] yes, external environment information, competitor's products, market trends, clippings... [...] there's also an informal information collection made by workers that (sic) "fish" something in the market and put it in the intranet – even rumors. (Siemens' Sales Manager)

[...] knowledge management is a strategic area hooked to the directorship, providing information to support decision making processes, its directorship's advisory. (CTC's Knowledge Manager)

[...] to implement a rigid taxonomy for all the organizational content. (Documental Research, CTC, 2005)

The interviewees were also inquired about the emphasis or priority aspects of knowledge management in their organizations. Data analysis revealed that the starting point for knowledge management initiatives – strategic information management – was reaching a stage of concept maturity, with consciousness that it is a permanent process. The organizations of this study were putting their efforts at advancing in aspects related to sharing, organizational culture and the creation of "Ba" or the enabling conditions. It's imperative to highlight the existence of many initiatives that are genuinely Brazilian initiatives,

Figure 6. Basic steps for the implementation of a knowledge management process (Alvarenga Neto, 2008, 2009)

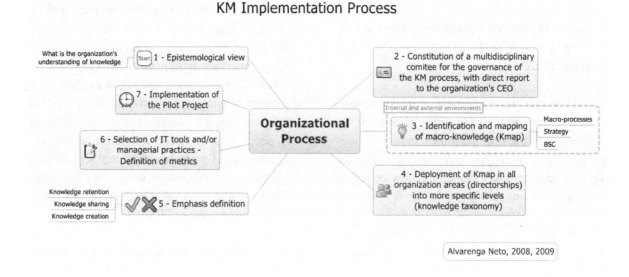

adopted to address the creation of "Ba", like the "Cultural Moment" at CTC and the "Knowledge Happy Hour" at Siemens. This last initiative is:

[...] it is an informal practice of conferences, where essential organizational knowledge is shared in a tacit, spontaneous way. It's a local specific initiative that fits general policies. The speeches last for one hour and are presented by the firms' personnel. (Documental Research, Siemens, 2005)

A CLOSER LOOK AT MAIN KNOWLEDGE MANAGEMENT PRACTICES IN THE BRAZILIAN ORGANIZATIONAL CONTEXT

In order to present the main practices and experiences of knowledge management in the Brazilian organizational context, they will be grouped into six categories, that is to say: a. environmental scanning, competitive intelligence, market research and activities alike, b. strategic information

management, electronic document management, process mapping and information technology (IT), c. intellectual capital management, competencies management, and intangible assets, d. communities of practices – real and virtual, e. organizational learning and f. the creation of the enabling context or 'Ba'.

1. environmental scanning, competitive intelligence, market research and activities alike:
    a. **formal and structured processes:** clippings, market research, competitor intelligence, competitive intelligence, environmental scanning, benchmarking, information systems and data bases (external ones, like '*Reuters, Factiva, Dow Jones*', among others). At CTC, pursuing the goal of establishing spectral behaviour patterns capable of identifying and quantifying cultivated areas with registered varieties of sugar cane, geoprocessing and satellite pictures are used (Figure 7);

Figure 7. Use of geoprocessing and satellite images at CTC, Brazil - Landsat (Alvarenga Neto, 2005)

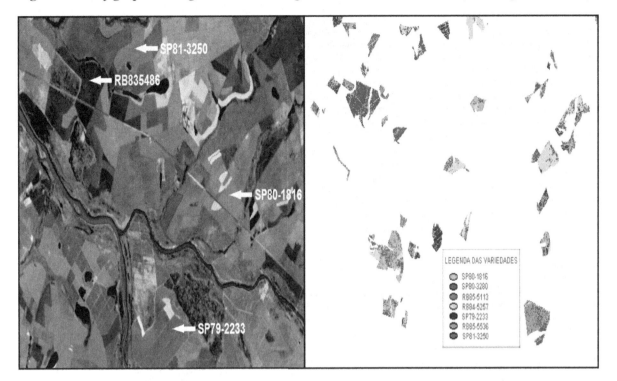

b. **informal and unstructured processes:** international trips, internet, rumours, networking and personnel's field work.

2. strategic information management, electronic document management, process mapping and information technology (IT):

a **strategic information management, electronic document management, process mapping:** electronic document management, workflow, establishment of central data repositories for all organizational content, taxonomies and ontologies, selective information dissemination processes, corporate libraries, archival and documentation centers, digital libraries, content management, project management, processes management, public archival mapping, among others;

b. **information technology (IT):** networks, intranets, software, digitaliza-

tion, information security management, data bases.

"[..]the main knowledge management projects at CTC: Document Management System −its goal is to create a unique repository to all documents, in order to provide sharing and facilitate access to explicit knowledge; development of an EDM – Electronic Document Management: the organizational memory was digitalized and taxonomies were defined (today: 15.000 documents stored), an average of 200 documents are included per month." (Figure 8, Documental Research, CTC,Alvarenga Neto, 2005)

3. intellectual capital management, competencies management, and intangible assets:

a. intellectual capital management and intangible assets: patents, royalties and registrations;

b. competencies management and retirement programs attendance;

Figure 8. CTC's Information General Flow and EDM Process - (Alvarenga Neto, 2008)

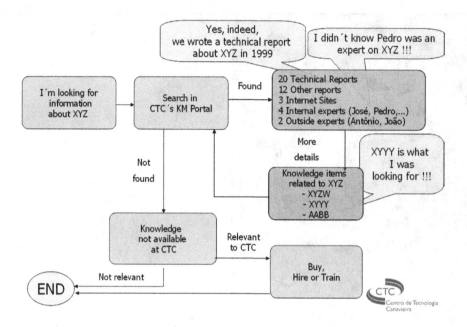

c.   programs/systems of ideas and suggestions (Figure 9) – ideas that strengthen the core competencies of the organizations and its knowledge portfolio;

d.   expertise locations systems, also known as *Yellow Pages*;

4.   Communities of practices:

a.   communities of practice: meetings, technical update sessions, chats;

b.   virtual communities of practice – virtual (Figure 10): workers are part of both internal and external communities; use of chats, conference calls, videoconference, news, knowledge libraries, discussion forums: best practices sharing and collective learning.

5.   organizational learning: a strong correlation between organizational learning and intellectual capital was revealed. Here's a comprehensive list of organizational learning practices:

a.   organizational support towards continued education: scholarships granted to workers in order to pursue MBA and

PhD degrees, language studies, among others. Workers are released from work for the period of time and still received their full wages;

b.   study groups and technical update sessions;

c.   e-learning;

d.   corporate universities and partnerships with universities;

e.   best practices databases/systems (Figure 11);

f.   training and development programs, self training centers and training programs with human resources, marketing and information technology.

6.   **The creation of the enabling context or 'Ba':** the results point out to relevant efforts towards the comprehension and creation of a favorable organizational context.

a.   layout;

b.   creation of organizational meeting points for conversations, information and knowledge sharing and learning. In this sense, there are genuine Brazilian

Figure 9. CTC's Innovation and Ideas' Program Evaluation (Alvarenga Neto, 2008)

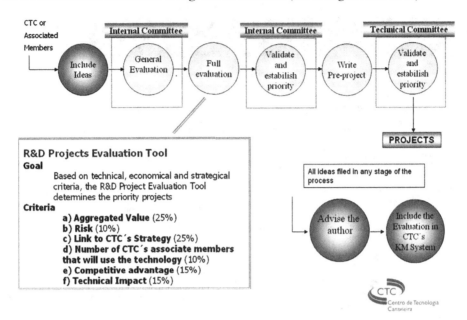

Figure 10. Communities of practice – Siemens' Sharenet (Alvarenga Neto, 2005)

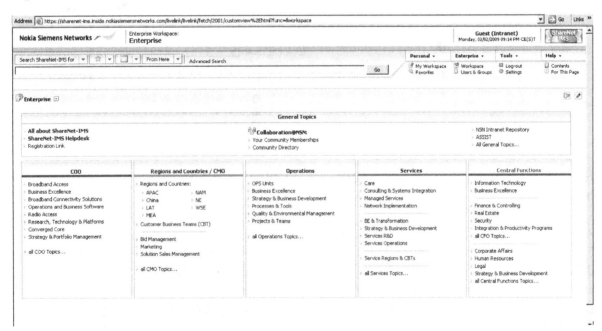

initiatives, such as the "*Cultural Moment*" (Figure 12) at CTC and the "*Knowledge Happy Hour*" at Siemens.

c. organizational culture and values;

d. creative chaos, empowerment, open management policies;

e. tolerance towards '*honest mistakes*'.

Figure 11. PwC's Global Best Practices (Alvarenga Neto, 2005)

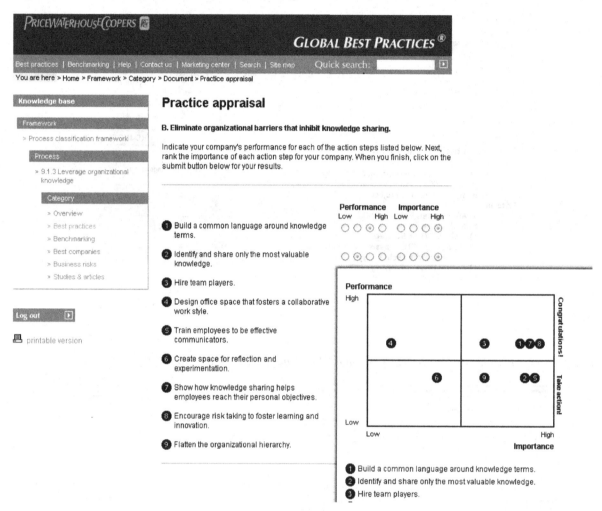

Results of Knowledge Management Initiatives

At last, the main results related to or generated by knowledge management were nominated by the interviewees: (i) innovation cycle reduction and faster time-to-market solutions; (ii) market share and portfolio increase; (iii) facilitation of expertise and people location; (iv) creation of an organizational memory and repository; (iv) increase in the learning capacity and (vi) ability to anticipate competitors' actions and movements.

CONCLUSION

This paper's main goal was to propose a conceptual integrative map for Knowledge Management. Far from proposing an ultimate solution or a hermetic model, it aimed to contribute for a better understanding of the field, its borders, scopes and connections. A knowledge management integrative model/map was elaborated starting from that proposed by Choo (1998), associated to the "Ba" or enabling conditions proposition conceived by Von Krogh, Ichijo & Nonaka (2001), in addition to the several managerial approaches and tools metaphorically denominated as the "knowledge

Figure 12. Invitation for CTC's "Cultural Moment" (Alvarenga Neto, 2008) - "Cultural Moment – Theme: Biosafety – Goal: to share information and tacit knowledge about relevant themes to CTC and the sugarcane industry. Come share with us! Knowledge Management."

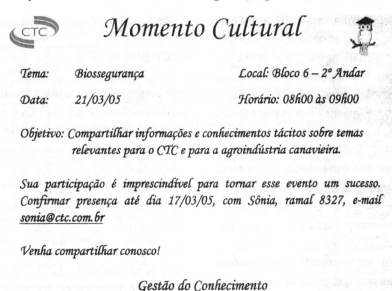

management conceptual umbrella". These three ideas interconnected are contributive for the construction of a theoretical framework as a starting point. Another corollary of this work assumed the task of confirming this integrative conceptual knowledge management framework through the discussion and analysis of a Brazilian research work in three Brazilian organizations committed to knowledge management.

Both the presuppositions and the theoretical framework presented in the literature review (Figures 1 and 2) were confirmed. This framework integrates the strategic, tactical and operational levels of the organizations concerning knowledge management initiatives, e.g.: the strategic concept "sense making" is driven into action by using managerial approaches or tools for this purpose – found in the "KM Conceptual Umbrella - such as competitive intelligence, market research or environmental scanning; the strategic concept "knowledge creation" is driven into action by using managerial approaches or tools such as "strategic

information management", "intellectual capital" and "communities of practices", among others. From strategy to action, "Ba" is needed to bridge the gap as it creates the favorable context for creativity, innovation, empowerment and creative chaos, among others. It is interesting to observe that the managerial approaches and tools considered in the "KM Conceptual Umbrella Metaphor" are also interconnected: strategic information management is the starting point that can lead to the strategic management of intellectual capital, the organization of communities of practice, the startup of organizational memory and organizational learning and so on.

The results confirmed the fact that knowledge management means a rethinking of the management of the knowing organizations or organizations of the information era. This statement has its origins in the comprehension that information and knowledge are the main factors of competitiveness for contemporary organizations and nations. It was also identified that the main challenges facing organizations committed to knowledge management have its focus on change management, cultural and behavioral issues and the creation of an enabling context that favors the creation, use and sharing of information and knowledge. Another remarkable challenge is the proposal or creation of a group of metrics and/or performance indicators to evaluate knowledge management. In this particular issue, Siemens' had already taken a step forward by introducing its own metrics, named "KS-Enabled" and "Strategic Skill Gap". The truth is that knowledge management must use both quantitative and qualitative metrics.

The conclusions suggest that knowledge management is an oxymoron, perhaps an impossibility. Knowledge as such cannot be managed; it is just promoted or stimulated through the creation of a favorable organizational context. The word "management" when associated with "knowledge" must be apprehended as promotion or stimulus for the creation and sharing of organizational knowledge and knowledge management assumes the meaning of a management from and to knowledge. There is strong qualitative evidence of a major shift in the context of the organizations contemplated in this study: from "knowledge management" to the "management of 'Ba' or the enabling conditions" that favors innovation, sharing, learning, collaborative problem solution, tolerance to honest mistakes, among others.

Knowledge management is highly political, demands knowledge managers and is an endless process that needs to be aligned with the organizations' strategy and highly in tune with leadership premises. Also, knowledge management is not the same as information technology (IT), but it can be a process supported by information technology. Not all knowledge management initiatives need IT, as demonstrated by CTC and Siemens with their "Cultural Moment" and "Knowledge Happy Hour" initiatives.

Further research is recommended to deeply understand the themes around knowledge management, as the concept of "Ba" and methodologies for the implementation of knowledge management processes.

REFERENCES

Alvarenga Neto, R. (2002). Gestão da Informação e do Conhecimento nas Organizações: análise de casos relatados em organizações públicas e privadas [Information and knowledge management in organizations: analysis of related cases in public and private organizations] Mestrado em Ciência da Informação [Masters in Information Science]. Belo Horizonte: PPGCI, Escola de Ciência da Informação da UFMG.

Alvarenga Neto, R. (2005).Gestão do conhecimento em organizações: proposta de mapeamento conceitual integrativo [Knowledge management in organizations: an integrative conceptual mapping proposition] Tese [Doctoral thesis in Information Science]. Belo Horizonte: PPGCI, Escola de Ciência da Informação da UFMG.

Alvarenga Neto, R., Souza, R.R. et al (2008). Strategic Knowledge Management: in search of a knowledge-based organizational model. *Comportamento Organizacional & Gestão, 14*(2).

Choo, C. (1998). *The Knowing Organization: How Organizations Use Information for Construct Meaning, Create Knowledge and Make Decisions.* New York: Oxford Press.

March, J., & Simon, H. (1975). Limites cognitivos da racionalidade. [Cognitive limits of rationality] In *Teoria das organizações* [Organizational Theory]. Rio de Janeiro: Fundação Getúlio Vargas.

Marchand, D., & Davenport, T. (2004). *Dominando a gestão da informação* [Mastering information management]. Porto Alegre: Bookman.

Miles, M., & Huberman, A. (1984). *Qualitative data analysis: a sourcebook of new methods.* Newbury Park, California: Sage Publications.

Nonaka, I., & Takeuchi, H. (1995). *The Knowledge-creating Company: How Japanese Companies Create the Dynamics of Innovation.* New York: Oxford University Press.

Nonaka, I., Toyama, R., & Konno, N. (2000). SECI, ba and leadership: a unified model of dynamic knowledge creation. *Long Range Planning, 33,* 5–34. doi:10.1016/S0024-6301(99)00115-6

Nonaka, I., Von Krogh, G., & Voelpel, S. (2006). Organizational knowledge creation theory:Evolutionary paths and future advances. *Organization Studies, 27,* 1179–1208. doi:10.1177/0170840606066312

Souza, R. R., & Alvarenga Neto, R. C. D. (2003). A construção do conceito de gestão do conhecimento: práticas organizacionais, garantias literárias e o fenômeno social [Building the concept of knowledge management: organizational practices, literary warranties and the social phenomenon]. In *Knowledge Management Brasil,* nov 2003, São Paulo. Anais. São Paulo, 2003. CD ROM.

Von Krogh, G., Ichijo, K., & Nonaka, I. (2001). *Facilitando a criação de conhecimento* [Enabling Knowledge Creation]. Rio de Janeiro: Campus.

Chapter 3
The Management of Knowledge Resources within Private Organisations:
Some European "Better Practice" Illustrations

Federica Ricceri
University of Padua, Italy

James Guthrie
University of Bologna, Italy

Rodney Coyte
The University of Sydney, Australia

ABSTRACT

National economies have rapidly moved from their industrial economic base and shifted towards a knowledge base, in which wealth creation is associated with the ability to develop and manage knowledge resources (KR) (see, among others, MERITUM, 2002; EC, 2006). Several national and international institutions have produced various Intellectual Capital (IC) frameworks[1] and guidelines (e.g. MERITUM, 2002; SKE, 2007; EC, 2006) to guide in the management, measurement and reporting of IC. However, there appear to be few studies of private company practices (Guthrie & Ricceri, 2009). The above informed the following two research questions of our study: (1) In what ways, did the private companies express their strategy and the role of KR within it? (2) What tools, including 'inscription devices', were used for understanding and managing KR within a specific organisation? This chapter answers these questions by providing illustrations of KR and their management in practice in a variety of private companies.

DOI: 10.4018/978-1-61520-829-6.ch003

INTRODUCTION

National economies have rapidly moved from their industrial economic base and shifted towards a knowledge base, in which wealth creation is associated with the ability to develop and manage knowledge resources (KR) (see, among others, MERITUM, 2002; SKE, 2007; EC, 2006; Guthrie *et al.,* 2007).

For instance, Drucker (1993, p.42) observed over a decade ago:

... knowledge is the only meaningful resource today. The traditional 'factors of production' — land (i.e., natural resources), labour and capital — have not disappeared, but they have become secondary. They can be obtained, and obtained easily, provided there is knowledge. And knowledge in this new sense means knowledge as a utility, knowledge as the means to obtain social and economic results.

The role of KR as the engine of organisational activities has become widely recognised and there is no doubt that successful organisations tend to be those that continually innovate, relying on technologies, and the skills and knowledge of their employees, rather than hard assets such as plants or machinery (Guthrie *et al.,* 2007).

It is widely recognised (e.g., Roos *et al.,* 2005) that the management of KR creates value; not so clear is the connection between their management and organisational performance. The need to investigate the management of KR in more depth is well established in the literature (Guthrie & Ricceri, 2009). According to Mouritsen (2004, p. 258) "... we struggle to specify how decisions can develop knowledge and translate this into desirable effects".

Several practitioners and academics have attempted to provide managerial and reporting tools that aim to facilitate an understanding of KR, their management, and links to organisational performance. These tools include 'inscription devices' that focus on understanding KR and making them manageable (Mouritsen *et al.,* 2001, p. 736) by using metrics, narratives and visuals, such as figures, tables and pictures.

Several national and international institutions have produced various Intellectual Capital (IC) frameworks[2] and guidelines (see, Ricceri & Guthrie, 2009). These frameworks aim to guide in the management, measurement and reporting of IC[3].

However, a gap exists in the literature as there are few examples of actual practices, rather than just reporting studies (Guthrie & Ricceri, 2009). Also there appear to be few studies of private company practices, however publicly listed and other types of organisations are represented in the literature (Guthrie & Ricceri, 2009). Therefore, the objective of the paper is to explore how a number of private companies are managing their KR. This will be the empirical focus of this chapter.

The above informed the following two research questions of our study:

1. In what ways, did the private companies express their strategy and the role of KR within it?
2. What tools, including 'inscription devices', were used for understanding and managing KR within a specific organisation?

This chapter answers these questions by providing illustrations of KR in practice in a variety of private companies. An analytical frame is used to examine each company (Ricceri, 2008). The illustrations were found in a variety of reporting media, including sections in Annual Reports, Corporate Responsibility Reports and stand-alone IC Statements. However, due to the difficulty of accessing internal documents such as strategic plans, business plans and financial resource plans, these were not examined. Therefore, the information set is limited to external documents provided by an organisation. These examples demonstrate how the management of knowledge resources (MKR) has been applied in actual organisations and the examination of these is invaluable in understanding how a group of private organisations translate the concept of MKR.

LITERATURE REVIEW

The following literature review elucidates several contributions relating to private companies. Understanding the research that has been conducted in this (or any) area is an important step in identifying any gaps in the literature and establishing possible paths for future progress.

The relevance of managing KR for achieving organisational sustainability is widely acknowledged in the IC field and several contributions focused on the MKR and related issues. According to the literature review of Guthrie and Ricceri (2009), the 39% of the (367) IC articles published in the last decade focused on 'management and strategy'. Within these, only 21% (30 articles) focused on private organisations, and therefore there is a significant space for further research on the management of knowledge resources in these organisations.

A central question in the field of strategic management is: why do some organisations perform better than others? (Barney, 2001, p. 644; Teece *et al.*, 1997, p. 509) This question forms the foundation of the debate surrounding the strategic relevance of KR and its management. This debate has seen the emergence of two main strategic views: the market-based view and the resource-based view. The main difference between these two views is the identification of factors that explain the organisation's performance and that need to be considered in strategy formulation. These two views will be briefly considered below, highlighting different approaches to strategy making and the relevance of KR within these.

In the market-based view, external environmental factors play an important role in explaining an organisation's performance and in determining its strategic choices. Within the market-based view

several theories and models have been developed for forecasting future conditions and for scenario building under the motto "predict and prepare" (Ackoff, 1983, p. 59). Among these, industry and competitor analysis, stimulated in particular by Porter's (1980) book, *Competitive Strategy*, have given rise to models that present a checklist of factors to be considered, often categorised as economic, social, political and technological (Mintzberg, 1994, p. 55).

The resource-based view is based on the assumption that organisational performance can be explained by an organisation's resources portfolio (Dierickx & Cool, 1989) and its deployment. Therefore, strategies should be defined around firm-specific resources, which provide abnormal returns to the organisation (Barney, 1991). Within the resource-based view, it is recognised that knowledge is a main strategic asset of the organisation (Itami and Roehl, 1987; Hall, 1993; Grant, 1996), and a shift towards a more internally focused approach to strategy formulation is proposed. Grant (1991, p. 129) expressed this as:

... the firm's most important resources and capabilities are those which are durable, difficult to identify and understand, imperfectly transferable, not easily replicated, and in which the firm possesses a clear ownership and control [...] The essence of strategy formulation, then, is to design a strategy that makes the most effective use of these resources and capabilities.

Within this resource-based view, two streams of thought can be identified: the 'static' stream and the 'dynamic' stream. The first stream, 'static', highlights the stocks of strategic relevant resources as the foundations of competitive advantage (see, for example, Barney, 1991; Amit & Schoemaker, 1993; Peteraf, 1993). For instance, Barney (1991) argues that sustained competitive advantage derives from the stocks of resources and capabilities controlled by the firm that are valuable, rare, imperfectly imitable and not substitutable.

Table 1. The group of European private companies examined

Organisations	Country	Type	Sector
Arkitema	Denmark	PR	Service
ATP Group	Denmark	PR	Service
CarlBro Group	Denmark	PR	Service
Cowi	Denmark	PR	Service
SentensiaQ	Sweden	PR	Service
Systematic	Denmark	PR	Service
Plastal	Italy	PR	Manufacturing

The second stream, 'dynamic', is based on the view that accumulating firm-specific assets, that is assets which may be non-tangible and respond to the characteristics highlighted above (Barney, 1991; Peteraf, 1993), are not enough to support competitive advantage, as these stocks of relevant strategic resources need to be appropriately managed. To achieve and maintain competitive advantage, organisations must learn dynamically to use their resources effectively (Prahalad & Hamel, 1990; Senge, 1990; Nonaka & Takeuchi, 1995) and to build and consolidate "competencies that empower individual business to adapt quickly to changing opportunities" (Prahalad & Hamel, 1990, p. 81). In other words, the dynamic capabilities approach links the market-based view and the resource-based view, and highlights the context according to which strategic resources, and in particular KR, have to be understood, managed and developed. Therefore, this dynamic approach can be considered as a useful approach for organisations focusing on enhancing their innovation capabilities. The MKR framework used in our analysis is informed by the dynamic approach, and several illustrations provided in this chapter will highlight ways in which a link between KR and the external environment is identified and used for the MKR.

RESEARCH

This section deals with several issues surrounding the selection of the organisations analysed[4], the reporting media and the frame used for analysis.

Organisation Selection

In identifying suitable examples of MKR, several academic articles highlighting practices were examined (e.g., Ordóñez de Pablos, 2002; Habersam & Piber, 2003; Leitner & Warden, 2004; Boedker *et al.*, 2005; Mouritsen *et al.*, 2005); also considered were workshops, seminars and conference proceedings (e.g., EIASM, 2005; OECD, 2005; 2006;, EIASH, 2007; 2008). Several recent books on the topic area were analysed (e.g., Bonfour, 2003; Andriessen, 2004; Roos *et al.*, 2005; Marr, 2006). Also, international and national policy bodies, green papers and other reports were examined (OECD, 1999; MERITUM, 2002; Mouritsen *et al.*, 2003; NIF, 2003; METI, 2005; SMIA, 2005; SKE, 2005; EC, 2006). Then a web search[5] was performed in order to download the relevant documents. A list of seven private organisations was extracted[6]. An overall table of the group of organisations analysed is provided in Table 1.

Private organisations are privately owned entities and generally do not have to make their financial information and management of operations available to a general audience or public shareholders.

Reporting Media

The reporting media considered in this chapter are documents specifically devoted to reporting MKR. These documents are stand alone reports (e.g., Intellectual Capital Statement) or a section of other reports (e.g., Annual Report or Corporate Responsibility Report). Only documents which specifically report MKR practices were used in the analysis. Clearly the documents considered are not the only reporting media used by organisations to disclose information. A variety of reporting media, including annual reports, websites, analysts' meetings, quarterly reports, etc., can be used (see, Unerman *et al.*, 2007). The documents analysed were mostly in English, one was in Italian (Plastal). The material used for the illustrations was extracted as accurately as possible from the original text.

The MKR Analytical Frame

The analytical frame used for examining the documents includes two main categories: Strategy and KR; and Managing KR. The first category is concerned with understanding the strategy of the organisation and the role of KR within this. In the second category, MKR is concerned with the identification, development and use of KR and how this is managed in the organisation.

KR are intangible resources embodied in: people (competencies, such as knowledge, skills, expertise and abilities); organisational structures and processes (such as practices, routines, patents and databases); and external relationships (such as with customers, markets, suppliers, investors and other stakeholders).

KR activities are those organisational activities that draw upon each of the KR categories to either create organisational value, or to further develop the value creating potential of KR. For example, intentionally structuring and facilitating dialogue amongst sales and marketing staff and with customers around customer needs constitutes a KR

activity designed to develop knowledge that can be applied to build relationship capital and more effectively use resources to increase customer value. Another example is provided by the KR activity of documenting improvements in standard operating procedures to enhance the quality and performance of organisational processes. A further example is derived from a common finding across the case studies presented below, where KR activities are performed to structure and facilitate networking between employees around business techniques, technologies and processes to enhance learning and develop competences.

The following fleshes out with illustrations what both of these categories represent and how they will be used in the results of our analysis. Concerning the first category Strategy and KR the following illustration highlights the importance of strategy within the organisation. For the private company ATP, the link between KR and strategic intent was represented by the development of employee competencies, which the organisation stated was a key factor in determining its competitive position and innovation capacity:

Competency development is a vital competitive parameter — both for ATP and for the individual staff member. This is clearly reflected in ATP's mission statement, setting out competitiveness and innovation as prioritised values. (ATP 2005; p.105)

The ATP report summarised the 2005 results achieved for the three main KR components (i.e., clients, staff, and business procedures). Results for clients are illustrated in Figure 1.

The second category, Managing KR, highlights how the organisation aims to 'create value' via KR and their management. Included in this are KR components and elements, which highlight how the organisation identifies and describes its KR. There is not a pre-defined set of KR elements that can act like a check-list, even if commonly accepted IC frameworks do exist[7]. Each organisa-

Figure 1. ATP 2005 clients challenges actions areas and results (ATP 2005; p.105)

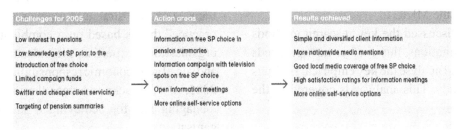

tion has its unique set of KR elements that are relevant for performing its activities and have to be managed within the context of that organisation. Without identifying specific KR elements, the organisation is unable to visualise or manage its KR.

An illustration of KR components and related elements is provided below:

- **Relational Capital:** represents the various relationships that the company has been able to develop with its customers.
- **Organisational Capital:** indicates the series of skills that exist within the structure of the company, our capacity for innovation, and the efficiency of our processes.
- **Human Capital:** consists of the know-how, skills and capacity of the persons who work within the organisation. Equally important in this area is the level of motivation and the sense of belonging to the company. (Plastal 2005, p. 2)

Also, the following illustrations of how ATP understood its KR was in terms of client surveys, which indicated the need to manage various client age segments:

The age targeting was prompted by client surveys that clearly demonstrated that older ATP members require more detailed information than their younger counterparts. While the basic versions have been retained, we took the age targeting a step further in 2004 and 2005 by further dif-

ferentiating the basic versions. In 2005, the age segments were the 16-27 year-olds, the 28-33 year-olds, the 34-49 year-olds and the 50-65 year-olds. (ATP 2005, p. 103)

Limitations Arising from the Research Methods Employed

As with all forms of research methods, there are several limitations inherent in the above methods. First, as the sample selection was based on the identification of 'better practice' private organisations, the selection was potentially biased to only those that had been reported in the policy and academic literature. However, as no statistical generalisations are being drawn from the data, this is not considered to be a major issue, although this limitation needs to be borne in mind when interpreting the data. Second, the researchers also encountered the usual issues associated with access to data. The information set is limited to external documents provided by an organisation. The research did not involve a study of internal processes and actions, but replied upon representations in public reports of KR and its management. Third, the analysis process involved coding the various media via our content categories as identified within the two categories. The researchers had regular meeting and email exchanges to ensure a degree of consistency on this matter. But ultimately, the insights provided in this paper are a distillation of many hours of reading of many hundreds of pages from the variety of media and anlysising this material into the several themes informed by the MKR.

Having discussed the key research methods used and limitations, this chapter now proceeds to provide and analyse the key empirical findings from this study. This analysis is covered in the next section.

ILLUSTRATIONS OF EUROPEAN PRACTICE

This section provides illustrations of practice from the group of European private companies, using the analytical framework, explained in the above section. Each of the companies is presented in alphabetical order as per Table 1.

Arkitema

Arkitema is a privately owned architectural consulting organisation based in Denmark. The document analysed was the "Knowledge Activities Account 2005"[8] (Arkitema, 2005). It was in English.

Arkitema's Knowledge Activities Account (KAA) focused on "our role as architects and business partners in a complex business industry" (Arkitema, 2005,p. 1). The report was produced both for internal and external purposes:

In relation to external readers the knowledge audit provides an insight into our processes, the expectations our clients have when they collaborate with us, and the results of our work.

In relation to internal readers – staff, partners, and the board of directors at Arkitema — the knowledge audit directs attention towards our ability to share knowledge and develop our skills in relation to the challenges we are presented with. This also applies to the relation between the structure of our organisation and our ability to develop knowledge and create learning. (Arkitema, 2005, p. 1)

In relation to strategy, the knowledge account focused on the "strategy for a new architectonic practice" that is based on a combination of the organisation's expertise, the industry dynamics, and social and economic responsibility (Arkitema, 2005, p. 1). It acknowledges the importance of managing KR for achieving a sustainable organisation:

We must combine our expertise within the building industry with social and economic responsibility. As an example, using our expertise to reduce the cost of construction will mean more and better schools, hospitals, factories, housing etc. But reducing costs means that we must revolutionise the building industry by increasing productivity and innovation, etc. (Arkitema, 2005, p. 1)

Arkitema's vision was contained in a knowledge narrative which analysed the business environment and expressed the organisation's "wishes and dreams for the future" (Arkitema 2005, p. 2). This narrative included industry background, which was characterised by an impasse determined by four main factors: "changing business partners" (e.g., instability of partnerships in the building projects); "routines and conventional thinking" (e.g., barriers to learning); "demand for generalists" (i.e., scarce specialisation of competencies and, therefore, scarce differentiation between competitors); "lack of innovation" (e.g., few research and development investments).

The report highlighted that Arkitema's vision was to "provide architecture with better conditions" and therefore to play an active role in helping the industry to overcome this impasse (Arkitema, 2005, p. 4). This was to be achieved by a vision of the role of Arkitema in the industry, incorporating the knowledge gained from its experience. Fostering active co-operation between different competencies and "combining the specialist's insights with the generalist's breadth view" (Arkitema, 2005, p. 6) will help in understanding customers' needs and proposing innovative solutions. Other parts of the vision included policies for employee development and retention, and also increasing the organisation's knowledge by developing "new methods for working on a procedural basis".

This vision was to be translated into practice via the identification of knowledge challenges and the definition of a set of "measures" that aim "to reduce the distance between what we wish for and what we do" (Arkitema, 2005, p. 11). Therefore, knowledge challenges and "measures" were defined by expressions of the way this organisation achieved its vision.

The KAA identified four main challenges that were summarised as: innovative management processes that focus on knowledge sharing; innovation in the production of architectural solutions; individual development through continuous learning; and the promotion of knowledge flows within the organisation (Arkitema, 2005, pp. 11–14). For instance, in relation to individual development the report addressed the importance of implementing learning in day-to-day operations. The extract below summarises Arkitema's challenge in regard to individual development:

Over and above training, the challenge therefore involves our ability to implement learning on an everyday basis. We must incorporate learning into far more situations; into all phases of projects, via evaluation, in technical and architectonic discussions. (Arkitema, 2005, p. 12)

Also, it was perceived as important to manage the organisational processes in order to provide space for individual development and initiative. The organisation focused on defining processes that would allow decentralised decision making and therefore enable employees to become actors for social responsibility. This is illustrated in the report as follows:

With our focus on the innovative design process, it goes without saying that the challenge is to develop skills that enable us to work on a procedural basis

and to make important decisions at decentralised level ... This would be the first step towards the development of the "socio-eco-responsible" employee, while the next step would focus on project management, professional cutting-edge skills, etc. (Arkitema, 2005, p. 12)

For Arkitema, knowledge is "not merely information stored in databases" — it is embedded in employees and can be shared within the organisation.

Arkitema's KAA reported managing KR through the identification of a set of areas for managerial intervention and related measures for achieving knowledge challenges. For instance, in relation to the challenge of knowledge sharing, Arkitema focused on the development of networks between employees, providing opportunities for learning. One way of supporting networking between employees was changing the physical layout of the workspace (Arkitema 2005, p. 13). Also, the organisation developed specific networking projects, such as the environmental network described in the illustration below:

Lars Kvist manages the environmental network and has environmental co-ordinators in all departments. The environmental network sharpens the focus on and disseminates the professionally qualified debate on the environment at the drawing office, and provides the various departments with help in connection to projects. In addition, the environmental network builds up and maintains our environmental tools. The environmental network generates new knowledge, finds new knowledge and, very importantly, passes it on to us. (Arkitema, 2005, p. 18)

The development of networking is one of the 18 focus areas for managerial intervention and relates to knowledge sharing. For each of the focus areas, the report highlights "measures" that were being implemented or that were to be implemented in the future. For instance, in relation to the focus area "creation of professional networks", the report identifies the need to develop an account of already existing networks and their main features in terms of aim, composition, etc.

In describing the measures for pursuing Arkitema's knowledge challenges, the report provides insights into the organisation's understanding of KR transformations. For instance, participation in international projects helps in developing employee competencies and skills (Arkitema, 2005, p. 21)

By working with other cultures and traditions we not only challenge our ability to listen and observe, but also challenge our working methods, and thereby our expertise and professional ability. In addition, we believe that international projects are of significance for our ability to recruit and retain the best employees. (Arkitema, 2005, p. 21)

Also, this statement highlights that the relational capital (represented by the element of international business partners) affects the human capital (and, in particular, the element employee competencies). In reporting each measure, the KAA names the person in the organisation who is responsible for implementation of the measure itself.

It was recognised in the report, that the production of a KAA enhanced the organisation's understanding of their working processes and methods, and that organisational learning was considered to be one of the main benefits of producing the KA. (Arkitema, 2005, p. 2)

Preparing the knowledge audit is a dynamic process that is continually influenced by what is happening, both internally and externally. New challenges and strategies focusing on particular issues are tested in various forums and processed, and as a result we acquire new knowledge and become wiser. It may therefore seem almost inconsistent to put the final full stop to such a

process. We do so however in the expectation that, in its final form, the knowledge audit will lead to a dialogue, both internally and externally. (Arkitema, 2005, p. 2)

In summary, Arkitema's KAA provides evidence of how the MKR can be positioned to achieve organisational sustainability. The KAA was a good illustration of a strategic document that was forward looking, however it lacked details, such as the identification of KR components and elements. Arkitema's KAA usefully illustrates how KR activities into day-to-day processes represent an important knowledge resource.

ATP (THE DANISH LABOUR MARKET SUPPLEMENTARY PENSION SCHEME)

The ATP group provides, in conjunction with the state-funded old-age pension system, basic pension and social insurance services. The ATP[9] Pension Fund is an independent organisation and, together with two other funds, the Temporary Pension Savings Scheme (DMP) and the Special Pension Savings Scheme (SP), forms part of the Danish pension system.

The document examined was the "Knowledge Activities" (KA)[10] section of ATP's 2005 annual report (ATP, 2005) and was in English. This KA section reports on challenges, strategy and results achieved in the management of KR. ATP used a Balanced Scorecard for managerial purposes and used the KA section to report externally about "significant activities and results" achieved by the group. Also, it was stated that the "KA represents a "supplementary report", that could be read independently from the rest of the annual report (ATP, 2005, p. 98).

The KA section reported on both our issues. In relation to strategy, the primary *foci* are on competitive position, through innovation and competency development, and on market stakeholders (i.e., clients and staff). However, in response to the growing interest from "outsiders" in ATP's social responsibility, attention has been paid to the internal working environment. Specific management challenges for KR are identified; reports on KR actions and resources transformations are included for managing KR for value creation, In particular, the KA highlighted how KR actions have helped ATP to identify new opportunities in the market and refocus the business.

In relation to the first MKR category, **strategy**, this was represented by the development of employee competencies, which the organisation stated was a key factor in determining its competitive position and innovation capacity:

Competency development is a vital competitive parameter — both for ATP and for the individual staff member. This is clearly reflected in ATP's mission statement, setting out competitiveness and innovation as prioritised values. (ATP, 2005, p. 101)

The main specific management challenges reported were "for client and staff satisfaction ratings to be high and in line with those of comparable Danish companies" (ATP, 2005, p. 99). Also, the KA section highlighted that ATP aimed to be a socially responsible group and established specific actions to achieve this.

Concerning the second category, managing KR, this report provided few examples of specific KR elements. One illustration was in terms of client surveys, which indicated the need to manage various client age segments:

The age targeting was prompted by client surveys that clearly demonstrated that older ATP members require more detailed information than their younger counterparts. While the basic versions have been retained, we took the age targeting a step further in 2004 and 2005 by further differentiating the basic versions. In 2005, the age segments were the 16-27 year-olds, the 28-33 year-olds, the

34-49 year-olds and the 50-65 year-olds. (ATP, 2005, p. 103)

Therefore, in this illustration the KR actions provided a better understanding of KR elements (e.g., clients) and identified areas for managerial intervention allowing the organisation to refocus the business. Also, this illustration highlights a link between KR and organisational processes, as an understanding of the age of clients led to changes in the way the organisation segmented its market.

Also, the staff challenge "establishing a healthy workplace" was translated into action. The KA section reported on the provision of stress management courses for staff and "affirmative programs" in which at least 5% of the workforce were from ethic minorities, people with disabilities, etc. The focus on social responsibility stemmed from increasing pressure from "outsiders" and also from the belief that this would be of benefit to the organisation's performance (ATP, 2005, p. 107).

The KA section included another 2005 ATP staff challenge, "competencies development", in which the organisation undertook both competency plans and CV management. These actions resulted in an increased amount of staff time devoted to competency development (ATP, 2005, p. 105)

Competency plans have been developed for all ATP staff members, describing their professional, social and personal competencies, while at the same time identifying desired developments. Loss of market value on account of insufficient competency development poses a large risk to the employee and therefore, the target is for ATP's staff to increase their market value by working for the company. ATP and the individual employees share a common interest in ongoing competency development, and the way to achieve that is through active CV management. (ATP, 2005, p. 105)

In summary, this report would be considered an excellent illustration of how a financial service industry could visualise and report its KR.

Carl Bro

Carl Bro Group is an international privately owned consulting engineering company based in Denmark. They offer consultancy in the fields of building, transportation, water, environment, energy and industry. This organisation has produced IC Accounts (ICA)[11] since 2001. The following analysis uses the 2005 annual report which has an ICA section (Carl Bro, 2005) and is in English.

The Carl Bro Group ICA produced information for external reporting that was also used for internal management processes. The stated purpose for producing an ICA was to "to establish the extent to which Carl Bro Group is developing the conditions for living up to its mission" (Carl Bro, 2005, p. 13). The data compiled for the external ICA was used for internal management purposes[12].

This report highlighted a clear strategy for each of the KR components, and used metrics, narratives and figures. The following will provide illustrations and narratives about how this was done by Carl Bro.

Concerning strategy, the report provided a clear understanding of the management of KR, which starts from the definition of the organisation's strategic intent. This is defined as the "overall objective" which is centred on KR (see Figure 2).

Carl Bro Group's overall objective is to be among the foremost consulting engineering companies in northern Europe. This objective will be achieved by building a company that combines knowledge, talent and initiative to create intelligent solutions for customers and society alike, centred around the Group's core competencies as consulting engineers. (Carl Bro, 2005, p. 3)

Therefore, for this organisation, the management of KR is seen as a way of creating value for

Figure 2. Carl Bro Group's mission, vision and values (Carl Bro, 2005, p. 12)

Mission:	We fuse knowledge, talent and energy to create intelligent solutions for clients and society.
Vision:	We aspire to be the intelligent choice.
Værdier:	We enjoy creating value – for clients, colleagues, society and owners. We insist on growth – in equity, intellectual capital and brand. We create opportunities – for people who have the courage to challenge their own capabilities. We are responsible – in our daily actions and through ethical, environmental and social practice. We are a colourful community – open to change, sharing across boundaries.

its stakeholders (e.g., clients, staff, society and owners) and for achieving organisational sustainability. The following illustration, which deals with the reasons for producing an ICA, indicates how Carl Bro approached MKR:

The purpose [of the ICA] is to establish the extent to which Carl Bro Group is developing the conditions for living up to its mission. Only by improving these conditions on a continuous basis can we ensure healthy and sustainable development of the business for the benefit of customers, employees and society at large. (Carl Bro, 2005, p. 3)

Carl Bro defines its intellectual resources as "the group combined Intellectual Capital" that are composed of three main components: customer capital; human capital; and structural capital. These were defined as follows:

Customer capital is defined as the value of the company's knowledge of and relations with customers. Human capital is defined as knowledge related to the company's employees. Structural capital is defined as knowledge related to the company's structures, which can be reproduced and shared with others, for instance processes and IT. (Carl Bro, 2005, p. 13)

Figure 3. Employees' General satisfaction: Carl Bro Group (Carl Bro, 2005, p. 14)

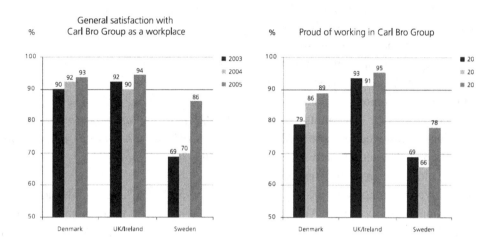

The strategic intent was detailed in terms of aims according to three main intellectual resources components. For instance, in relation to employees the reports stated:

Carl Bro Group aims to be a workplace that creates opportunities for people who have the courage to challenge their own capabilities and where knowledge, talent and initiative are developed for the benefit of employees, customers and society at large. (Carl Bro, 2005, p. 13)

The report makes clear that the organisation's view is that the development of employees' capabilities, knowledge and skills is functional not only for performing the business but also for benefiting society more broadly. Also, the organisation recognises the importance of human capital and it reports detailed measurements of satisfaction within the workplace and the feeling of employees towards the Group (see Figure 3). These indicators are reported over a three-year period and the accompanying narratives analyse the trends.

Customers' aims were addressed as follows: "The objective of Carl Bro Group is to create value for the customers in the form of intelligent solutions formulated in cooperation with the in-

dividual customer" (Carl Bro, 2005, p. 13). In order to achieve its aims, KR actions were implemented. The KR actions, for instance, related to "encouraging innovation and creativity" within its employees and "optimising project management". Therefore, the narratives provided an understanding of transformations within KR and related elements in organisational processes, where customer capital (i.e., customer satisfaction and loyalty) is affected by human capital (i.e., employees' creativity and innovation) and ("project management") internal capital. However, further details on the KR actions undertaken and on transformations were not provided in the report.

Most of the metrics and narratives were provided over at least a two-year period, and therefore allowed for establishing a trend in the reported metrics. For instance, in relation to customer loyalty the report stated:

Customer loyalty was measured at 98%, which exceeded the target of a customer loyalty rate of 97%. The last four years, customer loyalty has been in the range of 97 to 99%. (Carl Bro, 2005, p. 13)

This intellectual resources section of the annual report from this privately owned consulting organisation is a good example of how a knowledge service company can visualise and report its MKR.

In summary, the review of these first three cases has described approaches to managing KR activities aimed at upskilling and developing human competencies, primarily through recognition and documentation in IC reporting (sometimes termed 'knowledge activities accounts') and through facilitation of employee networking. The management of knowledge activities to support a strategy of developing core competences to enhance competitive advantage and ensure organisational sustainability is common. Although these themes and approaches are also common to the four case studies to follow, the emphasis of these is on the elaboration of indicators and explicit alignment models for exploiting the developed competencies to enhance customer value and relationship capital.

Cowi

Cowi is a Danish privately owned organisation that operates within engineering, environmental, science and economic consulting. The "Intellectual Capital Report 2005" (ICR)[13], which was considered in this analysis, was contained in a specific section of Cowi's Annual Report. This is the eighth ICR developed by the organisation and published within its annual report. The report is in English.

The ICR is provided in order to account "not only for our knowledge resources but also for our knowledge processes and their results" (Cowi, 2005, p. 56). For this organisation, knowledge is considered as an important resource and the ICR represents an account of its knowledge cycle.

In relation to strategy, the report highlights the focus on value creation for clients as the main *raison d'etre* of this organisation and knowledge is the main way to achieve this. The organisation's strategic intent is based on the knowledge and experience acquired by its employees while performing the day to day activities of the business and on the ability to transform this tacit knowledge into organisational knowledge. An illustration of this is:

Our most important resource is knowledge. Knowledge represents our intellectual capital ... which we manage and develop dynamically at COWI, tracking and reporting on key aspects of this asset in our Intellectual Capital Report (ICR). (Cowi, 2005, p. 56)

The ability of the organisation to pursue its strategy is related to the management of knowledge, as the IC report states that: "When Cowi's skills complement each other, we create synergy and total solutions for our clients. Our strength lies in our extensive, shared network" (Cowi, 2005, p. 60). Therefore, the integration of the knowledge of employees represents the main KR management challenge as it determines the organisation's ability to generate value for its clients and pursue its strategic intent.

Concerning the second category, managing KR, Cowi adopts a "Knowledge Cycle" model, which is used to identify the main transformations between KR, as illustrated in the following narrative and in Figure 4:

Our reputation, which depends on this satisfaction, provides the basis for sales, recruitment and commitment in our daily work. This in turn allows us to continuously generate and improve our knowledge resources, thus creating a perfect circle. We call this circle COWI's knowledge cycle. (Cowi, 2005, p. 56)

The report also provides a visual representation of Cowi's "Knowledge Cycle" and this highlights the transformations that happen between KR in the organisation (see Figure 4).

Also, Figure 4 provides a visualisation of the links between the various resources, and the Cowi working processes in achieving results. Three main relationships are highlighted: (1) Resources to

Figure 4. The "Knowledge Cycle" (Cowi, 2005, p. 56)

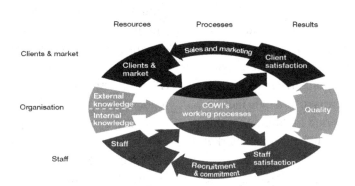

processes to results (e.g., the excellence of internal knowledge in the working processes affects the quality of the service provided); (2) Results to results (the quality of the service provided affects customer satisfaction); and (3) Results to processes to resources (client satisfaction affects the (actual and potential) clients in the market).

In summary, this ICR was brief and the initial part of the report was devoted to illustrating and explaining the "Knowledge Cycle"; therefore, little space was devoted to a more detailed identification and description of the issues that were reported. The fact that this was the eighth IC report produced by this private consulting firm clearly indicates their commitment to knowledge management and its role in organisational sustainability.

Importantly, Cowi's "Knowledge Cycle" model acts to explicitly align KR activities and their management with its organisational strategy. The causality modelled acts to raise awareness of the linkages between improvements in the quality of Cowi's working processes and development of key knowledge resources. Higher quality work processes lead to customer satisfaction, customer relationship development and learning from customers; and staff satisfaction, attraction and retention of talent, and internal knowledge development. The former, enhances relationship capital and the latter, employee competences and organisational capital. Done well, alignment

models such as Cowi's make clear the linkages between day-to-day decisions and actions and achievement of corporate strategy in the key customer and talent markets.

Plastal

Plastal is a privately owned organisation based in Italy. It is a manufacturing organisation that operates within the automotive industry. Plastal was one of the first private organisations producing IC reports in Italy. This is the sixth year that Plastal has produced an Intangible Capital Statement (ICS)[14] and this analysis considered the 2005 ICS (Plastal, 2005), available in Italian.

The ICS was used as an external communication device for improving relationships with stakeholders and informing them about the long-term drivers of the organisation: "the information provided by the Statement of Intangible Capital complements and integrates the data shown in the Financial Statements, demonstrates to our stakeholders the company's prospects for the long-term, and reinforces the faith of the clients and the markets" (Plastal, 2005, p. 3). Also, the ICS was seen to be an internal management tool, it: "provides important information to all those within the organisation for whom Intellectual Capital is an important factor giving information regarding trends in intangible variables" (Plastal, 2005, p. 3).

In relation to strategy, the report identifies the organisation's strategic focus as aligned with the three main IC components, that is relational, structural and human capital (see Figure 5). Also, it details these in terms of strategic factors. The strategic factors reported highlight that this manufacturing organisation focuses on market stakeholders.

Each IC strategic area highlighted strategic factors, for instance, for relational capital and the supplier and customer attributes which enhance it.

In regards to managing KR, the ICS reported briefly on KR actions that were undertaken in previous years, such as an "Intellectual Capital action plan". This plan aimed to use the ICS to define and promote improvements in the organisation and this is illustrated below:

During the course of 2005, we continued our activities aimed at bringing about improvements within the company by applying our Intellectual Capital Action Plan. This project involves working groups from across the organisation who analyze the data generated by the Statement of Intangible Capital in order to implement plans of action in certain strategic areas, such as relations with external customers, internal communications and involvement, incentives and organisation of the work. (Plastal, 2005, p. 3)

The "Continuous Improvement" plan has been implemented also this year to involve the employees in the organisation's plan for cost reduction via motivating and rewarding employees who contribute to reaching the aim(Plastal, 2005, p. 9).

Plastal implemented significant KR actions that involved management and the entire workforce. The report identified resources transformations, for instance, one of the metrics contained in the ICS related to the innovative ability of suppliers, and this metric can be seen as related to a

transformation between relational and structural capital. This means that the relationships with suppliers (relational capital) in the day-to-day organisational processes were considered as an important source of innovation (structural capital) (Plastal, 2005, p. 7). However, narratives in the report do not provide practical examples of this. Also, there was no attempt to identify, describe or map resources transformations in any other part of the report.

In summary, this report is performance assessment oriented as it devotes 11 out of 15 pages to illustrating and commenting on IC metrics. In regards to the second MKR category, the report provides interesting details on multi-year KR activities that had been undertaken to put KR management into practice and to drive change in the organisation. In regard to strategy, the report has both an internal and external focus, communicating long-term prospects to enhance relationship capital and, combined with other measures such as the re-alignment of employee rewards, to motivate and stimulate employee involvement and enhance human competencies and organisational capital.

SentensiaQ

SentensiaQ is a privately owned Scandinavian organisation that operates as an IT consultancy. The 2006 "Intellectual Capital Report" (ICR)[15] considered by this analysis is the organisation's second and is in English (SentensiaQ, 2006).

The stated reason for producing an ICR was to "give a holistic view of the company, based on well defined indicators on the basis of the company vision, strategy, basic values and goals" (SentensiaQ, 2006, p. 2). Also, the ICR and its indicators were seen as a managerial tool: "Comparison of indicators over time will give an opportunity to detect changes and developments and to help management to act correctly" (SentensiaQ, 2006, p. 2).

Concerning strategy, this was expressed in terms of the company's 'soul' and includes the mission, business concept, vision and strategy, goals

Figure 5. Company value and Intangible Capital (Plastal, 2005, p. 4)

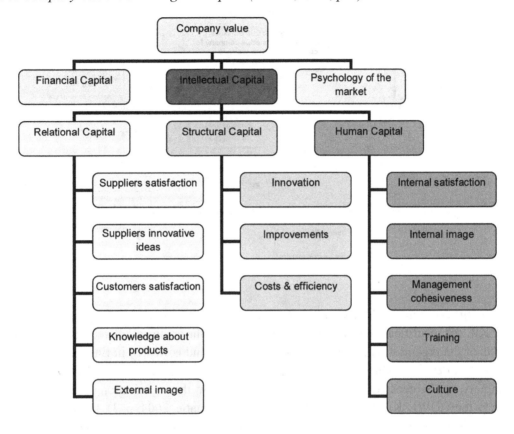

and basic values. The company uses a framework which includes KR and financial resources and this appeared on the front page of the 2006 ICR, as illustrated in Figure 6:

It is interesting to note that SentensiaQ sees value in terms of finance capital and IC. For this organisation IC was divided into three main blocks of assets: human capital, structural capital and customer capital.

For this organisation the basic business concept was stated as "Long-term customer relationships are a guiding point in everything we do. We always act in a business-like manner with a high degree of integrity and professionalism" (SentensiaQ, 2006, p. 4). Therefore, customers were seen as the main external stakeholders of the organisation. This understanding is supported by Figure 7, which identifies customers as the only external

Figure 6. SentensiaQ KR and strategy (Sentensiaensia, 2006, p. 1)

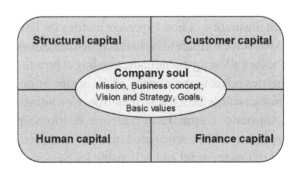

stakeholder group within SentensiaQ's strategic models.

The ICR states that the company's vision and strategy was to be the "most attractive knowledge-company for customers and co-workers (SentensiaQ, 2006, p. 5).

Figure 7. The strategic model of SentensiaQ (SentensiaQ 2006, p. 5)

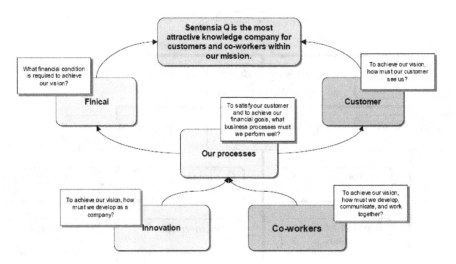

Concerning the second MKR category, managing KR, the identification of the main IC components of the organisation's "value" is not accompanied by a detailed discussion about these.

In summary, the SentensiaQ strategic model is similar to the COWI 'Knowledge Cycle' in making explicit the assumed causality between the continual enhancement of organisational processes through human competence development and innovation, and the strategic intent of success in the customer and talent markets. It is an excellent illustration of how to present metrics for KR. However, the failure to include detailed narratives does not allow a genuine understanding of how the metrics relate to the strategy of the organisation. In other words the KR activities to develop human competence (capital) and customer relationship capital should be articulated in a manner which is both meaningful and actionable by Sentensia co-workers.

Systematic

Systematic is a private organisation based in Denmark and provides IT solutions for information and telecommunication systems. The first "Intellectual Capital Report" (ICR)[16] was produced in 1999. This is the organisation's fourth ICR (Systematic, 2004) and is written in English.

The ICR was designed to provide insights into how the organisation is responding to its KR (Systematic, 2004, p. 3). However, Systematic's first ICR was developed to support the organisation's knowledge management and therefore was mainly aimed internally. With its second ICR, Systematic experienced the use of the report as a communication tool and, therefore the external motive became more prominent. The latest ICR provided a wider perspective on organisational performance as this was measured according to four main areas: customers, processes, employees and finance (Systematic, 2004, p. 2).

Concerning the first category, strategy, the issues are represented in the report. The ICR starts with the mission and vision of the organisation and a set of values that represent the foundation of organisational culture. Also, a number of these values relates directly to the organisation's "core competencies" and how they are managed. These are, for instance, "active knowledge – sharing", "constant change as a way of improving personal

Figure 8. Value chain and core competencies in Systematic (Systematic, 2004, p. 8)

Value Chain

Systematic's Core Competences

| Management Consultants | Software and Systems Development | Support and Hosting Services |

Business needs

Business analysis
IT strategy
Solutions concept

Development
Systems Integration
Test/Implementation

Operation
Support
Maintenance

IT based
service
deliveries

competence", and "partnership with customers" (Systematic, 2004, p. 33).

Systematic's core competencies are stated to be the link between the business needs and the IT service delivered to customers and end users. A visual representation of the organisation's value chain suggests the integration between KR and the different phases of the value chain (see Figure 8).

Systematic defines itself as a "knowledge intensive company" (Systematic, 2004, p. 11) that finds its value creation capability as "having the right knowledge resources based on close customer relationships, efficient processes and competent employees". Therefore, in its ICR, this organisation identifies the KR that produce value to the end user and also highlights KR management challenges. These are illustrated in Figure 9.

In relation to the second category, managing KR, the IC report provides illustration of the "measures that matter". For instance, "partnership with customers" is described as follows:

We intend to be the preferred partner for professional IT customers within our fields of expertise. Therefore, we want both parties to commit to co-operation. We will not be satisfied with merely being a good one-off supplier. Systematic attaches great importance to open co-operation. We report if anything fails, for example if the schedule is slipping. Likewise, we expect our customers to inform us if there are delays in the provision of

Figure 9. Systematic's Management challenges (Systematic, 2004, p. 11)

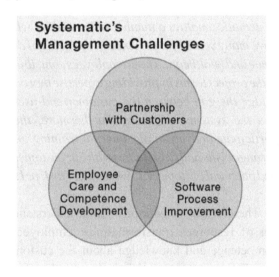

requirements, test data etc. Openness is fundamental to our ability to take corrective action in time. (Systematic, 2004, p. 13)

Results of a number of KR activities undertaken are illustrated in several graphs and tables, for instance, see Figure 10, which illustrates the results of an employee satisfaction survey.

It is recognised that, in order to foster "partnership with customers", actions may also be performed on other KR components, for instance, KR actions for maintaining and improving relationships with customer may relate to employees as highlighted in the following example:

Figure 10. Reported result of KR activity — Employee satisfaction survey (Systematic, 2004, p. 28)

Systematic employs a number of specialists who have many years of experience in the fields of defence and healthcare. These employees contribute to the project teams by providing expertise that can bridge the gap between the customer/end-users and the systems engineers. Furthermore, they participate actively in our internal training and arrange visits and field studies with our customers and potential customers. (Systematic, 2004, p. 15)

Therefore, Systematic provides an understanding of resources transformations: employees' competence and knowledge about the customers affect customer satisfaction and therefore the relationships between the customers and the organisation. Also, the narrative reported below highlights the relevance of human capital in determining the effectiveness of the core processes of the organisation (i.e., software production):

The ability to produce quality software on time is dependent on the knowledge and commitment of our employees. We therefore put a strong emphasis on attracting and retaining the best employees in the market. (Systematic, 2004, p. 26)

In the ICR analysed there was an understanding of resources transformations and also narratives about specific KR actions. Metrics and narratives

associated with them play an important part in Systematic's latest publicly available ICR.

In summary, this ICR, consisting of over 36 pages, provides a comprehensive understanding of the organisation's KR strategy and its management. Also, it outlines in detail its mission, vision and values in which knowledge and IC are central. It identifies that being a knowledge-intensive company means that value creation is dependent on having the right KR and performing KR activities that enhance their development. The organisation sees its KR priorities as close customer relationships, efficient processes and competent employees. More importantly, it provides illustration of the use of IC information for managerial purposes. It makes explicit the causal linkages between developing the key KR elements, value creation and the achievement of strategic objectives.

SUMMARY AND CONCLUSION

The general findings for private organisations are that they focus their KR activities on competitiveness in the talent and customer markets for their particular niches. A high recognition was found of causality between KR elements of human capital and relational capital. The former was developed by attracting the best talent and facilitating development through knowledge sharing in employee networks, and the latter by satisfying customers and drawing on their knowledge to design products and provide services better aligned to their needs. It was also found that the development of organisational capital (such as better work procedures and processes) was modelled as an outcome of success in human and relational capital development, while reinforcing that success in a 'virtuous cycle'. Usually, in these organisations, the "traditional" focus has been on owner interests and capital suppliers, and performance is limited to its economic and financial dimension, rather than KR. Also, as highlighted by recent scandals, a sustainable organisation cannot be achieved if economic, social and environmental matters are not addressed in the managerial and operational activities of the organisation (Ricceri, 2004). The management of KR is relevant for private organisations and therefore MKR is applicable to these organisational types.

In summary, this chapter aimed to provide a practical and informed understanding of how MKR were conceptualised and reported within a selected group of private European organisations considered to be "better practice". An analytical frame for examining MKR in practice was used and consisted of strategy and managing KR. The analysis of the group of seven private organisations indicates strongly how each individual organisation has varied narratives, visuals and metrics that have been used to report on their MKR. This supports the proposition that any attempt to construct general international KR, IC or innovation standards, guidelines or regulations needs to be aware that "black letter" prescription as to the identification of KR elements, the type of metrics and how they should be reported will not work, as although there are commonalities in high level strategic objectives amongst the private organisations discussed, the MKR is organisation specific. The idea underlying such a "black letter" approach, that IC can be treated as a stock of resources common to all organisations, is unsup-

ported by our examination of MKR in practice, which instead found tools designed to identify and guide the management of KR activities or 'flows' to achieve alignment of day-to-day actions with strategic objectives.

While the organisations examined have attempted to make visible the invisible sources of 'value creation', in most cases, this was not achieved via the use of a consistent framework. From the analytical reading of these 'better practice' documents, there is evidence of various approaches.

First, the IC documents examined generally indicated that KR information externally reported was used for internal decision making. Also, almost all of the organisations provided an understanding of the strategic relevance of MKR.

Second, as would be expected, all these 'better practice' illustrations outlined definitions of KR elements and KR actions that were specific to each organisation.

In conclusion, an important lesson from the analysis of practice was that there is a variety of ways to conceptualise MKR. Organisations employ a range of narratives, visuals and metrics which are specific to their organisational context.

REFERENCES

Ackoff, R. L. (1983). Beyond prediction and preparation. *Journal of Management Studies, 20*(1), 59–69. doi:10.1111/j.1467-6486.1983.tb00198.x

Amit, R., & Schoemaker, P. J. H. (1993). Strategic assets and organizational rent. *Strategic Management Journal, 14*(1), 33–46. doi:10.1002/smj.4250140105

Andriessen, D. (2004). *Making sense of Intellectual Capital: Designing a Method for the Valuation of Intangibles*. Oxford: Elsevier Buttherworth-Heinemann.

Arkitema (2005). Knowledge Account, sent by Arkitema's management to one of the authors.

ATP. (2005). Knowledge activities, Annual Report. Retrieved February 2007 from http://www.atp.dk/

Barney, J. B. (1991). Firm resources and sustained competitive advantage. *Journal of Management*, *17*, 99–120. doi:10.1177/014920639101700108

Barney, J. B. (2001). Resource-based theories of competitive advantage: A ten year retrospective on the resource-based view. *Journal of Management*, *27*, 643–650. doi:10.1177/014920630102700602

Boedker, C., Guthrie, J., & Cuganesan, S. (2005). An integrated framework for visualising intellectual capital. *Journal of Intellectual Capital*, *6*(4), 510–527. doi:10.1108/14691930510628799

Bozzolan, S., Favotto, F., & Ricceri, F. (2003). Italian annual intellectual capital disclosure: An empirical analysis. *Journal of Intellectual Capital*, *4*(4), 543–558. doi:10.1108/14691930310504554

Bozzolan, S., Ricceri, F., & O'Regan, P. (2006). Intellectual capital disclosure (ICD) in listed companies: A comparison of practice in Italy and the UK. *Journal of Human Resource Cost and Accounting*, *10*(2), 92–113. doi:10.1108/14013380610703111

Carl Bro. (2005). Intellectual Capital Account, *Annual Report*. Retrieved February 2007 from www.carlbro.com.

Cowi (2005). Intellectual Capital Report, *Annual Report*. Retrieved February 2007 www.cowi.com.

Dierickx, I., & Cool, K. (1989). Asset stock accumulation and sustainability of competitive advantage. *Management Science*, *35*(12), 1504–1511. doi:10.1287/mnsc.35.12.1504

Drucker, P. (1993) *Post-Capitalist Society*, New York: Harper Business European Commission (EC) (2006). *RICARDIS: Reporting intellectual capital to augment research, development and innovation in SME's*. Brussels: EC.

Grant, R. M. (1991). The Resource-Based Theory of Competitive Advantage: Implications for Strategy Formulation. *California Management Review*, *33*(3), 114–134.

Grant, R. M. (1996). Toward a knowledge-based theory of the firm. *Strategic Management Journal*, *17*, 109–122.

Guthrie, J., & Petty, R. (2000). Intellectual capital: Australian annual reporting practices. *Journal of Intellectual Capital*, *1*(3), 241–251. doi:10.1108/14691930010350800

Guthrie, J., Petty, R., & Ricceri, F. (2007). *Intellectual Capital reporting: Lessons from Hong Kong and Australia*. Edinburgh: The Institute of Chartered Accountants of Scotland.

Guthrie, J., & Ricceri, F. (2009). *Counting what counts: A decade of intellectual capital accounting research*. Paper presented at the British Accounting Association Conference, 21-23 April, Dundee.

Habersam, M., & Piber, M. (2003). Exploring intellectual capital in hospitals: Two qualitative case studies in Italy and Austria. *European Accounting Review*, *12*(4), 753–779. doi:10.1080/09638180310001628455

Hall, R. (1993). A framework linking intangible resources and capabilities to sustainable competitive advantage. *Strategic Management Journal*, *14*(8), 607–618. doi:10.1002/smj.4250140804

Itami, H., & Roehl, T. W. (1987). *Mobilizing invisible assets*. Cambridge: Harvard University Press.

Leitner, K. H., & Warden, C. (2004). Managing and reporting knowledge-based resources and processes in research organisations: Specifics, lessons learned and perspectives. *Management Accounting Research*, *15*, 33–51. doi:10.1016/j.mar.2003.10.005

Marr, B. (2006). *Strategic performance management*. Oxford: Elsevier.

MERITUM. (2002). *Guidelines for managing and reporting of intangibles*. Madrid: Fundacion Airtel Movil.

Ministry of Economy, Trade and Industry (METI) (2005). *Guidelines for disclosure of intellectual assets based management*. METI.

Mintzberg, H. (1994). *The rise and fall of strategic planning*. London: Prentice Hall.

Mouritsen, J. (2004). Measuring and intervening: How do we theorise intellectual capital management. *Journal of Intellectual Capital*, *5*(2), 257–267. doi:10.1108/14691930410533687

Mouritsen, J., Bukh, P., & Kaasgaard, B. H. (2005). *Understanding Intellectual Capital in an innovative medium-sized firm: The case of Maxon*. Copenhagen: The Aarhus School of Business.

Mouritsen, J., Bukh, P. N., Flagstad, K., Thorbjørnsen, S., Rosenkrands Johansen, M., Kotnis, S., et al. (2003). Intellectual Capital Statements — the new guideline, retrieved March 2008 http://www.videnskabsministeriet.dk/cgi-bin/theme-list.cgi?theme_id=100650&_lang=uk

Mouritsen, J., Larsen, H. T., & Bukh, P. N. (2001). Intellectual capital and the capable firm: Narrating, visualising and numbering for managing knowledge. *Accounting, Organizations and Society*, *26*(7/8), 735–762. doi:10.1016/S0361-3682(01)00022-8

Nonaka, I., & Takeuchi, H. (1995). *The knowledge creating company*. Oxford: Oxford University Press.

Olsson, B. (2001). Annual reporting practices: Information about human resources in corporate annual reports in major Swedish companies. *Journal of Human Resource Costing and Accounting*, *6*(1), 39–52. doi:10.1108/eb029071

Ordónez de Pablos, P. (2002). Evidence of Intellectual Capital measurement from Asia, Europe and the Middle East. *Journal of Intellectual Capital*, *3*(3), 287–302. doi:10.1108/14691930210435624

Organisation of Economic Co-operation and Development (OECD). (1999). *Guidelines and instructions for OECD Symposium*. International Symposium on Measuring and Reporting Intellectual Capital: Experiences, Issues and Prospects, June, Amsterdam.

Peteraf, M. A. (1993). The cornerstones of competitive advantage: A resource-based view. *Strategic Management Journal*, *14*(3), 179–191. doi:10.1002/smj.4250140303

Plastal (2005). Bilancio del Capitale Intangibile (Intangible Capital Report), sent by Plastal's management to one of the authors, Italian version.

Porter, M. E. (1980). *Competitive Strategy*. New York: Free Press.

Prahalad, C. K., & Hamel, G. (1990). The core competence of the corporation. *Harvard Business Review*, (May-June): 79–91.

Ricceri, F. (2002). *Intellectual Capital: between strategy and measurement*. Unpublished doctoral thesis, University of Venice, Italy.

Ricceri, F. (2004). Intellectual Capital (IC) statement: the case of an Italian "(non-)knowledge-intensive" company'. In A. Neely, M. Kennerley, & A. Walters (Eds) *Performance Measurement and Management: Public and Private*. (pp. 875-881) Cranfield: Center for Business Performance, Cranfield School of Management, Cranfield.

Ricceri, F. (2008). *Intellectual capital and knowledge management: Strategic management of knowledge resources*. London, New York: Routledge.

Ricceri, F., & Guthrie, J. (2009). Critical analysis of international KR guidelines for knowledge-intensive organisations. In Jemielniak, D., & Kociatkiewicz, J. (Eds.), *Handbook of research on knowledge-intensive organizations*. IGI Global.

Roos, G., Pike, S., & Fernström, L. (2005). *Managing intellectual capital in practice*. Oxford: Elsevier.

Senge, P. M. (1990). The leader's new work: Building a learning organization. *Sloan Management Review*, *32*(1), 2–18.

Sentensia, Q. (2006*). Intellectual Capital Report*, retrieved February 2007 www.sentensia.se.

Society for Knowledge Economics (SKE). (2005). *Australian guiding principles on extended performance management*. Sydney: SKE.

Society for Knowledge Economics (SKE). (2007). *Intangible drivers of organisational productivity and Prosperity*. Sydney: SKE.

Striukova, L., Unerman, J., & Guthrie, J. (2008). Corporate reporting of Intellectual Capital: Evidence from UK companies. *The British Accounting Review*, *40*(4), 297–313. doi:10.1016/j.bar.2008.06.001

Subcommittee on Management & Intellectual Assets (SMIA) (2005). *Interim report by subcommittee on management and intellectual assets*, August.

Sveiby, K. E. (1997). *The new organizational wealth: Managing and measuring knowledge based assets*. San Francisco: Berret Koehler.

Systematic (2004). *Intellectual Capital report*. Retrieved March 2007 from www.systematic.com

Teece, D. J., Pisano, G., & Shuen, A. (1997). Dynamic capabilities and strategic management. *Strategic Management Journal*, *18*(7), 509–533. doi:10.1002/(SICI)1097-0266(199708)18:7<509::AID-SMJ882>3.0.CO;2-Z

(The) Nordic Industrial Fund (Ed.). (2003). How to develop and monitor your company's Intellectual Capital — Tools and actions for the competency-based organisation. Retrieved March 2008 http://www.icframe.net/

Unerman, J., Guthrie, J., & Striukova, L. (2007). *UK reporting of Intellectual Capital*. London: Institute of Chartered Accountants in England and Wales Centre for Business Performance.

KEY TERMS AND DEFINITIONS

Financial Assets: Financial assets refer to the elements directly related to the measurement of the organisation's financial positions. It includes the $-value of financial assets (cash reserves, receivable balance, provisions, inventory balance), liabilities (loans, accounts payable, unearned revenue), and equity. It also includes elements such as: revenue, expenses, profit margin and cash-flows.

Human Resources: refer to the attributes related to individuals and include elements such as employees knowledge, abilities, skills, experiences and innovativeness. These resources will be within the organisation as long as the employee is staying with the organisation itself.

Structural Resources: consist in "all those things that remain in the organisation when the employees have left the building" (Leif Edvinsson), and are in some way owned or controlled by the organisation. Structural resources includes 'Intellectual property' and 'Infrastructural resources'. Intellectual property is owned by the company and protected by law, it includes elements such as patents, trademarks and copyrights. Infrastructural resources consist in the organisational characteristics as methods and procedures and the organisational support provided to individuals to achieve strategic objectives. Therefore, structural resources include, but are not limited to: culture, processes, routines, and information and networking systems.

Relational Resources: include the organisation brand and image in the marketplace, as well as relationships with external *stakeholders* (such as government, customers, partners and retailers, suppliers, residents, ecc.). These resources are not owned by the organisation but they can be at least managed considering *stakeholders* needs, along with the external environment opportunities and threats, in strategy formulation.

Intellectual Capital Statement or Report (ICS): The Intellectual Capital Statement is a reporting instrument that is made for informing the management of KR of the organisation, including objectives, actions and results. The Intellectual Capital Statement is a management tool used to generate value in a company and a communication tool to communicate to employees, customers, cooperative partner and investors how a company generates value.

Knowledge Resources (Intellectual Capital): Intellectual Capital (IC) is the organisational framework that is adopted to identify and address the management of knowledge resources. Knowledge resources are classified into three *components* and related *elements*, this tripartite classification is commonly known as Intellectual Capital (IC).

Knowledge Resources (Intellectual Capital) Information: Intellectual Capital information consists in IC metrics and Intellectual Capital narratives that relate to the management of KR of an organisation. Intellectual capital metrics are financial and non-financial indicators that refer to individual elements of the three IC dimensions Most of Intellectual Capital metrics are context specific and there are no widely accepted standards that help readers in understanding the meaning of the reported metrics. In other terms '[IC] numbers do not speak'). Therefore, knowledge resources metrics may be accompanied by narratives and visuals (i.e. figures, tables, maps) which explain the numbers meaning and explicit the relationships between KR, strategy and actions. IC metrics, narratives and visuals constitute the Intellectual Capital information.

Management of Knowledge Resources: The management of KR is concerned with the identification, development and use of KR in order to create value or to further develop the value creating potential of KR. It also includes the activities related to make KR manageable via the identification and use of Knowledge resources (IC) information.

Organisational Resources: Organisational resources are classified into two broad categories: Tangible Assets (which are composed by Financial Assets and Physical Assets) and Knowledge Resources (Intellectual Capital).

Physical Assets: Physical assets refer to tangible resources such as plant, property, equipment and inventory.

Strategic Intent: The strategic intent represents the strategic position the organisation aspires to, and it is normally expressed relative to the competitors, and/or to the distinctive KR resources of the organisation and/or in terms of perceived value by customers, and other *stakeholders*. The strategic intent should reflect the critical KR of that organisation as this helps in guiding behaviours (Hamel and Prahalad, 1989).

Strategy: Strategy determines and reveals the organisational purposes in terms of long-term objectives, action, programs, and resources allocation priorities; selects the business the organisation is in or is to be in; it is a coherent and unifying and pattern of decisions; defines the nature of the economic and non-economic contributions it intends to make to its stakeholders; is an expression of the strategic intent of the organisation; is aimed at developing and nurturing the KR of the firm; is a mean for investing selectively in tangible and intangible resources to develop the capabilities that are core for value creation.

Tangible Assets: Tangible asset are made up of *Financial assets* and *Physical assets*.

ENDNOTES

[1]   Several IC frameworks developed by national and international institutions to guide in the management and reporting of IC are analysed in more depth in Ricceri and Guthrie, 2009.

[2]   Several IC frameworks developed by national and international institutions to guide in the management and reporting of IC are analysed in more depth in Ricceri and Guthrie, 2009.

[3]   The key concepts of KR and IC are defined in more detail in Coyte, Guthrie and Ricceri, 2009.

[4]   The aim of the analysis was not to highlight the amount of information reported, as many previous academic studies on the reporting of IC have done (e.g., Guthrie & Petty, 2000; Olsson, 2001; Brennan, 2001; Bozzolan *et al.* 2003; Bozzolan *et al.* 2006; Guthrie *et al.* 2007; Striukova *et al.*, 2008), but to gain a general understanding of how organisations manage and report KR.

[5]   The web search was performed in English and in Italian and looked for the following words: intellectual capital, intellectual capital statement, intellectual capital report, intangible capital, intangible assets, intangible assets report, intangible assets statement, intangibles, intangible resources, knowledge, knowledge management, management of knowledge resources, knowledge assets, knowledge resources, knowledge reports.

[6]   A much wider sample of organisations including public listed, SME, public sector, etc were analysed and are reported in Ricceri (2008).

[7]   For some generalised checklists, see for instance, Sveiby (1997), Guthrie and Petty (2000), Bozzolan *et al.* (2003), Guthrie *et al.* (2007) and Ricceri & Guthrie (2009).

[8]   The "Knowledge Activities Account 2005" has been provided by the management of Arkitema to the authors. The report consisted of 23 pages.

[9]   ATP was named the Best European Pension Fund in 2005 by an international jury appointed by the magazine *Investment & Pensions Europe*.

[10] The report was available at: http://www.atp. dk/ and consisted of 13 pages (accessed in February 2007).

[11] The report specifies that Carl Bro UK/Ireland started producing ICS Statements in 2001 while Carl Bro Sweden started the process in 2003 (Carl Bro, 2005; pp.12-13). Also, since 2004 the ICA is not produced as a separate account and is included in a specific section (i.e., "Intellectual Resources") of the annual report. In 2006 Carl Bro was acquired by Grontmij (www.grontmij.com) and re-named Grontmij Carl Bro.

[12] The ICA is available at, www.carlbro.com and consists of 3 pages (pp.12-14). Page 3 of the annual report was also considered as it better explained the organisation's strategy. As in 2004, Intellectual Capital Accounts for 2005 will not be published in a separate form (Carl Bro, 2005; p.13).

[13] The Intellectual Capital Report 2005 (Cowi 2005) it is also available as a click-through report on the organisation's website (www. cowi.com). The Intellectual Capital Report considered in this analysis was a sub-section of the annual report and consisted of six pages (accessed in February 2007).

[14] The Intangible Capital Statement was made available by Plastal's management to the author. It consisted of 15 pages.

[15] The ICR was available as a stand-alone document on the organisation's website (www. Sentensia.se), accessed in February 2007. The report consisted of 13 pages and

includes a sub-section with a set of indicators which were developed in the PIP project (see, http://nhki.si.is/).

[16] ICR were produced in 1999, 2000, 2002 and 2004. The 2004 was the latest available on Systematic's website (www.systematic.com was last accessed in March 2007). The report consists of 36 pages and was included as it contained an audit opinion of the ICR.

Chapter 4
Knowledge Management and Project Management in 3D:
A Virtual World Extension

Steve Russell
Siemens Corporate Research, USA

ABSTRACT

Project management can be improved using modern interfaces that more naturally show work situations. Employees have deep real world knowledge that can be exploited, and a sense of common purpose among team members that can be enhanced. But, project efforts are currently guided only with structured charts and diagrams that show participants the state of their team's work activities. These charting tools have become more colorful and visually clear over time to reduce any uncertainty regarding task assignments, interdependencies, and any important schedule delays. However, a three dimensional environment extends the range of vision dramatically. Any team member can see what is currently being developed, the status of the process, and any pertinent actions needing focus, all in persistent and prominent wall displays. Discussions among remote collaborators are facilitated, focused on common views of pressing circumstances. Knowledge retention and transfer is more robust, and is illustrated in more compelling contexts keyed to current work activities. The immediacy of three dimensional world immersion will allow even forgetful workers to see at a glance the state of their contribution as well as the completion progress of those upon whom they depend.

INTRODUCTION

In this chapter, virtual worlds (VWs) are taken seriously as core elements in future work activities. Already useful in simulating and visualizing factories, in conducting meetings remotely, in

practicing maneuvers in military and space missions, and in delivering enriched training, VWs are mature enough now to be employed in planning and managing ongoing task activities among coordinated teams of contributors. The focus here is on an innovative implementation of Project Management (PM) in such an environment, and the issues involved in general adoption. The ideas,

DOI: 10.4018/978-1-61520-829-6.ch004

tools, and teamwork have already been moved in part into this domain, and there have been findings and lessons that are valuable as further VW project aids are institutionalized.

From a Knowledge Management (KM) perspective, there are also many exciting discoveries and powerful tools which are advancing our understanding of human know-how and shared expertise. Conceptualizations of work environments are already augmented and directed by computer applications and the by the electronically extended perceptions of reality that this involves. It is no stretch to say that workers and companies are becoming more and more thoroughly cybernetic – with crucial software and digital network components. Lessons gleaned slowly over decades of software experience are now solidified into digital rule-bases and best practice guides. Recent social networking platforms further bind those with similar needs and interests, using high-traffic electronic roadways for discussion, interpersonal query, and morale building. Knowledge has grown over the past sixty or seventy years along with the computer itself, and with the network of links that give light-speed connectivity to vast amounts of information. The breadth and fluidity of this knowledge-base sharing fundamentally changes the thought patterns of human contributors. The social nature of work, with collaborative outsourcing and readily available utilities, deeply alters the roles and duties of previously "individual" contributors. Group knowledge and the emergent intelligence of swarms of collaborators have become impossible to ignore for enterprises. So it is with the even deeper changes been promoted by Virtual Worlds.

Knowledge in a Virtual World has many facets. A worker immediately perceives the location setting, the current task situation, other actors, and potential courses of productive action. Just as in the real world (RW), the time and space dynamics are natural and intuitive and inherently social. This is a key point, so it is worth spending a moment on the differences between the VW capabilities and

current methods of understanding and managing work. A list of areas is offered in the following, where immersive, dynamic, and collective presence in a VW enriches and fundamentally extends the power of a worker and the overall workforce.

Project Management (PM) in a VW: Feasibility and Requirements Definition

The starting point of a project is the determination of a need or a desired change. Those responsible for building the project plan have to see the future state that is desired – its benefits as opposed to the current state and the path of changes that lead to it. There must be a company vision as well, where the money and time investments are justified in the context of competition, markets, and other enterprise needs. A conceptual vision is elucidated, and the costs and budgeting are financially checked. Affected stakeholders are carefully identified so as to ensure common purpose. While this step can be less formal than later PM steps, it is crucial to "cover the bases" in preparation for a successful project outcome. Enterprises have executed many projects concurrently, so aligning the resources and personnel among them over time is also important. The overall charter, steps, general deliverables, and timelines are discussed.

What can a computer product offer in this initiation stage? As opposed to trying to write out steps and dependencies by hand, a computerized tool gives formal layouts and steps for activities like scheduling, budget management, team communication and documentation. Rather than pasting charts along walls, the formal documentation is managed through a dedicated service. The development is stepped out, and there are sometimes narratives stored which briefly explain assumptions and objectives.

A Virtual World environment adds a deeper clarity regarding the succession of states in the development, and the final state of affairs. A rough drawing or artist's conception is extended

Figure 1.

into 3D with a miniature model that shows the stack of documents, physical product before-and-after, or the buildings in their incremental construction. Money flows and evolving risk profiles can be indicated by colors, pulsation of brightness, or the extrusion of part of an item. In Figure 1, a plot of flat land is converted into a set of virtual world buildings, according to plans that started as a pencil-and-paper sketch and then a flat color drawing, then rough 3D boxes and finally a detailed 3D plan for a set of buildings. Before detailed building, the project is sketched and modeled in the virtual space where alternative paths of spending and development can be explored. If needed, avatar representatives can walk around the miniature or full sized virtual layout to see if it meets the requirements for the eventual construction.

PM in a Virtual World: Artifacts

A standard computer application for Project Management can display various charts such as Gantt bar-chart sequencing, organization chart reporting, and so on. In the virtual world, many of these sorts of artifacts can be shown at the same time spread across the walls of a room. As mentioned above, the virtual room can also have 3D models of the development stages as they have progressed and as they are expected to occur. Even a database project or a software development project can have such 3D models, indicating structures, linkages, and dynamics shown to illustrate components and actions. Furthermore, a participant can point to or touch some of these artifacts which can be set up to react to this with further linked information or even animated illustrations.

It is worth noting that the appearance of a setting such as a project planning room is the same for all avatar-participants. However, displayed

Figure 2.

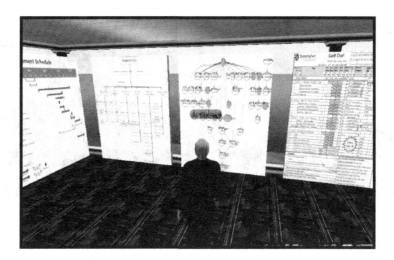

information can change by selecting, pressing, or even by the detection of a selected avatar. The attention of that actor can be thereby focused on just the items that most apply to them. This inter-activity and personalized liveliness is distinctly different from current static two dimensional (2D) software tools. Varying aspects of a project and differing viewpoints for distinct role players add a richness and intuitive navigation previously unavailable.

The clarity, coordination, and dynamism of artifacts are designed to match the visual and behavioral habits that are familiar to workers in the real world. Whereas many workers find complex text and graphics difficult to track, the virtual world setup's natural feel can be under-stood by anyone who can play a standard video game. Workers and their managers can even edit and add appropriate explanations, as with a wiki or blog – but pinned directly at the point in space where the addition will be most useful. When the pinned data is clicked on like a mashed-up Google map, the flow of text or illustrations will be displayed right next to the object in question, like a person on an organizational chart or a line on a product requirements document. Just as mashups enrich Google applications, RSS feeds, and of the Internet software, the result is a more

usable application. Such four-dimensional (4D, which is the solid 3D model plus behavior in time) interactivity, is 4D-I. 4D-I display artifacts are profoundly more knowledge-enriched with apt, terse, local in-context information on-demand and as-a-service, provided democratically. Projects thus enabled benefit from a steady accumulation of explanations, suggestions, and even mini-debate tweet-streams. This sociable modality is very modern, and in line with the dispersed talent sets of cooperating team members and support networks.

PM in a Virtual World: Meetings

In person, by telephone, and even tele-presence Cisco mega-screen meet-ups offer certain advan-tages as modes of remote person-to-person or group communications. To share digital applica-tions, additional tools exist such as Webex. Of course nothing is quite the same as being there. But a virtual world offers more – and certainly more than just a reduction on travel costs. As al-ready explained, there is a great deal of enhanced visual clarity, organized physical space, and strong interactivity in this dynamic environment. One example is that of a so-called "War Room" where there many project documents and artifact displays for discussion and interaction. In large product

Figure 3.

projects, military missions, and cold-case detective hunts, rooms can be set aside for maps, miniature table-top models, and interconnected issues and photographs. Of course the situation in a VW is richer, with videos and interactive exhibits that can convey behaviors. For example, ideas and issues can be mapped together by sticking cards on the virtual-room wall (the "COW" method) and connecting them with colored string or yarn like a 3D mind-map. In the VW, if a card is touched, however, it can be coded to zoom forward and to get larger, with its links to other cards highlighted. The issue and its connected issues are in this way hard to ignore even for a less-than-attentive project member.

Meetings can be held as walk-about affairs or sit-down formal sessions with a main speaker. Common office programs such as spreadsheets and slide-show displays can be brought in from external office computers for discussion, as well as movies and active 3D models, say of wind generation units.

PM in a Virtual World: Milestone Reviews and Deliverables

Walkthroughs with stakeholders and project team members can be guided by interesting Gantt charts with "touch-ability" that can show late items and critical dependencies. If a late item is in a physi-

cal unit like a building or a turbine, a model of that item can also be invoked for presentation and even dissection. For some participants, the "triple constraint" of tradeoffs (Time, Cost, and Scope) can be clarified. In order to get desired quality or cost targets, the time frame may need to be extended. Or, it could be that the delivery time and funding is inflexible and the number of high-quality-and-functionality features may need to be reduced. These tradeoffs can be made apparent in the virtual world by indicating quality and number of delivered functions in say a colored bar, and reducing this level (and perhaps turning it a pulsing red) when costs get too high and deadlines cannot be moved.

Returning to the Gantt chart, this iconic expression of project progress can be made a central focus of display. There can be a highly detailed chart, or it could be a series of charts, say starting from a high-level summarization with only ten or fewer high-level work areas. Clicking on a particular work area can then result in a new dynamically-produced drill-down display of this particular grouped-level-item broken out into the more-detailed Gantt charts for its sub-project work items.

A chart in 3D could show the WBS (Work Breakdown Structure) activities and actors and their current status, with animations that could show the patterns of involvement among contribu-

Figure 4.

Figure 5.

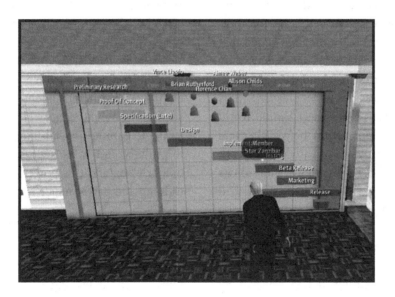

tors over the course of the project. Here again the visual and attractive nature of a large wall sized display can attract and sustain the attention of even unskilled and busy project contributors.

PM in a Virtual World: Training and Task Rehearsal

A dynamic virtual world is a natural platform for integrating new staff members. Showing the purpose, time course, physical flows, and current situation can visually convey the situation and any important problems. But just as in sports, it is good to practice. A common feature of modern military strategy is the war game and associated digital mission rehearsals. In a virtual world, unlike the real world, the construction of a duplicate setting for training is cheap. This is in part due to the near free duplication of graphical elements and also due to the extremely inexpensive purchase price of hand-made items in the "nano-economy" of VWs like Second Life which have a flourishing

Figure 6.

real-virtual currency exchange system. Similar to a football practice field or high-end digital basketball game system, work sessions can run through situations over and over. Some psychology theories of neural learning have stated that unlearning of inefficient modes and the learning of improved task performance modes can be enhanced by repeated sessions under pressure – as is seen in sports. IBM has developed a Virtual World Rehearsal Studio with the help of the WTRI virtual world research company, specifically for real work training. Using measured sessions of individuals and groups, this approach has resulted in published studies supporting significant and even surprising improvements in task performance. The areas of real world work-improvement addressed so far in this way have included transit systems, document handling, gold mining, and pharmaceutical operations. Below are screen captures of a Second Life Operations Center and its duplicate Rehearsal area built by WTRI for training and retraining command and control team members.

For project related tasks, similar VW-based training would be a serious adjunct to other training methods currently done with books, stand-up lectures, in-person team-building and web-based 2D training modules. The proven advantages of the VW rehearsal methods include the realism, multi-actor cooperation, rapid setup and reset, inexpensive alternate paths, and the ability to,

measure many more activities, decisions, timings, and motions. In addition to the wide variety of challenges and circumstances that can be presented to the learner, there are important issues of low overall cost and zero risk of personal harm.

Notably, the rehearsal sessions often have the flavor of popular computer games. Many younger employees are already adept in rapidly mastering such environments. The field of serious gaming or strategic gaming is well-understood and proven in military and space settings, so it is a natural matter to extend this power to business uses in training and performance improvement.

PM in a Virtual World: Value

The world of the second decade of the new millennium is steadily leaving the systems and outlooks of the 1980s and 1990s behind. There are global talent wars, massive Baby Boomer retirement headaches, economic downturns, population and climate challenges, compliance avalanches, and tidal waves of data coming from all directions. The Virtual World platforms offer a more understandable setting, natural parallels to familiar issues, remotely accessible collaboration and meeting places, and opportunities to componentize and partially outsource multi-specialty work team efforts. Scarce and infrequently needed resource skills are more readily made on-call in the ubiquitous social platforms for virtual societies. As smart phones and other small mobile computing platforms grow in power, virtual environments are becoming available on-demand in smaller app-sized mini-sessions. VW views of just the most pertinent project data at a given time and circumstance are in this way even more influential in reinforcing shared schedules and important deliverables.

The investments in these brave new worlds have been nominal in general, far less than the funds needed for real construction and travel. The returns on these investments (ROI) have matured from marketing promotions to improved products to better work teams. Their integration with legacy enterprise systems, the newer social media tools, and high end graphical and video applications are providing the grounds for rapid innovation, strategic vision, and competitive advantage. In the arena of Project Management, the adoption of these high-return and exciting virtual technologies is sure to accelerate. Since many projects are repeated in similar subsequent projects, a full lifecycle of project management (PML) can be considered – along with the associated Knowledge Lifecycle Management (KLM) issues. KLM in a Virtual World can include attention to project artifact appearances and interactive behaviors which are improved over project execution loops.

The form of VW adoption for Project Management will start with demonstration developments, followed by separate partially integrated VW add-ons. Finally, perhaps in the next five to ten years, there will likely be major PM tools that offer fully integrated systems with many of the capabilities detailed above. Over time, the superior areas of advantage using the VW tools and techniques will be financially measured and tracked more widely to justify PM software purchases, PM team member training, and increased adoption for the majority of significant project team efforts. Interfaces with Knowledge Management tools and methods will even further enhance the ROI, especially where the particular extensions

to KM in 3D and 4D and interactive 4D (4D-I KM) are included.

Virtual World Issues and Insights

Now that some of the areas of Project Management in a Virtual World setting have been explored, more attention can be devoted to considering the underlying characteristics of VWs where more study can yield deeper understanding and more success in implementations. The value in a deep dive into this new sea of information is that a common language of terminology is a foundational prerequisite. To apply the virtues of VW to any field, and to PM in particular, it will be necessary to take the time to consider many aspects of the novelty and promise – and the possible pitfalls. This seems to take a few months for most seasoned PM specialists, spent in roaming VWs and mulling the terms and fledgling developments pertinent to their needs. It may not be possible to bypass this needed immersion time, but the perhaps abstruse topics and pronouncements below are offered here in the belief that their value will go beyond an initial browse-through. It is hoped that a return to some of these expositions later may be of value in a PM endeavor with virtual world components.

Text and Graphics vs. Virtual World Immersion

Previous advances in storing work-related experience, in codifying understanding, and in sharing outlooks have generally involved portraying the situation with words or simple diagrams on paper or flat computer screens. This meant a complex of various coding and decoding activities and a severe reduction of the feature set. Events in the world are in this way expressed through mappings to a set of named ideas as words or idealized iconic images (semiotics). This transition to the language of words, both spoken and written, has certainly enabled the large-scale coordination of group activities and has cast in stone many useful human experiences. This nominal power has promoted societies of governance, belief, and work. But the partial representation of real events in linguistic characters also strips away many features and commits people to given patterns of conception. The sensibility of a situation is too often channeled by the patterned grammars, intentional rhetorics, and formal group coordination schemes. In a more naturalistic setting, some of these constraints can be eased for more accuracy and flexibility.

The coding and decoding involved in verbal and written communication are an intermediate step in seeing and synchronizing work. Intermediation through the focus of text, and the more recent on-screen computer charting, demands a certain mental agility. Each worker has to be able to grasp the importance of his or her particular role in a team effort, and to translate the layout and shading or coloring to glean their daily status. In a pre-computer setting, these coordinations would be more verbal and based on common patterns of interactivity which are learned incrementally. Many nonverbal situations such as military or hunting expeditions still revert to more positional, gestural, and projected-outcome forms of coordination. This will be the case in a virtual setting as well, with a naturalistic synchronizing of the shared sense in a situation and its outcomes. A more direct experiential interplay will replace many of the current verbal intermediaries through which workers communicate. Disintermediation of the text, by reducing the load of encoding and decoding words or other symbols, opens up the modes of idea sharing and common purpose in ways which are deep in human interactivity. Words are not the only way of trapping ideas. Pictograms, and more recent flow-charts and spreadsheet cells are also semiotic formats.

A virtual world offers an alternative to some of the language and graphics in a "semiotic disintermediation" that can be more accessible to more participants. Show-me systems in a virtual task illustration often require less long-winded linguistic explanations or checks with progress diagrams.

Since "visualization is a universal language", the 3D models and table-top geographic terrains are far more amenable to old and young, native and immigrant, and those with either extensive or only cursory formal education backgrounds. The visual cues in a realistic world setting in this way use a mode of sharing and coordinating that is older than computers, older than books, and even older than language itself.

Other knowledge about the forms and roots of human understanding is maturing. Many of these findings and new outlooks bear directly on why a Virtual World setting will be superior to current computerized Project Management tools. For instance, only recently has the degree of nonverbal communication among nonhuman species been apparent. From quorum sensing in bacteria to threat postures in predators, data exists in the layout of the actions and actors in a flowing scene. For eons, the ability to discern the meaning of such life-and-death scenes has had a survival value. The "eonic" intelligence shaped in this way is much more grounded and fundamental in humans that might be thought by those more adept in academics. Contrasted with the near-universal facility of humans in typical real-world situations is the fact that only a few people truly excel at producing and decoding text and business charts. These text-proficient people are often the leaders in a task effort, and they often assume that every other participant has the same facility in understanding complex intertwined goals as expressed on paper or a flat computer screen. Not coincidentally, these people are often those who have gotten the superior grades on the text-based academic institutions

As a side note, the growth in the business requirements to write and share, to publish and read, has encouraged a separation of influence based on literacy. When the outlook is thus dominated by the more successful persons who have stronger language skills, a phenomenon of narrowed interpersonal awareness can occur. Success can lead a person to believe that their way of conceptualization is the root cause of their advantages and that the modes of thinking in others are less optimal. Allospection, the ability to see the world through the eyes of another, can also become diminished. When this happens, some performance imperfections can be improperly attributed to poor mental agility or to patterns founded in relatively inferior reading skills. The altruism that is a foundational glue for team success is certainly not encouraged nor rewarded if such authority structures are based in differential capabilities in navigating complex project documentation. Also, given that "half of the world is below average" on any given ability measure, there will likely be many project participants whose interests in complex requirements might be less than desired. More will be considered later in this chapter on how VWs can naturally encourage the perception of work situations from others' viewpoints.

Efforts to improve employee adherence to chart-based planning and to extensive and abstruse project documents can be a doomed approach. Hounding employees who get behind according to a nest of deadlines or who fail to adhere to a buried policy can often discourage whole-hearted cooperation, rather than encourage compliance with all project artifacts. A case can be made for reducing the needed awareness at lower work-accomplishment levels, with managers being responsible for ensuring the pace of progress. Still, a VW's superior visibility can reduce this burden while encouraging buy-in on the part of even the ground-floor performers.

The Deeper Nature and Value of Virtual Platforms

A misunderstanding can occur in the adoption of a seemingly too-high-tech virtual world platform. The game-like look-and-feel can also be seen as alien and to be at odds with serious business operations. However it is perhaps worth considering another way to look at the emergence of a naturalistic, collaborative, and immersive simulated world.

Suppose that the only way to understand another nation or a newly discovered species was textual – no travel to see first-hand, no direct encounters with the life-forms, no establishing of residences for interaction. Just text. This collapse of the real world into a static two-dimensional shadow recalls the Platonic cave where all perception is indirect. Like the evil characters in a Superman movie, this is like a confinement to a flat "Phantom Zone" imprisonment. Recovering the 3D freedom of motion and perception is in this way actually an escape from the 2D prison's labyrinth of partial awareness. One could see the Virtual World then as simply a reinstatement of some of the more natural visibility and camaraderie. Far from being "too hard" for certain parties such as the elderly, people less familiar with technology, or even no-nonsense business executives, the realism in the platform more often proves to be refreshingly simple, natural, and even enjoyable.

The steady advance in interfaces and in the sharing of information has involved many signal developments. In recent Project Management history, the development of computerized tools linked with business circumstances has extended the ability to oversee huge pools of people and capital for successful outcomes. From Microsoft Project to tools like Primavera, these software aids have helped to institutionalize a management style for disciplined work. Before these, the invention of the computer and networked connectivity were central in coordinating distant and disparate teams in complex accomplishments. Yet earlier, the sciences of work itself were better considered using tools like Statistical Process Control (SPC) and Operations Research (OR). But far earlier, the simple recording of work on a two dimensional surface was found to be instrumental, as seen in ancient scrolls and wall glyphs. In between, the sharing of ideas in written form was revolutionized when movable type made printed works affordable and open to ownership by nearly anyone. The "Gutenberg-level" is how some are now describing the impending adoption of Virtual

Worlds, based on the ideas detailed here and in the worldwide press.

Time Magazine has made up a list of the most influential novels in most of the past century. This list includes two Virtual World-based books where the protagonists experience portions of their lives and work activities in mixtures and alterations between real and virtual domains. The influential nature of these works is attributed to their impact on subsequent works of fiction as well as on the thoughts for real directions for improvements in future work productivity. Given the profound successes already seen in the only the last five years when VWs have become mature, the outlook is bright for more productivity gains. For one thing, Linden Labs' Second Life platform touts a growing user base of over 70,000 simultaneously participating online in the same world, with over a million and a half logins over a single month span. One industry estimate predicts that one billion people will have experienced "life as an avatar" in at least one virtual world setting within the next eight years – one person in seven on earth. So some would say that "resistance is futile", regarding the adoption of VWs for real work. These may be for now, of course, extreme viewpoints on Virtual World valuation, but worth considering as counterpoints to any pooh-poohing of their potential value.

In any event, a reversion to the more natural and mutual forms of coordination would likely be welcome and effective. The guides, as enabled in a virtual version of the real world situation, will be more intuitive and efficient. Group behaviors, recently better understood as swarm or herd-like coordinations, can then be applied to make many group actions less stultified and less frictional. A degree of routinizing or automaticity can then be more readily instituted, where coordination is a part of the format of the facility and the equipment layouts. Then, the budgeted thinking capacity of a worker can be saved for use in those situations needing more dedicated attention like outages or emergencies.

The knowledge is then a part of the environment itself, embedded in the fabric and dynamics of the setting itself like geographic contours that favor some directions and pacing over others.

The population that is amenable to highly structured graphical displays and complex sets of documentation is a group of individuals who once would have been seen as being drawn from the right-hand portion of a bell curve of intelligence and dedication. The high-achievement crew has been a feature in many management styles and business school assumptions as the natural group for controlling projects. Linguistic facility was equivalent to task skill and to the understanding of group dynamics. It is often counter-intuitive, then, that a virtual world can be of value to a much wider population from this debatable bell curve. The "90% sweet spot" in the center of such a hypothesized curve are those who can hold down jobs, fight wars, elect leaders, and raise families – activities of great importance and complexity. It has only been the tools and politics of semiotic achievement that have barred this broader set of "eonically-smart" individuals from coordination roles in projects. With a virtual backdrop of natural-world sensibility at hand, however, this much greater pool of talent can be mined for effective task completions.

Virtual World Navigation and Perception

"The format is the message." This is akin to Marshall McLuhan's assertion that the medium of television conveys and constrains information by its very nature. The layout of text, the cadence of a harangue, the pagination of a project plan; these by their layout in space and time convey the importance and direct the serialization of states of consciousness. The intent of the writer is like that of a dynamic sculptor digging a river-bed to shape the flow of understanding by the reader. The form of the expression guides the reader's perceptions of the encoded material and the time course of mental states laid out by the author in a so-called "rhetorical" manner. In a virtual world, this is different, with authoring of settings themselves that convey areas of needed attention and perspectives in what should be a more natural manner. To run around obstacles and to avoid pitfalls is intuitive and normal in the daily world experience of anyone. The virtual world allows for the construction of settings and the channeling of understanding that appears more like this nature-given avoidance of trouble and optimization of outcomes. For example, lateness or poor quality in one participant's work product can be visually shown in its impacts on the utility and safety of the final goods – just in time for that person to take corrective action. If a lazy-day lapse in attention is resulting in defective bolts or code-modules for an automobile, a virtual display can just then emerge in view to clearly portray the possibly negative result of the eventually finished vehicle crashing and hurting people due to this particular inferior component.

In a virtual world as in the real world, people walk around. This peripatetic meandering can be tapped to better display information and share knowledge. Walls in real workplaces already are posted with notices and incentives to quality. As in the real world, the selection of messages and their discreet placement is crucial to their impact. Clutter, outdated materials, and uncoordinated messages are deadly in marketing products like soft drinks – so a unified messaging with regular rotations is similarly necessary. It is also important to accommodate the ways in which people perceive visual settings. From millennia of natural efforts like hunting and avoiding predators, humans have a set of exquisitely sensitive dynamic 3D senses for detecting alerts and opportunities. One example is peripheral vision. While looking ahead, a portion of one's subliminal attention is continuously dedicated to activities at the edge of the field of view. As in driving a car, events at the edge of the windshield such as animals or hazard signs are key to safe navigation. The presenta-

tion field of view in a virtual workplace should recognize this sensitivity to peripheral events. In a speaker-focused meeting, peripheral displays can be diffused or removed, whereas in some task displays the information content of the sidebar status indicators can be subtly adjusted to help indicate key circumstances and possible danger.

These sorts of recognitions of virtual world perceptions and expectations are like the ergonomic considerations applied to workplace comfort and safety. From fields such as Operations Research (OR), Industrial Engineering (IE), Efficiency Analysis, Human Factors and Human-Computer Interaction (HCI), the perceptions and motions of workers can be investigated. Improvements in performance can often be accomplished by simple alterations in the seating and in the timely display of useful information. These considerations in the virtual world involve a virtual version of ergonomics, or "vergonomics", as well as novel productivity or safety metrics and optimizations. The ways to express the virtual world issues in worker productivity are yet to be refined, but they will surely be cast in terms of the uniquely dynamic and immersive nature of these platforms. Workers' avatar-representatives can be measured for activities and outcomes that exist in the virtual setting, including the virtual versions of selected real world events that are mirrored there.

Virtual Work Measurement

In virtual worlds, work activities can not only be well-measured but these measurements can be a part of a targeted effort to improve performance on tasks ands strategies. A sports team can play their games in a stadium, yet have practice sessions in another field set up for that purpose. An orchestra can similarly rehearse outside of the finale performance venue. Such trials or "war-gaming" run-throughs involve repeated sessions that simulate the real performance activities and interactions that achieve targeted goals. Of course such run-throughs in a factory or laboratory or even in a document-centered negotiation cannot in general be duplicated in a practice-field manner. But in a virtual world such duplicate setups are natural and trivial to implement. Therefore, there have recently emerged formal ways to rehearse real work activities and collaborations in a virtual world environment. To be sure, virtual reality simulations of aircraft flight operations and aerospace missions have been used to instill skills and to explore risks. But the immersion of multiple simultaneous participants had been impossible or excessively expensive. With the advances fueled by Massively Multiplayer Online Role-Playing Games (MMORPGs), the technical architecture for remote casts of workers has become possible. Only in the past few years has this capability become more stable and commonly available. As opposed to virtual reality simulators or graphical story-board displays, such virtual worlds have a common stage for all participants at once where they can interact by moving, gesturing, sharing objects and documents, text-chatting, and even talking. Now it is possible to easily and cheaply run through immersive exercises of cooperation in ordinary and emergency situations. Also available is the ability to look more carefully at how actors in such spaces see the circumstances and make sense of the full scope of inputs. Sensemaking is a core framer for the knowledge needed in a situation, guiding the course of reactions, helping to find one's way (wayfinding), and planning for safe and efficient operations. The development of rapid or automatic situational awareness is the goal of repeated virtual world practice sessions. It has been seen that under pressure in repeated trials, individuals and work groups can discover new ways of approaching problems and measurements of their solution steps can be tracked and matched with the work effort outcomes. Some of the improvement comes from the unlearning of older and less efficient ways of conceptualization and action that is made possible by the time pressures and repeated trials. The natural "invisible hand" of re-organization for group participants is a realignment which is readily enabled in the VW "rehearsal studio" but which would have been difficult, expensive, and even unsafe on a RW (Real World) setting.

Computer games are a very successful market item, with advances in power and interfaces every year. More and more people spend time and billions of dollars on these contests and simulations, including popular virtual world games of warfare and fantasy realm quests. This acceptance has been noted by academic and enterprise analysts who predict that the employees now coming into the workforce ("millenials", and "Gen-i" Internet/iPhone youth) will have experience in online cooperation and strategizing that can be alien to most of their older pre-gaming managers. Harnessing the skillsets gleaned through the gaming exercises will be a challenge. This challenge will be more important as more of the factors covered above come into play in a convergent "perfect storm" of change such as digital youth, cybernetic acceptance, increased socialization, retiring Boomers, ubiquitous web, momentary-knowledge cell phone apps, blurring of simulation and reality, game-centered strategy development, virtualized computation and storage, and vast shared knowledge pools. The viral modernism here will be a social drift as opposed to a sudden market shift, resulting in a virtual-real or "virtureal" way of interacting with events and other cyber-solid citizens in daily life. This will be like the computer or cell phone or the Internet – not a new wave of temporary change, but a new way, a new standard.

Virtual Work Knowledge 4.0

In a less text-dominated world, knowledge and its transfer may well be more apprentice-like or incrementally shown on-demand and only as-needed. As in pre-literate societies, many modes of nonverbal signaling will return to importance as more than social lubricants or distractions. For instance, gestures such as acknowledgements and emphasis displays convey direct assertion with added force. Facial expressions also carry meaning and power. A frown from a project stakeholder may loom much larger than any progress chart red-box indicator. A virtual world avatar's expressions are controlled somewhat more consciously and deliberately at present. So, they may well be of great intentional communications value for determining agreement, or in indicting an affective inclination that can lead to disapprovals for certain milestone or deliverable checkpoints. Knowing the meaning of gestures and facial expressions is a newer field, particularly with respect to avatars.

Illustrations of skills and desired behaviors are conveyed to children by example. In a virtual world setting, a verbal explanation may be replaced with an animated walkthrough such as how to find your way around a virtual model of a hospital or new city or job site. Another example of non-book knowledge acquisition and application is seen in swarm insects and herd animals that "unconsciously" coordinate and share environmental knowledge. Human teams can also evince and optimize such emergent "trans-individual" understanding and can thereby benefit from improved collective performance skills. As a small extra example of non-literal dialogues, even blushing or reddening due to anger conveys human discomfort and emotional states – much like a squid in the ocean can change its colors when threatened. Some squid can also modulate ripples of beautiful colors along their bodies to send messages – a "squiddish" language which could have parallels in future avatar-communication or object-artificial-intelligence innovations.

So the honing and channeling of behavior in a shared setting like a work project can involve examples and group feedback and unspoken knowledge conveyance. Such "undocumented" coordination can direct and frame activities in a less thought-demanding manner. This sort of habituation and automaticity might well be possible to harness in complicated situations. Another application could be for integrating new employees, reducing the required cognitive loads and minimizing "on-boarding" delays and risks. Here as before, the virtual world shared platform gives a way to enact these benefits that cannot be duplicated in pre-millennial text and graphical project tools.

A point can also be made in favor of "KaaS" – Knowledge as a Service, where knowledge is available on-demand, from a remote expert with scarce expertise. If appropriate arrangements are made with, say a retired project tool expert, then that person might agree to be called for help. In the virtual PM setting, the avatar of the retired person would see the project status and indications of a root cause of a problem that they may have encountered in pervious decades of service. In future economic crunches, or talent shortages, or aging infrastructure related tasks, extending the lifespan of availability for expert knowledge in this manner could be of great value to the enterprise and its project workers.

Virtual Rules of Behavior

As in the real world, people may act inappropriately and perhaps in an undesired manner in virtual settings. On the internet, there is an expected etiquette or netiquette. In the virtual world, a kind of "vetiquette" should be expected. Good behavior is not only nice - it can be a matter of compliance with company rules and government regulations. Good citizenship can include cleaning up, helping others, keeping quiet, and reporting problems. This is really no different than the expectations in real world business settings. Since changes in the virtual world have enactors, responsible parties, and maintainers, there is a sense of ownership among individuals and teams that can be expected to encourage a continuously improved work context.

Virtual World History

The history of VWs consists of less than a decade of actual world-level implementations. In fact, only in the past five or so year have there been enough residents online to consider such worlds viable. The most popular virtual world at present is Linden Labs' Second Life (SL), the metaverse standard. A few of the other big world platform providers are Forterra, Teleplace, Photosphere, and Vast Park. Some of the worlds have higher quality graphics for more realism. Second Life has had residents and an economy, experimenting and maturing for over six years now. SL projects have included the construction of island-like domains focused on science and commerce and social interaction. Most U.S universities have hosted some form of island or event or course in SL. Other projects have used the visual power to help lay out buildings and activity plans, and to train first responders for emergencies. More recently, the power for business simulation has developed into full fledged rehearsal applications for trying out alternative business strategies. There are many interesting and important drivers, setbacks, and challenges for VWs, and the interested reader should refer to the references here or look online for more information.

Among the challenges in VW adoption are misconceptions regarding what they are. They are not simple User Interfaces (UIs), for one thing. The usage is also not a traditional User Experience (UE). Factors of immersion, physical realism, interactions with people and objects, and the ability to own, create, and sell are unlike older 2D screen applications. Building on preceding 3D systems such as Computer-Generated movie graphics (CG) and Virtual Reality (VR) simulations - which are normally single-user and less immersive and less interactive - VWs encourage individuals and groups to jump in to a much more world-like setting that has unique power based in its "realiness". Reputation, trust, confidence, and intent matter when one is "in-world", like when a person is in a new city in the real world. The very presence of another user or artificial-intelligence avatar promotes awareness, and users soon say "I am here" instead of "my avatar is in there".

There are novel interface and connectivity issues like the resolution of 3D moving images by the computer graphics card, or slow connection speeds, or company firewalls that block connections and images. Standards are emerging in many areas for interchangeability of objects between various virtual world platforms, and parts of the world look and feel. As shown in the pictures below, encounters with other avatar-users can be one-on-one or there can be a large group attending a project meeting. Note that the green indictor arcs above the head of the avatar in the left panel indicate that the avatar's human owner is using the Voice-Over-IP (VOIP) capability to talk to the other avatar's owner directly in the virtual scene.

There are developments for enhanced graphical quality, interfaces with video and office tools, and other business-friendly upgrades. The number of allowed simultaneous users at an event such as a meeting is increasing as well – over 80 or so avatars are currently the limit in a given server-generated island in SL.

The experience of being in the virtual world is normally like playing a game with a toy or a digital character. The role playing and adoption of the avatar characteristics are part of the experience. In a mixed real world and virtual world work situation such as a project planning session, a person exists in their mined partially or sequentially in both worlds. A fusion of the separate world experiences expands the viewpoint and the ways of determining context, and the ways of making sense of current circumstances.

Project Management in 4D-I: Additional Points

There are distinctions between projects, programs, and products. Each of these can be managed. Larger programs of sets of products and proj-

Figure 7.

ects would be a good next step in applying VW advantages. Product management can be a part off a larger lifecycle discipline or PLM, Project Lifecycle Management. The software for this purpose could also be augmented by 3D collaborative additions with good effect.

Some of the areas where a virtual world addition to Project Management would help right now are the subjects of strong corporate and governmental interest. These areas include Smart Grid, Green Buildings, Climate Response, Renewable Energy, and community changes like zoning or urban renewal. Some of these are likely places where a modern workforce might well benefit as early adopters. For example, projects in physical domains are natural candidates for digital simulations. A building's architectural design can be seen and shared over the Internet, a component of an automobile engine can be modeled, and a new food product can be tried out for handling and eye appeal. Software and conceptual products are harder to visualize directly, but there are already many graphical representations of situations like network connections, social networks, and algorithm operations. The steps in a schedule that flesh out these models can be cast in a large 3D model that is available for quick group consideration.

Also, in any area with diverse departments or areas of expertise such as a hospital, projects using a virtual world component could be effec-

tive. Ontologies from multiple fields can thereby be augmented with physical and visual examples and walkthroughs. Here as in other sensitive areas, there will likely be a demand for behind-the-firewall security in the platform as opposed to a universally open world like Second Life.

CONCLUSION

The discipline of Project Management would benefit from the intuitive and physical aspects of a remotely available Virtual World. The ability to see and understand more naturally will be very beneficial. Knowledge of the real physical situation will be portrayed in an obvious manner which reflects the concerns of the enterprise. Best practices for Knowledge Management in such a dynamic 3D interactive domain (4D-I) will help in ensuring the smartest developments that make maximum use of clear requirements and well managed human knowledge sources.

Some KM best practices for VW use in Project Management are:

- Develop realistic layouts related to the project at hand
- Engage participants in three dimensional (3D) world membership and remote telepresence discussions

- Allay the discomfort among participants less familiar with immersive online game platforms
- Reward the social skills of in-world expeditors who help other members to succeed
- Measure the utility of the added knowledge elements and virtual world clarity

The era of virtual world tools and platforms is emerging, and can only be expected to become more widespread in business and in project arenas.

REFERENCES

DiBello, L., Missildine, W., & Struttmann, M. (2009). The Long-Term Impact of Simulation Training on Changing Accountabilities in a Biotech Firm . In *Mind, Culture and Activity. Routledge Taylor&Francis Group*. Intuitive Expertise and Empowerment.

Forsberg, K., Mooz, H., & Cotterman, H. (2005). *Visualizing Project Management: Models and Frameworks for Mastering Complex Systems*. Wiley.

Gronstedt, A. (2008). *Training in Virtual Worlds*. ASTD Press.

Kerzner, H. (2005). *Project Management: A Systems Approach to Planning, Scheduling, and Controlling* (9th ed.). Wiley.

PMBOK (2008). *A Guide to the Project Management Body of Knowledge*.

Rymaszewski, M., Wagner, J. A., Ondrejka, C., Platel, R., Van Gorden, S., & Cézanne, J. (2008). *Second Life: The Official Guide* (2nd ed.). Sybex.

Weber, A., Rufer-Bach, K., & Platel, R. (2007). *Creating Your World: The Official Guide to Advanced Content Creation for Second Life*. Sybex.

Williams, M. (2008). *The Principles of Project Management*. SitePoint.

Chapter 5
Industrialisation of the Knowledge Work:
The Knowledge Conveyor Belt Approach

Dimitris Karagiannis
BOC Group, Austria

Robert Woitsch
BOC Group, Austria

Vedran Hrgovcic
University of Vienna, Austria

ABSTRACT

When analysing the transformation of the information society an industrialisation of knowledge work can be observed. The maturity, the quality, the process-orientation and the alignment of knowledge to personal or organisational requirements are industrialisation aspects covered by knowledge work. This chapter focuses on process-orientation, discusses the evolution of process-oriented knowledge management and sees the current industrialisation of knowledge work as a challenge that needs to be tackled not only on social and technical level but also on a conceptual level. Hence the so-called knowledge conveyor belt approach is introduced that is a realisation framework of process-oriented and service based knowledge management. This approach is seen as an answer for the requirements of industrialisation of knowledge work that keeps the "human in the loop" and enables the business and knowledge alignment. The realisation concepts and two implementation show cases are introduced.

INTRODUCTION

Knowledge work is becoming a mainstream activity in organisations and is emerging towards becoming a holistic critical success factor. Focusing on the business-aspects it can be stated that almost all areas of daily work within an organisation are affected by the way knowledge is treated.

Before discussing the knowledge work in more detail it is important to distinguish between Knowledge Engineering (KE), which is prioritizing machine interpretable knowledge, and Knowledge Management (KM) which is focused on the human interpretable knowledge.

DOI: 10.4018/978-1-61520-829-6.ch005

After both KE and KM already passed their hypes, both found their ways into applications although some of the original visions have not been realised yet. The technical KE approaches are prominently represented in the Semantic Web, whereas the human driven KM approaches can be found in Web 2.0 initiatives.

Today, knowledge techniques are used in everyday work by applying various methods and tools to steer, use or distribute knowledge. The challenge is to align knowledge with business requirements in a smart and flexible way. Hence the alignment between business requirements and knowledge provision is the topic of this paper.

This paper introduces the knowledge conveyor belt as a realisation framework for process-oriented knowledge management that is based on service-oriented knowledge management and is now strongly influenced by flexible and ad-hoc knowledge technologies.

In the conveyor belt approach the knowledge worker is seen as participant in a knowledge process that produces knowledge products. The knowledge product is a concept that defines the "knowledge" that is used by knowledge workers in a product-like way (cmp. (Make, 2005)). Each knowledge product can then be aligned with the consuming business process, similar to IT-Infrastructure which is now been aligned with business (Karagiannis, 2008).

Therefore the knowledge conveyor belt is based on the following concepts: (1) definition of the knowledge product that are as a result of the conveyor belt; (2) definition of the knowledge management processes that represent the knowledge conveyor belt; (3) formalisation of the knowledge in order to mediate between the human knowledge worker and the IT-based machines; and (4) the identification of required knowledge resources that are the tools and raw material that is used at the conveyor belt.

In the following, the overview of the evolution of the knowledge conveyor belt approach is discussed through a brief overview of the history of Knowledge Management –Engineering and then a discussion introducing the idea, the concept and the realisation approach is discussed. Praxis reports of the knowledge conveyor belt are then described, where one scenario demonstrates the realisation of a conveyor belt using KE and the second scenario explains the realisation of a conveyor belt using KM.

OBSERVATIONS OF KNOWLEDGE MANAGEMENT

The history of KE started in the 1940's with the first attempts of artificial intelligence. After the hype, disillusionment and first commercial success, KE can be found today in semantic technology (Karagiannis, 2001). A prominent sample is the Semantic Web.

KM in contrast evolved out of the KE community and has its origin in 1995 (Despres, 1999). KM is a holistic view on the knowledge space that considers human interpretation – more prominently, but also take account of machine interpretation (Woitsch, 2004a,b; Mak, 2005; v.Brocke, 2007; Beckman, 1999).

In both cases model-based approaches provide concepts for the formalization although the level of formalisms is different. Humans have the ability to interpret incomplete and partly corrupted models – such as mind maps, processes or textual guidelines - whereas machines require knowledge representations in a complete and correct manner – such as ontologies, workflows or rules. Hence in both cases it is reasonable to apply a model-based approach.

Process-oriented knowledge management is established since 2000 as an own discipline although the term has been mentioned earlier in the literature. From that time we observed three phases. The first phase was the introduction of the Process Oriented Knowledge Management (POKM) (Hinkelmann, 2002). The second phase was discussing the realisation of POKM via introduction of the Service Oriented Knowledge Management (SOKM) (Woitsch, 2004ab). In the third phase, the Knowledge Integration - the current goals of investigation - cover integration approaches mainly in form of Mashups or SOA (Schmidt, 2009; Maier, 2005).

Process Oriented Knowledge Management Approach

The process-orientation within knowledge management was mentioned since the start of knowledge management. During this time, there were several initiatives that made process-orientation the major part of the organizational dimension of knowledge management. A list of approaches includes (Gronau, 2003): (1) the Income approach which links knowledge resources to processes, (2) the Workware approach which distinguishes between tacit knowledge and explicit knowledge in a process, where tacit knowledge is aimed to be expressed in a different notation rather than process sequences; (3) the EULE2 is an agent based supporting system considering knowledge flows as processes; (4) the K-Modeller is a modelling method for knowledge-intensive business processes, whereas (5) the ARIS extension provided additional modelling elements for collaboration platforms like Hyperwave. Two research initiatives studied process-oriented knowledge management very intensively. DÉCOR (Abecker, 2001; Papavassiliou, 2002) was an EU-Project linking ontologies with business processes. The focus within the DÉCOR was the ontology support of business processes. PROMOTE (Karagiannis, 2000) was an EU-Project providing a holistic modelling language for process-oriented knowledge management based on the business process management paradigm (Karagiannis, 1995).

Today beside PROMOTE® which evolved from a series of research initiative towards a commercial product, there is also the KMDL approach that has reached the commercial level. KMDL (Gronau, 2003) focuses on key processes

and provides a dedicated model language for the analysis of processes. A reference framework for process-oriented knowledge management is provided from EuReKI, which classifies its different aspects and dimensions (Gronau, 2005).

Service Based Realisation of Knowledge Management

Following the Service Oriented approach available tools and resources have to be provided as services. Thus virtualisation will be applied to provide tool functionality as a service. Also human services can be integrated following the virtualisation approach. Service Oriented Knowledge Management (SOKM) is therefore based on the assumption that successful implementation and execution of knowledge management relies on tools, resources and humans that can be virtualised. The SOKM approach introduces the usage of Knowledge Services (K-S) that define KM Tools on a conceptual level independent of the actual technical implementation (Woitsch, 2004; Valente, 2001).

The service concept is therefore used for both the technical integration of different tools as well as the conceptual integration that considers the meaning of a service (Lindstaedt, 2009; Maier, 2005). This enables knowledge technology to participate in the trend towards the Internet of Services (FoI, 2009; Di Nitto, 2009) by providing encapsulated knowledge tools via services.

The key challenge is the definition of the "meaning" of knowledge services, which is approached by defining formal models for services (Woitsch, 2004) or practical codes (MATURE D1.1, 2009).

Knowledge Integration Frameworks

The Knowledge Bus is mentioned in MATURE (MATURE, 2009; MATURE D5.2, 2009) as an integration approach for K-S that can be realised following two integration approaches. One integration approach is the Service Oriented Approach which uses an Enterprise Services Bus (IBM, 2009) and Virtual Organisations to describe, orchestrate and enact sequences of services. The abstraction of concrete knowledge to so-called knowledge services is seen as the virtualisation of tools, resources or humans like in Skype Prime (SkypePrime, 2009). The goal is to bridge the gap between the traditional knowledge systems and the Service Oriented infrastructure. This so-called Service Oriented Knowledge Provisioning (SOKP) approach provides a way to channel the knowledge available directly to the knowledge intensive activities, and thus by implementing the knowledge management processes support the knowledge worker on an on-demand basis.

Alternatively the Enterprise Mashups (Jhingran, 2006; Daniel, 2007; Maximilien, 2008) approach enables similar frameworks to connect Web-resources and define data exchange. One of the major milestones in the SOKP is the research on delivery channels, in order to provide adaptivity and flexibility to the knowledge service delivery. The assumption of Mashups is to: (1) simplify the usage of the SOKP systems (Hoyer, 2009), (2) involve the end users into design of the SOKP systems (Fischer, 2009) and (3) enable knowledge discovery and creation by combining different knowledge sources (Heath, 2007).

Currently there is no coherent positioning between these two approaches although there are attempts to identify the differences (Hoyer, 2009). Both approaches aim for flexible usage, personalisation and user friendly handling.

The conveyor belt approach is a realisation framework that guides process-oriented knowledge management towards a SO realisation in this third phase of evolution. It aims at further formalizing KE and KM to enable knowledge industrialisation. The assumption is that the knowledge work carried out and steered by knowledge management methods can be seen as a conveyor belt.

THE KNOWLEDGE CONVEYOR BELT APPROACH

The knowledge conveyor belt has three abstraction levels. First the actual application scenario will be presented as the knowledge conveyor belt idea. Then the applied concepts are introduced before the realisation framework that describes, how organisations can use there conveyor belt is discussed.

Knowledge Conveyor Belt: The Idea

Knowledge workers have to face the challenges of simultaneously dealing with rapid change, uncertainty and emergence, dependability, as well as diversity, and interdependence (Boehm, 2008) of their daily work.

The answer to these challenges is to support the knowledge work with knowledge management processes, similar to a conveyor belt that supports the "industrial production" of knowledge. In such a scenario the knowledge worker requires a knowledge conveyor belt that provides the tasks to be done but also the knowledge support in a personalised manner. To tackle the assigned tasks the worker is provided with personalised knowledge, sources the worker is capable to deal with as well as with tools the worker is able to handle.

The knowledge-role concept in the conveyor belt distinguishes between knowledge manager, knowledge worker and knowledge administrator. Although the role-concepts separating the responsibility for tasks has been criticized in the Web 2.0 paradigm, we argue that the separation of roles is still valid but the fact that a person changes the role more frequently than in traditional role-concepts or works in parallel in two roles is a phenomenon that was massively boosted by the Web 2.0 philosophy.

The knowledge manager is responsible for the configuration of the knowledge conveyor belt and for the configuration of the orchestration of the services. The knowledge administrator is responsible for the technical deployment of the conveyor belt. Based on the experience of the knowledge worker, the template for knowledge management processes is selected. Appropriate tools and knowledge sources are selected at runtime based on the pre-selected parameters from the knowledge process used by the knowledge worker. The application scenario for the knowledge conveyor belt approach is the knowledge work in cases where (Hrgovcic, 2009) (a) knowledge is hybrid (implicit and explicit), (b) explicit knowledge is implemented in tools and (c) services and knowledge can be virtualized.

The knowledge conveyor belt has three layers: (1) The Application Scenario where knowledge workers are provided with required tools, sources and contacts to co-workers virtualised as knowledge services, (2) The Knowledge Middleware that is realised in form of the Knowledge Bus, allowing the configuration of the knowledge conveyor belt, and orchestration of the available knowledge services, and (3) Knowledge Resources layer, a massive flexible and hybrid collection of available knowledge that can be virtualised as services. Hence the knowledge resources may be used for the SO approach by virtualising the resources, but in case an alternative approach is used, the identified resources need not be virtualised.

Three basic principles enable the realisation of the knowledge conveyor belt, which are introduced in the next section.

Knowledge Conveyor Belt: The Concept

The knowledge conveyor belt requires then following three concepts for its realisation:

1. **Models to describe Business and Knowledge Alignment**

Models are used to describe the task and knowledge sources as well as to mediate the access of heterogeneous data and information

sources by introducing intelligent mechanisms into the system. Therefore semantic is used for the necessary alignment of available knowledge with the requested knowledge of the worker. Semantic has therefore different application scenarios on different levels. First the technical integration of different sources and formats is tackled via semantic technologies. Second, the semantic service discovery and orchestration of services is performed by semantic technology. Finally the description of skills, tasks, domain and usage – the so-called "context" of the requesting worker - uses semantic technologies for the alignment.

To achieve these goals of semantic services a number of approaches have been discussed in (Martin, 2007; Polleres, 2006; Cabral, 2004; Stollberg, 2007). One of the first initiatives in this regard that still attracts a lot of interest has been DAML-S that is now known as OWL-S (DAML, 2009; OWL-S, 2009). Another approach for the standardisation of integrating semantics into Web-Services descriptions, called SAWSDL (Semantic Annotations for WSDL) can be found in the Working Group for semantic annotations in Web-Service descriptions (SAWSDL, 2009).

Further related proposals for standards include WSDL-S (Akkiraju, 2005), WSML and the related ontology WSMO (Roman, 2005) and IRS-III (Cabral, 2006). The Internet Reasoning Service (IRS) (KMI, 2009) is built upon WSMO and provides the representational and reasoning mechanisms for implementing the WSMO metamodel to describe Web-Services.

An improvement of OWL-S is OWL-WS an extension of OWL-S that has been developed in research initiatives (Beco, 2005; Beco, 2006).

The conveyor belt approach is technology independent, hence the selection of the appropriate approach, depends on the given application scenario as well as on the legacy applications.

2. **Process-Orientation to describe Knowledge Work**

The knowledge work can be expressed in a process-oriented manner building upon the facts that (Karagiannis, 2001) knowledge is embedded in the business process and knowledge processes can be modelled. The POKM approach is specified by the following views on processes:

a. The first level in the POKM is covered by business process management. Here the business process is seen as a content making implicit organisational knowledge about working procedures explicit.

b. The second level sees the business process as a starting point and an integration platform to gain a common understanding, where knowledge is created and where it is required. Similar to Model Driven Architecture (MDA), the business process is seen as the starting point for knowledge management system requirements.

c. The third level interprets the process as a management approach, thus defining the sequence of performed knowledge activities. These so-called knowledge processes produce knowledge products that are consumed by business processes. Hence the conveyor belt is the implementation of these knowledge processes and deals with knowledge identification, accessing, usage, storage or distribution.

Service Orientation is a realisation approach for this process-orientation.

The OASIS article "Reference Model for a Service-Oriented Architecture" defines Service Oriented Architecture (SOA) as "a paradigm for organizing and utilizing distributed capabilities that may be under the control of different ownership domains" (OASIS, 2006).

SOA is considered to be a perspective of the software architecture which is used to support needs and requirements of the software users by defining the usage of loosely coupled software. According to (Erl, 2005) loose coupling "is a condition wherein a service acquires knowledge of another service while still remaining independent of that service".

In contrast to traditional architecture, where the components of a system know about existing interfaces and how to access them, in a SOA environment all services exist as loosely coupled, highly interoperable application services and are independent of the underlying platform and programming language. SOA is a conceptual and technology-independent concept on how to design a system in a heterogeneous environment.

As the aforementioned service oriented approaches discuss the technical aspects of service orchestration, the principle of "Virtualisation" has to be mentioned. Basically virtualisation is one of the key-concepts in the Grid (Foster, 2008), which had been adapted, so that today any resource – although resources that are not technical resources – are able to be virtualised and accessed through service interfaces (B4P, 2009). Applying the virtualisation in that sense enables to apply the SO approach to knowledge tools, resources and - assuming that humans can be virtualised to some extend – even human experts.

3. Modelling for Externalisation and Formalization

The model based approach uses graphics and pictures in supporting knowledge workers to express their knowledge, as this has been successful over the last decades when it comes to expressing knowledge. Graphical models have the advantage that besides the intuitive expressiveness of diagrams, there is a formalism that describes the meaning of the diagram.

Modelling is used to describe specific scenarios in such a way that it allows certain tasks, previously solvable only by humans, to be supported by machines.

Models can be basically classified into non-linguistic or iconic models which use signs and symbols that have an apparent similarity to the concepts of the real world and linguistic models that use basic primitives such as signs, characters or numbers. Nearly all models in computer science are of the linguistic type. Linguistic models can be further distinguished in being realized with textual and graphical / diagrammatic languages (Kalfoglou, 2003).

For the realisation of the conveyor belt three modelling layers are required:

- **Domain Knowledge Modelling:** To gather the requirements of the application scenario. Here PROMOTE® as the most comprehensive knowledge modelling language is proposed.
- **Ontology Modelling:** Ontology is used for the alignment of the business knowledge requirements and the available knowledge. There are various ontology representation languages; the most prominent one being used is the Web Ontology Language (OWL) (OWL, 2009).
- **Service and Workflow Modelling:** The services integrated into the conveyor belt will be described and registered with an orchestration language. Based on the requirements of the service handling the appropriate languages can range from BPEL including semantic extensions to OWL-WS or similar frameworks.

The applied models need to be integrated to a common knowledge conveyor belt model framework that is used for the design, documentation and configuration of the knowledge conveyor belt.

Knowledge Conveyor Belt: The PROMOTE Realisation Method

The challenge to realise the knowledge conveyor belt is to bridge the gap between the demands of the business-oriented end user and the available knowledge services, thus the alignment of the knowledge requirement and available knowledge

services. There are three assumptions for the realisation:

The first axiom states that the conveyor belt can be configured in a model-based way. A model is seen as an immaterial reflection of reality into a model system for the purpose of an individual (Kühn, 2003). This means, that modelling languages exist, or can be developed whose expressiveness is sufficient to describe all related aspects of the conveyor belt.

In the application scenarios the PROMOTE® tool was used as it provides a powerful and expressive modelling language for knowledge.

The second axiom states that a model needs to be formalised for machine interpretation. This means that the models consist of business graphs, execution graphs and evaluation graphs. The business graph defines the concept; the execution graph defines the technological mapping between the concept and the IT-infrastructure whereas the evaluation graph defines the monitoring of the execution.

In the application scenarios the semantic annotated WSDL approach was followed by using a combination of BPEL, WSDL and ontology languages such as OWL or OPAL to provide the required formalism in a pragmatic way.

The third axiom is to use the meta model concept for the implementation of the model. The new models are therefore defined on three levels. The meta2 model level defines the basic modelling constructs like in CDIF, MOF or UML Profiles. The meta model level implements the formalised business graph, execution graph and the evaluation graph using the constructs of the meta2 model.

In the application scenario the ADOxx® meta modelling platform has been applied, as it provides a well proven meta model that can be applied in a user-friendly way.

The three axioms are addressed by the PROMOTE® platform. PROMOTE® is a holistic modelling approach for process-oriented knowledge management that has been developed in the EC-

Project PROMOTE (IST Project 11658) (Woitsch, 2004) and improved in recent years during commercial and research projects. PROMOTE® has been successfully used and extended in the projects Akogrimo (Woitsch, 2006), AsIsKnown (Woitsch, 2007) and Brein (Woitsch, 2008), as well as in the Austrian military within the central documentation department (Mak, 2005) and the NBC-Defence School which is the school to teach the defence against nuclear, biological and chemical weapons (Goellner, 2008).

The Knowledge Graph

The highest layer of knowledge structuring in PROMOTE® uses the concept of Knowledge Product. A knowledge product is consumed by business processes while they are executed and produced by a knowledge management process.

Beside the Knowledge Management Process – that specifies the logical sequence of knowledge interactions, which produce the knowledge product - the Knowledge Environment needs to be described. PROMOTE® interprets skills, content-oriented roles and knowledge-depending access rights as the so-called Knowledge Environment in order to allocate responsibilities, access rights and roles to knowledge workers within an organisation.

Further Knowledge Resources are modelled, which capture the available tools, content and knowledge.

Figure 1 introduces the PROMOTE® model stack used to configure the knowledge conveyor belt. The knowledge product model describes the knowledge products like surveys, publications or the provision of expertise in form of consulting. In order to produce these knowledge products different knowledge management processes are executed. For example the process of a survey, the review process for quality assurance of publications or the process of creating and writing new knowledge. Each knowledge management process consists of several activities. These activities need to be performed by humans that may be supported

Figure 1. The knowledge graph of the conveyor belt

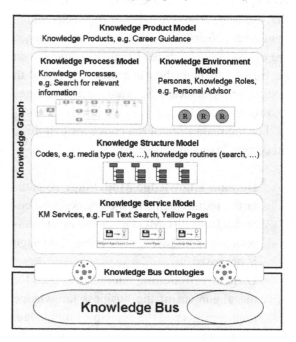

by machines. The domain of knowledge work can be classified using domain specific codes defined in knowledge structure model. Knowledge services are an abstraction of tools and resources, hence for the identification they are modelled in form of knowledge-services.

On the execution layer – represented as Knowledge Bus (K-Bus) - each service as identified on the conceptual layer – represented as Knowledge Graph - has to be provided in order to be executable at execution time. OWL is used to represent the knowledge graph in a standardised way in order to align the requested knowledge that is derived from the business process with the K-Bus. Therefore the "K-Bus ontology" integrates the domain knowledge models in a formalised way to be interpreted by the K-Bus models. This alignment between the knowledge domain and the technical K-Bus is not only a challenge of aligning requested knowledge with available knowledge but also to transform semi-formal models – that are commonly used to describe the domain knowledge by the domain experts – into formal

Figure 2. The execution graph of the conveyor belt

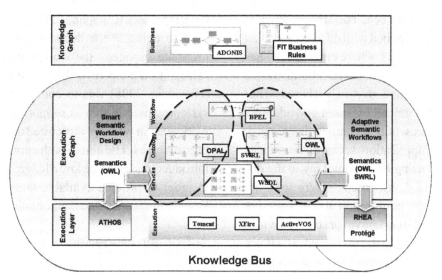

models – that are required by knowledge engineers and knowledge infrastructure such as the K-Bus.

The Execution Graph

The Knowledge Graph describes the domain knowledge and hence specifies the context of the conveyor belt. In order to execute the knowledge graph it has to be translated into a format that can be interpreted by IT-applications. Figure 2 provides a simplified description of the two different knowledge conveyor belts using either KE or KM.

The Knowledge Bus is depicted on two layers. First the execution graph describes executable models. Starting point is the orchestration of Web-Services, hence the workflow language BPEL is used to define the sequence of service invocations. The smart workflow approach applied in LD-CAST (Hrgovcic, 2008), uses an ontology – expressed in OPAL – to enable a loose coupling of concrete services – defined in WSDL – to the workflow. The adaptive workflow approach applied in FIT (Hrgovcic, 2008), used rules – expressed in SWRL – to describe so-called adaptive workflow sequences with a rule-based approach. The ontology – expressed in OWL – was used to

define the facts that are used for defining the rules. Hence there was a direct binding of concrete services to workflow items, but the sequence was adaptive due to enriched expressions of rules defined by the ontology.

The execution layer is a set of tools that can interpret the execution level model. Based on existing K-Bus configuration some tools are mentioned as samples, but the following tool-overview has only explanatory character. Tomcat and XFire are deployed as Web-Service container. ActiveOS is used for the deployment of the workflow engine. The interpretation of rules is executed by the rule engine RHEA. The ontology management system is different depending on the ontology dialect. Protégé is used for the OWL representation whereas ATHOS is used for the OPAL representation.

The next section introduces different application scenarios of the conveyor belt.

APPLICATION SCENARIOS OF THE CONVEYOR BELT

This section demonstrates two different application scenarios of the knowledge conveyor belt.

The first scenario uses KE techniques for a smart and adaptive conveyor belt. The sample which is discussed has been applied with different focus on eGovernment platforms, where citizens who has few knowledge about the concrete administrative procedures triggers the conveyor belt based on her knowledge and is guided by smart and adaptive workflows to successfully accomplish her request.

The second application scenario introduces a conveyor belt using KM technology in the domain of software development, where software developers request information about "software middleware" and the conveyor belt provides knowledge according to the users context. Hence the conveyor belt is an assistance system and leaves all major decisions to the user.

As the K-Bus is a framework and hence can support different applications scenarios. Most likely it will be a mixture between KE and KM technology, especially when transforming an existing knowledge management system to a higher maturity. The following two application scenarios therefore show the bandwidth of possible conveyor belts configurations. The difference between these two samples is that in the KE approach a workflow engine with an additional rule engine and an ontology management system is used in order to set of tool is responsible for the interpretation of the models and the correct orchestration of the knowledge conveyor belt. In the KM approach a so-called process-stepper – a trivial workflow engine that can only check the status of tasks – is applied that interprets to models only to a small extend but the knowledge worker needs to interpret and orchestrate the conveyor belt on its own. So both scenarios follow the vision of a knowledge conveyor belt, but in the KE scenario a set of tools steer the conveyor belt, and in the KM scenario the knowledge worker steer the conveyor belt.

The Conveyor Belt Realised with KE

The application scenario refers two e-Government EC research projects (LD-Cast, FIT) that realises the knowledge conveyor belt. In the case of LD-CAST project (Catapano, 2008) ontologies are used to delegate the decision on selecting appropriate services - the worker was not able to select - to the conveyor belt. The FIT approach (Hrgovcic, 2008) was to configure an adaptive system, which is able to support the knowledge work even in weakly –structured and thus changing processes. The aim in both approaches was to introduce and use the knowledge conveyor belt in order to provide available knowledge to the knowledge worker in an automatic way.

1. Domain Modelling

The first phase is the modelling of the application domain knowledge in form of business processes and domain models. This involves the configuration of the knowledge conveyor belt which is achieved by a set of executable models like workflow models, services description models as well as semantic models like ontologies – using OPAL and OWL – and rule models with SWRL. The combination of the executive models is seen as the semantic workflow model (Hrgovcic, 2009).

2. K-Bus Modelling

The FIT project involved first the creation of the ontologies in order to use that knowledge to define business rules and to enrich the workflows. The workflow was enriched with a so-called "adaptive" workflow item. An adaptive workflow item is not represented as a sequence but as a set of rules that have to be considered. During the execution the so-called adaptive workflow item was represented as a Web-Service – so conceptually treated by the workflow engine like any other service to invoke –, which implements a rule enactor. This enactor is responsible for translation of the application data provided by the workflow engine used for the invocation of the rule engine.

The LD-CAST project involved the creation of domain ontologies and abstract workflows.

The ontology was enriched with end user specific parameters. The next step was to bridge the gap between business processes and abstract workflows by using ontologies for the annotation. Finally the services required for execution had been bound to the abstract workflow via the enriched ontology. The binding of concrete services to abstract workflows took place during runtime (see (Catapano, 2008) for more details), which enables the binding of concrete knowledge resources based on the end user inputs.

3. K-Bus Deployment

The third phase is to deploy the executable K-Bus models into the K-Bus infrastructure. This includes either the use of legacy application or requires the integration of new tools like ESBs, workflows or rule engines depending on the IT-landscape of the organisation. In the aforementioned sample the K-Bus was deployed by the installation of workflow engines, rule engines, Web-Service containers and ontology management systems. There was additional effort in adapting some of the tools in order to fully realise the K-Bus.

The Conveyor Belt Realised with KM

This application scenario of the knowledge conveyor belt realises the K-Bus using KM technologies in the domain of software development. The aim was to involve external software developers – from the viewpoint of the project they were treated as novices – to highly interact, use and contribute with the open community of the project BREIN. This was a key success factor of the BREIN project (Woitsch, 2008) as it supports the use of the middleware in the way it was developed in BREIN. The project provided the environment for a public show case in a human driven setting, as the available knowledge was very complex, tightly coupled with details of the system and provided in form of implicit knowledge. Therefore the knowledge conveyor belt was not used for automation but was used to support human intensive interaction.

Similar to the KE supported knowledge conveyor belt the main goal in this scenario was to organize the knowledge about a software and provide access to the knowledge regardless of the nature of the knowledge sources.

1. Domain Modelling

The first phase specified the knowledge graph by modelling the software development process. Starting from a map of different software development processes two sub-processes have been identified for the realisation within the knowledge conveyor belt: (1) development of new services and applications and (2) integration of existing services and applications.

This knowledge graph was modelled starting from the business process and enriching the process with PROMOTE®.

2. K-Bus Modelling

The second phase the so-called process stepper instead of a workflow engine has been configured to realise the knowledge conveyor belt. The knowledge resources have been virtualised and provided as knowledge services (regardless of the tool or resource used) that can be bound to the process-stepper model. Knowledge services have been identified in an analytical manner like – but not limited to – UML Repository, that stores the UML diagrams, Bug Reporting Database, Yellow Pages that lists senior developer per topic, Java docs that is a special form of software documentation or Wikis that provide an overview of the whole software project.

3. K-Bus Deployment

The third phase is the deployment of the conveyor belt that is usually a configuration and integration of legacy application with the process stepper.

Figure 3. Web based access to the knowledge conveyor belt

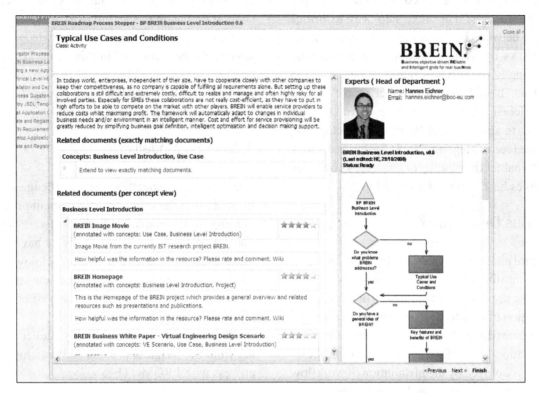

The binding of the knowledge services with the process-stepper has been achieved in a similar way than using workflows. As in the previous sample the underlying technology – like workflow engine or rule engines – is hidden to the user, the user of the process stepper directly interacts with the tool.

Access to the knowledge conveyor belt was provided to the end users utilizing a web based GUI to the process stepper that guided the users through the knowledge space, showed the underlying process model to the user and listed all annotated knowledge services as links as shown in Figure 3.

Through the binding of knowledge services with the process stepper, the knowledge worker gets guidance through the knowledge space that describe the software BREIN.

The aforementioned two scenarios demonstrate that the knowledge conveyor belt can be implemented in different application scenarios and with different focus. In the KE scenario the knowledge conveyor belt was implemented to semi-automatically produce knowledge products and decisions have been shifted from the knowledge worker towards the system. In the KM environment the knowledge conveyor belt was used as an assistant system that guided and supported the knowledge worker during software development.

SUMMARY

The knowledge conveyor belt is seen as the realisation framework for process-oriented knowledge management that applies service orientation to enable the execution of knowledge processes. Semantic technology is used to make the execution of knowledge processes smarter. Rules have been applied for adaptive workflows and ontologies have been used for service discovery and late binding of knowledge services.

The knowledge conveyor belt can be applied for knowledge systems which take over parts of human decisions or to guide the knowledge worker as an assistance system.

Upcoming challenges are the technical evolution of the current systems. This is reflected in new workflow technologies, improved semantic technologies and the challenges of integration.

On the conceptual layer the model-based approach seems to be appropriate but needs to consider that modelling is commodity today, hence the knowledge conveyor belt needs to deal with different modelling languages within different domains and different formal expressiveness.

On the knowledge level the knowledge conveyor belt needs to consider the monitoring of knowledge. Knowledge is generated, used and distributed based on the available resources, skills and processes to achieve a certain knowledge output. Based on the balanced scorecard approach (as described in (Woitsch, 2009)) the performance of the knowledge conveyor belt can be measured.

This paper outlines that, knowledge technologies both, in knowledge engineering and in knowledge management have reached such a maturity that industrialisation of knowledge work can be observed.

Appropriate tools and methods are applied, whose main concern is how to treat knowledge as a valuable resource of an organisation. This can be compared to traditional production processes, whereas the major raw material is kept within the human mind.

Therefore the conveyor belt approach aims to realize a smart assistant system to support knowledge workers. As the motivation of people to contribute to the knowledge system is essential, the knowledge worker should not only stay "in the loop" of the knowledge system but also needs to get efficient knowledge support.

REFERENCES

Abecker, A., Mentzas, G., Legal, M., Ntioudis, S., & Papavassiliou, G. (2001). Business Process Oriented Delivery of Knowledge through Domain Ontologies. In *Proceedings of DEXA conference, Munich.*

Akkiraju, R., et al. (2005). Web-Service Semantics - WSDL-S, W3C Member Submission, 7 November 2005. Retrieved March 12, 2009 from http://www.w3.org/Submission/WSDL-S

Beckman, T. (1999). The Current State of the Knowledge Management. In Liebovitz, J. (Ed.), *Knowledge Management Handbook* (pp. 1.1–1.22).

Beco, S., Cantalupo, B., Giammarino, L., Matskanis, N., & Surridge, M. (2005). OWL-WS: A Workflow Ontology for Dynamic Grid Service Composition. *First International Conference on e-Science and Grid Computing (e-Science'05).* (pp. 148-155) http://doi.ieeecomputersociety.org/10.1109/E-SCIENCE.2005.64

Beco, S., Cantalupo, B., & Terracina, A. (2006). The Role of Workflow in Next Generation Business Oriented Grids: Two Different Approaches Leading to a Unified Vision. In *Second IEEE International Conference on e-Science and Grid Computing (e-Science'06)* (p. 38). http://doi.ieeecomputersociety.org/10.1109/E-SCIENCE.2006.139

Boehm, B. (2008). Making a Difference in the Software Century. *IEEE Computer, 41*(3), 32–38.

BPEL4People (2009). WS-People Extension for People. Retrieved April 22, 2009 from http://www.ibm.com/developerworks/webservices/library/specification/ws-bpel4people

Cabral, L., Domingue, J., Galizia, S., Gugliotta, A., Norton, B., Tanasescu, V., & Pedrinaci, C. (2006). IRS-III: A Broker for Semantic Web-Services based Applications. In *Proceedings of the 5th International Semantic Web Conference, ISWC.*

Cabral, L., Domingue, J., Motta, E., Payne, T. R., & Hakimpour, F. (2004). Approaches to Semantic Web-Services: An Overview and Comparison. In *Proceedings of the European Semantic Web Conference*.

Catapano, A., D'Atri, A., Hrgovcic, V., Ionita, D. A., & Tarabanis, K. (2008). *LD-CAST: Local Development Cooperation Actions Enabled by Semantic Technology. 6th Eastern European eGovernment Days*. Prague, Czech Republic: OCG.

Daniel, F., Matera, M., Yu, J., Benatallah, B., Regis, S. P., & Casati, F. (2007). Understanding UI Integration. A Survey of Problems, Technologies and Opportunities. *IEEE Internet Computing, 11*(3), 59–66. doi:10.1109/MIC.2007.74

Despres, C., & Chauvel, D. (1999). A Thematic Analysis of the Thinking in Knowledge Management [White paper]. Graduate School of Business, Marseille-Provence and The Theseus Institute, Sophia Antipolis, France

Di Nitto, E., Sassen, A.-M., Traverso, P., & Zwegers, A. (2009). *At your Service, Service-Oriented Computing from an EU Perspective*. Cambridge, MA: MIT Press.

Erl, T. (2005). *Service-Oriented Architecture: Concepts, Technology, and Design*. Prentice Hall/PearsonPTR.

Fischer, T., Bakalov, F., & Nauerz, A. (2009). *An Overview of Current Approaches to Mashup Generation*. 5th Conference on Professional Knowledge Management, Switzerland, LNI GI-Edition.

Foster I. (2008). *What is Grid? A Three Point Checklist*. Retrieved November 10, 2008 from www-fp.mcs.anl.gov/~foster/Articles/WhatIs-TheGrid.pdf

Future of Internet. (2009). Retrieved April 20, 2009 from www.fi-bled.eu/

Goellner, J., Mak, K., Trattnig, G., & Woitsch, R. (2008). *Wissensmanagement und Wissensbilanz im ÖBH am Beispiel der ABCAbwS & ABCAbw*. Wien: Sonderpublikation, Schriftenreihe der Landesverteidigungsakademie.

Gronau, N. (2003). Modellieren von wissensintensiven Geschäftsprozesses mit der Beschreibungssprache K-Modeler. In Gronau N. Wissensmanagement: Potentiale – Konzepte - Werkzeuge, GITO Verlag, (pp, 3-30).

Gronau, N., & Bahrs, J. (Eds.), *Prozessorientiertes Wissensmangement – Strategien, Methoden, Erfahrungen und Werkzeuge*. Berlin: GITO Verlag.

Heath, T., & Motta, E. (2008). Ease of interaction plus ease of integration: Combining Web2.0 and the Semantic Web in a reviewing site. *Web Semantics: Science. Services and Agents on the World Wide Web, 6*(1), 76–83. doi:10.1016/j.websem.2007.11.009

Hinkelmann, K., Karagiannis, D., & Telesko, R. (2002). PROMOTE - Methodologie und Werkzeug zum geschäftsprozessorientierten Wissensmanagement. In *Geschäftsprozessorientiertes Wissensmanagement*. Springer-Verlag.

Homepage, D. A. M. L. (2009). Releases of DAML-S / OWL-S. Retrieved March 16, 2009 from http://www.daml.org/services/owl-s/

Hoyer, V., & Stanoevska-Slabeva, K. (2009). *Design Principles of Enterprise Mashups*. 5th Conference on Professional Knowledge Management, Switzerland, LNI GI-Edition.

Hrgovcic, V., Utz, W., & Woitsch, R. (2009). Knowledge Engineering in Future Internet. In Karagiannis, D., & Jin, Z. (Eds.), *Knowledge Science, Engineering and Management*. Springer. doi:10.1007/978-3-642-10488-6_13

Hrgovcic, V., & Woitsch, R. (2009). *Enhancing Semantic E-Government Workflows through Service Oriented Knowledge Provision*. 4th International Conference on Internet and Web Applications and Services, ICIW 09, Venice, Italy, IEEE.

Hrgovcic, V., Woitsch, R., Utz, W., & Leutgeb, A. (2008). *Adaptive and Smart e-Government Workflows - Experience Report from the Projects FIT and LDCAST. eChallenges e-2008 Stockholm*. Sweden: IOS Press.

IBM. (2009). Retrieved April 22, 2009 from www.ibm.com/developerworks/webservices/library/ws-esbia/

Jhingran, A. (2006). Enterprise Information Mash-ups: Integrating Information, Simply. In *Proceedings of the 32nd international conference on Very large data bases* (pp. 3-4). VLDB Endowment.

Kalfoglou, Y., & Schorlemmer, M. (2003). Ontology Mapping: the State of the Art. *The Knowledge Engineering Review*, *18*(1), 1–31. doi:10.1017/S0269888903000651

Karagiannis, D. (1995). BPMS: Business Process Management Systems: Concepts, Methods and Technologies, SIGOIS Special Issue. *ACM SIGGROUP Bulletin, 10-13*, 1995.

Karagiannis, D. (2009). *Modelling Semantic Workflows for E-Government Applications*. 3rd International Conference on Research Challenges in Information Science, RCIS 2009. IEEE.

Karagiannis, D., & Telesko, R. (2000). The EU-Project PROMOTE: A Process-oriented Approach for Knowledge Management. In *Proceedings of the 3rd International Conference on Practical Aspects of Knowledge Management.*

Karagiannis, D., & Telesko, R. (2001). *Wissensmanagement: Konzepte der künstlichen Intelligenz und des Softcomputing*. Oldenbourg Wissenschaftsverlag.

Karagiannis, D., Utz, W., Woitsch, R., & Eichner, H. (2008). *BPM4SOA Business Process Models for Semantic Service-Oriented Infrastructures. eChallenges e-2008*. Stockholm, Sweden: IOS Press.

KMI. (2009). Knowledge Media Institute, IRS - Internet Reasoning Service. Retrieved March 16, 2009 from http://technologies.kmi.open.ac.uk/irs/

Kühn., et al. (2003). Enterprise Model Integration. In K. Bauknecht, A.M. Tjoa, & G. Quirchmayer (Eds.), *Proceedings of the Fourth International Conference EC-Web 2003 – Dexa 2003, Prague, Czech Republic* (LNCS 2738, pp. 379-392).

Linsteadt., et al. (2009). Special Track on Knowledge Services, in conjunction with I-Know 2008. Retrieved April 20, 2009 from http://i-know.tu-graz.at/about/previous_conferences/i_know_08/special_tracks/ks

Maier, R., Hädrich, T., & Peinl, R. (2005). *Enterprise Knowledge Infrastructure*. Berlin: Springer Verlag.

Mak, K. (2005). *Der Einsatz des prozessorientierten Wissensmanagementwerkzeuges PROMOTE® in der Zentraldokumentation der Landesverteidigungsakademie*. Landesverteidigungsakademie Wien.

Martin, D., Domingue, J., Brodie, M., & Leymann, F. (2007). Semantic Web-Services, Part 1. *IEEE Intelligent Systems*, *22*(5). doi:10.1109/MIS.2007.4338488

MATURE D1.1 (2009). Results of the Ethnographic Study and Conceptual Knowledge Maturing Model. MATURE deliverable.

MATURE D5.2 (2009). Specification of the System Architecture. MATURE deliverable.

MATURE EU-Project. (2009). Retrieved April 22, 2009 from www.mature-ip.eu

Maximilien, E. M., Ranabahu, A., & Fomadam, K. (2008). An Online Platform for Web APIs and Service Mashups. *IEEE Internet Computing, 12*(5), 32–43. doi:10.1109/MIC.2008.92

OASIS. (2006). Reference Model for Service Oriented Architecture 1.0, OASIS Standard. Retrieved March 16, 2009 from http://docs.oasis-open.org/soa-rm/v1.0/soa-rm.html

OWL. (2009). Retrieved April 10, 2009 from http://www.w3.org/2004/OWL/

OWL-S. (2009). *OWL-S Specification*. Retrieved March 16, 2009 from http://www.daml.org/services/owl-s/1.1/

Papavassiliou, G., Ntioudis, S., Mentzas, G., & Abecker, A. (2002). Business Process Knowledge Modelling: Method and Tool. In *Proceedings of the Theory and Application of Knowledge Management*, Aix-en-Provence, France.

Polleres, A., Lausen, H., & Lara, R. (2006). Semantische Beschreibung von Web-Services. In *Semantic Web - Wege zur vernetzten Wissensgesellschaft*. Springer.

Roman, D., Keller, U., Lausen, H., de Bruijn, J., Lara, R., & Stollberg, M. (2005). *Web-Service Modeling Ontology* (pp. 77–106). Applied Ontology.

SAWSDL. (2009). Semantic Annotations for Web-Services Description Language Working Group Homepage. Retrieved March 12, 2009 from http://www.w3.org/2002/ws/sawsdl/

Schmidt, A., Ley, T., & Lindstaedt, S. (2009). Workshop on Knowledge Services & Mash-ups, In K. Hinkelmann, & H. Wache (Eds.), *WM 2009: 5th Conference on Professional Knowledge Management*, March 25-27, 2009, Solothurn, Switzerland, GI-Verlag, Bonn

SkypePrime. (n.d.). Retrieved from http://www.skype.com/allfeatures/skypeprime/

Stollberg, M., Hepp, M., & Fensel, D. (2007). Semantic Web-Services – Realisierung der SOA Vision mit semantischen Technologien. SWS – MKE conference.

Valente, A., & Housel, T. (2001). A Framework to Analyze and Compare Knowledge Management Tools. In *Proceedings of the Knowledge-Based Intelligent Information Engineering Systems and Allied Technologies* (KES2001). IOS Press.

vom Brocke, J. (2007). *Informationssysteme für Wissensnetzwerke*. HMD, Praxis der Wirtschaftsinformatik.

Woitsch, R. (2004). *Process Oriented Knowledge Management: A Service-Based Approach*. PhD thesis University of Vienna.

Woitsch, R., & Karagiannis, D. (2004). Process Oriented Knowledge Management: A Service Based Approach. In *Proceedings of the I-Know 04 from the Special Track BPOKI'04*, Graz, Austria.

Woitsch, R., Karagiannis, D., Fill, H.-G., & Blazevic, V. (2007). Semantic Based Knowledge Flow System in European Home Textile: A Process Oriented Approach with PROMOTE. In *Proceedings of I KNOW '07*, Graz, Austria.

Woitsch, R., & Leutgeb, A. (2008). The BREIN-Roadmap with PROMOTE®: A Use-Case Scenario of a Service-Based Knowledge Management Approach, I-Know 08, Graz, Austria.

Woitsch, R., & Utz, W. (2006). Roadmap to Akogrimo Convergence, A Sample of Process Oriented Knowledge Management with PROMOTE. In *Proceedings of I KNOW '06, Graz, Austria*.

Woitsch, R., Utz, W., Mak, K., & Göllner, J. (2009). *Intellectual Capital Management using Knowledge Scorecards: A Best Practice Implementation*. Paper presented at the Austrian National Defence Academy, 5th Conference of Professional Knowledge Management, (KM 09), Solothurn, Switzerland.

Chapter 6

Social Network Analysis as a Tool for Knowledge Management for Innovation

Claire Gubbins
University of Limerick, Ireland

Lawrence Dooley
University College Cork, Ireland

ABSTRACT

In today's changing environment, the competitiveness and sustainability of a modern organisation, be they global large scale enterprises (LSEs) or local small to medium scale enterprises (SMEs), depends on its ability to innovate. Innovation can be viewed as the combined activity of generating creative ideas and the subsequent successful exploitation of these concepts for benefit. Access to relevant and up to date information provides a critical competitive edge for organisations innovation efforts. Given that social relationships are key to enhancing the ability to gather knowledge and that creation of knowledge is primarily a social process among individuals, organisations' need to optimise the supporting mechanisms by which its people and processes accumulate, structure, and transfer knowledge effectively. Mechanisms such as social networks promote both organisational and collective learning and participation in these social networks are a significant source of knowledge, which subsequently leads to innovation. Consequently, this chapter will outline the innovation process with its knowledge management phases and extrapolate the role of social networks in this process. It will then outline the steps of the social network analysis tool and illustrate how it can be used to enhance knowledge management for innovation efforts.

INTRODUCTION

Innovation can be viewed as the effort to create purposeful change that has economic or social potential (Drucker, 1988). This potential can re-

alise itself in a number of ways, for example: new products, better service quality, reduced lead times, cost reduction and increased turnover. Innovation delivers economic growth and competitive advantage. The performance of an economy improves as a consequence of innovations that enhance design and manufacturing capabilities of organizations,

DOI: 10.4018/978-1-61520-829-6.ch006

nurture the development of new markets and business models and produce innovative products and services for global markets. Innovation not only increases the revenue streams into the economy but also provides employment and up-skilling opportunities to allow further movement up the value chain. Innovation contributes to economic growth by providing cost competitiveness within the industrial base and providing stimulus for entrepreneurial activity that will result in the creation of new ventures.

Today's organisations operate in an environment that is fast paced and uncertain, requiring them to continuously change and adapt. It is generally accepted that the driving forces behind such change are global competition, growth in mergers, acquisitions and alliances, organisational restructuring and advances in technology and telecommunication (Dowling & Welch, 2004). In such a changing environment, the competitiveness and sustainability of a modern organisation depends on its ability to meet these challenges through innovation. Organisations that have developed strong innovative capability have been able to grow in scale and market share, some developing from fledgling 'garage-based' operations to dominant global players in a matter of decades e.g. Microsoft, Apple and Dell. Innovation can be viewed as occurring within four dimensions of the organisation; product innovation; process innovation; market innovation and business model innovation. These types of organisational innovations transform the products the organisation offers to their customers, the way by which the products and services are produced and delivered, the markets to which they are focused on and even the structure of the business models by which the organisations generate profits and growth from the products and services they provide to the customer. Examples of the impact of organisational innovation types include the transformation of the Apple Corporation (and its share price) following development of the iPod product innovation; the

financial success and enhanced global reputation of Toyota due to their process innovations including equipment control and defect elimination; the reversal in fortunes (and market share) of the Lucozade drinks company following the market repositioning of their offering as a 'sports' drink and the growth and continued sustainability of Ryanair as a consequence of innovations in their business model. Also, as an example of innovation in an SME, following a strategic review by its management team, Creganna, an Irish based SME supplying to the electronics industry, undertook a significant market innovation. By applying its existing process capability in the areas of metal-forming and coatings, it was able to fulfil pressing needs of the medical devices industry. This innovation allowed the company move up the value chain in terms of market offering, which resulted in the organisation growing in terms of scale and profitability and ultimately establish Creganna as a leading player in the Irish medical device cluster.

Organisations (whether they are a LSE or SME) utilise their internal competencies and capabilities (including the creative capability of employees) to generate and develop suitable and appropriate innovative actions. The more effective an organisation is in controlling and influencing the outcome of this process (e.g. the organisations ability to manage its innovation process) then the greater the chance that it will be successful in developing innovative actions for the global marketplace. A well managed innovation process improves the organisations profitability and ultimately ensures its continued survival through constant renewal and adaptation.

Innovation can be viewed as the combined activity of generating creative ideas and the subsequent successful exploitation of these concepts for benefit (Roberts, 1988; von Stamm, 2003; O'Sullivan and Dooley, 2008). All innovations have creativity at their core; whether this creativity is in the originality of the initial idea or the way the idea is exploited by the organisation. The creative process relies on information, expertise and employee motivation and creative thinking skills as inputs to generate appropriate ideas. Access to relevant and up to date information (including information from external sources) can provide a critical competitive edge for organisations innovation efforts (Harris, 1999; Gunasekaran, 1999; Sveiby, 1997; Davenport et al, 1996). This requires an "ability to acquire, evaluate, store, use and discard knowledge and information" (Knock et al., 1997).

Given that social relationships are key to enhancing the ability of individuals to gather knowledge (Brown & Duguid, 2000; Cross, Rice & Parker, 2001; Smith and McKeen, 2007) and that creation of knowledge is primarily a social process among individuals (Berger & Luckman, 1966; Vygotsky, 1962; Wittgenstein, 1953), organisations' need to optimise collective knowledge and the supporting mechanisms by which its people and processes accumulate, structure, and transfer knowledge effectively (Miles et al., 2000). Collaboration between individuals and organizations is a key underpinning characteristic of knowledge exploitation and new knowledge development (McKenzie & van Winkelen, 2004). Research highlights that mechanisms such as social networks promote both organisational and collective learning and that participation in these social networks are a significant source of knowledge, which subsequently leads to innovation (Floyd & Woolridge, 1999; Tsai, 2001).

Cognisant of the importance of social networks for knowledge management for innovation, this chapter has the following objectives:

- To explain the terms information, knowledge, learning, their interrelationship and their role in innovation.
- To outline the innovation process with its knowledge management phases

- To extrapolate the role of social networks in the knowledge management for innovation process
- To outline the steps of the social network analysis tool and provide guidance for its implementation
- To illustrate with examples how to utilise the social network analysis tool to map and analyse the knowledge management for innovation efforts in a network.

BACKGROUND

The Key Terms: Information, Knowledge, Learning & Innovation

Knowledge can be defined as *information* acquired through implicit or explicit *learning* means and in the process combined with experience, context, interpretation and reflection (Davenport and Prusak, 1998). In essence, knowledge, within the context of innovation, is about making good information available to experienced individuals and groups who then take decisions based on that information. Knowledge is embodied in people; culture; procedures; routines; systems; processes and information systems. Knowledge is usually defined in relation to two other components: data and information. Data is words and numbers that may have some meaning to an individual (e.g. words in a paragraph or musical notes on a page). When this meaning becomes clear and useful, the data is transformed into information. Information can be stored in a variety of ways and can sometimes lose the original data that gave it meaning. When we store information in our minds about something, the original data often becomes forgotten but the meaning remains. When information is used with judgment and experience it can become knowledge. Thus although we are surrounded by a considerable amount of data, only some of it will be translated into knowledge (O'Sullivan &

Dooley, 2008). The genesis of innovation comes from new knowledge and ideas that are successfully transitioned into innovations. The ability of an organisation to access and apply appropriate knowledge for the purpose of generating new ideas or overcoming challenges during the exploiting of the idea is core to an organisations innovative capability (Tidd et al, 2007; Trott, 2005). As Roberts (1988) argues, innovation consists of two interrelated elements; the generation of the idea and the subsequent conversion of that idea into a useful application. Kanter (1983) views innovation as "the generation, application and implementation of ideas, processes, products and services".

The conversion of information to knowledge and knowledge to innovation begs the question as to what enables the conversion of information to knowledge so that innovation may occur. Sadler-Smith (2006; p.183) states that the root of knowledge creation is learning. It is acknowledged that this learning initially occurs at the level of the individual (Sadler-Smith, 2006) but it is also recognized that the knowledge of the group is greater than the sum of the individual members' knowledge (Senge, 1990). Thus it appears that the synergistic nature of knowledge and collective learning within networks of individuals is something that is of immense potential significance to organisations (Sadler-Smith, 2006). This collective learning is the 'dynamic and cumulative process of production of knowledge, which is due to interaction mechanisms typical of an area characterized by a strong sense of belonging and relational synergies' (Camagni, 1995, p.203). The learning component of 'collective learning' emphasises the production of knowledge whereas the collective component emphasises the social interaction mechanisms of a collective (Gubbins & MacCurtain, 2008). Recognition of the role of the collective social network for learning and knowledge sharing has resulted in changes in the way knowledge management systems are viewed and consequently in how innovation is nurtured.

Changes in the Nature of Knowledge Management Systems: Moves toward Social Networking Strategies

The focus on knowledge management (KM) initiatives has shifted from a strategy of capturing data and making the information explicit in portals and databases to one of promoting tacit knowledge sharing among people (Cross, Parker, Prusak, & Borgatti, 2001; Davenport & Prusak, 1998). Initial knowledge management initiatives were mostly information technology (IT)-based, including repositories that captured critical documents such as lessons learned and best practice. However, many of these early initiatives failed: some of the more common causes included out-of-date documents stored in the knowledge repositories; stored documents not fitting to the employee work process and needs; and the organisations culture, rewards and incentives operating in a manner that discouraged document sharing (Douglas, 2002). While IT certainly has been (and will remain) a critical component of an organisation's knowledge management systems, KM initiatives should also include strategic, process, and people components to achieve successful outcomes (Davenport, De-Long & Beers, 1998).

Increasing numbers of organisations are moving from traditional functional based structures to matrix, team-based and networked structures (Morton et al., 2006). These structures succeed in traversing traditional boundaries when they develop deep and collaborative relationships internally as well as with customers, suppliers, alliance partners and increasingly competitors (Neilson et al., 2004) or with colleges and universities. They thereby draw on the knowledge, experience and capabilities of diverse knowledge sources to generate value and facilitate the achievement of their objectives (Rothwell, 1992; Tidd et al, 2005). As a consequence such networked structures have a more effective and efficient innovation process than their traditionally structured, non relationship-driven counterparts (Rothwell,

1992). Astute organisations reconfigure their resource base to enhance existing networks or to create new network configurations to nurture and support the innovation processes. Consequently the locus of innovation and knowledge management is moving from stable, physically collocated functions to dynamic, competency-based, business networks (Voss, 2003; Walters, and Buchanan, 2001; Wright, and Burns, 1998).

This network perspective of innovation views the process as a continuous and cross-functional process involving and integrating a growing number of different resources inside and outside the organisation's boundaries (Boer et al, 1999). Networks link organisations, customers and suppliers to create adaptive value creating networks capable of exploiting emerging opportunities (Cormican and O'Sullivan, 2004; Venkatraman and Henderson, 1998). Such networks create value by synthesising information and knowledge, exploiting expertise and pooling resources across traditional boundaries in order to create new knowledge and achieve innovations outside of individual capabilities and the resource bases of individual organisations (Prasad and Akhilesh, 2002; Johnson et al, 2001; Ratcheva and Vyakarnam, 2001; Pawar and Sharifi, 2000).

These changes emphasise the increasing popularity and value of knowledge management initiatives that emphasise the connections among people (Parise, 2007). A key advantage of these people-focused strategies is that they enable the sharing of more relevant tacit knowledge (Polanyi, 1983), such as employees' experiences, know-how, and other similar or complementary expertise that cannot be captured in documents. The increasing relational, interdependent and collaborative nature of knowledge management initiatives points to the insights that can be gained from understanding the social network component of these knowledge management initiatives. The social network perspective is an appropriate lens through which to examine interactions among employees (both within and outside the organization) that enable

work to be accomplished (Cross & Parker, 2004), or in this case, that enable knowledge management for the purposes of innovation. A social network perspective permits conceptualizing the whole, rather than the parts (Storberg & Gubbins, 2006). Through work carried out at the Power & Systems Laboratory, Oshry (1996) found that individuals, groups, processes, and organizations always exist in relationship, and he suggested that artificially separating a thing (person, process, or group) from its system will produce a flawed understanding. A social network is a set of people or groups, called 'actors', with some pattern of interaction or 'ties' between them. These patterns can typically be represented as graphs or diagrams illustrating the dynamics of the various connections and relationships within the group (the group being that selected for exploration).

In this modern era of competition, managing either an organisation's internal knowledge assets within networks or those obtainable through an organisations network e.g. suppliers, alliances, partnerships or research collaborations with universities, and converting it into commercially successful innovations through effective collaboration is a critical component of competitive success (Roberts, 2002), however this process is intricate, complex and difficult to manage (Cormican and O'Sullivan, 2003a; Jaffe, 1989; Balconi et al., 2004). It is therefore important to a) understand the knowledge management phases within the innovation process b) understand the role of social networks in these knowledge management phases and c) be able to analyse the social networks of knowledge networks for innovation so as to determine how they can be managed for improved knowledge management for innovation efforts.

The Social Network Perspective of Knowledge Management Phases of the Innovation Process

Innovation is about knowledge, creating new ideas and possibilities through combining different knowledge sets. For an organisation to optimize the way new knowledge is developed and existing knowledge is exploited, it needs to facilitate the capabilities for converting the knowledge available to structures, processes, products and systems that allow the value, in this case innovation, to be exploited (McKenzie & van Winkelen, 2004). Such knowledge may be from the insights and competences of individual people (the source of new knowledge), found in experience or could be from a process of search- such as research into technologies, markets, competitor actions etc. This knowledge could be codified in such a way that others can access it, discuss it, transfer it etc. or it can be in tacit form, know about but not actually put into words or formulae. A key contribution to our understanding of the kinds of knowledge involved in different kinds of innovation is that innovation rarely involves dealing with a single technology or market but rather a bundle of knowledge which is brought together into a configuration. Successful innovation management requires that we get hold of and use knowledge about components but also that we understand how those can be put together, the architecture of an innovation.

Tranfield et al. (2006) outline the phases of the innovation process and extrapolate the knowledge routines in each of the innovation phases- discovery, realisation and nurture. Table 1 explains these innovation phases and the knowledge routines evident in each phase.

Discovery

The first phase of any innovation process is referred to by Tranfield et al. (2006) as discovery and involves searching the external environment to identify potential shifts and unfulfilled needs that provide the opportunity for potential innovations. The knowledge inputs for this phase of the innovation process necessitate the organisation spreading as wide a net as possible to capture information from relevant knowledge sources. Opportunities can originate from knowledge

sources such as existing customers, suppliers, lead-users, government legislation, developments in technology and related industries, competitor action, university research or even communities of practice. The broadness of the domain makes it impossible for any one individual (or even organisation) to adequately search all potential sources. Consequently, the models of the innovation process are evolving from linear, self contained processes to one which embraces the power of networks. The use of social networks to search for and access knowledge regarding emergent shifts in the external environment improves the organisations searching ability to identify appropriate opportunities for innovation.

The social network literatures provide insight and empirical evidence which informs practice on how best to search for and access valuable knowledge through social networks. For example, Granovetter (1973) proposes through his weak tie theory that weak ties, defined as relationships that are emotionally distant and based on infrequent communication, enable a focal individual to contact another who resides in a different social circle and hence access non-redundant knowledge. Burt (1992) proposes, through his structural hole theory, that boundary spanners, defined as those individuals in a network who connect otherwise unconnected individuals, gain privileged access to novel knowledge in a timely fashion, as well as bargaining power in the knowledge exchange process.

Once the *search* process is complete, the more effectively an organisation can *capture* and *articulate* the knowledge from these networks, the richer the opportunities they have to feed their innovation efforts. In order for meaningful knowledge transfer and learning to occur, the social networking process requires direct and intense interaction between individuals with relevant knowledge and expertise, within the structure of the network (Hansen, 1999; Swan, 2001). This ensures that knowledge can be internalised in the organisation and given expression in a form understood by those

Table 1. Innovation phases, knowledge management routines within & social networks in use

Innovation Phases	Description	Knowledge Management Routines	Description	Social Networks in Use
Discovery	Searching & scanning the environments to pick up & process signals about potential innovation, such as needs, opportunities arising from research, regulatory pressures, or the behaviour of components.	Search	The passive & active means by which potential knowledge sources are scanned for items of interest	Casting a broad search net through the available social networks. The larger the network, the wider the search net will be cast.
		Capture	The means by which knowledge search outcomes are internalised within the organisation	Access to a greater pool of diverse competencies of relevance to the knowledge accessed will enhance the absorptive capacity of the network & thus its ability to capture & articulate the knowledge
		Articulate	The means by which captured knowledge is given clear expression	
Realisation	How the organisation can successfully implement the innovation. It involves selecting from the potential innovations those which the organisation will commit resources.	Contextualise	The means by which articulated knowledge is placed in particular organisational contexts	Selection decisions on which potential innovations to pursue are based on available knowledge & expertise so having access to a greater network of expertise, knowledge and diverse perspectives to enlighten the selection process improves the selection decisions.
		Apply	The means by which contextualised knowledge is applied to organisational challenges	
Nurturing	This is the phase of nurturing the chosen option through providing resources, developing the means for exploration.	Evaluate	The means by which the efficacy of knowledge applications is assessed	The opening of this phase of the innovation process to input from knowledge sources available throughout the immediate and external social networks of the organisation enhances the expertise & knowledge available, increases the creative capability to solve problems encountered and ensures that relevant stakeholder requirements are incorporated into the design & development activities. Potential errors are minimised by collective knowledge sharing, collaborative routines have the potential to develop technologically superior innovations & reduce the cost & time of development.
		Support	The means by which knowledge applications are sustained over time	
		Re-innovate	The means by which knowledge & experience are reapplied elsewhere within the organisation	

Adapted from Tranfield et al., (2006)

tasked with exploring its innovative potential. The requirement for intense interaction emphasises the importance of the strength of the relationships.

The requirement for individuals with relevant competencies emphasises the need to investigate the absorptive capacity of the network. Absorptive capacity relates to the "ability to recognise the value of new external knowledge, assimilate it and apply it to commercial ends" (Van den Bosch et al., 2003).

Initial empirical studies grounded on weak tie theory (Granovetter, 1973) and structural hole theory (Burt, 1992) focused on *access* to social network benefits, such as knowledge. However, advancements in research indicate that *access* to the knowledge of contacts does not guarantee *mobilisation* or transfer. Hansen (1999), for example, identified that weak ties are more likely to facilitate access to non-redundant information by comparison to strong ties due to the ability of weak ties to reach outside an individuals immediate social circle. However, it is strong ties that are most likely to facilitate *transfer* of such information, particularly where that information is complex. This is due to relationships characterised as strong ties being more likely to be closer, more trusting (Hansen, 1999) and more reciprocal. Levin (1999) found that weak ties characterised as trusted weak ties are the most effective network configuration for access to and transfer of valuable knowledge due to their ability to reach and search beyond an individuals' immediate social circle for novel knowledge and the presence of sufficient trust that will enable the knowledge to be transferred.

The effectiveness of interaction for knowledge exchange between individuals is also influenced by the absorptive capacity (Cohen and Levinthal, 1990) of both individuals and their parent organisational. Antecedent factors that affect absorptive capacity include cognitive distance and mutual related knowledge (such as foundation skills and learning experience) between individuals, mutual understanding of partner and network objectives (Balconi et al., 2004; Hussler and Ronde, 2002), and compatible organisational factors (structure, communication infrastructure and knowledge distribution) (Van den Bosch et al., 2003). If the network is to enhance the knowledge store of the network and consequently deliver innovation, they must possess the capability to recognise the op-

portunities within the transferred knowledge and also be able to assimilate the acquired knowledge into their own systems and models to manipulate and adapt it. A network which provides a diverse pool of expertise, knowledge, perspectives and competencies combined with mutual related competencies and understanding of network objectives improves the absorptive capacity of the network and consequently the ability to capture and articulate the knowledge.

Realisation

The second phase of the innovation process relates to *realisation*. This involves firstly screening and selecting appropriate actions to be progressed along the innovation process. Not all opportunities identified are equally attractive. The organisation must decide which concepts from the search phase should be progressed and which abandoned. This is often the most subjective and uncertain phase of the innovation process as the organisation endeavours to estimate the future value of the concept, their ability to develop and exploit it and the alignment of the concept with the organisation's strategic direction. Selection decisions are based on available knowledge and expertise so the adoption of a team-based, consensus approach to decisions is facilitated by having access to a greater network of expertise, knowledge and diverse perspectives to enlighten the selection process. The organisation must strive to identify and access all pertinent information and absorb this knowledge to enhance their decisions. Better informed decisions regarding which concepts are approved will enhance the likely success of the innovative actions pursued.

Nurturing

The third phase of the innovation process relates to nurturing the innovative actions approved from the realisation phase. The challenge of this phase is to transform the concept into a reality and align it with the needs of the market. This phase integrates technology and market information together with the organisations capability to develop the prospective innovation. The further along this phase an action is then the more difficult it is to alter the design. Consequently organisations need to access information to ensure the design and subsequent development is correct. The use of concurrent engineering and co-design teams are common in this phase of the process to enhance the knowledge flows and eventual output. Concurrent engineering brings together all relevant stakeholders (e.g. design, manufacturing, logistics, sales, etc.) to collaborate on the development of the action; co-design engages the capability of suppliers and other independent organisations to work together on the design of the future innovation. The opening up of this phase of the innovation process to input from knowledge sources external to the organisation enhances the expertise and knowledge available, increases the creative capability to solve problems encountered and ensure that relevant stakeholder requirements are incorporated into the design and development activity. Since potential errors are minimised by collective knowledge sharing, such collaborative routines have the potential not only to develop technologically superior innovations but also to reduce the cost and time of development. Such leveraging and integration of necessary resources from the social networks facilitates successful exploitation of the 'new' knowledge opportunity.

Finally, this phase is concerned with the exploitation of value from the developed actions. The concepts identified in the realisation phase of the innovation process are pursued to increase revenues, expand markets, reduce costs or enhance the organisations competitive advantage in some tangible way. Many organisations succeed in making substantial technological breakthroughs during the nurture phase, only to be unable to secure benefit from the development. The ability to commercialise developed actions is essential to the long term sustainability of any organisation.

Knowledge inputs for this phase of the process relate to how the organisation can ensure the market adopts the innovation and what mechanisms can be used to protect intellectual property from competitors. Organisations must be careful when securing intellectual property that the associated secrecy does not adversely affect the necessary knowledge flows to the innovation process. Many issues of exploitation overlap with the preceding development phase, as the organisation must ensure the developed action is both technologically capable and what its prospective market requires. The identification of alternative applications for technology or knowledge created as part of the innovations journey along the innovation process may become an input for the discovery phase of future processes

SOCIAL NETWORK ANALYSIS AS A KNOWLEDGE MANAGEMENT FOR INNOVATION TOOL

This chapter has discussed the collaborative nature of knowledge management efforts for innovation and emphasised the role of social networks in the phases of innovation. Successful knowledge management for innovation requires an understanding of the characteristics of a given knowledge network for innovation so as to determine how it can be managed for improved knowledge management efforts. For example, new-product development or process improvement team initiatives can be assessed in terms of how the team is integrating its expertise and the effectiveness of this integration for innovation. Social network analysis (SNA) facilitates such an assessment. Social network analysis (SNA) facilitates analysis of relationships among individuals in a network. It describes a number of social network metrics or indices that are useful in mapping and analysing overall network structures and the characteristics of these structures with a view to identifying the positive and/or negative impact of the social net-

Table 2. Name generator questions for investigating innovation networks

Name Generator Questions for Investigating Innovation Networks: Ego or Personal Network Analysis	
Please list (by first initial and last name or by initials) up to 15 people whom you have gone to, to obtain help to initiate, design, develop and/or implement the project/innovation "specify innovation".	To focus on a successful innovation which has already occurred and to focus the investigation on a network which, demonstrated evidence of past success.
Please list (by first initial and last name or by initials) up to 15 people whom you would go to for help you initiate, design, develop and/or implement a new idea or innovation.	To identify and investigate the potential perceived social network available to those with innovative ideas.
Name Generator Questions for Investigating Innovation Networks: Whole Group Network Analysis (names to be collected in a pre-survey & incorporated in the final design of the social network survey)	
From the list of names provided, please answer each question asked, for each individual listed. If you do not know the individual listed, leave your answer blank.	To collate answers to social network questions for each and all the members of the network from each and all members of the network.

work on knowledge management for innovation efforts. By exploring a knowledge management for innovation driven social network in this way, one can identify strategies for developing the network and improving its performance. This section will explicate the stages involved in social network analysis, identify and explain the SNA metrics that can be calculated and explain how these metrics provide insight into the dynamics of network operations in its efforts to innovate.

The Steps of Social Network Analysis

The process of conducting a social network analysis typically involves the following steps:

1. Determining the type of analysis
2. Identifying an important group
3. Identifying the key relationships in the network
4. Collecting network data
5. Measuring the relationships
6. Including individual attribute information in the analysis
7. Analysing the network data
8a. Analysing the results: Visually
8b. Analysing the results: Quantitative Descriptive Indices

Step 1: Determining the Type of Analysis

The first consideration where social network analysis will be conducted relates to what form of analysis to conduct (Wasserman & Faust, 1999). There are two types of SNA analyses that can be conducted; *whole or group network analysis* and *ego or personal network analysis*. The broadest level is concerned with comparing entire social structures. Whole group network data requires collecting measurements from *all* the people in a group. It involves the SNA analyst identifying all the members of the group. This can be done by a simple pre-survey to get known members of the group to identify and list all the other members of the group. This generates names for the remaining network analysis questions (a name generator question). Table 2 illustrates some examples of name generator questions that can be utilised for the purposes of analysing innovation networks. The combined list of names is then used in the final SNA survey; each person in the group is asked about his/her relationship with every other member of that group as listed on the survey (See example questionnaire 1). The boundary of the group, in terms of who does and does not constitute the group is determined by what the researcher is interested in studying. For example, if one is concerned with promoting product or process innovation, a SNA analyst may investigate a relevant Research and Development (R&D) team, a university-industry research and development team or a number of R&D teams who ideally should be interconnected. The boundary is therefore defined by the membership of the team.

There are obvious difficulties associated with collecting whole network data, most notably the need for close to a 100 percent response rate, it is time consuming for large groups and does not account for relationships outside the defined group. A narrower approach is concerned with the relationships that exist from the point of a particular individual. This approach is referred to as ego-centric or personal network data. This method focuses on specific individuals and enumerates the local networks surrounding them. An ego-centred network consists of a focal individual, termed *ego*, a set of *alters* (individuals) who have ties to ego and ego estimated measurements on the ties between these alters. The focal person is asked to identify the other people whom are important to him/her for a given function/purpose/task (which is determined by the nature of the study). For example, an SNA analyst may be interested in investigating a top manager and his/her connections for the purposes of commercialising innovations or enabling the conversion of innovative ideas into products or new processes or an SNA analyst may be interested in investigating an academic researcher's links with industry and how they are utilised for technology transfer.

Within these social networks, a researcher can focus on a number of different units of analyses; the *dyadic* level (individual tie to another individual), *monadic* level (cases of individuals and the sum of their connections) and *network* level (the ties across the group). The dyadic level is concerned with relationships between pairs of individuals. For example, the strength of the relationship, extent of information shared in the relationship. Monadic is concerned with cases of individuals and the sum of their ties to others or distances to others. For example, to identify a key source of information,

the goal would be to locate someone who is central to the network (see measure of centrality), that is has a high number of ties to him/her. The network level is concerned with cases of whole groups such as a department, team or organisation and the ties that exist among them. An SNA analyst may be concerned with the number of ties in the network, the average distance between individuals or the extent of centralisation.

The precise areas investigated and metrics chosen will be determined by the nature of the questions the SNA analyst wishes to answer and by the context in which the SNA will be conducted.

Step 2: Identifying an Important Group

In combination with step 1, determining the type of analysis, an SNA analyst in consideration of the question/problem/area/topic s/he wishes to investigate, must consider which group to utilise for this investigation. In the context of an SNA analyst being interested in investigating how social networks and the individuals within social networks facilitate or hinder innovation and what can be done to develop or enhance the social network to encourage innovation, the SNA analyst needs to identify a strategically and operationally important group, which yields or is expected to yield innovation benefits for the organisation. Most importantly innovation is a collaborative endeavour, both in conception and implementation. SNA can be useful for revealing how a network is integrating its expertise, how aware the network is of others expertise, whom is in communication with whom and in what direction, who is accessing information from whom, who facilitates information transfer, how effective is the network at integrating its expertise with others in the organisation and utilising the expertise of others outside of the organisation etc. For example, an SNA analyst could investigate a geographically dispersed research and development team, a department, a team or a university-industry partnership network.

Step 3: Identifying the Key Relationships in the Network

Once a strategically important group for innovation is identified, the next step is to collect the information needed to map the relationships which help explore and understand how social networks influence knowledge access, transfer, combination and innovation initiation, development and exploitation. This step is thus concerned with determining how the relationships will be defined. For the purposes of exploring the process of innovation, elements such as collaboration, awareness of expertise, access to knowledge and expertise, facility for transfer and combination of knowledge, opportunities for innovative ideas to be realised are important. Thus questions concerned with relationships such as communication relations (e.g. who speaks to whom), information sharing relations (e.g. who shares information with whom), instrumental relations (e.g. who asks whom for help in implementing a new innovation), are useful. Table 3 provides a list of possible relationships and the questions that can be asked when investigating the influence of social networks on innovation. By focusing on such defined relationships, it is possible to explore the structure of that particular network and how individuals work together to achieve optimal performance or in this case innovate. It is recommended that 2-4 questions are selected which are closely linked to the goals of the investigation (Cross & Parker, 2004). By exploring a number of defined relationships, the SNA analyst gets a greater understanding of the innovation networks. For example, individuals who often communicate with each other in a communication network may not necessarily share information with each other in an information sharing network.

By collecting social network data on communication and information flow and combining it with social network data on more specific relationships of significance, for example, to the innovation generation process, it provides more complete and contextually relevant information. The most important things are; to pick relationships that are strategically important; provide thorough information on the topic of interest, such as innovative capability; and which can be actioned on once areas for development/improvement are recognised.

In posing these questions, it is particularly valuable and more reliable if whole group network data is collected and each member is asked questions pertaining to each and all the other members. This ensures that where member A is asked about the extent of knowledge sharing between himself and member B., member B is asked about the extent of knowledge sharing between himself and member A. This helps clarify the true extent of knowledge sharing rather than that perceived by one member who may over-inflate his own independence by suggesting low knowledge sharing or over-inflate the extent to which he is collaborative by suggesting high knowledge sharing.

Step 4: Collecting Network Data

The techniques used to collect network data are determined by a number of factors. The questions that need to be asked, access to the network members, availability of network members, time available for conducting the study and willingness of members to participate in such a survey. The options one can choose from, while cognisant of the factors influencing the choice of network data collection instrument, include paper based survey questionnaires, on-line survey questionnaires and interviews. Table 4 summarises the benefits and disadvantages of utilising each of these methods for social network data collection.

Step 5: Measuring the Relationships

Further to determining which relationships to focus on and how those relationships will be defined, this next step pertains to determining how the relationships will be measured. A network rela-

Table 3. Questions to identify key relationships in an innovation network

Relationship of Interest	Social Network Question	Purpose of Question
Relationships that Reveal Knowledge Sharing Potential		
Knowledge Awareness	I am aware of the knowledge, skills and expertise possessed by this person. This does not necessarily mean that I understand or possess the same knowledge or skills but I am aware of his/her knowledge, skills and expertise.	To determine the extent to which people are aware of others' expertise. Where people know others' expertise, they know whom to contact for help and whom they can potentially combine with to develop innovative ideas.
Absorptive Capacity	I possess similar knowledge, skills and expertise to this person, to the extent that I would find it relatively easy to combine my knowledge and skills with theirs.	To determine the likelihood the information/ knowledge shared can be combined. Individuals with similar knowledge, skills and expertise have a greater capacity to absorb each others' knowledge/information.
Access	When I need information or advice on a problem, this person is generally accessible to me within a sufficient amount of time to help me solve the problem.	To determine the ease with which a person can gain access to another.
Engagement	If I ask this person for help, I am confident that s/he will actively engage in helping me as far as s/he has knowledge and skills to do so.	To determine the extent to which an individual will engage with another to ensure transfer of information, understanding and/or combination.
Knowledge Access	When I need information or knowledge on a problem, which this person possesses, s/he is generally accessible to me.	To determine a person's ability to can gain access to another with the required knowledge/information for a particular problem/task etc.
Potential for Knowledge Transfer	When I need information or knowledge on a problem, which this person possesses, I am generally confident that s/he will provide me with it and work with me until I understand it and can integrate it into my work.	To determine the extent to which an individual will willingly provide information/knowledge and subsequently engage with another to ensure effective and complete transfer of information, understanding and/or combination.
Relationships that Reveal Value and Reliability of Knowledge Sharing		
Evidence of Knowledge Transferred	This person has provided me with information or knowledge in the past on a project or idea I was working on.	To assess *actual* information/knowledge transfer.
Value of Knowledge Transferred	This person has provided me with information or knowledge in the past on a project or idea I was working on, which was of value in developing the idea or project.	To assess the real value of information/knowledge *actually* transferred.
Competence Based Trust	I can trust that any information and knowledge provided by this person is well founded in his/her experience or education or research and where she/he does not know the answer to my questions or does not possess the competence to help me, s/he he will not provide incorrect information or knowledge.	To determine an individuals perception of the degree of trust in the information/knowledge providers competence.
Benevolence Based Trust	I can trust that any information or knowledge provided by this person will not cause me any harm or problems.	To determine and individuals perception of the degree of trust in the information/knowledge providers benevolence for the other person.
Relationships that Reveal Communication and Collaboration		
Communication	How often to you talk to this person about *"topic"*?	To determine who speaks to whom and how frequently.
Information Sharing	How frequently have you acquired information from this person to do *"task"*, in the past 3 months?	To determine who acquires information from whom for a specific task with whom and how frequently.

continued on following page

Table 3. continued

Relationship of Interest	Social Network Question	Purpose of Question
Information Giving	How frequently have you provided information to this person to do "*task*", in the past 3 months?	To determine who gives information to whom for a specific task and how frequently. The network of those who acquire information is not necessarily the same as that of those who give information. This can illuminate who are the information providers and information sharing barriers.
Collaboration	How frequently have you engaged in a discussion with this person on a new or innovative idea or "*idea specify*"?	To determine who the key contact people are in a network for individuals with innovative ideas and how frequently these are contacted.
Collaborative Problem Solving	How frequently have you engaged in a problem solving discussion with this person for the purposes of developing an innovative idea or "*idea specify*".	To determine who the key contact people are in a network for individuals with innovative ideas that need to be discussed, explored and solved and how frequently these are contacted.
Innovation Implementation	Whom would you speak to if you wished to initiate implementation of or commercialisation of an innovative idea?	To determine who the key contact people are in a network for facilitating implementation or commercialisation of an innovative idea.

Table 4. Data collection techniques

Approach	Benefits	Disadvantages
Paper based survey	• Hard copy so highly visible. • Traditional and low barrier to use. • More user friendly. • No PC access required • No PC skills required	• Difficulty of re-entering names generated from name generator question • Expensive due to mailing costs. • Labour intensive reminder system. • Social network questionnaires in this format are long & cumbersome
Online Survey	• Cost efficient way to distribute survey. • Can re-use data from earlier questions (name generator) in later questions to avoid need for re-entry. • Software can facilitate question skipping based on answers given to reduce participant burden • Ease of introducing reminder system. • Respondent can fill in survey over number of days by constant saving. • Data entered in electronic form which facilitates analysis stage.	• Possible barrier of the technology. • Not as visible as paper based survey.
Interviews	• Facilitates correct understanding of questions. • Allows collection of 'deeper' information. • Ensures all questions are answered.	• Can be more repetitive & more time consuming than respondent self-completion • Expensive due to travel costs. • Time pressure to respond in the face-to-face situation can reduce respondents' time to think & result in forgetting network members

tion can be measured as either binary or valued. Binary measures are simply indicated by a 0 or 1. The lack of a relationship between two individuals is represented as a "0" and a "1" represents the presence of a relationship. Utilising binary measurement is sufficient for determining, for example, who does/does not interact with whom or who does/does not know whom. Binary mea-

Table 5. Measuring key relationships in an innovation network

Measuring Relationships that Reveal Knowledge Sharing Potential			
Relationship of Interest	**Social Network Question**	**Measurement**	**Meaning**
Knowledge Awareness	I am aware of the knowledge, skills and expertise possessed by this person. This does not necessarily mean that I understand or possess the same knowledge or skills but I am aware of his/her knowledge, skills and expertise.	**Binary:** Please indicate your answer to this question by placing a tick next to the name of the persons, from the list of names provided, for those for whom you agree with this statement.	A tick is scored "1" to represent the presence of a relationship and no tick is scored "0" to represent no relationship
		Valued: Please rate each of the individuals listed on the question provided using the following scale: 1 not aware at all; 2 limited awareness; 3 partially aware; 4 mostly aware; 5 very aware	A rating of 5 indicates that the respondent is very aware of the knowledge, skills and expertise possessed by a person. A rating of 1 indicates that the respondent is not aware at all of the knowledge, skills and expertise possessed by a person.

surement is basically sufficient if the SNA analyst is only concerned with determining connections and lack of connections between people. If the SNA analyst is interested in the strength of relations and interactions, a valued measure should be utilised as this helps determine the extent of the relationship or interaction between two people. To do this, the SNA analyst uses a Likert type scale which allows the respondent to rate their relationship or interaction on a scale of 1 to 5 or 1 to 7. Table 5 provides an example based on a question presented in Table 1.

Step 6: Including Individual Attribute Information in the Analysis

It is also possible to collect attribute characteristics about the individuals in the network. Such attributes as age, gender, educational attainment, martial status, number of children, years of work experience, religion, performance record and competency record provides information about the individuals whom the respondent engages with, which may inform the SNA analyst about the respondent in terms of the homogeneousness or heterogeneity of the network. For example, where the respondent engages with others who are high performers, then they may encourage the respondent to perform highly also. Where a respondent engages with others with higher education or more years of work experience then they may find it easier to access new knowledge. Where a respondent engages with others of the same gender it may suggest something about the diversity of their network. Essentially, the attribute characteristics of the respondents' network may predict something about the respondent or help explain why innovation occurs in one group but not in another.

Step 7: Analysing the Network Data

Once the data is collected, you can analyse it using a social network analysis software package. A variety of packages are available. Some facilitate the drawing of networks, some do quantitative analysis and some do both. The most commonly used packages are UCINET, NetDraw, Pajek and another package used by business people is Inflow. A comprehensive list of and descriptions of these software packages is available on http://www.insna.org/software/index.html.

Step 8a: Analysing the Results: Visually

The network diagrams produced from the social network analysis software packages present some interesting results when analysed. Table 6 explains some of the basic concepts as illustrated in Figure 1.

Table 6. SNA concepts on visual network diagrams

Network Concept	Representation	Figure 1.	Analysis Meaning
Each symbol; triangle, circle, square	Represents a person or 'node' in the network	▲ represents the person/node Eamon	Number of nodes in the network; Who is in the network
A line between two people or nodes	Represents a relationship between these people	If, for example, Figure 1. depicts answers to the question "How frequently have you engaged in a discussion with this person on a new or innovative idea?", then the line between Eamon & Steven represents an innovation idea discussion relationship. The rating of "5" indicates that on a scale of 1 to 5, where 5 represents "very frequently", Steven "very frequently" engages in a discussion with Eamon on new or innovative ideas.	Which nodes are connected and which are unconnected; number of connections possessed by each node.
A number/rating for each line	Represents the strength/ frequency/rating of the relationship which that line depicts.		The strength/frequency/rating of the relationship. This is only measured if the strength of the relationship is something of importance and of interest to the analyst. The meaning of lines depends on the questions asked. Where the SNA question is based on a non-valued or binary measure, a line indicates a relationship and no line indicates no relationship. Such binary measures say nothing about the strength of the relationship etc.
Arrowhead lines	Represent the direction of the relationship and reciprocity	In the case of Steven and Eamon, the relationship is not reciprocal. Steven frequently goes to Eamon to discuss new ideas but Eamon does not go to Steven.	Directionality can mean many things and will vary with the nature of the question asked. Someone attracting a lot of arrows may be an expert, a key source of information or a bottleneck. Someone radiating out a lot of arrows may be in a role that requires obtaining information, may be good at sourcing information to facilitate knowledge combination or may be a drain on other people's time.
The shape of the symbol	Represent a characteristic about the person	In Figure 1, people have been coded into three groups, research, manufacturing & marketing. This is indicated through the use of three different symbols; triangle, square, circle. Additionally, the size of some of the symbols varies. The larger symbols represent managers & the smaller symbols represent non-managers.	Symbol shape can be utilised to represent any characteristic selected by the SNA analyst, for example any demographic or other information can be presented in this way; age, gender, function, hierarchy, tenure, organisation etc. Drawing diagrams that show such characteristics can reveal splits and then the meaning and implications of these splits can be explored. In Figure 1, the results provide indications of; who has a relationship with the managers, whether these relationships are reciprocal and in which direction; how many connections each manager has, who has a relationship with groups outside their own; how may connections there are between different groups and through whom etc. This information can be utilised by the SNA analyst to explore its implications for the network depending on the question asked.
Position in overall network: central or on boundary	Represent the centrality (high number of connections) or lack of centrality of a node (low number of connections)		Where the SNA software utilised includes an algorithm for positioned the nodes in the network according to their connectivity to other networks, it generally places highly connected people in the centre of the diagram and weakly connected people on the edges of the diagram, though this is not always completely possible with very large networks.

Figure 1. Example social network diagram

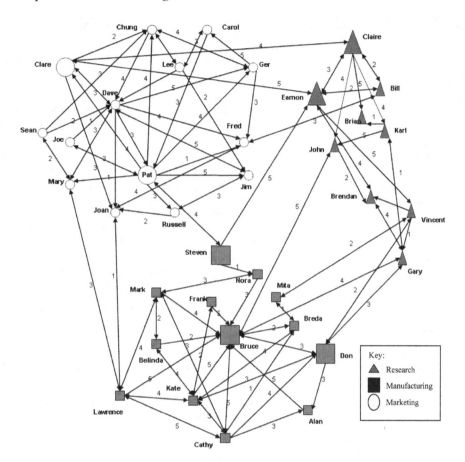

Step 8b: Analysing the Results: Quantitative Descriptive Indices

For large networks, network diagrams can be difficult to read, thus quantitative analysis is useful. Also, utilising the quantitative method, the number of measures and types of analyses that can be conducted is extensive.

The formal theoretical properties in the network perspective can be categorised as follows: centrality (betweeness, closeness and degree), position (structural), strength of ties (strong/weak, weighted/discrete), cohesion (groups, cliques) and division (structural holes, partition) (Hatala, 2006). These elements represent the building blocks for developing and conceptualising network theory (White, 1997). Measurement and analysis of these

elements presents some insightful information from which to identify means for the development or enhancement of knowledge management for innovation processes'.

Table 7 presents key network measures, an explanation of the purpose of the measure, how it is illustrated and its informative capacity for the purposes of knowledge management for innovation. Previous empirical studies concerned with these social network measures and their implications for knowledge management and innovation provide some insights into how SNA analysts can use these measures to explore their knowledge networks. With regard to the *centrality* measure, it was found that "a units innovative capability is significantly increased by its centrality in the intraorganisational network, which provides op-

Table 7. Network measures

Network Concept & Meaning	Variations of the Concept	Interpreting the Measure
Centrality: Centrality refers to the position of a node within a network.	**Local centrality:** deals with the number of direct ties with all the nodes in the network.	A high local centrality number represents a more centralised location of the node. This suggests that information can flow easily around the network through these nodes. If these nodes do not exist then there will be a structural hole, which will prevent information flow between groups or information will only flow through an individual who connects these groups thus conferring on that individual a high degree of power and control (Burt, 1992; 1997).
	Global centrality: relates to the connections between nodes via paths.	Global centrality measures highlight nodes which are not highly connected but provide links from one set of nodes to the other.
	Betweenness centrality: relates to the extent to which a particular person lies "between" the various other people in the network	High betweenness represents someone who is very important to information flow and the network is vulnerable to disruption if this person leaves or if there are power plays. Low betweeness represents someone who may play an important intermediary role and as a result will be very central to the network (Scott, 2000).
	In-degree centrality: The number of incoming ties a person has for a given relationship (e.g. information access, potential for knowledge transfer)	A high number of incoming ties to a person could indicate someone who is sought after for information, perhaps an expert. It may signify someone who would be a big loss to the company if they left. It can also indicate someone who is so sought after that too much of their time is taking up with providing information (or responding to whichever relationship the tie measures).
	Out-degree centrality: The number of outgoing ties a person has for a given relationship (e.g. information access, potential for knowledge transfer)	A high number of outgoing ties may suggest someone who is resourceful at obtaining information (or obtaining that which the relationship question measured) or someone who lacks knowledge. A person with a high number of outgoing ties but few incoming ties may signal someone who is an information hoarder or someone whose expertise is not being sought after by others as effectively as it could be. Those with a low number of incoming and outgoing ties are isolates.
	Closeness centrality: the extent to which a person lies a short distance to many other people in the network.	Persons who are highly central in terms of closeness have more efficient access for a given relationship (e.g. quicker access to information, faster potential for knowledge transfer).
	Brokerage Measures: **Coordinators:** those who broker connections within same group **Representatives & Gatekeepers:** Those who broker connections between their own group & another **Liaisons:** Those who broker connections between two different groups	
Density Density is a measure of the level of connectivity within the network. It represents the number of actual links as a proportion of the total possible links that can exist.		If each person in a network was connected to every other person density would be 100 percent and if their were no connections, network density would be 0 percent. Density is obviously affected by group size; it is easier to be connected to everyone in a group of 10 than every person in a group of 100. Thus density measures for a group should be compared to similar groups or determine an ideal network pattern depending on the objective of the analysis. For example, comparing density within the functional department of research and development and within the functional department of new product marketing and the density between these two functions. While you would not expect the between function density to be as high as the within group density, it would be necessary that some between function relationships exist. In general the density measure suggests that the greater the density the greater the cohesiveness in the network and the lower the density, the poorer the connectivity in the network. However, the optimum density level is only determined by assessing the function of the network and determining whether it needs to be more or less tightly connected.

Table 7. continued

Network Concept & Meaning	Variations of the Concept	Interpreting the Measure
Cohesion The average of the shortest paths between every pair of people in the network	**Clique:** is a subset of nodes that are completely connected and do not appear in any other cliques (Scott, 2000).	To identify cliques, the n-clique procedure is utilised. A strong clique may be defined as any node that is 1 degree from another node. Thus a 1-clique procedure is utilised to identify those individuals with 1 degree of separation. The degree of separation gives an indication of the strength of the relationships within the clique. Anything over 2 degrees is considered less reliable (Hatala, 2006). Cliques are highly connected and thus knowledge residing in the clique is likely to be known by everyone (Granovetter, 1973).
	Reciprocity: a 'give and take' relationship between members	A measure of reciprocity can give indications as to the extent to which two individuals will engage with each other to facilitate transfer of knowledge. Higher reciprocity is argued to be more conducive to the transfer of complex knowledge, whereas low reciprocity may suffice for simple knowledge (see Hansen, 1999). Bidirectional ties are illustrated in Figure 1 show reciprocity. These ties can also be valued.
Strength of Ties The strength of a relationship between two individuals.	**Strong Ties:** emotionally intense, frequent and involving multiple types of relationships (Granovetter, 1973). **Weak Ties:** not emotionally intense, infrequent and restricted to one narrow type of relationship (Granovetter, 1973).	A number of measures exist but the most accepted measure utilises a Likert type scale on closeness (Marsden & Campbell, 1984). A high closeness score indicates a strong tie and a low closeness score indicates a weak tie.
Structural Holes A structural hole is said to exist between two contacts who are unconnected to each other & circulate in different networks.	Redundancy: The impact of structural holes can be measured using a measure of redundancy; a person's ego network has redundancy to the extent that his/her contacts are connected to each other as well.	A low redundancy score or low constraint indicates a network with many structural holes. A high redundancy score or high constraint indicates a network with few structural holes.

portunity for shared learning, knowledge transfer and information exchange" (Tsai, 2001, p.1002). Central organisations become better informed about what is going on in the network, which increases the possibility for the central organisation to initiate the formation of new alliances (Gnyawali and Madhavan, 2001). Similarly their timely access to information and structural power within the network structure increases their bargaining position and improves the possibility of higher benefit from alliances than less central firms (Gilsing et al 2008). As network centrality increases so does an individuals' knowledge of the network's structural power and systems which enhances their innovative capacity (Ibarra, 1993). However, empirical studies also found some difficulties for central organisations. Central organisations that search for knowledge through non-redundant ties have to deal with higher volumes of more diverse information and this may result in random drift in a central organisations knowledge base (Gilsing et al 2008). Also, research highlights that there does not appear to be a significant association between an organisations centrality position and its business performance which highlights that some of the benefits of centrality may not outweigh the associated costs, such as coordination efforts (Tsai, 2001)

Knowledge brokers are found to be valuable as they initiate learning activities between organizations, establish new linkages for enriching knowledge and connect the innovation activity with wider networks (Powell et al, 1996; Murray, 2002). Further still knowledge brokers that bridge structural holes or bridge unconnected networks are found to improve the productivity of their teams by providing access to rich sources of novel knowledge (Regan and Zuckerman,2001).

Dense networks are found to possess certain advantages and disadvantages for knowledge management for innovation processes. Density through direct ties and indirect ties plays an important role with regard to assessing the reliability of (technologically distant) sources of novel knowledge as well as understanding and evaluating these sources. In essence density enhances the absorptive capacity of each individual firm in the network and builds up the shared absorptive capacity, however it may then begin to impede the possibilities for search and novel creation (Gilsing et al 2008). This can occur as dense networks can enable reputation effects and yield opportunities for sub-groups within the larger network to form coalitions that can constrain behaviour and lead to a desire by network members to conform rather than be cognitively distant from the sub-group (Coleman, 1988; Kraatz, 1998).

CONCLUSION

This chapter identified the key phases of innovation, that is discovery, realisation and nurturing and recognised that the knowledge management process as the central process through which organisations create innovation. The interrelated knowledge management process for the purposes of innovation consists of three integrated phases broadly corresponding to the phases of innovation, each with a number of such elements. These include the search for and the capture and internalisation of knowledge, which relates to the discovery phase of innovation. The knowledge management phases of articulation, contextualising the knowledge in an organisational context and then applying the knowledge for the purposes of innovation relate to the realisation phases of innovation. Finally an evaluation of the efficacy of

the knowledge relates to nurturing the knowledge transferred. Further to this the knowledge management process considers support for knowledge applications over time and the extent to which the knowledge is used for further re-innovation efforts, which again emphasise the nurturing of the knowledge transferred. This chapter suggests that organisations and individuals concerned with innovation should investigate not just the phases but the characteristics that enable these phases. Specifically, this chapter focuses on the enabling characteristics of social networks for the phases of knowledge management.

The search capability of an organisation or individual is enhanced through its social network and the size, diversity and access potential of this network to non-redundant knowledge. The capture and articulation potential of the individual or organisation is further enabled through access to a strong knowledge network with a bank of knowledge or access to a bank of knowledge to facilitate absorption of the new knowledge. Similarly, the potential of the individual/organisation to contextualise and apply the new knowledge is enhanced by the ability of the networks of which they are part to utilise their personal bank of knowledge capital to correctly and efficiently make decisions regarding the value of the new knowledge and consequently its application, evaluation and use in the future. Identification of the characteristics of the social networks influencing the knowledge management phases facilitates the development of strategies to improve the capabilities of social networks to facilitate knowledge management.

Specifics regarding the social networks enable management of these networks and consequently improved knowledge management capability.

The social network analysis tool provides a means for such an analysis of knowledge management for innovation networks and subsequent consideration of the networks enabling and inhibiting characteristics for innovation. The design of the precise social network analysis tool to be utilised must take careful account of the purpose of the analysis, as explicated in this chapter. For example, consideration needs to be given to membership of the network both current and desired, whether the network analysis should focus on internal or external knowledge or both, the type of knowledge requiring transfer, such as is it explicit and easy to transfer or tacit non codified knowledge such as that which resides in individuals heads, the key purpose of the knowledge management process for a specific organisation, such as is it about accessing knowledge or transferring it or combining knowledge in new ways. Once the key purpose of the investigation are identified and key considerations reviewed, SNA is a powerful tool for identifying relational patterns that influence the knowledge management process or phases within it. It provides the vehicle for mapping out the social structures of an organisation that will allow for identification of relational facilitators and barriers to knowledge management for innovation.

REFERENCES

Balasubramanian, R., & Tiwana, A. (1999). Supporting collaborative process knowledge in new product development teams. *Decision Support Systems*, *27*(1-2), 213–135. doi:10.1016/S0167-9236(99)00045-7

Balconi, M., Breschi, S., & Lissoni, F. (2004). Networks of inventors and the role of academia: an exploration of Italian patent data. *Research Policy*, *33*(1), 127-145.

Bassi, L. (1998) Harnessing the power of intellectual capital. *The Journal of Applied Manufacturing Systems*, Summer, 29-35.

Bennett, R., & Gabriel, H. (1999). Organizational factors and knowledge management within large marketing departments: an empirical study. *Journal of Knowledge Management*, *3*(3), 212–225. doi:10.1108/13673279910288707

Berger, P. L., & Luckman, T. (1966). *The Social Construction of Reality*. London: Penguin Books.

Blackler, F. (1995). Knowledge, Knowledge Work and Organizations: An Overview and Interpretation. *Organization Studies*, *16*(6). doi:10.1177/017084069501600605

Blake, P. (1998) The knowledge management expansion, *Information Today, 15*(1).

Bohn, R. (1994). Measuring and managing technological knowledge. *Sloan Management Review*, (Fall): 61–73.

Braha, D., & Bar-Yam, Y. (2004). Information flow structure in large-scale product development organizational networks. *Journal of Information Technology*, *19*(4), 244–253. doi:10.1057/palgrave.jit.2000030

Brass, D. J. (1984). Being in the right place: A structural analysis of individual influence in an organization. *Administrative Science Quarterly*, *29*(4), 518–540. doi:10.2307/2392937

Brown, J. S., & Duguid, P. (1991). Organizational learning and communities-of-practice: Toward a unified view of working, learning, and innovation. *Organization Science*, *2*(1), 40–57. doi:10.1287/orsc.2.1.40

Burt, R. S. (1992). *Structural Holes: The social structure of competition* (1st ed.). Cambridge, MA: Harvard University Press.

Camagni, R. (1995). Global network and local milieu: towards a theory of economic space. In Conti, S., Malecki, E., & Oinas, P. (Eds.), *The Industrial Enterprise and Its Environment: Spatial Perspectices* (pp. 195–214). Aldershot: Avebury.

Cohen, W. M., & Levinthal, D. A. (1990). Absorptive Capacity: A New Perspective on Learning and Innovation. *Administrative Science Quarterly*, *35*(1), 128–152. doi:10.2307/2393553

Coleman, J. S. (1988). Social Capital in the creation of human capital. *American Journal of Sociology, 94*(Supplement), S95–S120. doi:10.1086/228943

Cormican, K., & O'Sullivan, D. (2003a). A Collaborative Knowledge Management Tool for Product Innovation Management. *International Journal of Technology Management, 26*(1), 53–67. doi:10.1504/IJTM.2003.003144

Cormican, K., & O'Sullivan, D. (2003b). A Scorecard for Supporting Enterprise Knowledge Management. *International Journal for Information and Knowledge Management, 2*(3), 191–201. doi:10.1142/S0219649203000395

Cross, R., Parker, A., Prusak, L., & Borgatti, S. P. (2001). Knowing what we know: Supporting knowledge creation and sharing in social networks. *Organizational Dynamics, 30*(2), 100–120. doi:10.1016/S0090-2616(01)00046-8

Cross, R., Rice, R. E., & Parker, A. (2001). Information seeking in social context: Structural influences and receipt of information benefits. *IEEE Transactions on Systems, Man and Cybernetics. Part C, Applications and Reviews, 31*(4), 438–448. doi:10.1109/5326.983927

Cross & Parker. (2004). *The Hidden Power of Social Networks: Understanding How Work Really Gets Done in Organisations*. Boston: Harvard Business School Press.

Currall, S. C. (2003). *Observations and recommendations regarding university technology commercialization programs in England and Scotland. Rice University*. Houston, TX: Sponsored by Invest-UK.

Davenport, T. H., De Long, D. W., & Beers, M. C. (1998). Successful knowledge management projects. *Sloan Management Review*, (Winter): 43–57.

Davenport, T. H., Jarvenpaa, S. K., & Beers, M. C. (1996). Improving Knowledge Work Processes. *Sloan Management Review*, (Summer): 53–65.

Davenport, T. H., & Prusak, L. (1998). *Working Knowledge: How Organisations Manage What They Know*. Boston: Harvard Business Press.

de Boer, M., Van Den Bosch, F. A. J., & Volberda, H. W. (1999). Managing Organizational Knowledge Integration in the Emerging Multimedia Complex. *Journal of Management Studies, 36*(3), 379–398. doi:10.1111/1467-6486.00141

Douglas, P. (2002). Informational technology is out-knowledge sharing is in. *Journal of Corporate Accounting & Finance, 13*(4), 73–77. doi:10.1002/jcaf.10072

Dowling, P. J., & Welch, D. E. (2004). *International Human Resource Management: Managing people in a multinational context* (4th ed.). United Kingdom: Thomson.

Drucker, P. (1993). *Post Capitalist Society*. New York: Harper Business.

Duysters, G., & Lemmens, C. (2003). Alliance group formation. *International Studies of Management and Organization, 33*(2), 49–68.

Gilsing, V., Nooteboom, B., Vanhaverbeke, W., Duysters, G., & van den Oord, A. (2008). Network embeddedness and the exploration of novel technologies: Technological distance, betweenness centrality and density. *Research Policy, 37*, 1717–1731. doi:10.1016/j.respol.2008.08.010

Gnyawali, D. R., & Madhavan, R. (2001). Cooperative networks and competitive dynamics: A structural embeddedness perspective. *Academy of Management Review, 26*, 431–445. doi:10.2307/259186

Granovetter, M. S. (1973). The Strength of Weak Ties. *American Journal of Sociology, 78*(6), 1360–1380. doi:10.1086/225469

Gubbins, C., & MacCurtain, S. (2008). Understanding the Dynamics of Collective Learning: The Role of Trust & Social Capital. *Advances in Developing Human Resources, 10*(4), 578–599. doi:10.1177/1523422308320372

Gunasekaran, A. (1999). Agile manufacturing: A framework for research and development. *International Journal of Production Economics, 62*(1-2), 87–105. doi:10.1016/S0925-5273(98)00222-9

Hansen, M. T. (1999). The Search-Transfer Problem: The Role of Weak Ties in Sharing Knowledge across Organization Subunits. *Administrative Science Quarterly, 44*(1), 82–111. doi:10.2307/2667032

Hatala (2006) Social Network Analysis in Human Resource Development: A New Methodology. *Human Resource Development Review, 5*(45), 45-71.

Hussler, C., & Ronde, P. (2002). *Proximity and academic knowledge spillovers: New evidence from the networks of inventors of a French university*. EUNIP Conference 2002, Turku, Finland; Dec 5-7

Ibarra, H. (1993). Network centrality, power and innovation involvement: Determinants of technical and administrative roles. *Academy of Management Journal, 36*, 471–501. doi:10.2307/256589

Inkpen, A., & Tsang, E. (2005). Social capital, networks and knowledge transfer. *Academy of Management Review, 30*(1), 146–165.

Jaffe, A. B. (1989). Real effects of academic research. *The American Economic Review, 79*, 697–970.

Johnson, P., Heimann, V., & O'Neill, K. (2001). The "wonderland" of virtual teams. *Journal of Workplace Learning, 13*(1), 24–30. doi:10.1108/13665620110364745

Kanter, R. M. (1983). *The Change Masters*. New York: Simon & Schuster.

Knock, N., McQueen, R., & Corner, J. (1997). The Nature of data, information and knowledge exchanges in business processes: Implications for process improvement. *The Learning Organization, 4*(2), 70–80. doi:10.1108/09696479710160915

Kraatz, M. S. (1998). Learning by association? Interorganizational networks and adaptation to environmental change. *Academy of Management Journal, 41*, 621–643. doi:10.2307/256961

Krackhardt, D., & Hanson, J. R. (1993). Informal networks: the company behind the chart. *Harvard Business Review, 71*(4), 104–111.

Lengnick-Hall, M. L., & Lengnick-Hall, C. A. (2003). *Human Resource Management in the Knowledge Economy: New Challenges, New Roles, New Capabilities*. San Francisco: Berrett-Koehler.

Levin, D. Z. (1999). *Transferring knowledge within the organization in the R&D arena*. Unpublished doctoral dissertation, Northwestern University, Illinois.

Marsden, P. V., & Campbell, K. E. (1984). Measuring Tie Strength. *Social Forces, 63*(2), 482–501. doi:10.2307/2579058

McKenzie, J., & Van Winkelen, C. (2004). *Understanding the Knowledgeable Organization: Nurturing Knowledge Competence*. London: Thomson.

Miles, R. E., Snow, C. C., & Miles, G. (2000). The future.org. *Long Range Planning, 25*(6), 28–35.

Morton, S. C., Dainty, A. R. J., Burns, N. D., Brookes, N. J., & Backhouse, C. J. (2006). Managing relationships to improve performance: a case study in the global aerospace industry. *International Journal of Production Research, 44*(16), 3227–3241. doi:10.1080/00207540600577809

Murray, F. (2002). Innovation as co-evolution of scientific and technological networks: exploring tissue engineering. *Research Policy, 31*(8/9), 1389–1404. doi:10.1016/S0048-7333(02)00070-7

Neilson, G., Gulati, R., & Kletter, D. (2004) Organizing for success in the 21st century. Booz Allen Hamilton-Kellogg School of Management, Fortune 1000 survey findings. Retrieved from http://www.boozallen.com/bahng/SilverDemo

O'Sullivan, D., & Dooley, L. (2008). *Applying Innovation*. Sage Publications.

Oshry, B. (1996). *Seeing systems: Unlocking the mysteries of organizational life*. San Francisco: Berrett-Koehler.

Pagel, M. D., Erdly, W. W., & Becker, J. (1987). Social networks: we get by with (and in spite of) a little help from our friends. *Journal of Personality and Social Psychology, 53*, 794–804. doi:10.1037/0022-3514.53.4.793

Parise, S. (2007). Knowledge Management and Human Resource Development: An Application in Social Network Analysis Methods. *Advances in Developing Human Resources, 9*(3), 359–383. doi:10.1177/1523422307304106

Pawar, K. S., & Sharifi, S. (2000). Virtual collocations of design teams: coordinating for speed. *International Journal of Agile Management Systems, 2*(2), 104–113. doi:10.1108/14654650010337104

Podolny, J. M., & Baron, J. N. (1997). Resources and Relationships: Social Networks and Mobility in the Workplace. *American Sociological Review, 62*(5), 673–693. doi:10.2307/2657354

Polanyi, M. (1983). *The tacit dimension*. New York: Doubleday.

Powell, W., Koput, K. W., & Smith-Doerr, L. (1996). Inter-organizational collaboration and the locus of innovation: Networks of learning in biotechnology. *Administrative Science Quarterly, 41*, 116–145. doi:10.2307/2393988

Ratcheva, V., & Vyakarnam, S. (2001). Exploring team formation processes in virtual partnerships. *Integrated Manufacturing Systems, 12*(7), 512–123. doi:10.1108/EUM0000000006231

Reagans, R., & Zuckerman, E. (2001). Networks, diversity and productivity: The social capital of corporate R&D teams. *Organization Science, 12*(4), 502–517. doi:10.1287/orsc.12.4.502.10637

Roberts, E. M. (1988). Managing invention and innovation. *Research-Technology Management, 31*(1), 11–29.

Sadler-Smith, E. (2006). *Learning and Development for Managers: Perspectives from Research and Practice*. Oxford: Blackwell Publishing.

Scott, J. (2000). *Social Network Analysis: A Handbook*. London: Sage.

Senge, P. (1990). *The fifth discipline: The art and practice of the learning organisation*. New York: Doubleday Currency.

Storberg-Walker, J., & Gubbins, C. (2007). Social Networks as a Conceptual and Empirical Tool to Understand and "Do" HRD. *Advances in Developing Human Resources, 9*(3). doi:10.1177/1523422306304071

Sveiby, K. E. (1997). *The New Organizational Wealth: Managing and Measuring Knowledge Based Assets*. San Francisco: Berrett-Koehler.

Tidd, J., Bessant, J., & Pavitt, K. (2005). *Managing Innovation: Integrating Technological, Market and Organisational Change*. Chichester, UK: John Wiley & Sons.

Tranfield, D., Young, M., Partington, D., Bessant, J., & Sapsed, J. (2006). Knowledge management routines for innovation projects: developing a hierarchical process model. In J. Tidd (2nd ed.). *Knowledge Management to Strategic Competence* (pp. 126-149). London: Imperial College Press.

Trott, P. (2005). *Innovation Management and New Product Development* (3rd ed.). Prentice-Hall.

Tsai, W. (2001). Knowledge Transfers in Intra-Organizational Networks. *Academy of Management Journal, 44*(5), 996–1004. doi:10.2307/3069443

Uhl-Bien, M., Graen, G. B., & Scandura, T. A. (2000). Implications of leader-member exchange (LMX) for strategic human resource management systems: Relationships as social capital for competitive advantage. In Ferris, G. R. (Ed.), *Research in personnel and human resource management* (*Vol. 18*, pp. 137–185). New York: JAI Press.

Umpress, E. E., LaBiance, G., Brass, D. J., Kass, E., & Scholten, L. (2003). The role of instrumental and expressive ties in employee's perceptions of organizational justice. *Organization Science, 14*(6), 738–753. doi:10.1287/orsc.14.6.738.24865

Van den Bosch, F. A. J., Van Wijk, R., & Volberda, H. W. (2003). Absorptive capacity: Antecedents, Models and Outcomes. In Easterby-Smith, M., & Lyles, M. A. (Eds.), *Handbook of Organizational Learning & Knowledge Management* (pp. 278–301). Oxford: Blackwell Publishing.

Von Stamm, B. (2003). *Managing Innovation, Design and Creativity*. Wiley.

Voss, C. A. (2003). Rethinking paradigms of service. *International Journal of Operations & Production Management, 23*(1), 88–104. doi:10.1108/01443570310453271

Walters, D., & Buchanan, J. (2001). The new economy, new opportunities and new structures. *Management Decision, 39*(10), 818–834. doi:10.1108/EUM0000000006524

Wasserman, S., & Faust, K. (1994). *Social network analysis: Methods and applications*. New York: Cambridge University Press.

Wenger, E. C., & Snyder, W. M. (2000). Communities of practice: the organizational frontier. *Harvard Business Review, 78*, 139–145.

White, D. R. (1997). *What is network theory?* Retrieved May 2, 2005 from http://eclectic.ss.uci.edu/drwhite/netsy196.htm.

Wittgenstein, L. (1953). *Philosophical Investigations*. Oxford: Basil Blackwell.

Wright, D. T., & Burns, N. D. (1998). New organisation structures for global business: an empirical study. *International Journal of Operations & Production Management, 18*(9), 896–923. doi:10.1108/01443579810225513

Zack, M. (1999). Managing codified knowledge. *Sloan Management Review*, 45–58.

Chapter 7
Change Knowledge Management:
Transforming a Ghost Community into a Real Asset

Alberto Carneiro
Autonomous University of Lisbon, Portugal

ABSTRACT

Besides being a basic way to understand the world and an appropriate behavior to survival and development of organizations, the knowledge – acquisition, updating, and use – must be managed to increase creativity, and should be taken as a force to drive the human being in the field of competitive innovation. In this chapter the potential contribution of knowledge workers is discussed. Considering an assets approach, these reflections may enable the organization to promote and use the creativity of their knowledge workers, which are seen as a specific set of assets in the organization. This specificity should be considered in the policies of human resources management and also in the formulation of competitive strategies. Some suggestions are made for improving the utilization of knowledge workers to increase the level of productive creativity.

INTRODUCTION

The accumulated knowledge is invisible when it is not being used to produce useful activities that may enhance the organizational functioning. So if a company is unable to harness the knowledge of some workers, it is supporting a group of people which is almost equivalent to a ghosts community that can not show life during its existence.

In order to keep alive their competitiveness levels, organizations should adopt measures related to implementation of innovative practices and new technologies in several sectors. But it is well known that purchasing advanced technologies does not necessarily lead to success. Enterprise performance critically depends on how these technologies are adopted and successful adoption processes require a knowledge workers strategy to develop the necessary worker skills.

A better knowledge management can improve productivity by enabling "organisational inno-

DOI: 10.4018/978-1-61520-829-6.ch007

vation". Economic and social innovations are generated by the creative application of technical knowledge. The greatest benefits from knowledge management appear to be realised when ICT investment is combined with other organisational assets, such as better knowledge workers skills, new business processes, and new organisational structures.

Organizational changes may improve performance enhancement of firms through their capacity to take advantage of their knowledge workers skills, guiding their efforts to facilitating new organisational strategic movements. Knowledge workers may enable firms to introduce significant organisational changes in the areas of re-engineering, decentralisation, new products, new services, and flexible work arrangements.

When they are strongly motivated they allow organizations to produce with greater flexibility to satisfy shifting consumer preferences. In fact, organisational innovation and knowledge workers may be regarded as complementary factors. For instance, multinational corporations in the chemical and pharmaceutical industry increasingly explore global innovative networks also based on research activities conducted by their best knowledge workers.

To plan initiatives around organizational innovation or to bolster innovation requires a solid grasp of the innovation process in which knowledge workers can play a decisive role.

BUILDING ORGANIZATIONAL INNOVATION

The organizational abilities to generate and gain from innovation are sources of durable advantages of firms. As technological innovation is an organized process, more research on the existence, diffusion and effectiveness of organizational innovations and new management practices is needed.

As a complex concept "Organizational innovation" includes several dimensions, such

as competitive strategy (i.e. role of innovation, costs, knowledge, personnel, and technologies); structural characteristics of the organization such as hierarchy, functional lines, and organizational boundaries; work processes including the use of different production inputs, the flow of work, job design, work allocation, and use of suppliers and subcontractors; and industrial relation practices involving the strategies and institutional structures affecting the labour-management relationship.

In another perspective, organizational changes include three broad streams:

1. the restructuring of production processes, which include business reengineering, downsizing, flexible work arrangements, outsourcing, greater integration among functional lines, and decentralization;
2. product/service quality-related practices emphasizing total quality management and improving coordination with customers/ suppliers; and
3. human resource management practices, which include performance-based pay, institutional structures affecting the labour-management relations, flexible job design, employee involvement, and improving employees' skills.

By improving the employees' skills in what concerns knowledge acquisition, top management can attract and retain better qualified knowledge workers, that is, technicians charged with creating and evaluating knowledge, thinking creatively, analyzing and solving business problems, and contributing to organizational innovation.

Scientific knowledge and its resulting advances constitute decisive factors into an arena for organization development, namely, organizational innovation. Nowadays the characteristics of the economy and its movements demand that scientific and technological knowledge assets should be managed in a creative way. The fundamental unit of this new economy will no longer be the corporation but the individual, and according to this perspective, the presence of knowledge workers has to be attentively considered.

This interest in a more focused knowledge contribution has led to a concentrated evaluation of knowledge worker concept. Sometimes, the conceptualization of this type of worker is not very clear definition (Joseph, 2004), nevertheless, we assume that knowledge workers should integrate a continuous process in order to help their organizations to organize and transfer important information and expertise necessary for activities such as problem solving, dynamic learning, strategic planning and decision making.

Who is the knowledge worker? Which groups of employees engage in high-skill, knowledge-based work? Knowledge worker has been a term coined by Peter Drucker in 1959, which means that this worker is someone who works mainly with information or who develops and uses knowledge within their tasks context. This knowledge and the experiences that exist in the employees have to be considered as a real asset that should be used as a resource available for others in the organization. Knowledge workers can be seen as agents of a fluid mix of experience, values, contextual information, and expert insight that provides a framework for building new activities or new information that has value for business (Davenport & Prusak, 1998; Elliott, 1996).

The recognition of the pivotal role of the individual in the knowledge economy and its focus on helping and supporting individual leads to the need to develop the knowledge-working competencies. In fact, for organizations to prosper, knowledge workers need to learn how to better work together and how to harness their collective knowledge.

Knowledge workers can be best understood by the way managers use information and creativity in their organizations. Managers may involve and motivate their knowledge workers by using workshops and brainstorming – and asking them, to what use could this knowledge inventory be put. These initiatives are potential instruments for supporting knowledge worker induction and may result in a list of issues which can be reviewed to isolate and secure strategically important knowledge. To improve the effectiveness of knowledge workers, information systems groups at several organizations have started creating databases for knowledge, information maps and custom-made applications.

The presence and the real contributions of knowledge workers are more relevant to enterprises that are operating in knowledge intensive areas. Consulting firms are the ultimate example of organization selling knowledge directly. However, there are certain indicators for an organization's ability to create, disseminate and apply knowledge. Organizational culture is an important aspect for facilitating sharing, learning, and knowledge creation. An open culture with incentives built around integrating individual skills and experiences into organizational knowledge will be more successful.

Management should express their wishes to apply creative thinking at work to try processes that have never been done before in order to improve performance and unleash the creative potential of knowledge workers. They can learn proven creative thinking techniques to generate new ideas and get a blueprint for establishing a climate of innovation in their firms. For example, they can be able to:

- Turn existing problems into opportunities for growth;
- Apply creative thinking techniques to foster innovation and improve systems, products and processes;
- Produce, evaluate, and selecting new ideas, for instance, models for analyzing options.

It is needed a dynamic view of skills to understand how the knowledge acquired in professional experience or in university degrees is transformed into organizational asset. There are four critical skills that a knowledge worker needs to be effective:

- To be awake, self aware and intrinsically motivated;
- To take responsibility for working lives;
- To search for adequate information to build up the right solution;
- To set their own objectives;
- To focus and maintain their attention on those objectives.

Organizational innovation will be more succeeded if the organization has invested in intellectual capital and in the development of knowledge workers. However, because it is not enough to find new talents, management should also to focus the organizational innovation effort in the existing community of collaborators, because they are not mere invisible ghosts, they have to be treated as living sources of new products / services proposals. This can be reached by two different strategies: a) improving the qualification of present knowledge workers and b) providing adequate working conditions in order to support the development of the creativity. It is decisively important for leaders of organizations to understand who has knowledge, what competencies can be used, and how to develop support systems for its creation and application.

To manage themselves effectively, knowledge workers have to put some important questions within their professional reflections:

- Am I really a living knowledge worker? My specialized knowledge and my creative skills are taken into account by my top managers?
- Are they looking for my opinions about innovation policy in our organization? Or aren't they feeling that my knowledge is an asset that can be used as a contribution for organizational innovation?
- Am I moving my real skills noiselessly like a ghost? Am I a fictitious employee without having the motivation to suggest,

to propose, to participate decisively in innovative processes?
- Are my technical skills used to base innovative suggestions?

It is truly important to identify knowledge workers according to the type of industry and company size. Their functions may differ according to the situations and the environment of their activities. It is essential to convince top managers of the need to educate all knowledge workers in order to obtain from them a better contribution to the positive evolution of organizations (Carneiro, 2004). We believe that we need to sell the benefits of having knowledge workers to the board members of our companies. In fact, top management has to realize that these workers can be faced as a true gold vein that has to be significantly explored.

Knowledge workers must face surroundings where the technological transformations arise with great speed, reason why the industrial competitiveness has a very hard impact in organizations (Carneiro, 1995). Management should look for solutions to enable their knowledge workers to develop adequate competences, i.e., the skills that make possible to promote and to protect their intellectual products as a significant part of their professional responsibility.

KNOWLEDGE WORKER AND ICT: A BINOMIAL APPROACH

The value of new Information and Communication Technologies (ICT) is more and more intense within organizations that are operating in sectors that are highly developed technically. It constitutes a basic tool in many processes and influences the internal relationships between the functional areas and external relationships with markets' actors. Therefore, it is possible therefore to ask how these new technologies influence the acquisition of knowledge and performance management.

Basic ICT infrastructure is required to bring the tools to a company allowing workers to gain the knowledge, skills, and training needed to function in the modern competitive world. Access to and knowledge of basic ICT can make a substantial and positive difference to the technical performance of developing companies and business processes. Access to technology and ICT knowledge has a proven positive impact on productivity and business success. That is why knowledge workers should be stimulated to participate in every organizational innovation decisions.

ICT architectures should be designed accordingly to achieve competitive levels of flexibility and responsiveness, moving away from outdated conceptions of information systems.

Organizational knowledge and ICT refer to distinct sets of conceptions and establishing their relationships is far from trivial. The question then is how to assess the relationship between ICT and knowledge workers. Several variables to be considered when answering this question have been identified in the literature, namely, the enabling role of ICT for knowledge processes, the sate of the ICT infrastructure, and the level of knowledge required for using ICT

The users of these new technologies must have the necessary knowledge to use efficiently and effectively the diverse agents (Carneiro, 2005). Competence is one of the problems that this approach should face because it demands an advanced knowledge level from knowledge workers. In this domain, a competence strategy should have the following key targets:

- To transform ICT and information networks into tools which should be able to contribute for the renewal of strategic business units;
- To use the information to consolidate production technologies and processes;
- To intensify the competitiveness and to create excellence in ICT capacities.

According to an ICT perspective, we can also say that knowledge management is a new way of thinking about information systems within the organization. In fact, some traditional ICT organizations operate and think in terms of systems and processes, but knowledge management involves an interactive approach to thinking about ICT emphasizing a network of relationships among different sorts of information and between information and people.

When implementing a knowledge-management system based on a relational database, a cost analysis of the hardware and software acquisition costs and system administration and management is considered. The time spent before and after on certain management activities is measured and there is usually considerably less time spent on those tasks after the knowledge-management system goes in. That means that the same number of people can do more work on the systems-administration and management side. And this can be translated into more goods or services produced and delivered, and more profits for the company.

Knowledge-management systems typically involve e-mail, groupware and collaborative-computing software, document management and workflow, databases, and text-search and retrieval engines coupled with Internet access and a Web-browser interface. Knowledge management may be faced as the next step in the evolution of today's groupware, document-management, and workflow systems.

The Web and collaboration groupware products are the two most important technologies currently driving knowledge-management systems. Collaboration groupware products, for instance, provide for collaboration and the interchange of ideas, while the Web provides not just a ubiquitous interface to all types of information but also a way for users to see the relationships that exist between different information assets.

The Web is particularly valuable because it is a tool to establish links between pieces of information through hypertext, and part of knowledge is really coming from the relationships among different pieces of information.

Knowledge Management: a Key Factor for Creative Productivity

Early in the industrial era, organizations improved their efficiency, effectiveness and hence, their competitive edge by automating manual labor and reducing redundancy. However, now, in the age of the knowledge worker, many organizations have gone through massive restructuring to eliminate redundant workers and jobs. This movement has been swept up by the Business Process Re-engineering movement. To stay competitive, companies must still be innovative in reducing their costs and expanding their markets. Thus, organizations are streamlining their processes. KM enters the picture at this point. KM emerged with not only the need to be cost efficient and managerially effective in problem solving, decision making, innovation and all other elements that organizations need to maintain and develop their competitive edge, but also more specifically, to capture, catalogue, preserve, disseminate the expertise and knowledge that are part of organizational memory that typically resides within the organization in an unstructured way.

Moreover, KM means management of the intangible assets that generate value in the organization. The majority of these intangible values are related to processes that demand a real catching, structuring and transmission of knowledge. Therefore, KM has in the organizational learning its main tool and it is a dynamic concept, i.e., it is drastically linked to a knowledge flow. In addition we can say that the productive factor par excellence of the present era is the knowledge. It is this factor that sustains the leverage to the technological change.

KM is the management of corporate knowledge that can improve a range of organizational performance characteristics by enabling an enterprise to be more "intelligent acting" (Wiig, 1993). It is

not a new movement per se, as organizations have been trying to harness their internal processes and resources that have resulted in various movements over the years as total quality management, expert systems, business processes re-engineering, the learning organization, core competencies, and strategy focus (Shukla, 1997). Good managers in organizations have been using the know-how of people they hired with skills and experience, and processes for effective management on an ad-hoc, casual basis. However, only recently have organizations begun to focus their interest on this aspect in more systematic and a deliberate manner.

In a world of fast changes and innumerable sources of information, the more human resources a company has that may learn quickly bigger competitiveness it can sustain (Carneiro, 2000). The way for success is not mechanistic anymore: it requires creative capacities from managers and executants who deal with key processes in the field of the organization core businesses. Moreover, this way for success also needs a careful attention in order to permit an integrated sharing level in what concerns goals and management practices.

Many authors have already suggested that learning can be our competitive weapon. But it is possible to consider models that show the benefits of the construction of collaborative advantages. In practice, one of the most difficult challenges is the creation of an innovation culture in which knowledge is evaluated and shared effectively. One of the first influences can really be the competitive environment that if has developed throughout the years. Knowledge economy seems to offer an abundance of resources capable to support the appearance of innovative proposals in what concerns products, services and processes.

Knowledge economy creates a chance for (re) defining the true notion of the innovation process (Carneiro, 2008). In a certain sense, competitiveness can be considered as an inexact or unhappy term, since the creation of wealth within knowledge economy depends on the creation of market niches in a cooperative infrastructure. Innovation should be present in the form to work of all the participants in the system. It does not mean that all are expert in technology and expert in marketing at the same time. It does mean that everybody knows the whole innovation system and its particular paper in this process. This means that there are some common languages and shared objectives and frontiers tend to disappear among functional areas, departments, industries and cultures in our present world. This would mean that a basic belief in the potentialities of innovation, mutual respect and competences would exist, having even a constant engagement to learn.

The links between innovation and prosperity are complex and perhaps they are not entirely understood due to the existence of multiple variables, to the speed of change and to the fact that relationships cause-effect are not linear. Innovation demands a mentality, a spirit state in which creativity, entrepreneurship, ability to face calculated risks and an acceptance of social and professional mobility are combined. The actions and the attempts that can be undertaken to create an innovation culture in a company should take into account the following considerations:

- Training and education processes can be guided in the sense of stimulating creativity and an entrepreneurship mentality since childhood;
- To facilitate the mobility of technicians and researchers to contribute for the success of technology transfer projects;
- To demonstrate to efficient approaches of innovation mentalities, involving citizens, collaborators and industries into a debate on technological alternatives;
- To promote better management practices and methods to control organization's performance so that companies become more agile in its adaptation movements to changes of the situations and the markets;
- To stimulate the design and the practice of innovative modifications in the pub-

lic sector and governmental organisms through training courses and mentalization processes.

If it stays isolated, R&D is not enough to support innovation. In fact, it is necessary to consider that:

- An innovation policy involves marketing tools, development of services given to the market, technologies of communication processes, incremental modifications, and reengineering of production processes;
- Entrepreneurship mentality must be encouraged;
- It is advisable to build a differentiation culture (distinctiveness);
- To develop a highly motivated state of mind to keep sustainability of competitive positions that have achieved in the market place.

Managers have to concentrate on the way of tailoring a knowledge strategy. This strategy has to be formulated in the Why (the value of the knowledge), what (elements of the architecture) and How (knowledge innovation strategy) of an architecture of knowledge innovation. Knowledge architecture has various aspects that must be considered in an integrated way: performance, structure, people, processes and technologies. A company's innovativity depends on the implementation of a strategy that has as objective the integration of these aspects experienced by all the functional areas.

We think that knowledge levels are so valuable for an organization that companies must convert this knowledge into a permanent structural capital. That is really important for all companies, but especially for the firms that assumed its direction in the context of information society. If a manager intends to remain in the competition, then it is necessary to constantly increase the level and the spectrum of knowledge in the organization. We can point out another reason: if an organization is capable to capture the knowledge of its collaborators, probably it can not capture their capacities.

Total Quality Management (TQM) and Business Process Reengineering (BPR) are not enough to increase the chances of organization success. So, what other factors can we consider? Nowadays, we are entirely convinced that knowledge plays a significant role. The only sustainable source of organization success is the ability to learn, to acquire more knowledge and skills, and to transform them into competitive and innovative offerings and processes. Collective (i.e. team and organizational) learning require skills for sharing information and knowledge, particularly implicit knowledge. The following abilities can be considered as key skills:

- Communication, especially across organizational boundaries;
- Listening and observing;
- Mentoring and supporting colleagues;
- Taking a holistic perspective - seeing the team and organization as a whole;
- Coping with challenge and uncertainty (Senge *et al.* 1994).

Managing Knowledge for Competitive Creativity: Tools and Techniques

Some basic elements for knowledge management can be pointed: survey and categorize knowledge; appraise and evaluate value of knowledge; synthesize knowledge related activities; and activities of conceptualizing, reflecting, specifying and reviewing (Wiig, 1993; Wiig *et al.*, 1997). Knowledge management covers the following aspects:

- Identifying what knowledge assets a company possesses: Where is the knowledge asset? What does it contain? What is its use? What form is it in? How accessible is it?

- Analyzing how the knowledge can add value: What are the opportunities for using the knowledge asset? What would be the effect of its use? What are the current obstacles to its use? What would be its increased value to the company?
- Specifying what actions are necessary to achieve better usability & added value: How to plan the actions to use the knowledge asset? How to enact actions? How to monitor actions?
- Reviewing the use of the knowledge to ensure added value: Did the use of it produce the desired added value? How can the knowledge asset be maintained for this use? Did the use create new opportunities?

The KM tools may provide different components such as knowledge maps, groupware, data-mining, databases, e-learning, workflow, portals, structuring of data, and intranet which aid in knowledge-sharing within an organization. The growth of ICT-based tools for KM is leading to shift in thinking in many firms, whereby explicit knowledge bases are being faced as real assets. Usually, managing knowledge process requires techniques to capture, to organize, to store the knowledge of the workers, to transform it into intellectual assets that give benefits and it is possible to be shared. The general concept of KM basically implies the development of the strategic management of the following areas:

- Information management;
- Intelligence management;
- Documentation management;
- Human resources management;
- Innovation and change management;
- Work organization.

If they want to transform their knowledge workers into a real asset, top managers have to remain decisively interested in the definition of objectives about all the talented people in the organization. It

Table 1. Practical ways to turn your knowledge workers into a real asset

Goals that you want to reach	How to conduct such community
Revitalization of the creative potential	1. Make your knowledge workers believe on their own values 2. Persist on consolidating their commitment
Techniques and tools for creativity and emotional intelligence	1. Creativity requires domain expertise 2. Do not permit excessive work 3. Give them time to invent new products and different procedures
Generation of new ideas	1. Recruit creative persons 2. Create an internal "innovation habitat" 3. Schedule brainstorming sessions 4. Implement better ideas
Problems' solutions in creative and flexible ways	1. Try to look at problems in different ways 2. Don't let your knowledge workers focus on a single solution 3. Quantify the value of each solution 4. Stimulate internal competitiveness among innovative solutions 5. Be provocative to your knowledge workers
Overcome the barriers to creativity	1. Ask for solving problems in new ways 2. Influence positive thinking 3. Barriers may be understood as motivators of creativity 4. Create adequate opportunities to encourage and reward knowledge workers for their creativity's results
Increase the capacity for self-confidence and motivation to realize goals.	1. Respect their autonomy 2. Give them freedom to present new contributions

is known that many top managers are constantly saying that knowledge workers are their most valuable asset. However, many times what they say and what they do don't hang together. We have been intensively defending that management has to focus all efforts on developing and applying the relationships between knowledge and creativity with the following purposes:

- Expand and revitalize the creative potential;
- Learn the techniques and tools for creativity and emotional intelligence;
- Discover and generate new ideas;
- Solve problems in creative and flexible ways;
- Overcome the barriers to creativity;
- Increase the capacity for self-confidence and motivation to realize goals.

As an effective manager, are you able to help your collaborators improve their innovative contributions and increase their creative skills? Can you transform your knowledge workers into a valuable asset? This subject is complex, we know. Let me call your attention to some points requiring our awareness and that may guide our personal reflections (Table 1).

Tools and techniques to manage knowledge acquisition and use are too numerous to cover in detail, but include a wide range of learning and creativity skills in the following groups:

- **Inquiry:** interviewing, seeking information;
- **Creativity:** brainstorming, associating ideas;
- **Making sense of situations:** organizing information and thoughts;
- **Making choices:** deciding courses of action;
- **Observing outcomes:** recording, observation;
- **Reframing knowledge:** embedding new knowledge into mental models.

What techniques can be used to increase the levels of contribution of the knowledge to enter-

Table 2. Stimulus to creativity

1. **Physical environment:** pleasant, with lighting, furniture and adequate ventilation.
2. **Communication:** existence of communication channels that allow the democratization of information.
3. **Challenges:** assignments and challenging tasks that stimulate the expression of creative potential.
4. **Organizational structure:** limited number of hierarchical levels, flexible rules, less bureaucracy, decentralization of power.
5. **Freedom and autonomy:** freedom to decide how to do the work, a sense of responsibility on the work.
6. **Participation:** evaluation of personal initiative, greater power of decision in their areas of activity, participation in decision-making and in the solution of organization problems, as ways of stimulating the expression of the creative potential of employees.
7. **Technological and material resources:** availability of equipment and miscellaneous equipment to facilitate the process of generating new ideas.
8. **Salaries and benefits:** adequate remuneration level, benefits policies, rewards system, as ways to stimulate innovative ideas.
9. **Support from managers**: posture of receptivity, flexibility, openness, acceptance, encouragement for new ideas, and respect for divergent views of employees.
10. **Support from the working group:** acceptance from colleagues, interpersonal relationships and stimulating favorable to new ideas, work in groups, meetings with exchange of experiences, dialogue and trust between people, space for relaxation and joy.
11. **Organizational support:** stimulating creativity, recognition of creative work, mechanisms for the development of new ideas, planning and setting goals for work, culture focused on innovation.
12. **Training:** motivation and training of employees for the development of their creative potential, enabling them to work and preparing them to be open to innovations.

Adapted from Alencar (1997)

prise's growth? What tools can managers use to stimulate innovation's efforts based on knowledge increase and to explore the relationships between knowledge and productivity? There are some tools that can stimulate the creativity, whether personal characteristics include some interest for the innovation (Table 2).

The strategies for acquiring and using knowledge already are one set of the many tools and techniques that can be developed to manage the relations between knowledge and organizational performance. In this process, many tools and techniques may be deployed in order to increase knowledge contribution for the improvement of business performance, leading to:

- A better understanding of markets nature and respective dynamics;
- A faster time-to-market in what concerns new products;
- The improvement of the value of products and services;
- To improve the quality of client service;
- Higher quality production processes.

An entire understanding of the mechanisms through which individuals, teams, and organiza-

tions improve their knowledge processes is the essence of an efficient knowledge management. These processes include:

- To create and to collect information;
- To assimilate and to organize the knowledge increase that this information provokes;
- To apply this new knowledge in innovation systems;
- To embed new knowledge into mental models and managerial practices that make possible a new understanding of business' realities;
- To transmit acquired knowledge as a factor of creation of innovative modifications.

There are several techniques that can be used to facilitate the production of new ideas and reach new solutions. One of them, which is also a valuable resource to reach a greater number of ideas or solutions to a given problem, is the list of verbs presented in Table 3, based on proposals of Osborn (1957).

The images and the performance of most organizations would benefit from these capacities for knowledge accumulation and utilization. A

Table 3. Some verbs that help the production of new ideas

1. **Modify.** What can be modified? Meanings change? Uses? Movements? Sounds? Odors? Ways? Qualities? Plans?
2. **Increase.** What can be added, multiplied or expanded? More time? Stronger? Longer? More often? More ingredients? Higher value?
3. **Decrease.** What can be eliminated? Condensed? Reduced? Omitted?
4. **Replace.** What can be replaced? Other ingredient? Other material? Other process? Another approach? Another person? Another place?
5. **Adapt.** What else is like this? Does this suggest other ideas? What could be copied? What else could be adapted?
6. **Reverse.** Seek the opposite, front to back, on the contrary, reverse roles.
7. **Combine.** What ideas, objectives, parts, colors, materials, functions, etc. can be combined?
8. **Rearrange.** Change components, sequences, rhythms, timing, etc.

Adapted from Osborn (1957)

wide range of useful tools for maximizing the advantages of knowledge workers demands a balance between organizational needs and individual capacities.

We can indicate some levers that knowledge management must have into account to develop the creativity based on intangible assets:

- Innovation policies and strategies: if the company will include in its objectives the innovation of technologies, processes, and products, this fact will constitute a work environment which creates requirements of talents recruitment and, over all, contributes to the creation of a mentality open to accumulate knowledge with the goal of transforming it into profitable innovations;
- Innovative proposals: to stimulate the elaboration of a variety of innovative proposals made by knowledge workers;
- R&D of innovation: the value given to technical research and the development of new products contribute to increase in creativity.

From a practical point of view and to maximize the intellectual assets of an organization, top management should be decisively compromised with an adequate set of daily tasks, behaviors and attitudes to stimulate and motivate their knowledge workers.

FUTURE RESEARCH DIRECTIONS

KM research will enhance understanding of creativity processes by both building upon existing frameworks and offering additional perspectives, focusing on competency based issues serving as both competitive advantages and catalysts of competitive creativity. We advise our readers to read an excellent article where a critical review on research on employee creativity has been made (Zhou & Shalley, 2003). If innovation and knowledge management are key factors in determining successful creativity activities, then investigation of pertinent new techniques should be encouraged towards a deeper comprehension of organizations and knowledge workers' relationship.

CONCLUSION

Organizations should commit to a new vision of knowledge workers and recognize and harness their value to improve technical progress and to increase the performance level of some industries. Knowledge workers can e should be used by management boards to offer to the organizations' functioning performance their qualifications, skills, and creative potential. Many knowledge workers are treated as if they were invisible presences, almost as if they were ghosts, memories of inactive people who no longer exist. It should not, it cannot be like that. It would be an entirely wrong way to manage the global resources of an organization. KM should be aware that this type of workers are an indispensable asset with an indefinite value, because, often it not easy to quantify the consequences of their intellectual production. There are techniques and tools to encourage the practical use of knowledge and to provoke creativity and the emergence of new ideas. KM has to teach managers in any hierarchical level to use these tools to transform knowledge workers in real assets, i.e., capable of contributing decisively to enhance organizational competitiveness.

REFERENCES

Alencar, E. S. (1997). *A gerência da criatividade*. S. Paulo: Makron Books

Carneiro, A. (1995). *Inovação – Estratégia e Competitividade*. Lisboa: Texto Editora, Colecção "Textos de Gestão".

Carneiro, A. (2000). How Does Knowledge Management Influence Innovation and Competitiveness? *Journal of Knowledge Management*, *4*(2), 87–98. doi:10.1108/13673270010372242

Carneiro, A. (2004). Teaching Management and Management Educators: some considerations. *Management Decision*, *42*(3 / 4), 430–438. doi:10.1108/00251740410521800

Carneiro, A. (2005). How technologies support winning strategies and productivity. In *Handbook of Business Strategy* (pp. 257-263).

Carneiro, A. (2008). When Leadership means more Innovation and Development. *Business Strategy Series*, *9*(4), 176–184. doi:10.1108/17515630810891843

Davenport, T. H., & Prusak, L. (1998). *Working knowledge: How Organizations Manage What They Know*. Cambridge, MA: Harvard Business School Press.

Elliott, S. (1996). APQC conference attendees discover the value and enablers of a successful KM program. *Knowledge Management in Practice*, *5*, 1–8.

Osborn, A. F. (1957). *Applied Imagination*. New York: Scribner's.

Senge, P., Kleiner, A., Roberts, C., Ross, R., & Smith, B. (1994). *The Fifth Discipline Fieldbook – Strategies and Tools for Building a Learning Organization*. London: Nicholas Brealey Publishing.

Shukla, M. (1997). *Competing Through Knowledge – Building a Learning Organization*. London: Sage.

Wiig, K. (1993). *Knowledge Management Foundations – Thinking about Thinking – How people and Organizations Create, Represent and Use Knowledge*. Arlington, VA: Schema Press.

Wiig, K., Hoog, R., & van der Speck, R. (1997). Supporting knowledge management: a selection of methods and techniques. *Expert Systems with Applications*, *13*, 15–27. doi:10.1016/S0957-4174(97)00019-5

Zhou, J., & Shalley, C. (2003). Research on employee creativity: a critical review and directions for future directions. *Research in Personnel and Human Resources Management*, *22*, 165–217. doi:10.1016/S0742-7301(03)22004-1

ADDITIONAL READING

Bontis, N. (2001). Assessing Knowledge assets: A review of the models used to measure intellectual capital. *International Journal of Management Reviews*, *3*(1), 41–60. doi:10.1111/1468-2370.00053

Carlsson, B. (2006). Internationalization of innovation systems: A survey of the literature. *Research Policy*, *35*(1), 56–67. doi:10.1016/j.respol.2005.08.003

Collison, C., & Parcell, G. (2005). *Learning to Fly: Practical Knowledge Management from Leading and Learning Organizations* (2nd ed.). USA: Capstone.

Davenport, T. H., & Prusak, L. (2000). *Knowledge Management* (2nd ed.). Cambridge, MA: Harvard Business School Press.

Fuller, A., Unwin, L., Felstead, A., Jewson, N., & Kakavelakis, K. (2007). Creating and using knowledge: an analysis of the differentiated nature of workplace learning environments. *British Educational Research Journal, 33*(5), 743–759. doi:10.1080/01411920701582397

Garavan, T., Morely, M., Gunnigle, P., & Collins, E. (2001). Human capital accumulation: The role of human resource development. *Journal of European Industrial Training, 25*, 48–68. doi:10.1108/EUM0000000005437

Gibbons, M. (2003). Competition processes and the management of innovation. *Prometheus, 21*(4), 449–465. doi:10.1080/0810902032000144655

Hislop, D. (2003). Linking human resource management and knowledge management via commitment, a review and research agenda. *Employee Relations, 25*(2), 182–202. doi:10.1108/01425450310456479

Ibert, O. (2007). Towards a geography of knowledge creation: The ambivalences between "knowledge as an object" and "knowing in practice". *Regional Studies, 41*(1), 103–114. doi:10.1080/00343400601120346

Ichijo, K., & Nonaka, I. (2006). *Knowledge Creation and Management: New Challenges for Managers*. USA: Oxford University Press.

Joseph, R. (2004). The Knowledge Worker: Getting the Organizational and Informational Balance Right: A review. *Innovation: Management. Policy & Practice, 6*(1), 85–97.

Liebowitz, J. (2006). *What They Didn't Tell You about Knowledge Management*. USA: The Scarecrow Press, Inc.

Murmann, J. P. (2003). *Knowledge and Competitive Advantage: The Coevolution of Firms, Technology, and National Institutions*. Cambridge, UK: Cambridge University Press.

Ordonez de Pablos, P. (2003). Knowledge management and organizational competitiveness: A framework for human capital analysis. *Journal of Knowledge Management, 7*(3), 82–91. doi:10.1108/13673270310485640

Peters, M., & Besley, T. (2008). Academic Entrepreneurship and the Creative Economy. *Thesis Eleven, 94*(1), 88-105.

Rothman, J. (2004). *Hiring the Best Knowledge Workers, Techies & Nerds: The Secrets & Science of Hiring Technical People*. USA: Dorset House Publishing Company, Inc.

Serenko, A., Bontis, N., & Hardie, T. (2007). Organizational size and knowledge flow: A proposed theoretical link. *Journal of Intellectual Capital, 8*(4), 1469–1930. doi:10.1108/14691930710830783

Stankosky, M. (2005). *Creating the Discipline of Knowledge Management: The Latest in University Research*. USA: Butterworth-Heinemann.

Thompson, P., Jones, M., & Warhurst, C. (2007). From conception to consumption: Creativity and the missing managerial link. *Journal of Organizational Behavior, 28*, 625–640. doi:10.1002/job.465

Section 2
Knowledge Management in NPD

Chapter 8
Product Innovation as a Result of Knowledge Development Processes in Organisations

César Camisón-Zornoza
Universitat Jaume I, Spain

Montserrat Boronat-Navarro
Universitat Jaume I, Spain

ABSTRACT

The main purpose of this chapter is to conduct a theoretical analysis of how product innovation is influenced by the process of knowledge management, and to show that it is necessary to complete the entire process in order to develop incremental as well as radical innovations. Other studies have associated different knowledge development processes with different types of product innovation by specifically linking radical innovation with exploration processes, and incremental innovation with exploitation processes. We differ from this point of view, since we consider both processes as being necessary to the development of the two kinds of innovations.

INTRODUCTION

Product innovation is one of the visible results of the capability to create knowledge (Un and Cuervo-Cazurra, 2004), since the knowledge that is created must be justified by introducing innovations (Nonaka, von Krogh and Voelpel, 2006). Schumpeter (1934) already claimed that new combinations of knowledge and of learning were transferred to the creation of innovations in the enterprise. An innovative context is going to require the combination of different knowledge

bases, as well as the creation of new knowledge. Thompson (1965) defined innovation as the generation, acceptance and implementation of new ideas, processes, products or services, while the definition put forward by Zaltman, Duncan and Holbeck (1973) states that innovation is an idea, practice or material artefact perceived to be new by the relevant unit of adoption. In this chapter we will focus on product innovation, which may be radical or incremental. Radical (or disruptive) innovation is *an innovation that has a significant impact on a market and on the economic activity of firms in that market* (OECD, 2005: 58), but *it is important to recognise that an innovation can also*

DOI: 10.4018/978-1-61520-829-6.ch008

consist of a series of minor incremental changes (OECD, 2005: 40). Thus, following this idea and also following definitions put forward by Dewar and Dutton (1986), Ettlie, Bridges and O'Keefe (1984) and Gopalakrishnan and Damanpour (1997), we consider radical innovation as that producing fundamental changes in the activities of an organisation and incremental innovation as that which produces minimal changes. Radical and incremental outcomes are thus considered as two dimensions. Consequently, we understand that innovation outcomes must include radical and incremental innovations (Damanpour, 1991; Gopalakrishnan and Damanpour, 1997). Knowledge created by an organisation may be reflected in the whole range of these outcomes.

Furthermore, the knowledge development process in organisations requires exploration and exploitation activities. Initially, the concepts of exploration and exploitation were proposed from the literature on Organisational Learning. More specifically, March (1991) defines exploration as those activities related with searching and experimenting, whereas exploitation is the expansion of existing competencies, technologies and paradigms. Both activities are necessary for the continuous development of learning (Bontis, Crossan and Hulland, 2002; March, 1991) and therefore for the development of organisational knowledge.

Nevertheless, some authors conceptualise exploration and exploitation as outcomes and not as capabilities, and they specifically associate exploration with radical and exploitation with incremental innovation (e.g. Benner and Tushman, 2002). The framework that we propose here departs from those studies and suggests that the degree of novelty is not the aspect that differentiates exploration and exploitation activities. Our approach considers exploration and exploitation as two types of activities that are both necessary for successful knowledge development, and therefore for the development of innovations. Those ideas help to further our comprehension of how

knowledge management facilitates innovations in firms. It is not enough to direct and foster processes within the organisation that are aimed at just exploration or exploitation separately, as can be deduced from studies that associate these processes with different types of innovation; rather, both of them must be fostered.

Thus, the main objective of this chapter is to analyse how product innovation is one of the outcomes of the process of creating organisational knowledge and, how all the phases of the process are required to develop both incremental and radical innovations. In the section that follows, we shall examine what the process of knowledge creation is like, associating it with the terms exploration and exploitation. We will then review the conflicts that exist in the use of these two concepts, in order to highlight the need to treat them as ex-ante variables, which together exert an influence on another variable that can be considered as their result, i.e. innovation. Following that, future lines of research will be proposed and last section will contain the conclusions drawn from the study.

BACKGROUND

The ability to innovate on a continuous basis is important to be able to maintain a competitive advantage in such a changeable environment as the one that firms have to work in today. Innovation in the firm will depend on its capability to apply and to develop new knowledge (Cavusgil et al., 2003). The importance of analysing what organisational knowledge is like and how it is developed, so as to be able to understand how the enterprise can learn continuously, has given rise to a number of theoretical approaches that are now becoming especially relevant in the specialised literature. The Knowledge-based View (Grant, 1996; Nonaka, 1994; Nonaka and Takeuchi, 1995; Spender, 1996) and Organisational Learning (Argyris and Schon, 1978; Brown and Duguid, 1991; Easterby-Smith, 1990) have analysed and underlined the fact that continuous learning must take place in the organisation to generate knowledge. Because it is intangible and embedded in the processes and routines of the organisation, this knowledge is difficult for competitors to imitate.

From these approaches, several authors have analysed the process of knowledge generation so that attempts can be made to foster the organisational processes that further it. The model by Nonaka (1994) and Nonaka and Takeuchi (1995), proposes an explanation of how individual knowledge is expanded inside the organisation thanks to interactions among individuals. Tacit knowledge, which cannot be explained because it is embedded in the know-how of the organisation and its individuals, is gradually transformed into explicit knowledge (that is to say, knowledge that can be codified and explained) through interactions among individuals or due to observing others at work. And this transformation also runs in the opposite direction. Explicit knowledge must be combined with the different knowledge bases of the organisation and the members of the organisation must learn it and internalise it so that it interacts with their previous knowledge and thus becomes tacit again.

All this conversion allows organisational knowledge to develop, that is to say, it makes it possible to generate new ideas that arise throughout this process in which knowledge expands from the individual level to the organisational level and also the other way round. For all the process to generate new knowledge, there has to be a conceptualisation phase, where new ideas are generated thanks to the interaction of tacit knowledge and its later transformation into explicit knowledge. Furthermore, these new ideas must crystallise in a second phase in which the new ideas are applied to products or processes that incorporate the new concepts in a real application in the organisation. This must be performed in such a way that the organisational knowledge is expanded. Therefore, a key element in this second phase is explicit knowledge, and its being combined and inter-

nalised by individuals, so that when it is integrated into the prior knowledge base they are capable of applying the new concepts that are generated. All the different ways of converting knowledge are necessary to be able to finally integrate the new ideas into a real application in the enterprise. The first phase would correspond to what the author calls generation or acquisition, whereas the second implies knowledge implementation or exploitation. As we shall propose later, these two phases correspond to our conception of the terms exploration and exploitation.

Another of the development models, this time put forward from the Organisational Learning perspective, is the model suggested by Crossan, Lane and White (1999) and Bontis, Crossan and Hulland (2002). This is a framework that incorporates and extends previous research by combining the different elements that make up the overall organisational learning system. It also takes into account both the learning stocks that are to be found at the individual, group and organisational learning levels and the flows that occur within and between levels, and which allow this learning to develop. Although they come from two different approaches, the parallelisms between them are quite apparent, since learning is able to expand in order to ultimately create new knowledge due to interaction and the expansion of knowledge from the individual to the organisational levels and vice-versa.

Their model considers four phases that take place on the different levels that exist in learning, namely, individual, group and organisational. The passage from individual to group and then on to organisational is what is considered to be a process of assimilating new learning or exploration or feed-forward; in the opposite direction, on the other hand, we would have process of exploitation or feedback, that is, of using what has already been learned. These processes can only take place if there are interactive relations between cognition and action. The four phases of the model are intuiting, interpreting, integrating and institutionalising, which is why it is known as the 4I model. The first of them takes place on the individual level, since it involves experiences, images or metaphors, which entails recognition of the pattern that exists in a personal experience (Weick, 1995). Interpreting occurs at both the individual and group levels and is the explanation of an idea by means of language. Third, integrating goes a step further as it deals with the construction of shared understandings through coordination and mutual adjustment, and is therefore a process that links the group level with the organisational one. Lastly, institutionalising, which only occurs on the organisational level, consists in embedding the learning that has occurred by individuals and groups into the organisation by means of routines, rules and procedures (Crossan, Lane and White, 1999). These phases do not necessarily take place sequentially; instead it is a recursive model that functions at and between different levels, and which also underlines the dynamic nature of learning by highlighting the fact that is occurs over time, between levels and through both exploration and exploitation.

The two models thus demonstrate the need for exploration and exploitation for the development of organisational knowledge. Many other authors have stated the need to have both processes in order to accomplish organisational learning and the creation of new knowledge. March (1991) suggests that it is necessary to reach a balance between the two for learning to develop. Zollo and Winter (2002) also claim that both concepts are necessary in their model of the development of dynamic capabilities.

CAPABILITIES AND INNOVATION RESULTS

Issues, Controversies, Problems

Considering exploration and exploitation as two parts of the process of generating knowledge

therefore implies that both are necessary for the whole process to be completed and finally become apparent in innovations. In accordance with the models of the development of knowledge and organisational learning presented in the previous section, exploration and exploitation can be associated with two stages of a single process. Additionally and following the conceptualisation of the terms proposed by March (1991), we define exploration as the capability an organisation has to experiment with new alternatives, that is, with the creation of a new concept. This is reflected in feed-forward processes. For the organisation to be able to create a new concept, the tacit knowledge of the group members has to be converted into explicit concepts (*externalisation*). A process of *socialisation* must also be performed by sharing mental models among the members of the group. This will make it possible to carry out the process of conceptualisation of new ideas. Moreover, exploitation implies the organisational capability to refine, extend and crystallise new concepts in real applications in the firm. It is at this point, then, that the feedback processes of the organisation become particularly important, since this is where organisational knowledge is transferred and internalised within the individuals of the organisation. The aim here is to put into practice the concept that was created earlier, that is, the process of *internalisation* is vital for crystallisation to take place, that is to say, for the transformation of newly created concepts into a real application in the firm, or into a new product or system (Nonaka, 1994). In our view, another essential point is the *combination* of explicit knowledge of the organisation, since for the idea to be transformed into a real application, documenting and articulating the knowledge will make it easier to specify and apply it, as pointed out by the author himself when defining *combination*. The table below outlines these ideas, how they correspond to the models analysed in the previous section, and also the main organisational processes that would be

Table 1. Concepts of exploration and exploitation and their correspondence with the models of the development of learning and organisational knowledge

March, 1991	Correspondence with the model byBontis, Crossan and Hulland (2002)	Correspondence with the process of knowledge creation (Nonaka, 1994)	Processes that activate them
Exploration: activity based on experimenting with new alternatives	Feed-forward learning: how individual learning flows towards the group level and continues until the organisational level.	Creation of a new concept (*conceptualisation*): For the organisation to be able to create a new concept, the process of *externalisation* must take place in order to convert the tacit knowledge of the group members into explicit concepts. *Socialisation* must also be performed by sharing the mental models among the members of the group. This will allow the process of *conceptualisation*, or articulation of concepts, to be carried out.	The modes of conversion *socialisation* and *externalisation*, in particular, require fluent interaction among the individuals in an organisation. To achieve this, the mechanisms associated with shared experience, dialogue and organisational culture will play a key role. The capabilities associated with mechanisms that facilitate cohesion, dialogue and fluent interaction will favour both types of conversion.
Exploitation: refinement and extension of the existing competencies, paradigms and technologies	Feedback learning: how the learning that is embedded in the organisation affects the group and individual levels.	Putting the concept that has been created into practice (*crystallisation*): the process of *internalisation* is vital for *crystallisation* to take place, that is to say, for the transformation of new concepts that have been created into a real application in the firm, or into a new product or system (Nonaka, 1994). In this concept we consider that *combination* also plays an essential role, since for the idea to be transformed into a real application, documenting and articulating the knowledge will make it easier to specify and apply, as pointed out by the author himself when defining *combination*.	The transformation required to produce *crystallisation* is carried out after confirming that the different departments in the enterprise are capable of producing and applying the concept that has been created. Therefore, if we consider together the two forms of knowledge conversion that are mainly involved in this part of the process, i.e. *combination* and *internalisation*, the capabilities that are involved will be those related with the mechanisms for internally evaluating and applying knowledge, its integration within the enterprise, and also the actions that drive individual development and learning in the members of the organisation.

involved in the two phases, following the ideas of the authors cited in each case.

In some studies, however, exploration is associated to radical innovation, and exploitation is linked to incremental innovation. The logic underlying these studies is the idea that exploration entails a search for new capabilities, which are different from those currently available, and implies a change to a different technological trajectory. The further it is removed from the knowledge used in previous innovations, the more exploration it will be, whereas exploitation entails a local search that builds on existing technological capabilities. It therefore implies improvements in existing components and is constructed on the technological trajectory of the organisation

(Benner and Tushman, 2002). According to this conception, exploration involves a higher degree of novelty than exploitation, and hence a parallelism with radical and incremental innovation is created. This association is produced, for example, in the study by Jansen, van den Bosch and Volberda (2006).

Nevertheless, what distinguishes radical from incremental innovations is the degree of novelty, but this is not the characteristic that distinguishes exploration from exploitation. In accordance with the proposal in the previous section, both are necessary for organisational knowledge to develop. Each of them will be associated to certain processes, skills and an organisational atmosphere that favours them, but the firm needs to enhance both of them if knowledge is to develop. This is a premise that is implicit in all the studies that view exploration and exploitation as two parts or dimensions of organisational learning and that analyse the ambidexterity hypothesis (e.g. He and Wong, 2004). According to this hypothesis, organisations that manage to integrate exploration and exploitation within the same organisation will achieve higher performance. Furthermore, they are considered to be capabilities and, although some studies do define them as capabilities, most of them later measure them as outcomes, since they associate them with innovation.

The table below outlines a number of studies that analyse different aspects of exploration and exploitation. It can be seen how the definitions and ways of measurement that have been adopted vary widely from one work to another. Whereas some authors define exploration and exploitation as capabilities and measure them as such (e.g. Bontis, Crossan and Hulland, 2002; Gibson and Birkinshaw, 2004), other scholars also define them as capabilities, or at least as antecedent variables, but measure them as outcomes (e.g. Auh and Menguc, 2005). Finally, in some cases they are defined and measured directly as innovation outcomes (e.g. Jansen, van den Bosch and Volberda, 2006).

Few studies, however, include capabilities and their most direct results in their models. Of the studies presented in Table 2, only the authors He and Wong (2004) and Tsai et al. (2008) have defined exploration and exploitation as ex-ante variables, and later included innovation as an ex-post variable.

The controversy becomes even more pronounced if we consider authors who go as far as to state that there is no new learning or knowledge in exploitation (e.g. Rosenkopf and Nerkar, 2001; Vermeulen and Barkema, 2001; Vassollo, Anand and Folta, 2004). Nevertheless, the underlying idea in these studies breaks away from the essential meaning of exploration and exploitation. The terms, initially put forward by March (1991),

reflect two dimensions or two aspects of organisational learning. They go together to make up this learning and thanks to both of them it is possible for knowledge to evolve.

Previous concepts developed in studies of innovation can help us to better understand exploration and exploitation with a view to their application. Although these studies only deal with innovation, which is the visible result of the development of knowledge, and do not refer specifically to knowledge as the antecedent of innovation, different stages to adopt innovations could be classified in the same way. Damanpour (1991) distinguishes between the initiation stage and the implementation stage. As proposed in our conceptual framework, exploration is related to the generation of new ideas, i.e., to conceptualisation, whereas exploitation refers to the processes involved in applying and incorporating new knowledge into an organisation via crystallisation. Therefore, the initiation stage could be assimilated into the exploration, since it refers to the perception of the problem and of information gathering, whereas the implementation stage is similar to exploitation, since it is defined as all activities related to modifications in innovations and in organisation to successfully apply the innovation in the firm. Nevertheless, it must be borne in mind that knowledge and the development of knowledge, and therefore exploration and exploitation, are antecedents of innovation, and that studies of innovation usually treat them as an outcome.

Solutions and Recommendations

Once the controversies surrounding the terms *exploration* and *exploitation* have been analysed, we believe that they should both be treated as part of the process of knowledge creation, in line with what was outlined in previous sections. Exploration and exploitation are two capabilities that together represent organisational learning and make the organisational knowledge evolve. With-

Table 2. Studies that have analysed exploration and exploitation from different perspectives

Conception and method of measuring exploration and exploitation and main results
Benner and Tushman (2003)   • These authors consider exploration with radical innovation, with *architectural* innovation and with innovation for groups of potential consumers.   • They consider exploitation as being incremental innovation and innovation for today's consumers.   They propose the theory that management practices related with TQM techniques stabilise and rationalise organisational routines and favour exploitation innovation to the detriment of exploration innovation. Nevertheless, within a context of ambidextrous organisational structures, both types of activities that lead to exploration and exploitation innovations can coexist; moreover, TQM-related management practices do not produce a negative effect on exploration innovation within the context of ambidextrous organisations.
Bontis, Crossan and Hulland (2002);Crossan, Lane and White (1999)   • These authors associate exploration with the 'feed-forward' flows of their 4I model: how individual learning flows towards the group and the organisational levels. And they measure it as the degree to which the lessons learned by one group are actively shared by others; individuals supply the organisational strategy with input; the results of the group are used to improve products, services and processes; the recommendations of the groups are adopted by the organisation; we do not reinvent the wheel.   • Exploitation is associated with the 'feedback' flows of their 4I model (how the learning that is embedded in the organisation affects learning at group level and individual learning) and they measure it as the degree to which policies and procedures help individual work; the aims of the enterprise are communicated throughout the organisation; the organisation's files and databases provide the information needed to carry out our work; the group decisions are backed by individuals.   They conduct analyses and show that individual, group and organisational learning has a positive influence on performance and that the imbalance between stocks and learning flows is negatively associated with performance. They do not have explicit, differentiated results as regards exploration and exploitation because the two are part of the model (more specifically of the flows), which together are tested to see whether their maladjustment with stocks exerts an effect or not.   They consider exploration and exploitation to be two parts of organisational learning.   Performance is taken as their dependent variable.
Gibson and Birkinshaw (2004)   • Adaptation capabilities: management systems that encourage individuals to change their traditions and practices, that are flexible so that they can respond quickly to changes in the market, and that evolve quickly to adapt to changes in business priorities.   • Adjustment capabilities: management systems that work coherently to support the goals of the organisation, that endeavour not to waste resources on non-productive activities, and that do not propose conflicting goals.   The higher the level of ambidexterity is, the higher the level of performance will be.   No direct reference to exploration and exploitation is made, but they do discuss the conflictive tensions and demands between them.   Other variables in the model include the social context of the firm, as antecedents, and the performance of the unit as the dependent variable.
Hill and Birkinshaw (2006)   • **Exploration:** development of new capabilities measured as how important the creation of new resources and technologies is for the work of the unit.   • **Exploitation:** use of existing capabilities, which is measured as the importance the unit grants to utilising the assets and skills of the firm that they are a subsidiary of (since it is a study of corporate venture units).   Units that carry out both exploration and exploitation are found to have a higher performance and this ambidexterity is favoured by the relationships among members of management in the parent enterprise, the relationships with other business units and the relationships with the venture capital community, all of which is included within what they call the relational context of the unit.

continued on following page

out exploitation, exploration does not fully make sense, as the new ideas that are generated are not crystallised in a product, process or organisational innovation within the enterprise. The new concepts need to be crystallised in a real application in the organisation in order to justify the efforts made in exploring knowledge. And, furthermore, without exploration, exploitation alone does not open up

Table 2. continued

Conception and method of measuring exploration and exploitation and main results
Lubatkin et al. (2006) • **Exploration:** involves those activities that make it possible to respond actively to changes in the environment by carrying out revolutionary innovations, and it is measured as exploration orientation (whether the enterprise searches for new technological ideas, whether it bases its success on the skill to explore new technologies, whether it creates products or services that are innovative for the firm, whether it searches for creative ways to satisfy its consumers' needs). • **Exploitation:** involves carrying out activities related with refining the existing technological or marketing trajectories that attempt to adapt themselves to the conditions of the environment and the firm's customers. It is measured as exploitation orientation (whether the firm attempts to improve quality and cut costs, whether it continuously improves the reliability of its products or services, whether it increases the level of automation of its operations, whether it constantly conducts surveys among its consumers to determine their degree of satisfaction, whether it refines what it has to offer in order to keep its customers satisfied, whether it penetrates further into its customer base). Small and medium-sized enterprises with a management team that behaves in an integrating manner have a greater capability to pursue both an exploration and exploitation orientation and attain higher levels of performance. In the model they include other variables such as size, uncertainty or the composition of the management team, performance being taken as the dependent variable.
He and Wong (2004) • **Exploration:** behaviours characterised by searching, experimenting, innovating and risk taking, and it is measured as the strategy or the exploration goals of innovation projects (whether the goals of the firm are oriented towards introducing new generations of products, expanding the range of products, opening up new markets, or entering new technological fields). • **Exploitation:** activities characterised by refinement, implementation, efficiency, production and selection, and it is measured as the strategy or the exploitation goals of innovation projects (whether these goals are related with improving the quality of existing products, improving productive flexibility, cutting production costs, or improving or reducing the consumption of materials). They consider exploration and exploitation as being two dimensions of organisational learning. The interaction between the innovation strategies of exploration and exploitation is positively related with the sales growth ratio, and the imbalance between the two is negatively related with the sales growth ratio, which thereby confirms the ambidexterity hypothesis. The sales growth rate is used as the dependent variable, but innovative performance is also included as an intermediate variable. This is measured as the intensity in product innovation and the intensity in process innovation.
Jansen, van den Bosch and Volberda (2006);Jansen et al. (2008) • **Exploration:** radical innovations designed to fulfil the needs of emerging markets or customers and which are somewhat removed from the firm's existing products, services or technologies. • **Exploitation:** incremental innovations designed to fulfil the needs of existing markets or customers and which are therefore closer to existing products, services and technologies. They associate exploration and exploitation with innovation. The firm must exploit its existing competencies and explore new ones. In the authors' first study, they confirm how centralisation has a negative effect on exploration, formalisation has a positive effect on exploitation, and the degree of connectedness or interaction among members of the organisation has a positive effect on both, whereas dynamism of the environment and competitiveness moderate the relationship between exploration and exploitation and performance. The other variables in the model include antecedents of the organisation such as centralisation, moderating variables such as environmental dynamism, and performance taken as the dependent variable. In the second study, they analyse and confirm how the characteristics of the senior team and leadership behaviour play a decisive role in achieving exploration and exploitation (ambidexterity). In this case, interaction between exploration and exploitation is the dependent variable, while other antecedents (such as the shared vision of the senior management team) are included because the article analyses the attributes of the members of the senior team as antecedents to achieving both exploration and exploitation in the firm.

continued on following page

new paths by offering new ideas that make it possible to continue advancing in the development of organisational knowledge.

Innovation is the tangible result of the capability to create knowledge (Bontis, Crossan and Hulland, 2002; Un and Cuervo-Cazurra, 2004). The development of new ideas is the antecedent to

Table 2. continued

Conception and method of measuring exploration and exploitation and main results
Auh and Menguc (2005); Menguc and Auh (2008) • **Exploration:** concerned with questioning existing ideas with new, innovative concepts. The variable is measured as the extent to which firms use different learning methods that include efforts to improve the efficiency of the organisation. • **Exploitation:** concerned with refining and extending existing capabilities in order to ensure the current viability of the firm. They measure the variable as the degree to which firms use different learning methods related to spending on R&D and on marketing techniques, but also as the product innovation ratio. Hence, they include both ex-ante and ex-post variables in this variable. Exploration and exploitation are conceived as different modes of organisational learning, although they include both efforts or skills and innovation outcomes in their measurements. In the first study, the authors propose and demonstrate how firms classified as different strategic types, such as defenders and prospectors, account for some of the differences in the relationship between exploration and exploitation and performance. They show that, for defenders, exploration is positively related with effectiveness in performance, whereas exploitation will be negatively related when competition becomes more intense. For prospectors, on the other hand, exploration is negatively related with effectiveness, whereas exploitation is positively related when competition becomes more intense. In the second study, they claim that the impact of ambidexterity (the combination of the two capabilities – exploration and exploitation) on performance is less negative among firms that are classified as prospectors, which add exploitation to exploration, than among defenders, which add exploration to exploitation. Their findings are rather mixed, however. Other variables in the model include moderating variables, such as competitive intensity in the first paper or market orientation in their second article, but in both cases performance is taken as the dependent variable.
Tsai et al. (2008) • **Exploration:** proactive market orientation that is characterised by behaviours related to discovery, variation, innovation and risk-taking; it is measured as the degree to which the firm attempts to understand and satisfy customers' latent needs. • **Exploitation:** market orientation that is characterised by behaviours related to proximity, refinement, efficiency and implementation; it is measured as the degree to which the firm attempts to understand and satisfy the needs expressed by its customers. They propose curvilinear relationships between the types of market orientation of the enterprise and the performance of new products, depending on the turbulence of the environment or on the competitive intensity; mixed results were obtained. Exploration and exploitation are conceived as the firm's market orientation, and new product performance is used as the dependent variable. Other variables in the model include moderators, such as technological turbulence or competitive intensity.

innovation (Van den Ven, 1986). Papers that deal with exploration and exploitation should include both the processes involved in each of them and their outcome, that is to say innovation, in order to prevent the terms from being confused, as occurs in some studies in which they are defined as input but they are measured through output or outcome (e.g. Benner and Tushman, 2002).

Managers need to be aware of the consequences of the ideas developed in this chapter. Nowadays, the dynamic environment involving complex variables and with rapid global changes also demands rapid innovations. Innovations are the result of knowledge development in organisations, and therefore managers should encourage the evolution of capabilities in exploration and exploitation. Firm success depends on the creation of a suitable context that fosters both of these capabilities, and it is here that managers play an important role by strengthening the context in order to develop these capabilities and to arrive at a situation in which all organisational members work together to create new knowledge. Furthermore, the distinction proposed between exploration and exploitation, although both are equally necessary to the development of knowledge and, in turn, of innovations, implies that managers should create the right organisational contexts in which both capabilities can flourish. Although the two capabilities require different contexts, both these contexts should be easily connected within the firm through its culture and through dialogue between all organisational members. Finally, the chapter also highlights the need for both capabilities to successfully create product innovations, regardless of whether the firm wants to develop radical or incremental innovations. Therefore, managers must trigger the development of exploration and exploitation to ensure that generation of innovations is successful. Without exploration capabilities, new ideas are not developed, but organisations that only focus on exploration can not transform their new ideas into marketable product innovations.

FUTURE RESEARCH DIRECTIONS

In this chapter we have defended, theoretically, the posture that exploration and exploitation are two phases that together make organisational knowledge evolve; at the same time the concepts have been associated with the process of knowledge creation described by Nonaka (1994). Future research should concentrate on finding a way to operationalise both exploration and exploitation in order to reflect these two phases of the process of knowledge development. Measuring different organisational capabilities as an outcome is a tendency that is observed in a number of studies in the Knowledge Based View and even in Organisational Learning. This is a result of the difficulties involved in measuring capabilities and concepts associated with the intangible, which is why proxies are used to measure them. Efforts therefore need to be made to analyse the potential of organisations by measuring their capabilities. Several of the studies analysed here do introduce exploration and exploitation into their models as antecedents (e.g. Lubatkin et al., 2006). Carrying out a thorough review of the studies that measure these two capabilities may therefore be a good starting point for developing scales that clearly reflect the importance of these two constructs in their relationship with the different phases in the knowledge creation process.

We now make some suggestions about what the main components of these capabilities might be, in the light of an initial review of these studies

and the processes that activate them, as presented in Table 1. This initial approach on how to measure exploration and exploitation can help managers to understand what processes they should encourage in their organisations. The first aspect that firms need in order to develop exploration capabilities is a leadership strategy that encourages an organisational context in which change and innovation are favoured, that supports new initiatives, and that promotes creative orientation on problem resolution. Moreover, the organisation should develop a culture of knowledge creation by stimulating continuous improvement and learning. All organisational members should feel they share a context that encourages innovation and should perceive that their ideas are useful and incorporated into new processes or products. A further component required to develop exploration capabilities relates to coordination mechanisms and processes that also favour the development of new ideas, such as flexible processes or the stimulation of dialogue between organisational members. Moreover, exploitation requires that all organisational resources favouring research and development be integrated and coordinated if new ideas are to be successfully transformed into new products or processes. The firm must assign specific financial and human resources to R&D to this end. The transformation required in crystallisation also demands organisational processes that enable the articulation and documentation of knowledge. Information systems and technologies are important here to help organisational members to share, systematise and distribute information. Finally, exploitation also requires the internalisation of knowledge by all the actors in the organisation, and therefore it is also important to encourage mechanisms that stimulate competence development and support individual learning and actions to identify employees' knowledge needs. Future studies should refine the proposal made here regarding the specific organisational mechanisms that comprise exploration and exploitation capabilities.

Furthermore, in order to corroborate the theoretical arguments proposed here, future research should analyse the different effects that exploration and exploitation have on radical versus incremental innovation. The idea put forward here is that both exploration and exploitation should be related to the two types of innovation, and that both capabilities are needed for any kind of innovation to be produced. Future studies should therefore include empirical models that propose hypotheses about these relationships. All this could help gain a better understanding of the processes and the organisational environment that favour both exploration and exploitation so that the enterprise can finally produce innovations.

CONCLUSION

Knowledge development in organisations requires processes that include exploration and exploitation activities. March (1991) defines both concepts as two necessary sides in the improvement of organizational learning. Exploration is characterised by searching and experimenting, and exploitation involves activities related to refinement and application. Although exploration is typically used by authors in the sense of activities carried out in pursuit of new knowledge, there is no consensus on whether the concept of exploitation implies knowledge and learning or just the application of what has already been learned. According to Gupta, Smith and Shalley (2006), both concepts involve learning. March (1991) explains exploitation as the refinement and extension of existing competencies, technologies and paradigms. Even by replicating past actions, an organisation accumulates new learning (Gupta, Smith and Shalley, 2006), an idea that becomes stronger if we take the entire organisation as the unit of analysis because of variation in knowledge from one individual to another. Since organisational learning includes exploration and exploitation (Bontis, Crossan and Hulland, 2002), both concepts entail learning

and thus the development of knowledge. Jointly, the activities and processes of exploration and exploitation complete the process of knowledge development.

Innovation is the most immediate and visible result of these knowledge development processes, exploration and exploitation. We draw a distinction between radical and incremental product innovations because several authors have associated exploration with radical innovation and exploitation with incremental innovation. In our framework, however, we depart from previous studies in which the authors have made such associations (e.g. Benner and Tushman, 2002

) and also from studies that define innovation as exploratory and exploitative (e.g. Jansen, van den Bosch and Volberda, 2006). In our approach the concepts of exploration and exploitation are not differentiated by the degree of novelty; rather, they are seen as two types of processes that are both necessary for successful knowledge development. Therefore, innovation requires activities to be included in both of them.

The process of knowledge creation has thus been analysed in order to understand what stages it is made up of, and the concepts of exploration and exploitation have been associated with two different phases of this process. The controversies surrounding the terms exploration and exploitation were then reviewed in a summary of the way different authors deal with these concepts. This review made it clear that the models of analysis need to deal with and incorporate the processes that are included in exploration and exploitation, as antecedent variables, and also their radical and incremental innovation outcomes. Therefore, suggestions for future lines of research include a thorough measurement of the two concepts, treating them as antecedents, as ex-ante variables, as well as carrying out a comparison to analyse their effects on innovative outcomes. In this chapter, we have advanced what the main components of the two capabilities should be in order to facilitate understanding about which organisational processes managers should encourage. Leadership and culture towards change and innovation, coordination mechanisms to integrate all organisational members and their ideas, resource assignation to transform new ideas into innovations, information systems and the support of individual learning are the main activities and processes that should be encouraged in the firm. Future research should concentrate on how to develop these processes.

This chapter is therefore the start of a new kind of analysis to determine what processes are implicit in exploration and exploitation, by associating them explicitly with the process of knowledge generation. By so doing, we help to cast light on the differences between processes and outcomes, which can also help management to understand which processes must be reinforced in the organisation in order to contribute to the development of innovations.

REFERENCES

Argyris, C., & Schön, D. (1978). *Organizational learning: a theory of action perspective*. Reading, MA: Addison-Wesley.

Auh, S., & Menguc, B. (2005). Balancig exploration and exploitation: the moderating role of competitive intensity. *Journal of Business Research*, *58*(12), 1652–1661. doi:10.1016/j.jbusres.2004.11.007

Benner, M. J., & Tushman, M. (2002). Process Management and Technological Innovation: A Longitudinal Study of the Photography and Paint Industries. *Administrative Science Quarterly*, *47*, 676–706. doi:10.2307/3094913

Benner, M. J., & Tushman, M. L. (2003). Exploitation, exploration, and process management: the productivity dilemma revisited. *Academy of Management Review*, *28*(2), 238–256. doi:10.2307/30040711

Bontis, N., Crossan, M. M., & Hulland, J. (2002). Managing an Organizational Learning System by Aligning Stocks and Flows. *Journal of Management Studies*, *39*, 437–469. doi:10.1111/1467-6486.t01-1-00299

Brown, J. S., & Duguid, P. (1991). Organizational learning and communities-of-practice: toward a unified view of working, learning, and innovation. *Organization Science*, *2*(1), 40–57. doi:10.1287/orsc.2.1.40

Cavusgil, S., Calantone, R., & Zhao, Y. (2003). Tacit knowledge transfer and firm innovation capability. *Journal of Business and Marketing*, *18*(1).

Crossan, M. M., Lane, H. W., & White, R. E. (1999). An organizational learning framework: from intuition to institution. *Academy of Management Review*, *24*(3), 522–537. doi:10.2307/259140

Damanpour, F. (1991). Organizational innovation: a meta-analysis of effects of determinants and moderators. *Academy of Management Journal*, *34*, 555–590. doi:10.2307/256406

Dewar, R. D., & Dutton, J. E. (1986). The adoption of radical and incremental innovations: An empirical analysis. *Management Science*, *32*(11), 1422–1433. doi:10.1287/mnsc.32.11.1422

Easterby-Smith, M. (1990). Creating a learning organization. *Personnel Review*, *19*(5), 24–28. doi:10.1108/EUM0000000000779

Ettlie, J. E., Bridges, W. P., & O'Keefe, R. D. (1984). Organization strategy and structural differences for radical versus incremental innovation. *Management Science*, *30*, 682–695. doi:10.1287/mnsc.30.6.682

Gibson; C.B., & Birkinshaw, J. (2004). The antecedents, consequences, and mediating role of organizational ambidexterity. *Academy of Management Journal*, *47*(2), 209-226.

Gopalakrishnan, S., & Damanpour, F. (1997). A review of innovation research in economics, sociology and technology management. *Omega, 25*, 15. doi:10.1016/S0305-0483(96)00043-6

Grant, R.M. (1996). Toward a knowledge-based theory of the firm. *Strategic Management Journal, 17*(Winter Special Issue), 109-122.

Gupta, A. K., Smith, K. G., & Shalley, C. E. (2006). The interplay between exploration and exploitation. *Academy of Management Journal, 49*(4), 693–706.

He, Z. L., & Wong, P. K. (2004). Exploration vs. exploitation: an empirical test of the ambidexterity hypothesis. *Organization Science, 15*(4), 481–494. doi:10.1287/orsc.1040.0078

Hill, S.A. & Birkinshaw, J. (2006). Ambidexterity in Corporate Venturing: Simultaneously using Existing and Building New Capabilities. *Academy of Management Proceedings*, C1-C6.

Jansen, J. J. P., Van Den Bosch, F. A. J., & Volberda, H. W. (2006). Exploratory Innovation, Exploitative Innovation, and Performance: Effects of Organizational Antecedents and Environmental Moderators. *Management Science, 52*, 1661–1664. doi:10.1287/mnsc.1060.0576

Jansen, J. P., George, G., Van den Bosch, F. J., & Volberda, H. W. (2008). Senior team attributes and organizational ambidexterity: The moderating role of transformational leadership. *Journal of Management Studies, 45*(5), 982–1007. doi:10.1111/j.1467-6486.2008.00775.x

Lubatkin, M. H., Simsek, Z., Ling, Y., & Veiga, J. F. (2006). Ambidexterity and Performance in Small- to Medium-Sized Firms: The Pivotal Role of Top Management Team Behavioral Integration. *Journal of Management, 32*, 646–672. doi:10.1177/0149206306290712

March, J. G. (1991). Exploration and exploitation in organizational learning. *Organization Science, 2*(1), 71–87. doi:10.1287/orsc.2.1.71

Menguc, B., & Auh, S. (2008). The asymmetric moderating role of market orientation on the ambidexterity-firm performance relationship from prospectors and defenders. *Industrial Marketing Management, 37*(4), 455–470. doi:10.1016/j.indmarman.2007.05.002

Nonaka, I. (1994). A dynamic theory of organizational knowledge creation. *Organization Science, 5*(1), 14–37. doi:10.1287/orsc.5.1.14

Nonaka, I., & Takeuchi, H. (1995). *The knowledge-creating company*. New York: Oxford University Press.

Nonaka, I., von Krogh, G., & Voelpel, S. (2006). Organizational knowledge creation theory: evolutionary paths and future advances. *Organization Studies, 27*, 1179–1208. doi:10.1177/0170840606066312

OECD. (2005). *The measurement of scientific and technological activities. Proposed guidelines for collecting and interpreting technological data* (3rd ed.). Paris: Oslo Manual, OCDE.

Rosenkopf, L., & Nerkar, A. (2001). Beyond Local Search: Boundary-Spanning, Exploration, and Impact in the Optical Disc Industry. *Strategic Management Journal, 22*, 287. doi:10.1002/smj.160

Schumpeter, J. A. (1934). *The theory of economic development*. Cambridge, MA: Harvard Business Press.

Spender, J.C. (1996). Making knowledge the basis of a dynamic theory of the firm. *Strategic Management Journal, 17*(Winter Special Issue), 45-62.

Thompson, V. A. (1965). Bureaucracy and innovation. *Administrative Science Quarterly, 5*(June), 1–20. doi:10.2307/2391646

Tsai, K. H., Chou, C., & Kuo, J. H. (2008). The curvilinear relationship between responsive and proactive market orientations and new product performance: A contingent link. *Industrial Marketing Management, 37*(8), 884–894. doi:10.1016/j.indmarman.2007.03.005

Un, C. A., & Cuervo-Cazurra, A. (2004). Strategies for knowledge creation in firms. *British Journal of Management, 15*(Supplement 1), 27–41. doi:10.1111/j.1467-8551.2004.00404.x

Van den Ven, A. H. (1986). Central problems in the management of innovation. *Management Science, 32*(5), 590–607. doi:10.1287/mnsc.32.5.590

Vassolo, R. S., Anand, J., & Folta, T. B. (2004). Non-Additivity in Portfolios of Exploration Activities: a Real Options-Based Analysis of Equity Alliances in Biotechnology. *Strategic Management Journal, 25*(11), 1045–1061. doi:10.1002/smj.414

Vermeulen, F., & Barkema, H. (2001). Learning through Acquisitions. *Academy of Management Journal, 44*(3), 457–476. doi:10.2307/3069364

Weick, K. E. (1995). *Sensemaking in organizations*. New York: McGraw-Hill.

Zaltman, G., Duncan, R., & Holbek, J. (1973). *Innovations and organizations*. New York: Wiley.

Zollo, M., & Winter, S. G. (2002). Deliberate learning and the evolution of dynamic capabilities. *Organization Science, 13*(3), 339–351. doi:10.1287/orsc.13.3.339.2780

Chapter 9
New Product Development Based on Knowledge Creation and Technology Education

Haris Papoutsakis
Technological Education Institute (TEI) of Crete, Greece

ABSTRACT

The aim of this chapter is to investigate if and to what extend the process of New Product Development, today, is based on Knowledge Creation and Technology Education. The value chain and the way it allows the company to achieve and sustain competitive advantage is used, in this chapter, in a way that facilitates the exploration of the relationship between technology and competitive advantage. This is done under the competence-based perspective of the organization, where knowledge is the point of departure and the individual – in this case the industrial employee– the relevant unit of analysis. With knowledge and knowledge creation being the reference point, their influence on new products and on the product life cycle has been investigated. The significance of the technology education background of each individual has also been examined in an effort to determine whether there is a need to strengthen Technology Education in existing national curricula. Surveys collected from 486 employees, of 51 industrial companies in Spain, were analyzed in order to test our hypothesis. The results of this study support our main hypothesis and allow us to draw conclusions on the significance of the relationship under investigation.

INTRODUCTION

The hypothesis under investigation in this chapter is that New Product Development (NPD), in the 21st century, is increasingly based on Knowledge Creation (KC) and Technology Education (TE).

DOI: 10.4018/978-1-61520-829-6.ch009

The research presented in this chapter was conducted under the competence-based perspective of the organization, where knowledge is the point of departure and the individual the relevant unit of analysis. The main objective is to investigate the ways individuals in their professional lives use the subjective and experience based knowledge they bring with them, and how they build upon their

TE background in order to create new knowledge aiming to design innovative new products.

In this introductory section the concept of technological literacy is introduced, and the meaning of knowledge explored. Then the competence-based theory, the theoretical framework of this research, is put forward. The complementary dimensions of competencies and capabilities are extensively examined and the concept of fit is introduced. In the following section, the research enablers are introduced: the KC process is analyzed and TE and its relationship with industry are examined from an economic and industrial understanding perspective. In the third section, the value chain is used as a facilitator to approaching the NPD process. The impact of KC and TE in every phase of this process is discussed in the fourth section, both through the literature and a questionnaire-based survey. The study results are analytically presented, and finally, in the last section, our conclusions are presented together with some suggestions for future research.

Technological Literacy

In the modern organization, effective use of technology is considered among the key variables that drive competitiveness. Because technology is employed, to some degree, in every value creating activity, changes in technology can impact competitive advantage by progressively changing the activities themselves or by making possible new configurations in the value chain. Companies, in their desire to innovate, reduce cost and protect or sustain competitive advantage, often resort to changes regarding their production technology, lean manufacturing, internet marketing activities, customer relationship management, and other technological developments.

However, this investigation concerns not technology itself, but the technological literacy of the industrial employees. Dyrenfurth (1991) considers that technological literacy is 'a multi-dimensional concept' and as such it is addressed, in terms of its

curricular implementation, in subsection TE and Industry, in the following section. For Dyrenfurth, technological literacy is essential for everyone, while specific technical education only for those pursuing specific occupations. Modern organizations increasingly recognize the significance of TE in general schools, for reasons associated with the development of future employees.

Knowledge

There is no unanimity concerning the definition of knowledge. The difficulty in doing so originates in the very intangible meaning of the term: knowledge, wisdom, intelligence are concepts constantly revised and redefined as parts of cognitive psychology and the philosophy of science.

Davenport and Prusak (1998) underline that knowledge, data, and information, are not identical concepts. Knowledge transcends both data and information in a number of ways. It derives from information, in a similar way that information derives from data, via a transformation that takes place in and within persons. Von Krogh, Ichijo and Nonaka (2000) define knowledge as a "justified true belief". When somebody creates knowledge, he or she makes sense out of a new situation by holding justified beliefs and committing to them. This interesting approach matches the perspective of this study. According to Sveiby (2001) this definition is building on Plato and arguing against the Descartian body and mind split. In previous works, Sveiby (1994, 1997) building on contemporary philosophers, Polanyi and Wittgenstein, defines knowledge as a capacity-to-act which may or may not be conscious. The emphasis of the definition is on the action element: A capacity-to-act can only be shown in action. Each individual has to re-create his or her own capacity to act through experience. The last two definitions provide ideal ground for approaching knowledge under the perspective of the investigation hypothesis.

In the related literature, it is first Polanyi (1966) who makes the critical distinction between tacit and explicit knowledge, by noting that "we can know more than we can tell". The most comprehensive distinction is the one proposed by Nonaka and Takeuchi (1995) which, as they acknowledge, derives from Polanyi's work.

- *Tacit knowledge* is subjective and experience based knowledge that may not be expressible in words, sentences, numbers or formulas, often because it is context specific. This also includes cognitive skills such as beliefs, images, intuition and mental models as well as technical skills such as craft and know-how.
- *Explicit knowledge* is objective and rational knowledge that can be expressed in words, sentences, numbers or formulas (context free). It includes theoretical approaches, manuals and databases.

Both tacit and explicit knowledge have a significant input in the way technology education curricula are developed. It is for this reason that they have been selected as the two knowledge enablers, in this study.

The Theoretical Framework

In the last decade of the 20th century a resource-based theory of the firm (Prahalad & Hamel 1990; von Krogh & Roos, 1995) has received attention as an alternative to the traditional product-based or competitive advantage view (primarily of Porter, 1985). Both theories have served, equally well, as the basis for new product development, for almost a decade each. Prahalad & Hamel (1990) define *core competences* as the "collective learning in the organization, especially how to coordinate diverse production *skills* and integrate multiple streams of technologies" and they add that: "the force of core competence is felt as decisively in services as in manufacturing". Competence, according to

the Webster Dictionary (1981) is defined as the "quality or state of being functionally adequate or of having sufficient knowledge, judgment, skill or strength for a particular duty".

Evans et al (1992), with a tendency to dispute and complete the above definition, emphasize the difference between competence and capability and the way the two concepts relate to each other:

competencies and capabilities represent two different but complementary dimensions... But whereas core competences emphasize technological and production expertises at specific points along the value chain, capabilities are more broadly based, encompassing the entire value chain. In this respect, capabilities are visible to the customer in a way that core competencies rarely are. (Evans et al, 1992)

The authors base their remarks on a well-documented case study of Honda in comparison with Ford.

Von Krogh & Roos (1995) note that the above definition is based on the pre-existence of a particular knowledge and a particular task, and referring to the Latin origin of the term *competencia*, actually meaning agreement, they state: "Only where there exists an agreement or *fit* between knowledge (or subject) and 'task' may we speak of competence". And they conclude that "... it is only meaningful to discuss competence in a specific knowledge-task context, or put another way, competence is both knowledge specific and task specific". Tasks are carriers of information, and may vary in degree of complexity. There might be multiple paths leading to a desired end, and there might also be multiple desired ends, not always totally independent among themselves. Consequently 'competences' have been selected as the first of the TE Enablers in this study.

Pearson and Young (2002) give the following characteristics of the technologically literate citizen, the industrial employee, in this study, in connection to his/her skills: (a) has a range of hands-on skills, such as using a computer and operating a variety of home and office appliances; (b) can identify and fix simple mechanical or technological problems at home or work; (c) can apply basic mathematical concepts to make informed judgments about technological risk and benefits. In line with this approach, 'skills' have been added as the second TE Enabler.

There is clarity and quasi unanimity amongst researchers in recognizing the importance of commitment in accomplishing a certain task. Fit, on the other hand, has not always had unanimous interpretation, although it has served as an important element for theory construction in many research areas. Venkatraman (1989) notes that although theorists are "using phrases and words such as *matched with, continent upon, consistent with, fit, congruence,* and *coalignment,* precise guidelines for translating these verbal statements to the analytical level are seldom provided". And he cites Galbraith and Nathanson's (1979) observation in order to further support his statement: "although the concept of fit is a useful one, it lacks the precise definition needed to test and recognize whether an organization has it or not". Despite the three decades that have passed since this observation, it is still partially valid today. As we consider 'commitment' and 'fit' valuable to this study, we selected them as the last two TE Enablers.

Finally, von Krogh and Roos, in a well-documented comparison of the resource and product-based theories, have gone one step further and proposed the competence-based theory, where:

...the point of departure is knowledge, implying that the relevant unit of analysis in a competence-based perspective is the individual. This is different from the unit of analysis used both within the competitive strategy perspective (the industry) and the resource-based perspective (the firm). Here knowledge is not seen as a resource in a traditional meaning and differs from these types of resources in many ways. (Von Krogh and Roos, 1995)

This particular distinction is the main reason why the competence-based theory has been adopted to guide this research.

RESEARCH ENABLERS

Having introduced the research enablers for Knowledge (tacit and explicit) and Technology Education (competences, skills, commitment and fit), the research enablers for Knowledge Creation are now discussed.

Knowledge Creation in the Value Chain

Innovation and knowledge share a tight relationship that has been noted by Drucker (1985). The innovation process can be better described as a reoccurring activity in which inventors swing between ideas and objects. The real meaning of invention seems to be the dynamic interplay of mental models with mechanical representations (Gorman and Carlson, 1990). The above mentioned relationship is noticeable in the area of industrial competitiveness as a factor of development and as a fundamental element for the creation of value. In order to explore innovation and R&D from a knowledge management perspective, we have to understand the flow of knowledge in the industry. We consider the spiral of knowledge model proposed by Nonaka and Takeuchi (1995) as the best tool for doing so. Let us briefly present the historic evolution of the model.

Porter (1985) was the first to introduce the concept of the *value chain,* by dividing the firm into the discrete activities it performs in designing new products, producing, marketing and distributing them. He describes (ibid) how a company – using the value chain as the basic tool for understanding technology – can choose and implement a generic strategy in order to achieve and sustain *competitive advantage.* He further explores the relationship between technology and competitive advantage (ibid). Technology is pervasive in the value chain and plays a powerful role in determining competitive advantage, in both cost and differentiation prospects. He describes the variables that shape the path of technological change in an industry and demonstrates how technological change can influence both competitive advantage as well as the entire industry structure.

A few years later, Nonaka (1991) opens his article with the statement: "In an economy where the only certainty is uncertainty, the one sure source of lasting competitive advantage is knowledge". He defines knowledge creation, dissemination and quick embodying it in new technologies and products as the activities that define the *knowledge-creating company*. He also describes such a company as the environment where "inventing new knowledge is not a specialized activity – the province of R&D It is a way of behaving, indeed a way of being, in which everyone is a knowledge worker – that is to say, an entrepreneur" (ibid)..

There is a dynamic cycle of knowledge, which Nonaka and Takeuchi (1995) present in the form of a spiral of knowledge within the industry, which reflects the process of generation and its consolidation: create >> capture >> organize >> share. It is a never-ending process, which is continuously being updated, generating new spirals of knowledge creation. According to Nonaka and Takeuchi, the KC process, which is continuous and cumulative, consists of four main modes:

- *Socialization* is the process of sharing experiences and thereby creating new *tacit* knowledge which can be acquired directly from others without the use of language. The key, therefore, to acquiring tacit knowledge is experience.
- *Externalization* is the process of converting tacit knowledge into *explicit* concepts. This requires both technological and verbal aptitudes, and it is here where a strong technology education background can prove to be of significant importance.

- *Combination* is the process of combining different bodies of explicit knowledge through written or oral means of communication. Knowledge creation carried out in Technology Education and Vocational Training usually takes this form.
- *Internalization* transforms explicit knowledge into tacit through experiences, where individuals absorb knowledge through *learning-by-doing*, a fundamental method developed in every technology education classroom.

In a later article, Nonaka and Konno (1998) named this ongoing process of interactions between tacit and explicit knowledge, the SECI model, which serves as an outline for knowledge creation. The four modes of knowledge conversion described by the SECI model have been used as the KC research enablers in this study.

During the same time, Porter's concept of the value chain has gone one step further. Through his new management paradigms, Drucker (1998) extends the concept of business relationships beyond traditional enterprise boundaries and seeks to organize the entire business processes throughout a value chain of multiple companies. During the past decades, outsourcing, globalization, and information technologies have enabled many organizations, such as Dell and Hewlett Packard, to successfully operate solid collaborative supply networks in which each specialized business partner focuses on only a few key strategic activities.

In the 21st century, changes in the business environment have contributed to the development of supply chain networks. First, as an outcome of globalization and the proliferation of multinational companies, joint ventures, strategic alliances and business partnerships, proved to be significant success factors, following the earlier 'Just-In-Time' and 'Lean Manufacturing' practices. Second, technological changes, particularly the dramatic fall in information communication costs, a significant component of transaction costs, have transformed the ways by which members of the supply chain network coordinate (Coase, 1998).

Many researchers have recognized this kind of supply network structures as a new organization form, using terms like 'Extended Enterprise' (Tapscott, 1996) or 'inter-organizational networks' (Fine, 1998; Kelly 1998). Akkermans (2001) defines these structures as "a group of semi-independent organizations, each with their capabilities, which collaborate in ever-changing constellations to serve one or more markets in order to achieve some business goal specific to that collaboration". And Fine (1998), emphasizing the capability of the multiple company value chain, states that "there is no competency more critical than that of superior design of one's capability chain—from the final consumer all the way upstream to the sources of raw materials and new technological concepts". The question that still has to be answered is who is responsible for the management and the performance of the organizations entire value chain, under these circumstances.

In the relevant literature, the position of a value chain manager appears only sporadically, within the hierarchy, and in most cases they do not manage the whole chain and their job is confined to a particular function and department. De Giovanni (2009), in a study that analyzes the role and tasks of a knowledge manager and his suitability to manage successfully the entire value chain, concludes that mainly general managers and managing directors carry out this role and tasks. Prajogo and McDermott (2005) agree with the above statement and recognize the conflict among other senior managers who fulfil all or part of this role and tasks. If we agree that the knowledge created within the value chain plays an important role in the organizational performance, then we also have to consider that there can be no significant knowledge created without someone able to manage it. Under this perspective, successful value chain managers should effectively manage the knowledge sparse across their organization and, at the same time, handle and coordinate the

knowledge belonging to the value chain of the cooperating multiple organizations.

Technology Education and Industry

In many countries, technology is taught as a compulsory or sometimes optional subject in one or more of primary, secondary or upper-secondary schools. TE is intended to develop competences, skills and insights for citizens in a society dominated by continuous change and, as an essential discipline, technology ought to be provided at all levels of the educational system, as well as by continuing and life-long educational programs (Dyrenfurth, 2003). The author believes that "The primary outcome of participating in technology education is technological literacy –a characteristic that encompasses both understanding and capability" (p.120). Some TE curricula have been based upon the implementation of educational ideas, usually fuelled by socio-economic concerns, structured in fields of action: work and production; transportation and traffic; supply and waste management; information and communication; construction and built environment.

Recently revised curricula have been influenced by ideas like preservation of nature, technology and social conditions, equality for women and men, political, cultural and economic freedom. A turn towards more society-oriented curricula is noticeable. The following three propositions, made by Eggleston involve society and the education system in a very realistic way and they further support our investigation assumption:

1. Every society and every government wants more technology education because it is seen to be the key to a developed economy and to growth in national income.
2. Every individual wants more of the products of technology for their personal satisfaction, security, comfort, leisure and entertainment. The goods that consumers, in every town and city, desire are remarkably similar.

3. *In consequence every education system is trying to develop technology education from the early years through to higher and post graduate education for boys and girls.* (Eggleston, 1995)

The pedagogical approach regarding technology education starts with children at the age of 5 to 6 and continues with the education of students from 7 to 11 and 11 to 16 on the above described fields. Technology education is also present within the university sector, where the focus of attention is the development of new technology education programs that seek to mould the next generation of engineers and technologists.

According to McCormick (2004) "almost any technology education curricula will have problem solving as an important part". He, nonetheless, notices differences among the various national curricula. In the USA the emphasis is on 'problem solving', while in UK 'design' is the central point. But McCormick considers both design and problem solving as kinds of procedural knowledge, although he distinguishes problem solving as "the most important procedural knowledge that occurs in technology, and indeed, in many other areas of activity". He also notices "the desire to teach a general problem-solving skill. In Britain there is a notion of 'key skills' with problem solving being one such skill" (ibid).

Benson (1995) defines the concept of Economic and Industrial Understanding (EIU). She argues that EIU plays a very important role in the life of both adults and young children, who "will become consumers, workers and producers and it is important therefore that the experiences that they have at school prepare them for their economic and working lives". According to Benson, "EIU is broader than 'making money' through mini-enterprises and it is important that a broad interpretation of EIU is promoted if children are to gain from its inclusion in the curriculum". Finally Benson refers to case studies in UK, aiming at examining among other factors the skills and the organization of the production line that are needed in a mini enterprise within a school. The results were not always positive as "often the pupils saw it just as a way to make money for the school funds".

So, the links between TE and Industry are not equally developed in every society. In countries with strong tradition in TE there have been organizations that played a major part in supporting these links. The United Kingdom is a good European example. Innes (1995) refers to SCSST (The Standing Conference on Schools' Science and Technology) and its national network SATRO (Science and Technology Regional Organization) as examples of two such organizations, which "have played a major part in supporting industry links by exciting young people about science and technology". To illustrate this, Innes (ibid) brings up three examples:

- Experienced engineers working on real and relevant projects in the classroom.
- *Young Engineers*, a national SCSST program where students, members of school clubs for the 11 to 18-age range, become actively involved in real projects. Their achievements are recognized each year through National Awards Finals where their work is displayed and prizes presented.
- The designation of 1986 as the Industry Year in the UK, which focused public attention on the value of Industry-Education links.

Nevertheless, the UK is not a typical European example. International approaches to technological education justify its implementation on the basis that it supports development of the human capital of the country where it is being applied.

NEW PRODUCT DEVELOPMENT

Let us follow step-by-step the development, birth and critical first year of a new product's life. Focus will be on phases previous to what is commonly referred to as the Product Life Cycle (PLC) in relevant bibliography. We shall only enter the very first phase of the PLC which Porter (1980) calls "the grandfather of concepts for predicting the probable course of industry evolution". Porter relates the PLC concept to the industry and not only to individual products.

For the purpose of this investigation the first PLC phase has been divided into five sub-phases. Individuals, industrial employees in Spain, to whom our survey has been addressed, were asked to evaluate the impact of knowledge, KC and TE enablers in each and every one of the following PLC sub-phases.

Phase One: Ideas for new products can arrive from any number of sources: the scientist in the laboratory, the inventor who approaches the company, the irritated customer or a competitor's innovation. Heavy technological background as well as capability for knowledge creation is of significant importance in each of the above four possible sources.

Phase Two: Key managers, with their best both technological and financial judgment, among other data sources, approve the idea, thus giving the green light to generate forecasts and other planning documents. If positive market and financial performance is predicted for the new product, the idea wins a place in the design laboratory.

Phase Three: Management approval is not enough to launch the project. In addition, market research, that is useful in defining and positioning the new product and helps to forecast demand, has to be conducted. In this phase, technology is strongly supported by the creation and sharing of knowledge among the departments involved: marketing, research and development (R&D), quality control and manufacturing.

Phase Four: A prototype is produced and the design for the final product is finalized. This is a phase where technological literacy plays a vital role and the analogy between the industry's prototype laboratory and the TE classroom is easily recognized.

Phase Five: Production is launched and improvements have to be made as the sales force meets resistance from both the distribution channels and customers. Production problems occur with the first full run. In this phase, technology is present in the entire value chain of the company, as sales and distribution departments are now involved.

However, the emergence of new technologies and the increased rate of change in existing technologies tend to shorten the PLC. As new products emerge more rapidly to satisfy similar consumer needs, existing ones decline more quickly. Shortened life cycles put time pressure on the organization to plan and launch the next-generation product.

THE RESEARCH

Two previous studies have triggered this investigation. Dyrenfurth (1998) surveyed approximately 200 businesses in the region of Kansas City, USA and found technological literacy as an 'increasingly important capability' assessed almost as high a need as the basic skills of arithmetic, communication and cooperation capabilities. These basic skills competences were cited by the research responders with frequencies ranging from 53 to 78 percent, compared to some 51 to 60 percent cited for the technological literacy competences, included in the study. The author even considers technological literacy as fundamental to being able to transfer knowledge and skill to unknown or new operational situations. Another important finding of this study is that specialized technical and industry-specific competences, like computer literacy, were all cited by the responders with frequencies below 50 percent.

The second study (Oskarsdottir, et al. 2000), in which we have also participated, is a comparative analysis on developments and skill requirements in 20 non-professional jobs in four European countries: France, Greece, Iceland and Italy. We interviewed, by means of a questionnaire, a total of 1600 individuals: 15 employees and 5 supervisors in each of the 20 jobs in every country. The results were similar to those in the above study. Basic skills (mathematic, communication, cooperation) were reported as very important by a 47 to 86 percent of the employees and 51 to 93 percent of the supervisors, whereas 52 percent of the employees and 63 percent of the supervisors opted for information mastery, the only technological literacy competence included in the study.

The individual, in our case the industrial employee, was the unit of analysis in the present investigation. The source for sampling was 82 major Spanish companies, covering 5 industrial sectors. Staff members and experienced employees working in production, new product development (or R&D) and quality departments were asked to participate in the study. Due to the nature of the investigation we adopted both interviews and a questionnaire-based survey, the latter being our principal research instrument.

During the interviews the objectives of the investigation were explained to the above mentioned department managers and a two-page explanatory text was handed out to be distributed to all potential respondents. The text, apart from a brief description of the research project, provided definitions of the ten enablers and the five PLC sub-phases. The guideline was that only employees who, due to their everyday professional activities, were fully aware of the meaning and significance of all enablers should participate in the survey. Although data collected during the interviews are not analyzed statistically, they were valuable for our interpretations and conclusions.

Following the interviews, the questionnaire survey was conducted. Questionnaires, as shown in Table 1 were administrated via e-mail to a total of 876 staff members and experienced employees of production, new product development (or R&D) and quality departments within the 82 companies of our sample.

Six to twelve employees from each company were surveyed depending on its size. Finally, 486 responses from 51 companies were received and analyzed. Table 2 shows the industrial sectors represented, the number of companies contacted and those who finally participated, as well as the number of employees who received and finally responded to the questionnaire.

The participation rates achieved in the research (62% at company level and 55% at the unit of analysis level) were satisfactory. Table 3 shows the respondents' characteristics in terms of sector, company and departments.

Reliability and Validity

Cronbach's *alpha* has been used to test the reliability of the measurement instrument. As all enablers have higher than 0.7 cut-off *alpha* values (in Table 4, below, they range from 0.8375 to 0.9254), they meet the criteria set by Nunnally (1978) for previously adopted instruments. As only single-item enablers were used, there was no need for convergent and discriminant validity tests to be applied.

THE IMPACT OF KC AND TE ON NPD

The relationship between KC, TE and NPD – the focus point of our study – has not been sufficiently investigated up-to-date, especially regarding the contribution of TE. In this section first we present the overall research findings in Table 5 and then, in Tables 6 and 7 we summarize and highlight those findings that best support the investigation hypothesis.

Table 1. Questionnaire

Use the following scale to evaluate the impact of the Knowledge, Knowledge Creation and Technology Education enablers in each and every one of the PLC sub-phases:

1	2	3	4	5	6
Very Weak	Weak	Moderately Weak	Moderately Strong	Strong	Very Strong

1. Knowledge enablers	
Enabler	Question
	In our organization, possession and management of Tacit and/or explicit knowledge, in each of the five PLC phases, is evaluated:
Tacit	Phase 1: Phase 2: Phase 3: Phase 4: Phase 5:
Explicit	Phase 1: Phase 2: Phase 3: Phase 4: Phase 5:
2. Knowledge Creation enablers	
Enabler	Question
	In our organization and in the course of the Knowledge Creation process, I assess the appropriate use of Socialization, Externalization, Combination and Internalization in each one of the five PLC phases, as:
Socialization	Phase 1: Phase 2: Phase 3: Phase 4: Phase 5:
Externalization	Phase 1: Phase 2: Phase 3: Phase 4: Phase 5:
Combination	Phase 1: Phase 2: Phase 3: Phase 4: Phase 5:
Internalization	Phase 1: Phase 2: Phase 3: Phase 4: Phase 5:
3. Technology Education enablers	
Enabler	Question
	In our organization, I assess the development of Competences, Skills, Commitment and Fit (all four due to Technology Education background) in each one of the five PLC phases, as:
Competences	Phase 1: Phase 2: Phase 3: Phase 4: Phase 5:
Skills	Phase 1: Phase 2: Phase 3: Phase 4: Phase 5:
Commitment	Phase 1: Phase 2: Phase 3: Phase 4: Phase 5:
Fit	Phase 1: Phase 2: Phase 3: Phase 4: Phase 5:
4. An Additional Question	
4.1 Have you had any kind of Technology Education at:	
	a) Primary School?: YES NO
	b) Secondary School?: YES NO
4.2 Have you had University studies and/or Vocational Training on a	
	Technological subject?: YES NO

The investigation hypothesis was that there is a constructive impact of KC and TE on the process of NPD and this assumption has been scrutinized under both theoretical and empirical perspectives.

Tables 6 and 7 bond the literature remarks made previously upon describing the NPD phases with the research findings, in a way that supports the

Table 2. Research participants by sector and unit of analysis

Sector	Companies		Employees	
	Contacted	Participated	Contacted	Participated
Automotive	8	6	83	51
Chemical & Pharmaceutical	7	5	63	36
Electro-Mechanical	25	18	339	182
Food & Beverages	26	14	212	112
Textile	16	8	179	105
Total	82	51 (62%)	876	486 (55%)

Table 3. Study participants by sector, company and department

Sector	Number of Companies	Respondents per Department			Total
		Production	NPD-R&D	Quality	
Automotive	6	17	22	12	51
Chemical & Pharmaceutical	5	14	12	10	36
Electro-Mechanical	18	60	78	44	182
Food & Beverages	14	55	37	20	112
Textile	8	81	6	18	105
Total	51	227	155	104	486

Table 4. Descriptive statistics and reliability test

Enablers	Mean	S.D.	Reliability (Cronbach's *alpha*)
Knowledge enablers			
Tacit	4.2307	0.4476	0.9235
Explicit	5.0125	0.4149	0.9136
Knowledge Creation enablers			
Socialization	3.8642	0.3956	0.8534
Externalization	4.1327	0.4176	0.8375
Combination	3.9468	0.4064	0.8963
Internalization	3.6534	0.5743	0.8766
Technology Education enablers			
Competences	5.5432	0.5287	0.9254
Skills	4.1542	0.5367	0.8688
Commitment	3.8534	0.4098	0.9142
Fit	4.3482	0.5268	0.8653

hypothesis. This will be further demonstrated in the conclusions section.

Table 6 summarises research findings regarding the impact caused upon each one of the five

Table 5. Research results

Enablers	New Product Development				
	Phase One: Ideas	Phase Two: Approval	Phase Three: Market Research	Phase Four: Prototyping	Phase Five: Product Launch
Knowledge enablers					
Tacit	**HIGH 72.4** MEDIUM 16.7 LOW 7.9	HIGH 9.8 MEDIUM 12.6 **LOW 65.6**	HIGH 12.5 **MEDIUM 70.4** LOW 10.1	**HIGH 61.1** MEDIUM 10.2 LOW 21.7	HIGH 9.4 **MEDIUM 66.9** LOW 16.7
Explicit	HIGH 8.2 MEDIUM 11.3 **LOW 70.5**	**HIGH 56.4** MEDIUM 17.1 LOW 22.6	**HIGH 81.3** MEDIUM 10.5 LOW 3.2	**HIGH 74.3** MEDIUM 18.4 LOW 2.3	**HIGH 85.1** MEDIUM 8.4 LOW 2.5
Knowledge Creation enablers					
Socialization	**HIGH 62.8** MEDIUM 11.7 LOW 20.5	**NA 36.7**	**NA 74.5**	**NA 82.4**	**NA 54.9**
Externalization	HIGH 10.5 **MEDIUM 72.8** LOW 9.7	**NA 54.5**	**NA 64.3**	**HIGH 56.2** MEDIUM 13.2 LOW 20.6	HIGH 13.5 **MEDIUM 65.9** LOW 8.6
Combination	**NA 65.8**	HIGH 9.3 **MEDIUM 66.9** LOW 16.8	**HIGH 67.9** MEDIUM 15.4 LOW 10.7	HIGH 11.8 **MEDIUM 76.7** LOW 1.5	**NA 49.7**
Internalization	**NA 72.5**	**NA 47.9**	**NA 87.9**	**NA 33.2**	**HIGH 67.7** MEDIUM 18.8 LOW 4.5
Technology Education enablers					
Competences	**HIGH 88.4** MEDIUM 6.8 LOW 1.8	HIGH 11.6 **MEDIUM 77.5** LOW 4.9	**HIGH 68.8** MEDIUM 21.6 LOW 2.6	**HIGH 67.5** MEDIUM 12.8 LOW 10.7	HIGH 11.7 **MEDIUM 65.2** LOW 10.1
Skills	HIGH 7.7 **MEDIUM 80.6** LOW 5.7	HIGH 8.5 **MEDIUM 56.7** LOW 30.8	**HIGH 75.6** MEDIUM 12.9 LOW 4.5	**HIGH 65.4** MEDIUM 18.5 LOW 9.1	HIGH 8.7 MEDIUM 17.4 **LOW 56.9**
Commitment	HIGH 5.5 MEDIUM 9.2 **LOW 79.3**	**HIGH 70.9** MEDIUM 15.6 LOW 7.5	HIGH 11.3 **MEDIUM 58.8** LOW 20.9	HIGH 5.8 MEDIUM 7.9 **LOW 74.3**	**HIGH 69.8** MEDIUM 11.1 LOW 12.1
Fit	HIGH 12.7 **MEDIUM 61.8** LOW 17.5	HIGH 14.7 **MEDIUM 71.8** LOW 8.5	**HIGH 81.9** MEDIUM 9.7 LOW 2.4	**HIGH 60.7** MEDIUM 10.6 LOW 15.7	**HIGH 73.8** MEDIUM 11.7 LOW 4.5

NPD phases by the two knowledge and the four KC enablers. The use of a three-grade range (Low, Medium, and High) has been adopted for simplicity purposes. Its relation to the six-point Likert scale stands as follows: 1 & 2 = Low, 3 & 4 = Medium, and 5 & 6 = High. Adoption of a six-point Likert scale, which does not include the midpoint About Average, prevents respondents from using a neutral default option. The rating Low, Medium or High, depicted in the cells of

Tables 6 and 7 for each one of the enablers, is the dominating one according to the research findings presented in Table 5. KC enablers that do not appear in the cells of Table 6 were considered as Not Applicable (NA) by more than 30% of the respondents, for the relevant phase.

Table 7 summarizes research findings regarding the impact caused upon each one of the five NPD phases by the four TE enablers: competences, skills, commitment and fit.

Table 6. The impact of knowledge and KC upon NPD

Enablers	New Product Development				
	Phase One: Ideas	**Phase Two: Approval**	**Phase Three: Market Research**	**Phase Four: Prototyping**	**Phase Five: Product Launch**
Knowledge & Knowledge Creation Impact	*Tacit* **HIGH 72.4%** *Explicit* LOW 70.5 *Socialization* **HIGH 62.8%** *Externalization* MEDIUM 72.8	*Tacit* LOW 65.6 *Explicit* **HIGH 56.4%** *Combination* MEDIUM 66.9	*Tacit* MEDIUM 70.4 *Explicit* **HIGH 81.3%** *Combination* **HIGH 67.9%**	*Tacit* **HIGH 61.1%** *Explicit* **HIGH 74.3%** *Externalization* **HIGH 56.2%** *Combination* MEDIUM 76.7	*Tacit* MEDIUM 66.9 *Explicit* **HIGH 85.1%** *Externalization* MEDIUM 65.9 *Internalization* **HIGH 67.7%**

Table 7. The impact of TE upon NPD

Enablers	New Product Development				
	Phase One: Ideas	**Phase Two: Approval**	**Phase Three: Market Research**	**Phase Four: Prototyping**	**Phase Five: Product Launch**
Technology Education Impact	*Competence* **HIGH 88.4%** *Skill* MEDIUM 80.6% *Commitment* LOW 79.3% *Fit* MEDIUM 61.8%	*Competence* MEDIUM 77.5% *Skill* MEDIUM 56.7% *Commitment* **HIGH 70.9%** *Fit* MEDIUM 71.8%	*Competence* **HIGH 68.8%** *Skill* **HIGH 75.6%** *Commitment* MEDIUM 58.8% *Fit* **HIGH 81.9%**	*Competence* **HIGH 67.5%** *Skill* **HIGH 65.4%** *Commitment* LOW 74.3% *Fit* **HIGH 60.7%**	*Competence* MEDIUM 65.2% *Skill* LOW 56.9% *Commitment* **HIGH 69.8%** *Fit* **HIGH 73.8%**

An additional question inquiring about the TE responders had during their primary or secondary schooling, as well as the possible technological nature of their University studies and Vocational Training, demonstrated that: Only 3.4% of the responders had contact with TE at primary school level, while a significant percentage (42.6%) had TE during secondary school. Finally 58.5% of the responders had either a University degree or Vocational Training related to technology. The latter high percentage is explained by the fact that in the industrial sectors under investigation staff members are typically engineers, chemists, physicists, doctors or economists, with a technical orientation.

CONCLUSION

Research findings, as presented in Tables 5, 6 and 7, prove that New Product Development (NPD), in the 21st century, is increasingly based on Knowledge Creation (KC) and Technology Education (TE). To demonstrate this more clearly we are 'interpreting' Tables 6 and 7, here below, in reference to each one of the ten research enablers used in this study.

Regarding the two knowledge enablers: 'tacit knowledge' is reported as highly beneficial in the NPD phases of Ideas and Prototyping, while possession of 'explicit knowledge' is recognized as such in four out of the five NPD phases (Approval, Market Research, Prototyping and Marketing). The nature of explicit knowledge, as described in the Introduction under subsection Knowledge, is a good reason why it is not considered beneficial in the Ideas phase, where tacit knowledge plays the dominant role.

In reference to the four KC enablers: 'socialization' is considered highly beneficial in the Ideas phase; 'externalization' in the Prototyping phase; 'combination' during Market Research and 'internalization' in the Product Launch. Here again, the nature of the four enablers, as described in Research Enablers under subsection Knowledge Creation in the Value Chain, explains why that happens and why some enablers were considered as Not Applicable (NA) by more than 30% of the respondents, in certain phases. For example, this complies with Nonaka & Takeuchi's interpretation that socialization ranks high in the Ideas phase (tacit to tacit knowledge), while it receives low rating in every other phase, where explicit knowledge is relatively dominant.

Finally, interpretation of results regarding the four TE enablers is a little more complex. 'Competences' rank high during Market Research and Prototyping (which is in accordance with the theoretical perspectives), but is also considered essential in the Ideas phase, this time challenging theory. 'Skills' are considered essential during Market research and Prototyping; 'commitment' is reported as highly required for Approval and Product Launch; 'fit' is believed to be beneficial for Market Research, Prototyping and Product Launch. They all abide by theory, although interpreting Venkatraman, one would expect 'fit' to be beneficial during the Ideas phase, as well.

The previously presented analysis allows us to observe the three concepts under investigation (KC, TE, and NPD) not as three unrelated entities, but as parts of an equilateral triangle, as it is shown in Figure 1. It is difficult to decide which one of the three comes first, but if the triangle is seen as the rotating heart of a Wankel motor, then the problem vanishes.

Research findings indicate that knowledge, KC and TE have, each one on its own and all three combined, a very constructive impact on NPD. On the other hand, authors from both the market-

Figure 1. The Wankel motor analogy

ing standpoint (Kotler, 1991) and the industrial engineering perspective (Porter, 1980 and 1985) of NPD emphasize on the positive impact that active participation in NPD teams has on the knowledge sharing or KC capabilities of the individuals. Combining this observation with the results of the present research we can conclude that there is freewheeling among KC, TE and NPD. Knowledge sharing and KC combined with a strong TE background can positively influence NPD; this in turn, nourishes knowledge sharing and KC and improves the technological literacy of individuals participating in NPD teams. Long-established tools, like brainstorming, and contemporary ones, like groupware, keep facilitating the flow in this exchange of knowledge, experiences and innovative ideas across the entire value chain.

Although the results of this study are based on a large sample, two issues of concern remain. First, the constructive impact that knowledge, KC and TE have on NPD was evaluated at a static point in time (spring 2005) whereas the basic enablers vary over time. And second, the study was conducted in a single country, Spain. A future multinational study, and if possible periodically repeated, would be of greater value for the research and the TE communities.

REFERENCES

Akkermans, H. A. (2001). Renga: A systems approach to facilitating inter-organizational network development. *System Dynamics Review, 17*(3), 179–193. doi:10.1002/sdr.215

Benson, C. (1995). Economic and Industrial Understanding as Part of Design and Technology Education in the Primary Curriculum. In K. Langer, M. Metzing, & D. Wahl (Ed.), *Technology Education, Innovation and Management* (pp. 224-232). Berliln/Heidelberg: Springer-Verlag.

Coase, R. (1998). The New Institutional Economics. *The American Economic Review*, 88(2), *Papers and Proceedings of the Hundred and Tenth Annual Meeting of the American Economic Association*, 72-74.

Davenport, T. H., & Prusak, L. (Eds.). (1998). *Working Knowledge: How Organizations Manage what they Know*. Cambridge, MA: Harvard Business School Press.

De Giovanni, P. (2009). The Knowledge Manager's Role and Tasks for Supply Chain Management Success. *Journal of Knowledge Management Practice, 10*(1).

Drucker, P. F. (1985). The Discipline of Innovation, *Harvard Business Review*, 63(3), and re-published in 1998 as HBR Classic in *HBR*, 76(6), 149-157.

Drucker, P. F. (1998, October 5). Management's New Paradigms. *Forbes*.

Dyrenfurth, M. J. (1991). Technological Literacy Synthesized. In M. J. Dyrenfurth & M. Kozak (Eds.), *Technological Literacy* (pp. 138-183). Fortieth yearbook of the Council on Technology Teacher Education, International Technology Education Association. Peoria, IL: Glencoe.

Dyrenfurth, M. J. (1998). *Final Report-State Fair RTEC Region Project to Conduct a Collaborative Targeted Technical Education Needs Assessment. Columbia, MO: Research Institute for Technical Education & Workforce Development*. Columbia: University of Missouri.

Dyrenfurth, M. J. (2003). Technology Education for Developing Nations. In Graube, G., Dyrenfurth, M. J., & Theuerkauf, W. E. (Eds.), *Technology Education: International Concepts and Perspectives* (pp. 119–124). Frankfurt am Main: Peter Lang.

Eggleston, J. (1995). Are We Making Technology Education Attractive to Our Students? In Langer, K., Metzing, M., & Wahl, D. (Eds.), *Technology Education, Innovation and Management* (pp. 216–223). Berlin, Heidelberg: Springer-Verlag.

Evans, P., Shulman, L. E., & Stalk, G. (1992). Competing on Capabilities: The New Rules of Corporate Strategy. *Harvard Business Review, 70*(3), 57–69.

Fine, C. (1998). *Clockspeed: Winning Industry Control in the Age of Temporary Advantage*. New York: Perseus Books.

Galbraith, J. R., & Nathanson, D. (1979). The Role of Organizational Structure and Process in Strategy Implementation. In Schendel, D., & Hofer, C. W. (Eds.), *Strategic Management: A New View of Business Policy and Planning* (pp. 249–283). Boston: Little, Brown.

Gorman, M., & Carlson, B. (1990). Interpreting Invention as a cognitive process: The case of Alexander Graham Bell, Thomas Edison, and the Telephone. *Science, Technology & Human Values, 15*(2). doi:10.1177/016224399001500201

Innes, S. (1995). Working with Industry to Enhance Technology Education. In Langer, K., Metzing, M., & Wahl, D. (Eds.), *Technology Education, Innovation and Management* (pp. 233–240). Berlin, Heidelberg: Springer-Verlag.

Kelly, K. (1998). *New Rules for the New Economy*. London: Fourth Estate.

Kotler, P. (1991). *Marketing Management* (7th ed.). Englewood Cliffs, NJ: Prentice Hall.

McCormick, R. (2004). Issues of Learning and Knowledge in Technology Education. *International Journal of Technology and Design Education, 14*(1), 21–44. doi:10.1023/B:ITDE.0000007359.81781.7c

Nonaka, I. (1991). The Knowledge-Creating Company. *Harvard Business Review, 69*(6), 96–104.

Nonaka, I., & Konno, N. (1998). The Concept of 'Ba': Building a Foundation for Knowledge Creation. *California Management Review, 40*(3), 40–54.

Nonaka, I., & Takeuchi, H. (1995). *The Knowledge-Creating Company*. New York: Oxford University Press, Inc.

Nunnally, J. C. (1978). *Psychometric Theory* (2nd ed.). New York: McGraw-Hill.

Oskarsdottir, G. G., Busetta, P., Ginestie, J., & Papoutsakis, H. (2000). *Employability Skills in non-Professional Occupations. A four-country comparative research project*. Reykjavik, Iceland: University Press, University of Iceland.

Pearson, G., & Young, T. (2002). *Technically Speaking. Why all Americans need to know more about technology*. Washington, DC: National Academy Press.

Polanyi, M. (1966). *The Tacit Dimension*. London: Routledge & Kegan Paul Ltd.

Porter, M. E. (1980). *Competitive Strategy. Techniques for Analyzing Industries and Competitors*. New York: The Free Press.

Porter, M. E. (1985). *Competitive Advantage. Creating and Sustaining Superior Performance*. New York: The Free Press.

Prahalad, C. K., & Hamel, G. (1990). The Core Competence of the Corporation. *Harvard Business Review, 68*(3), 79–91.

Prajogo, D. I., & McDermott, C. M. (2005). The relationship between total quality management practices and organizational culture. *International Journal of Operations & Production Management, 25*(11), 1101–1122. doi:10.1108/01443570510626916

Sveiby, K. E. (1994). *Towards a Knowledge Perspective on Organization*. PhD Dissertation, University of Stockholm.

Sveiby, K. E. (1997). *The New Organizational Wealth – Managing and Measuring Knowledge-Based Assets*. San Francisco: Berrett-Koehler.

Sveiby, K. E. (2001). A Knowledge-based Theory of the Firm to Guide Strategy Formulation. *Journal of Intellectual Capital, 2*(4), 344–358. doi:10.1108/14691930110409651

Venkatraman, N. (1989). The Concept of Fit in Strategy Research toward Verbal and Statistical Correspondence. *Academy of Management Review, 14*(3), 423–444. doi:10.2307/258177

Von Krogh, G., Ichigo, K., & Nonaka, I. (Eds.). (2000). *Enabling Knowledge Creation*. London: Oxford University Press.

Von Krogh, G., & Roos, J. (1995). A perspective on Knowledge, Competence and Strategy. *Personnel Review, 24*(3), 56–76. doi:10.1108/00483489510089650

Webster (1981). *Third New International Dictionary*. Chicago: Meriam-Webster.

Section 3
Process Innovation

Chapter 10
A Novel Practical Triangular Approach to Process Innovation:
VDF Model

Daniela Butan
University of Limerick, Ireland

Emma O'Brien
University of Limerick, Ireland

Mark Southern
University of Limerick, Ireland

Seamus Clifford
University of Limerick, Ireland

ABSTRACT

This chapter presents a novel Knowledge Management model - VDF (Variation Mode and Effect Analysis & Design of Experiments & Finite Element Analysis) for process innovation and efficient problem solving in enterprises. To date there is no practical unified tool that enables companies to switch from engineering chaos to a structured, sustainable process. Unlike process improvement the current method creates a multidisciplinary framework which promotes innovation into the organizations processes. The VDF triangulated approach uses the company's tacit knowledge asset, convert it into explicit knowledge (through a Variation Mode and Effect Analysis) and it couples it with engineering scientific tools (Design of Experiments and Finite Element Analysis) to solve problems and innovate inside the organization. The unified model was validated through multiple company case studies one of which is presented in this chapter. The use of this model resulted in a robust, controllable, innovative process which could be sustained due to the development of key knowledge.

DOI: 10.4018/978-1-61520-829-6.ch010

THE NEED FOR A PRACTICAL APPROACH TO PROCESS INNOVATION FOR MANUFACTURING COMPANIES

"Process creation is an innovation process that emphasises the need to design and redesign products in a way to match organisational needs with emergent technology" Zumd (1984). Its importance is founded in a study conducted by Yamin et al. (1997) that discovered that process innovation was the stronger predictor of performance over product innovation.

"A process innovation is the implementation of a new or significantly improved production or delivery method. This includes significant changes in techniques, equipment and/or software." (OECD, 2005)

Despite the perception that it does not provide significant economic benefits, process innovation is as important as product innovation to a company. Process innovation requires a significant amount of knowledge of the internal workings and processes of the company as well as potential machinery and technologies that can enhance the process.

Within companies engineers often feel that they have a thorough knowledge of their processes. However, this is often not the case, many times continuous problems in products such as a high rate of defects; low productivity and yield are due to problems with the production process and a lack of understanding of its capability and limitations. Often engineers spend time tweaking the process or machinery to try to address such problems which often result in new problems occurring. Taking the steps to innovate the process can often solve many of these underlying problems permanently, resulting in a more sustainable process.

To date the research in product innovation has been limited to the debate on which type of innovation is suitable for what type of companies and barriers to process innovation. There have been few practical models to assist companies to adopt process innovation in a scientific, structured method. There are tools available to support process innovation however companies are often unaware of which tools to select based on their suitability, furthermore as a standalone these tools have their limitations.

Within companies process innovation is often chaotic, based on trial and error or instinct. The need for a practical approach to guide companies in the area of process innovation is long overdue.

As mentioned previously process innovation is greatly concerned with the knowledge of the internal processes of the companies, much of this knowledge is undiscovered and people are unaware that it is required. Thus it involves a large amount of knowledge creation is required. This chapter outlines a novel model for process innovation that brings together the existing tacit knowledge of all stakeholders in the process convert it into explicit knowledge and it couples it with engineering scientific tools to solve problems and innovate inside the organization.

The chapter will first discuss tools used in the process innovation and their limitations; it will then discuss a novel model that provides a practical approach to process innovation. It will then illustrate the successful use of this model using a case study.

2. EXISTING APPROACHES AND THEIR LIMITATIONS TO PROCESS INNOVATION

There are plenty of tools that can be used to facilitate process innovation but companies are unaware what tools to select to ensure the maximum efficiency during process innovation. Some of the most common engineering tools that have been used to improve and optimise processes are:

- Variation Mode and Effect Analysis (VMEA)

- Design of Experiments (DOE)
- VMEA and DOE Combined
- Finite Element Analysis (FEA)
- DOE and FEA Combined

The following sections will discuss the use of these tools in the context of process innovation and outline their limitations

2.1 Variation Mode and Effect Analysis (VMEA)

Variation Mode and Effect Analysis (VMEA) is a variation risk management tool that 'statistically aims at guiding engineers to find critical areas in terms of the effects of unwanted variation' (Johansson et al., 2006).

It was failure mode and effect analysis (FMEA) and fault tree analysis (FTA) that initially inspired the development of VMEA. Failure mode and effect analysis was concerned with determining potential failures in a product and assessing them.

VMEA was first introduced by Chakhunashvili et al., 2004 but the salient features were comprehensively described later (Johansson et al., 2006). VMEA was developed to systematically determine the noise factors within a process and evaluate their affects on key product characteristics (KPCs) such as diameter, length, shape etc.

VMEA uses group techniques coupled with the statistical model in order to elicit the tacit knowledge in the minds of the people involved in the process and transform it into explicit knowledge. Group dynamics, often poorly understood by engineers, management and operatives, can be controlled by using brainstorming techniques along with voting and ranking algorithms. These techniques guarantee that all staff and researchers have contributed to the analysis and feel that they are part of the problem solving process. This all inclusive technique promotes holistic ownership over the problem and provides a motivational incentive for everyone to contribute positively. Functional barriers within organisations can be

lowered using this technique meaning that the multifunctional team operates with constancy-of-purpose that is common to all involved.

'Conducted on a systematic basis, the goal of VMEA is to identify and prioritise noise factors that significantly contribute to the variability of important product characteristics and might yield unwanted consequences with respect to safety, compliance with governmental regulations, and functional requirements' (Chakhunashvili et al., 2004).

Often in process innovation engineers believe they are aware the main causes of variation but in many cases it is one of the unsuspecting parameters which is not high on the list of offenders is the main cause of process problems and variation. VMEA provides a scientific method to discover the actual main causes of variation.

The VMEA is concerned with a team of engineers, designers and technicians brainstorming regarding the product and causes of variation. Firstly the product characteristics for which variation can be a major company problem are identified. The team then identifies the potential elements of variation on each product characteristic so for example Smoothness might be a product characteristic, potential elements that may cause the variation may be the temperature etc, these are known as sub-KPCs. They are then prioritised (assigned a priority number according to a specific table used for VMEA). For each sub KPC the noise factors associated with it are identified and again prioritised according to the table. For example a noise factor for temperature may be the length the of time the machine is on or the cooling element of the machine. Then the facilitator calculates a variation risk priority number (VRPN) thus indicating areas where reasonably anticipated variation might be detrimental. Based on the VRPN, practitioners can determine the product characteristics that are mostly influenced by variation. The variation is often some aspect of the process such as machine settings, raw material composition, temperature etc.

The VMEA allows you to pinpoint potential causes of variation using a structured method and collating the knowledge of several professionals. However there is one main limitation of this methodology. VMEA does not provide a model to allow you to explore the effect of specific process parameters (or the causes of variation) on the product. It merely provides an insight to the engineer on what he/she may alter to innovate the process.

Furthermore because VMEA is reliant on group dynamics and brainstorming there may be issues with dominant characters in the brainstorming session forcing their opinion on the rest of the group.

Another limitation of VMEA is it may provide a basis for company politics. Some departments or individuals opinions may be viewed as in superior because of their position in the company and thus their contribution may not be given any weight in the VMEA.

In addition to companies politics in many organisations there are some employees which fail to share key knowledge because it provides them with a status in the organisation. Such individuals may not share this knowledge in the VMEA as they feel it will dethrone them from their organisational rank.

As a result of such limitations the outcomes of the VMEA need to be validated in some way.

2.2 Design of Experiments (DOE)

People execute experiments in their everyday lives in order to learn or develop knowledge. When one wishes to achieve a particular response in an unfamiliar act they often do so through trying various actions. For example if a person is learning to use a new washing machine they may try pressing different buttons to figure out which one starts the machine. The same occurs in engineering. Engineers conduct experiments to gather knowledge about a particular product or process. Often they conduct experiments like in real life on a "trial and error" basis, this approach

is known as one factor at a time (Clements, 1995) in which engineers alter one factor of the production process while keeping the others constant and run a product through to determine the effect. It is a slow procedure with very little methodological reasoning and is costly to conduct yielding little scientific knowledge. Often it only provides a temporary fix to a problem however it is still widely used in organisations today (Anthony et al, 2003).

A more structured approach to experimentation is Design of experiments (DOE). "Design of experiments is one of the most powerful quality improvement techniques for reducing variation, enhancing process effectiveness and process capability in the twentieth century" (Anthony, 2006). Variation is an element in any production process that can lead to low quality products, increased costs and reduced yield. By designing products to take account of variation it permits the production of a product as close as to the required specification as possible. Design of experiments allows engineers to determine which process settings can minimize variation.

Variation is as a result of a number of factors two of which are controllable. Signal factors are those parameters which are input into the production process such as the settings on a machine, control factors are upper and lower limits of the product as set by the product developer. Phadke (1989) The third set of factors are uncontrollable and are known as noise factors, these factors are often unknown as they occur during production, they can be due to variation in the raw material, variation in the conditions during the production process such as temperature or variation as a result of overuse of machinery deteriorating or over operating. (Kackar 1985; Taguchi 1986; Phadke 1989; Clausing 1994). Design of experiments allows engineers to determine the optimal process settings which minimises noise.

DOE is a technique that can readily be used in the design and development of new products and their processes (Ellekjaer and Bisgaard,, 1998).

Furthermore DOE can assist the modification of existing processes and lead to the incremental improvements in such products. Thus it is useful for both radical and incremental innovation and product and process innovation. "Radical innovations are fundamental changes that represent revolutionary change in technology. They represent clear departures from existing practice. In contrast, incremental innovations are minor improvements or simple adjustments in current technology". This is significant in light of the way businesses operate today. Stalk (1993) highlights that with the fast moving pace of today's business world, product lifecycles are constantly reducing, as a result it is important that companies address this issue with the ability to replace products with better versions.

DOE focuses on the improvement and identification of new processes regardless. "Process creation is an innovation process that emphasises the need to design and redesign products in a way to match organisational needs with emergent technology". (Zumd, 1984)

However DOE is not without its limitations. A lot of economic recourses can be consumed through poorly designed experiments thus adequate preparatory work is needed when approaching DoE (Johansson et al., 2006). Furthermore badly designed experiments often generate little knowledge. (Franceschini and Macchietto, 2008) There have been a number of procedures for effectively planning and conducting DoE (Coleman and Montgomery, 1993; Montgomery, 2001), however, none of these tells us how assess and prioritise Noise Factors (NF) and determine their impact on important response variables. Often engineers perceive that they know what factors cause variation however what they perceive is not always the case. As a result it is important to introduce a methodology that can objectively and scientifically prioritise noise factors.

Traditionally DOE focused on conducting of experiments by varying inputs or factors to determine their effect on the output and statistically analyse the results to determine the correlation between factors and responses (Viles et al 2009). However in later years DOE, particularly in Montgomery's model (2005) guidelines have been included in the model to take account of how to determine a problem to be solved by experiments and select potential variables which may cause the variation. However this is not conducted in a scientific manner and there are no predefined methods or standards of how to scope the problem and select variables. This is worrying considering such inputs can significantly affect the success of the experiment.

Sufficient preparation is often reliant on the perspectives of a number of key stakeholders in the organisation who often have different yet complimentary knowledge of the process, for example the product designer may have a detailed knowledge of how the product works, the engineer a knowledge of the limitations of the manufacturing process, the manager a knowledge of the customer requirements or process capacity. DOE when applied is often conducted by individual engineers within companies and lacks consensus building between individuals who all have key knowledge that may significantly influence the product or process. Even Montgomery (2009) highlighted that experimenters have an opinion of the most appropriate experimental model this is often based on their opinion of the most significant factors on variation. However, it is possible that after running the experiment that the projected model is wrong. The success of the experimental model depends on experience and knowledge.

Another limitation of DOE is it is seen as largely an academic phenomenon which is difficult to apply in the real world due to what is felt its statistical nature; it is seldom taught to undergraduate engineers thus the transfer of the method to industry is difficult. (Anthony et al 2003) The use of a model that reduces the threatening statistical terminology of DOE and increases the awareness of its potential would assist in the use of DOE in industry by all stakeholders in the production and product design process.

2.3 Finite Element Analysis (FEA)

It is already known that there is a strong link between Process innovation and New Process design. So often to increase their competitiveness on the market companies require a redesign of their current process or adopting a completely new process. Finite Element Analysis (FEA) plays an important role during process modelling.

Shinar (1978) defined process modelling as the relation between 'outputs' and 'inputs', (feed conditions, design parameters and process adjustable parameters) in view of scale up from lab to industrial scale, prediction of process dynamics and optimization of operating conditions.

According to one of the well established Engineering Finite Element Analysis providers – Ansys (2010) 'In nearly every industry, driving product and process development through engineering numerical simulation technology has become a key strategy to develop more innovative products, reduce development and manufacturing costs.'

Hastings et al. (1985) also showed that 'The introduction of Finite Element Analysis (in product and process modelling) has substantially decreased the time to take products (and processes) from concept to the production line.'

The FEA embeds specialized software that can manage both the complexity of modelling and the analysis of a system. FEA allows entire designs to be analysed, constructed, refined, and optimised before the design is manufactured. Numerical simulation covers a large range of engineering analysis starting from the analysis of an individual part, such as a rivet to the simulation of an entire system such as an industrial processing plant. It can involve structural and electromagnetic, fluid dynamics, simulation process and data management.

FEA is a powerful engineering tool and the results of the simulations might look great but one thing needs to be remembered all the time: *after performing a FEA analysis, the findings need to be compared with the experimental results.. That might be considered one of the major drawbacks of the FEA analysis, the predictions will not be considered valuable until they are experimentally validated.*

Many companies use dedicated Finite Element Analysis packages (i.e. Ansys, DEFORM, ABAQUS, NASTRAN etc) to optimise or create new design features for their products and processes.

However, using the FEA package during the process innovation might have a major disadvantage. When building a model with FEA the designer has to make several assumptions and assume some restrictions about the real world structure. If the assumptions are not a good representation of the real engineering system and if the limitations and constraints are not well understood, then there is a real danger that the model generated by the FEA is completely wrong.

Another disadvantage of using the FEA is related to the engineer's level of experience in modelling. According to Vince Adams (2009)

'Specific to FEA, remember that a finite element solver simply processes data to provide a solution. It doesn't possess any additional insight, can't prompt a user to consider other options, or in most cases, point out flawed inputs. In a manner of speaking, your FEA solver trusts that you know what you're doing. To many newer users, this may be one of its biggest limitations.'

As can be seen previously the common tools currently used for process innovation have many limitations when used in isolation. To overcome some of these problems some of the tools have been combined, however even when used together there are still some drawbacks. In this section we will look at how these tools have been combined in practice and their limitations.

2.4 The Use of VMEA and DOE

As mentioned previously due to political issues, knowledge struggles and the lack of ability to provide concrete results the findings of the VMEA need to be validated in some way.

On the other hand the expense of DOEs, poorly designed experiments and the academic perception of it are all limitations associated with the design of experiments methodology.

The introduction of a statistical tool such as VMEA can be significantly beneficial when undergoing traditional industrial designed experiments. It is important to consider that there have been a number of recent applications of the technique in industrial settings which highlight its many benefits associated with product/process optimisation, [36, 38]. None have been used in conjunction with DoE. However the two tools can complement each other efficiently.

VMEA can provide a structured method to provide an indication of key problem areas in the production process which may require further investigation reducing the number of experiments that need to be run. Furthermore it gathers knowledge from a number of key areas rather than the perspective of one engineer. In turn DOE validates the findings of the VMEA and eliminates any bias.

VMEA has been successfully used with DOE in an applied research project. A small commodity based engineering company wished to operate in the highly regulated medical device sector. The company needed to innovate its processes so it would consistently produce high quality products within a very narrow specification in line with the Food and Drug Administration (FDA) guidelines.

Time and cost were a significant factor in the project as a result it was decided to adopt a VMEA prior to designing the experiment. A new machine was purchased for the purposes of developing new products (a variation of their existing products expect on a smaller scale) to break into the medical devices sector.

The experiment focused only on seven of the eighteen potential factors that were expected to cause variation, the VMEA conducted was responsible for determining the factors that were the cause of 75% of the variation in the product responses. Furthermore the VMEA acquired excellent R^2 values in a small amount of time.

The VMEA assisted the engineer to collate knowledge from a number of departments and build a consensus gaining 'buy in' from all departments into the project. It identified the problem in lay mans terms using a structured scientific method which minimised the use of threatening statistical terminology. Furthermore it determined the most important factors influencing variation allowing a smaller number of experiments to be run reducing costs.

As a result of the project the engineering company in the case study is top of its class in the medical devices sector and understands its process more than even the largest manufacturing companies in its sector.

2.5 The Use of DOE and FEA

Some researchers have seen the advantages of using a combined model DOE and FEA for process optimisation and innovation, overcoming the limitations of the FEA described in Section 2.3.

Al-Momani and Rawabdeh (2008) found out that the combination of both techniques (DOE+FEA) resulted in a reduction of the necessary experimental cost and effort in addition to getting a higher level of verification. They concluded that the method used provided a good contribution towards the optimisation of sheet metal blanking process.

Chen and Koc (2007) concluded that the combined DOE and FEA approach provided a rapid and accurate understanding of the influence of the random process variation on the springback variation in forming of advanced high strength steels, eliminating the need for lengthy and costly physical experiments.

Figure 1. VDF model: Going from engineering chaos to a optimised, robust, innovative process

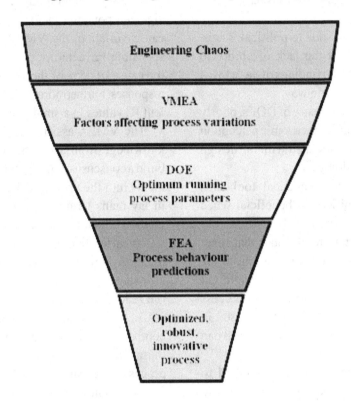

Engineering Chaos

VMEA
Factors affecting process variations

DOE
Optimum running
process parameters

FEA
Process behaviour
predictions

Optimized,
robust,
innovative
process

Koc and Arslan (2003) studied large and non-asymmetric precision forming tooling where conventional shrink-fit solutions cannot be applied effectively and economically. They proposed and validated an effective use of stress pins through a combined FEA and DOE analysis as an innovative approach to support the precision forming dies for reducing the amplitude of tensile stresses and deflections induced by the forming loads.

However the limitations of this approach are obvious. If the DOE uses a large range of process parameters that will not only have an impact on the total experimental analysis cost and quality but it might also increase the FEA simulation time.

3. THE VDF MODEL: DESCRIPTION

To overcome the limitations outlined in the previous section, a unified model is proposed.

The new VDF model is combining the three engineering tools: Variation Mode and Effect Analysis & Design of Experiments & Finite Element Analysis, in one powerful KM practical framework which is capable of using the existing tacit knowledge, converts it into an explicit knowledge package and uses that in the most efficient way to solve problems, optimise and innovate in companies.

The first component of the VDF model, the VMEA uses a brain storming- like technique in order to elicit the tacit knowledge in the minds of the team involved in the process and transforms it into explicit knowledge. Then using dedicated ranking algorithms, the VMEA finds and prioritises the process characteristics for which the unwanted variation is detrimental. Those with the highest priority number are chosen for further investigation i.e. DOE. The right process parameters and the optimum number of inputs that will feed the DOE are determined which will ensure a minimum cost for the DOE analysis. In this way, the limitations of the DOE analysis described in Section 2.2 are overcome.

After the VMEA, a statistical DOE analysis will be performed to determine the process optimum running parameters and the most suitable combination of these parameters which will ensure maximum efficiency of the process.

After the VMEA and DOE were performed, the FEA analysis comes into play, underpinning the process (see Figure 1). Using the combined VMEA+DOE approach prior to the process modelling, overcomes the Finite Element Analysis limitations described in Section 2, providing realistic process conditions and parameters for constructing the model.

Using specialised modelling packages and dedicated engineering principles, FEA then simulates and predicts the process behaviour and finds out factors that went undetected by the VMEA and DOE methods. At the end of the simulation, the FEA results will be compared and evaluated with the results of the experimental DOE and the predictions will be validated.

The three components of the VDF model act as feeds to one another and their complementary approaches produce the most efficient analysis of the process, creating a structured and sustainable platform for robust process and innovation into the company with minimum cost involved: the VMEA outputs constitute the starting point for the DOE analysis, the DOE inputs and outputs are then used to construct and validate the FEA model and in the end the results from the DOE and FEA are disseminated to the original brainstorming group in a final VMEA using the findings of the experiments and analysis and through discussion (see Figure 2), in this way the VDF model allows the knowledge to come back full circle to the individuals. A comprehensive body of knowledge is created which can be used later on by the company for further development on their process.

Figure 2. VDF model: Component elements

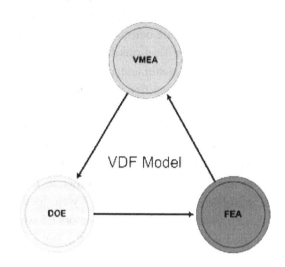

4. BENEFITS OF USING THE VDF MODEL: CASE STUDY

The engineering company in this case study is a medical company which presented itself with a product failure due to the unknown causes during the fabrication process.

Due to confidentiality issues, the company cannot be named, as well as their product and fabrication process. The names will be kept confidential but the procedure will be explained to you in detail. To investigate the process and the root cause of the product's failure the proposed approach was the VDF model. The VDF model's procedure was described to you in detail in Section 4 above.

The VMEA analysis was pursued first. The critical areas in the process, in terms of the effect of unwanted variation were identified through a brain storming session which involved a cross functional team with people from various areas in the company, i.e. Managerial team, Engineering department, R&D, Technical and Quality department. The VMEA technique is described in detail in Section 2.1.

Firstly the Key Product Characteristics KPCs for which variation can be a major company problem were identified. In this case study the KPC was defined by the team as: 'The Lack of Performance due to Product Failure before its prescribed time outlined in the Specifications due to the unknown causes during the manufacturing process'.

The team then identified the potential process elements of variation on the product characteristic, which is called the KPC casual breakdown and it involved separating of the KPC into a number of Sub-KPCs. The Sub-KPCs were broken down further into key process factors known as noise factors (NFs). Factor 1 to Factor 7 were identified as Sub-KPCs, Factors 1.2 to Factors 1.5 were identified as noise factors (NFs) for the Sub-KPC named Factor 1. Factor 2.1 was identified as NF corresponding to the Sub-KPC Factor 2 and so on.

The impact of the Sub-KPCs sensitivity on the KPC, the NFs sensitivity on the Sub-KPC and the NFs variation size was assessed by the cross-functional team and assigned a weight according to the criteria given in Tables 1, 2 and 3.

Based on the given weightings, the Variation Risk Priority Number (VRPN) is calculated which computes the effect of noise factors on KPC/Sub-KPCs and determines the portion of variation contributed from each Sub-KPC to the KPC. It indicates the sub-KPCs that need to be further investigated.

Using the equation, $VRPN_{NF} = S_1^2 S_2^2 V_1^2$, the VRPN was calculated for a specified noise factor. where, S_1 is the KPC sensitivity to the Sub-KPC (assessment criteria Table 1); S_2 is the Sub-KPC sensitivity to the NF (assessment criteria Table 2); V_1 is the variation size of the NF (assessment criteria Table 3).

Then a total variation risk priority number was calculated for each Sub-KPC by summing up all the VRPNs for the NFs influencing the corresponding Sub-KPC as it can be seen in Table 4 below (Note: the highest the total VRPN number - the greater the influence of that Sub-KPC on the product failure).

Table 1. Criteria for assessing sensitivity of KPC to action of Sub-KPC

Sensitivity of KPC to Sub-KPC	Weight
Very low sensitivity: Variation of Sub-KPC is transmitted to KPC to a very small degree.	1-2
Low sensitivity: Variation of Sub-KPC is transmitted to KPC to a small degree.	3-4
Moderate sensitivity: Variation of Sub-KPC is transmitted to KPC to a moderate degree.	5-6
High sensitivity: Variation of Sub-KPC is transmitted to KPC to a high degree.	7-8
Very high sensitivity: Variation of Sub-KPC is transmitted to KPC to a very high degree.	9-10

Table 2. Criteria for assessing sensitivity of Sub-KPC to NF

Sensitivity of Sub-KPC to NF	Weight
Very low sensitivity: Variation of NF is transmitted to Sub-KPC to a very small degree	1-2
Low sensitivity: Variation of NF is transmitted to Sub-KPC to a small degree.	3-4
Moderate sensitivity: Variation of NF is transmitted to Sub-KPC to a moderate degree.	5-6
High sensitivity: Variation of NF is transmitted to Sub-KPC to a high degree.	7-8
Very high sensitivity: Variation of NF is transmitted to Sub-KPC to a very high degree.	9-10

Table 3. NF variation assessment criteria

Variation size	Weight
Very low variation of NF: NF is considered to be almost constant in all possible conditions.	1-2
Low variation of NF: NF has small fluctuations or lies within a small interval in all possible conditions.	3-4
Moderate variation of NF: NF exhibits visible but moderate fluctuations in all conditions.	5-6
High variation of NF: NF exhibits visible and high fluctuations in all conditions.	7-8
Very high variation of NF: NF exhibits very high fluctuations in all conditions.	9-10

Table 4. VMEA table

Process:	Process ABC					Revision level	1.0
KPC	Sub-KPC	KPC sends to Sub-KPC	NF	Sub-KPC sends to NF	NF variation size	VRPN (NF)	VRPN (Sub KPC)
The lack of performance due to product failure before its prescribed time outlined in the specifications	Factor 1	6	Factor 1.1	6	6	46656	90040
		5	Factor 1.2	5	6	22500	
		4	Factor 1.3	6	6	20736	
		3	Factor 1.4	2	2	144	
		2	Factor 1.5	1	1	4	
	Factor 2	8	Factor 2.1	3	3	5184	5184
	Factor 3	8	Factor 3.1	3	3	5184	6482
		4	Factor 3.2	3	3	1296	
		1	Factor 3.3	1	1	1	
		1	Factor 3.4	1	1	1	
	Factor 4	1	Factor 4.1	1	1	1	1
	Factor 5	10	Factor 5.1	4	2	6400	
		8	Factor 5.2	4	2	4096	
		8	Factor 5.3	4	2	4096	
		8	Factor 5.4	4	2	4096	
		8	Factor 5.5	2	2	1024	
		2	Factor 5.6	2	2	64	
	Factor 6	5	Factor 6.1	2	2	400	400
	Factor 7	9	Factor 7.1	8	7	254016	1730396
		9	Factor 7.2	8	7	254016	
		10	Factor 7.3	8	6	230400	
		9	Factor 7.4	8	6	186624	
		7	Factor 7.5	8	7	153664	
		8	Factor 7.6	8	6	147456	
		8	Factor 7.7	8	6	147456	
		8	Factor 7.8	5	8	102400	
		9	Factor 7.9	7	5	99225	
		6	Factor 7.10	5	8	57600	
		5	Factor 7.11	5	8	40000	
		9	Factor 7.12	4	3	11664	
		9	Factor 7.13	4	3	11664	
		9	Factor 7.14	6	2	11664	
		9	Factor 7.15	3	3	6561	
		9	Factor 7.16	3	3	6561	
		9	Factor 7.17	2	3	6561	
		9	Factor 7.18	2	2	1296	
		9	Factor 7.19	2	2	1296	
		3	Factor 7.20	2	2	144	

continued on following page

Table 4. continued

| | | 2 | Factor 7.21 | 2 | 2 | 64 | |
| | | 2 | Factor 7.22 | 2 | 2 | 64 | |

Table 5. Extract from the VMEA: VRPN calculation Sub KPC Factor 1

Process:	Process ABC					Revision level	1.0
KPC	Sub-KPC	KPC sends to Sub-KPC	NF	Sub-KPC sends to NF	NF variation size	VRPN (NF)	VRPN (Sub KPC)
The lack of performance due to product failure before its prescribed time outlined in the specifications	Factor 1	6	Factor 1.1	6	6	46656	90040
		5	Factor 1.2	5	6	22500	
		4	Factor 1.3	6	6	20736	
		3	Factor 1.4	2	2	144	
		2	Factor 1.5	1	1	4	

Table 5 is an extract from the VMEA Table above and it illustrates the calculation of the VRPN number of the Sub-KPC named Factor 1:

$$VPRN_{1.1} = 6^2 \times 6^2 \times 6^2 = 46656$$

$$VPRN_{1.2} = 5^2 \times 5^2 \times 6^2 = 22500$$

$$VPRN_{1.3} = 4^2 \times 6^2 \times 6^2 = 20736$$

$$VPRN_{1.4} = 3^2 \times 2^2 \times 2^2 = 144$$

$$VPRN_{1.5} = 2^2 \times 1^2 \times 1^2 = 4$$

$$VPRN_{total} = \sum_1^5 VPRN_{1.x} = 46656 + 22500 + 20736 + 144 + 4 = 90040$$

From Table 4 it can be seen that the calculated highest VRPN total number (1730396) corresponded to the Sub-KPC Factor 7. It was concluded that the Factor 7 process characteristic, by its variation, has the greatest influence on the product failure.

Therefore a DOE was planned to be performed on the process stage named Factor 7 to determine the process optimum running parameters and the most suitable combination of these parameters which will ensure the product meeting the life outlined in the Specifications. As there were too many factors in this process stage which would make the DOE experiment very expensive, the most significant measurable factors had to be taken into consideration. Out of the 22 factors having an influence on the variation of the Factor 7 process stage only 7 factors were identified as being significant and measurable.

The statistical package Wisdom and a Placket-Burman Design with two centre points and one replicate were chosen for the DOE experiment (see Table 6).

Good R^2 values, over 80%, were obtained for all of the factors from the DOE experiment. The R^2 value indicates how much of the variation was attributed to that factor. Therefore, almost all experiments found at least 80% of the causes of variation.

The acquisition of the above R^2 values was attributed to good factor selection, experimental array design, factor level selection and measurement system.

An optimum process set up was found by the statistical package and a validation run took place.

Table 6. DOE design table

Plackett-Burman Design						
Factors: 7	Replicates: 1					
Base runs: 14	Total runs: 14					
Base blocks: 1	Total blocks: 1					
Center points 2						
Factor 7.4	Factor 7.12	Factor 7.13	Factor 7.15	Factor 7.14	Factor 7.3	Factor 7.19
1.45	7.7	2.7	8	50	26.2	40
1.45	6.3	2.7	8	40	23.2	30
1.45	7.7	3.3	8.3	50	23.2	40
1.45	7.7	3.3	8.3	40	23.2	30
1.45	6.3	2.7	8.3	50	26.2	30
1.45	6.3	3.3	8	40	26.2	40
2	7	3	8.15	45	24.7	35
2	7	3	8.15	45	24.7	35
2.55	7.7	2.7	8	40	23.2	40
2.55	6.3	2.7	8.3	50	23.2	40
2.55	7.7	2.7	8.3	40	26.2	30
2.55	6.3	3.3	8	50	23.2	30
2.55	6.3	3.3	8.3	40	26.2	40
2.55	7.7	3.3	8	50	26.2	30

The prediction equation provided by the Wisdom Package also showed that the product exhibited a non-uniform microstructure after fabrication and that was considered a possible cause for the product failure. This finding was confirmed by an SEM experimental microstructure analysis

Still more research had to be done to capture all of the process factors that have an impact on the product behaviour.

In the meantime, a FEA analysis was performed to simulate the product behaviour in order to get an understanding of the product parameters that were most likely to be influenced by the variation into the fabrication process and which could contribute to the failure.

The FEA Ansys multiphysics package was used to simulate the product behaviour – a thin metallic plate vibrating at a very high frequency. Different vibration mode shapes were found for different values of the Plate Natural Frequency (NF)

The results were compared with the literature models and experimental readings. Good correlation was found as shown in Figure 3.

Therefore the FEA model was declared valid and its predictions were taken into consideration.

The model predicted that:

- There is a direct relationship between the stiffness of the material and the natural frequency
- An inverse relationship exists between the plate dome diameter and natural frequency
- There is a direct relationship between the thickness of the material and natural frequency
- The presence of cracks in the plate contributes to a decrease in the natural frequency

Figure 3. FEA simulation: Comparison with literature models (top) and experimental readings (bottom)

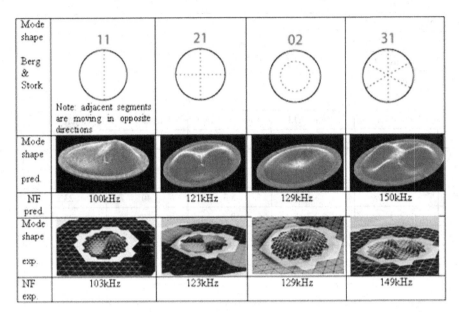

Figure 4. FEA simulation, process behaviour

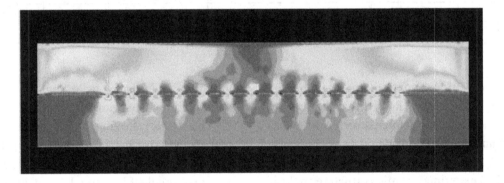

- A complete change in mode shape could occur if a material with a very low or very high elastic modulus is employed

The relationships above could not be identified by the VMEA and the DOE analysis described earlier.

After the product behaviour was modelled, the same FEA package simulated the process behaviour using the Ansys multiphysics Fluid option and the optimum setting parameters found through the DOE analysis.

A lot of variation during the fabrication process was predicted due to the flow behaviour Figure 4, factor that was not possible to be identified by the VMEA and the DOE analysis and that could contribute to the premature failure of the product and to low yield.

Based on the FEA results above, a new feature of the fabrication process was designed to ensure a more uniform flow distribution (see Figure 5). A more consistent product's microstructure and higher yield were expected.

The new process design feature along with the knowledge captured by modelling the product

Figure 5. FEA simulation, new process design feature

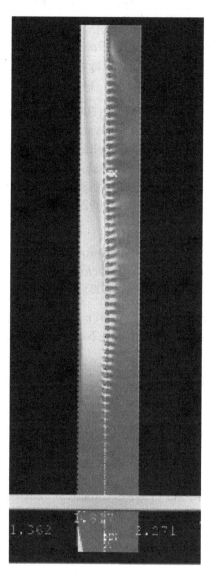

behaviour and the DOE analysis were implemented into the process.

A better product's microstructure uniformity was achieved, the product met the life expectancy outlined in the Specifications, the process became fully controllable and an increase in yield by 80% was recorded.

In the final stage of the VDF approach, the results from the DOE and FEA were disseminated to the original brainstorming group in a final VMEA using the findings of the experiments and analysis and through discussion, allowing the knowledge to come back full circle to the individuals.

5. CONCLUSION

The VDF multidisciplinary approach proved its efficiency and validity through the successful case study results described in the Section 4 above. It also created a comprehensive body of knowledge which can be used later on by the company for further development on their process. Rather than having to conduct additional experiments blindly the FEA can simulate the effects of changes on the process and on the product.

The VDF unified model enabled the company to switch from engineering chaos to a structured, sustainable process and considerably improved the company's competitiveness on the medical device market. Unlike process improvement the current method created a multidisciplinary practical framework which promoted innovation into the organization. The VDF triangulated approach used the company's tacit knowledge asset, converted it into explicit knowledge (through a Variation Mode and Effect Analysis) and it coupled it with engineering scientific tools (Design of Experiments and Finite Element Analysis) to successfully solve problems and significantly contribute to process innovation inside the company. Furthermore significant knowledge is generated through the model which can help to sustain and embed knowledge in the organisation.

REFERENCES

Adams (2009). Retrieved from http://www.nafems.org/downloads/public/nafems_-_the_role_of_simulation_in_product_development_-_whitepaper.pdf

Al-Momani, E., & Rawabdeh, I. (2008). An Application of Finite Element Method and Design of Experiments in the Optimisation of Sheet Metal Blanking Process. *Jordan Journal of Mechanical and Industrial Engineering*, *2*(1), 53–63.

Ansys (2010). Retrieved from www.Ansys.com

Antony, F. (2006). Taguchi or classical design of experiments: a perspective from a practitioner. *Sensor Review*, *26*(3), 227–230. doi:10.1108/02602280610675519

Antony, F., Tzu-Yao, C., & Ghosh, S. (2003). Training for design of experiments. *Work Study*, *52*(7), 341–346. doi:10.1108/00438020310502642

Chakhunashvili, A. Johansson, P., & Bergman, B. (2004). Variation Mode and Effect Analysis. In *Proceedings of the annual reliability and maintainability symposium*. Piscataway, NJ: IEEE Press.

Chen, P., & Koc, M. (2007). Simulation of springback variation in forming of advanced high strength steels. *Journal of Materials Processing Technology*, *190*, 189–198. doi:10.1016/j.jmatprotec.2007.02.046

Clements, R. B. (1995). *The Experimenter's Companion*. Milwaukee, WI: ASQC Quality Press. Coleman D.E. and Montgomery D.C., A systematic approach to planning for a design industrial experiment. *Technometrics*, *35*(1), 1–12.

Ellekjaer, M. R., & Bisgaard, S. (1998). The use of experimental design in the development of new products. *International Journal of Quality Science*, *3*(3), 254–274. doi:10.1108/13598539810229230

Franceschini, G., & Macchietto, S. (2008). Model-based design of experiments for parameter precision: State of the art. *Chemical Engineering Science*, *63*, 4846–4872. doi:10.1016/j.ces.2007.11.034

Hastings, J. K., Juds, M. A., & Brauer, J. R. (1985). *Accuracy and Economy of Finite Element Magnetic Analysis*. Paper presented at 33rd Annual National Relay Conference.

Johansson, P. (2006). Variation Mode and Effect Analysis: a practical tool for quality improvement. *Quality and Reliability Engineering international*.

Kackar, R. (1985). Off-Line Quality Control, Parameter Design, and the Taguchi Method. *Journal of Quality Technology*, *17*(4), 176–188.

Koc, M., & Arslan, M., A. (2003). Design and finite element analysis of innovative tooling elements (stress pins) to prolong die life and improve dimensional tolerances in precission forming processes. *Journal of Materials Processing Technology*, *142*, 773–785. doi:10.1016/S0924-0136(03)00647-2

Montgomery, D. C. (1999). Experimental design for product and process design and development. *The Statistician*, *48*(2), 159–177. doi:10.1111/1467-9884.00179

Montgomery, D. C. (2001). *Design and Analysis of Experiments* (5th ed.). New York: John Wiley & Sons.

(2005). *OECD* (3rd ed.). Guidelines for Collecting and Interpreting Innovation Data.

Phadke, S. M. (1989). *Quality Engineering Using Robust Design*. Englewood Cliffs, NJ: Prentice Hall.

Shinnar, R. (1978). Chemical reactormodeling—The desirable and the achievable. In Luss, D., & Weekman, V. Jr., (Eds.), *Chemical reaction engineering reviews, ACS symposium series* (*Vol. 72*, p. 1).

Taguchi, G. (1986). Introduction to Quality Engineering, Asian Productivity Organization (Distributed by American Supplier Institute Inc., Dearborn, MI).

Viles, E., Tanco, M., Unai Artecheb, I., & Sagartzazub, X. (2009). Applying Design of Experiments to a Lift Test Rig. *Quality and Reliability Engineering International*, *26*(2), 157–165.

Yamin, S., Mavondo, F., Gunasekaran, A., & Sarros, J. (1997). A study of competitive strategy, organisational innovation and organisational performance among Austrian manufacturing companies. *International Journal of Production Economics, 52*(1). doi:10.1016/S0925-5273(96)00104-1

Zumd, R. (1984). An Examination of 'Push–Pull' theory applied to process innovation in knowledge work. *Management Science, 6*.

Section 4
Marketing Innovation

Chapter 11
Knowledge Management in SMEs:
A Mixture of Innovation, Marketing and ICT: Analysis of Two Case Studies

Saïda Habhab-Rave
ISTEC, France

ABSTRACT

Global economy is transforming the sources of the competitive advantages of firms, especially for firms embedded in local manufacturing systems. Based on the theoretical contributions to knowledge management and industrial districts, this paper describes alternatives firm's strategies and upgrading options by exploring the relationships among innovation, marketing and network technologies. Starting from the analysis of the global competitiveness report and the European Innovation Scoreboard, this paper focuses on the case of firms specializing in "furniture and textile" industries (fashion, mode, home products) to outline a framework explaining the new competitive opportunities for SMEs. Through a qualitative analysis, this paper presents two case studies of French firms that promote successful strategies based on a coherent mix of R&D based innovation, experienced marketing and design, by leveraging on ICT.

INTRODUCTION

Global economy is transforming the sources of firms' competitive advantages and especially for firms embedded in local manufacturing systems. As in the case of France, small and medium enterprises (SMEs) localized in industrial districts and specializing in low or medium-tech industries have built their success on productive flexibility, quality certification and incremental innovation.

DOI: 10.4018/978-1-61520-829-6.ch011

Literature on industrial districts has provided evidence of the sources of competitiveness of local systems (Porter, 1990). As opposed to large multinational corporations, district SMEs emphasize an alternative model of economic organization (Porter, 1998), in which external economies support distributed production processes within the local networks of firms. From this perspective, on the one hand, scholars focused on the advantages offered by proximity in terms of technology spillovers and economic externalities (i.e., Krugman, 1991) (collective goods). On the other hand, studies on the knowledge economy (Arora et al., 1998) consider industrial districts as knowledge management systems, where the local context is able to sustain and facilitate creation, exploration and exploitation of knowledge, rooted into social practices (Nonaka and Takeuchi, 1995).

In the actual environment, SMEs are now facing competitive forces that impact on the sustainability of their strategies in the next years. First, manufacturing internationalization pushes firms operating in local supply chains to extend their networks beyond local boundaries to catch the opportunities of global value chains (Gereffi et al., 2005). While, on the one hand, a growing part of local productive activities may be transferred internationally with cost advantages, on the other hand, those paths may reduce a small firm's control over economic processes with negative influence on learning-by-doing innovation.

A second major challenge refers to the development and management of sales networks on a global basis, in a framework of stronger connections with the market. As many scholars have outlined, the interaction between customers and the firm through sales networks, as well as the web, is crucial in order to understand the market and anticipate demand trends. More important, building relationships with active customers (lead users and communities of customers) is part of a firm's innovation strategy, to obtain profitable knowledge for product and brand management (i.e. Sawhney, Prandelli, 2000). From this perspective, SMEs have to improve their competencies in interaction with customers at the international level, overcoming local, social and cultural boundaries as well as their traditional manufacturing approach. Such strategic options require more sophisticated marketing competencies, which are not usually available within SMEs operating in local productive systems.

Thirdly, the evolution of information and communication technologies (ICT) contributes to the debate about the transformation of the district firm model and the advantages of local embeddedness.

Global supply chains and international commercial outlets ask the firm to increase control on processes at the organizational level and within the firm's extended value system. From this perspective, network technologies can strengthen information sharing, process transparency and interaction among players in the value system (final customers included). Large multinational companies were able to fill the gap with the flexible SME model in the 1990s, thanks to network technologies. These tools supported distance cooperative work, also increasing process monitoring, knowledge management and communication within a renovated firm model (Scott Morton, 1991). In the present scenario, SMEs are asked to update their strategies benefiting from network technologies. SMEs have to overcome the local environment as the prime source of innovation – local tacit knowledge mainly manufacturing-oriented and informally managed - by developing new capabilities to manage extended networks including research centers, designers, and customers.

Based on the theoretical contributions to knowledge management and industrial districts, this paper describes alternative firm's strategies and upgrading options by exploring the relationships among innovation, marketing and networks technologies. The paper focuses on the case of firms specializing in "furniture" and "clothes and shoes" industries (fashion, mode clothes, and equipments, home products) to outline a framework explaining new competitive opportunities for SMEs. Our hypothesis is that the learning-by doing innovation model that has characterized district firms in the past is no longer sufficient to sustain their competitive advantage. The RD based innovation, efficiently adopted in large corporations, can offer new strategic options to face international competition. However, it cannot be implemented easily in all district SMEs. Moreover, innovation cannot be limited to scientific knowledge management, but can benefit also from customer input and experience related to technical features as well as associations and symbols the product incorporates (Krippendorf, Butter, 1984). From this perspective, the capabilities of SMEs to manage networks of relationships and to translate customers' needs into products may open new competitive opportunities, under the condition of a well-defined ICT strategy.

In the first section, this paper analyzes the district SMEs' model and its impact on French competitiveness, based on the contributions and approaches to innovation of the Global Competitiveness Report and the European Innovation Scoreboard. The second section focuses on the drivers of competitive advantage and strategies of firms in terms of science-driven and market-driven innovation, also considering the role of ICT. Through a qualitative analysis, in the third section, this paper discusses two case studies of French firms that promote successful strategies based on a coherent mix of R&D based innovation, experienced marketing and design, by leveraging on ICT.

1. SMES' COMPETITIVENESS IN THE INTERNATIONAL SCENARIO

Despite scholars' interests in the emerging countries economic model based on competitive local systems of SMEs, international analysis stresses the marginal role of France in the global arena as regards SME's capabilities to manage codified innovation. The Global Competitiveness Report of the World Economic Forum put France out of top 10, 16th in the international ranking. This study emphasizes the dynamics of growth and competitive factors of countries (with a focus on technology innovation, economic systems and institutional framework) through a comparative approach and identifies the competitive potentials of firms localized in each country. As opposed to success during the '80s and '90s, French economic system, and specifically SMEs specializing in "furniture" and "clothes and shoes" industries (home products, fashion, equipment…), seem to

lack competitiveness, due to low investments in R&D and patents. Even in the European Union Framework, the tool used to evaluate competitiveness and performances of nations and regions – the European Innovation Scoreboard- describes a quite negative picture of French firms, based on a few indicators on firm's expenditure on R&D, the numbers of patents registered, and investments in advanced services.

As stressed by analysts, the prevalence of small and medium firms in the economic system is the principal reason for French weakness in managing innovation successfully. According to the data of European researchers, the French SMEs are characterized by learning-by-doing innovation. Thus, SMEs are not able to translate new knowledge into patents and codified outputs. Moreover, SMEs do not approach (formal) innovation with strategic intent and, hence, do not invest a relevant amount of resources in R&D, training and new technologies. Despite this negative picture, those studies mention a few French SMEs' strengths related to organizational innovation and strategic control on technical activities such as product design.

From our perspective, the explanation of such contradictory results can be explained by considering a broader approach to innovation, which does not cover only R&D based activities. Instead, innovation can also be linked with the development of intangible features of the product and customer experience as the main drivers of value creation. From this standpoint, there are many different ways through which innovation can be deployed: the value created through innovation and its impact on competitiveness is rooted in the variety of forms and processes of the innovation each firm is able to design in its own original way. Following this approach, recently, the European Union has upgraded its framework of analysis by creating the Innovation Diversity Index, which is a measure oriented to capture the alternative forms of innovation characterizing countries and regions. Such an index is influenced not only by innovative firms that invest in R&D and patents, but also firms that have positive performances based on organizational innovation and innovation in marketing and design.

From this point of view, the competitive advantage of France becomes clearer. Despite their specialization in low or medium-tech industries, French SMEs and their leadership in the area of technological innovation (16th in the innovation pillar) are important attributes that have helped to boost the country's growth potential with regards to innovation management processes that develop and transform informal knowledge into value for the market. France's labour market flexibility continues to be ranked very low (131st) because of the rigidity of wage determination, high nonwage labour costs and the strict rules on firing and hiring. Another area of concern is macroeconomic stability (65th): the government budget deficit and the related public-sector debt ratio remain large, and the national savings rate, while growing, still remains low by international standards.

In this scenario, of near formalized procedures that lead to innovation –typically used in large corporations- one should also evaluate, on the one hand, the openness of the innovation cycle (innovation inputs beyond scientific knowledge and R&D) and, on the other hand, the results of innovation (outputs) and its use. Based on the Innovation Diversity Index of the EU, French SMEs show strong ability in the management of networks and collaboration. Traditional innovation drivers (R&D, skilled labor force and lifelong training) are weak in SMEs (ranked 21 out of 25). Instead, small firms are stronger in new knowledge generation and implementation.

According to the categories developed by the EU, French firms are classified as "modifier" in their innovation strategy because they capture and transform external knowledge into products through informal processes. Such approach is perceived either negatively, as it is not codified (and represents incremental innovation) or positively, as SMEs are flexible in knowledge management. Firms can reinvent products and processes in many

original ways thanks to their reactivity to market inputs and demand and by developing differentiation strategies. This capability is supported by specific professional practices focused on product specialization available at the territorial level. We explain those results by referring to the economic district model, where small businesses belonging to local networks of production organize knowledge management through distributed innovation systems, instead of a large organization.

During the fordism paradigm, the large firm model has been considered the best way and scientific knowledge (and R&D) was the main driver of innovation. In the open innovation paradigm, distributed networks sustain innovation (Chesbrough, 2003) and customers can contribute with their knowledge (Von Hippel, 2005). Moreover, customers are available to pay for products that offer not only new features (technological innovation), but also which offer them an experience and the tangible value linked to associations with sensemaking supported by brand strategy, design and social participation (Prahalad, Ramaswamy, 2003). From this perspective, innovation cannot be limited to technological innovation, but should also include aesthetic and intangible elements created through marketing strategy (communication) (Bettiol, Micelli, 2005). According to this perspective, French firms may improve their position in the international competitive arena because of their specific capacity to face innovation.

2. STRATEGIES, KNOWLEDGE MANAGEMENT AND ICT

In low or medium-tech industries such as textile or furniture, the competition is increasing and requires firms to choose either cost leadership in the mass market or niche differentiation, while positioning in the middle-market is becoming more and more unsustainable (Silverstein, Fiske, 2003). As opposed to high-tech industries, in which the role of patents and collaboration with research institutions is crucial for product innovation, in the mentioned industries innovation cannot usually be perceived as patent-driven. Instead, innovation is linked to creativity, a firm's ability to manage variety (innovation as organizational capability), and mix inputs coming from the market, designers and marketing (Schmitt, Simonson, 1997). From this perspective, an evaluation of a firm's innovation performance and its strategy should not be limited only to R&D activities and its outputs. Rather, from our perspective, in the open-innovation paradigm (Chesborugh, 2003) it should also consider the extension and characteristics of the networks that sustain a firm's innovation (as inputs of knowledge) as well as innovation outcomes. Marketing scholars emphasize the role of the intangible as part of the innovation process and a result of the value offered to customers. Products are not sold only because of their new features and functionalities, but also, and often, due to the meaning they transmit through their shapes (design) and the experience they give to customers (Pine and Gilmore, 1999).

Studies on innovation process have stressed the role of codified knowledge in knowledge management cycles, while the analysis of social dynamics (Brown and Duguid, 2000) has outlined the situated learning system and the relevance of experience as a driver to develop and share complex knowledge. According to this point of view, SMEs operating in local manufacturing systems benefit from physical proximity to customers, suppliers and relevant communities of practices embedded into local contexts. However, the global competitive scenario forces SMEs to upgrade and develop new strategies where innovation processes are sustainable on an international level. In a complex and global market, where leading customers are far from the firm and there are numbers of potential knowledge sources for a firm's innovation (Tapscott & Williams, 2007), the local economic and social system is inadequate to offer SMEs all the relevant and useful knowledge to compete. On the one hand, modularity

and codification can guarantee a more open and extended circulation and use of knowledge, across contexts. On the other hand, the more complex knowledge to manage, the higher the difficulties in codification and the need for promoting more sophisticated sharing strategies based on "pragmatic collaboration" (Helper, MacDuffie, Sabel, 2000) (people-to-people by face-to-face interaction or web-based).

Based on this distinction and the literature contributions on the topic, we can represent the sources of firms' competitive advantage (Grant, 1996; Kogut & Zander, 1996) by comparing the different role of knowledge developed by firms and the alternative strategies of knowledge management adopted. We identified alternative models (Table 1). On the one side, we can identify firms that compete by leveraging on R&D and scientific knowledge. Codification allows firms to enter into global networks of innovation and exchange knowledge on a broad scale with universities and research centers (regional innovation systems, Asheim Coenen, 2006). Local dynamics are supported by international connections, through which the firm is able to explore opportunities and exploit knowledge. On the other side, competitive advantage is based on customer relationship management built on experience. The firm is interested in selecting lead users and involving customer communities into the innovation processes, aiming at their sharing relevant knowledge (Von Hippel, 2005). It is a form of entrepreneurial innovation, with a strong role of marketing, as the firm's organization and processes are oriented to the market and to interact with external players (customers and lead users) to co-develop the product and the meaning related to it (Muniz & O'Guinn, 2001). Our hypothesis is that in the complex competitive scenario, firms may develop sustainable competitive advantage by mixing the strengths of the opposite models, where patents and R&D based innovation may be enhanced through marketing based innovation and vice versa.

Table 1. Competitive advantage and firm strategy

Technology	Organization	Marketing
R&D (patents)	Mix of different types of knowledge	Brand strategy design
Human Capital	Management of extended manufacturing and Commercial networks	communication and interaction with customers (lead Users, community)
Technological Innovation	Distributed innovation	
Science-based Innovation	Non technical – Marketing based innovation Entrepreneurial innovation	

Focus on research   *Focus on organizational Processes*   *Focus on communication*

- **Technology & R&D:** R&D within the traditional corporate value chain has been regarded as a function closely related to product development or manufacturing. However, there are indications that this is changing through the introduction of knowledge management and the fact that R&D is more often performed within networks across traditional corporate boundaries. Griffin and Hauser (1992a, 1992b) focus their research on the interaction of marketing and the R&D interface. Additionally, customers are rising as potential innovators, which should be included into the R&D process as early as possible. Based on the above discussion we suggest in this paper that a more market- and customer-oriented approach to R&D could be obtained by applying a radically different view of R&D activities. We propose a relationship marketing approach based on knowledge management.

- **Organization:** Attempts to define KM mirror and reflect the intangible, fragmented and multifaceted nature of knowledge itself. KM has thus been defined in a whole host of ways that vary in scope and focus. In terms of scope, the term has been used broadly to refer to "the capacity (or processes) within an organization to maintain or improve organizational performance based on experience and knowledge". In terms

of focus, definitions emphasize, variously: organizational processes and routines; performance improvement outcomes; processes for networking and collaboration; practices for harnessing, storing and distributing expertise; specific tools and methodologies such as data-mining and storage systems. These definitions suggest a variety of practices and organizational processes "a skillful blend of people, business processes and IT". However, research and practice in KM has been dominated by a focus on using Information Technologies (Its) to store, search and transfer knowledge within and across organizations. The logic behind this technocratic approach to managing knowledge is that by implementing various kinds of IT (databases, intranets) coupled with relevant search engines, knowledge can be captured and transferred from place to place. The assumption here is that if knowledge is transferred via technology, it can be used for innovation in other parts of the organization and so means that the chances of needlessly what has already been done elsewhere will be minimized. The notion that knowledge can be extracted from where it lies, codified and moved, using Its, en masse from one place to another has been challenged for failing to adequately address the problems of managing tacit knowledge.

Tacit knowledge by definition is, at best, difficult or, at worst, impossible to articulate, values and experiences that give tacit knowledge its meaning. Moreover, it is precisely because tacit knowledge is tacit that makes it difficult to for other organizations to imitate or import and therefore makes it an important organizational resource for securing competitive advantage. But the cognitive model of KM adopts a partial view of knowledge, assuming that knowledge lies with individuals and largely ignoring the socially constructed and socially mediated nature of knowledge. So, organizational knowledge is thus both widely distributed and embedded in collective systems of meaning and action. The aim is to discover the best practice in KM. with the development of the field of KM there has been a massive outpouring of articles and books dealing with these issues from a prescriptive standpoint. The problem is that many of these best practice prescription assume a direct, functional relationship between knowledge, marketing and innovation, despite evidence to suggest that this is over-simplistic.

- **Marketing:** The importance of marketing for business success is not new. Highly respected scholars like Peter Drucker and Theodore Levitt published their classic writings on these subjects as early as 1974 and 1975 respectively. Drucker (1974) argued that the only purpose for a business is to create a customer and that is achieved through marketing and innovation. Levitt (1975) argued that marketing is largely ignored because top management is wholly transfixed by the profit promises of technological R&D. Levitt also argued that product-orientedness in high technology works well where firms are pushed into new frontiers where they did not necessarily have to find markets but to fill them. Based on the above discussion we suggest in this paper that a more market-and customer-oriented approach to innovation could be obtained by applying different view of innovation activities.

In such competitive scenario, the analysis of a firms' strategy about innovation management cannot be developed without the study of their approach to information and communication technologies (ICT). On the one hand, these technologies support information management at a distance, by stressing the advantages of efficiency. On the other hand, thanks to multimedia tools, ICT allow the development of a virtual, interactive environment, where participants live the experience and are involved in social interaction on line. This environment offers opportunities related to knowledge creation and sharing, even in the case of complex knowledge (i.e. product innovation).

It is not our aim to describe the debate on the impacts of ICT on knowledge management in detail. We would outline the SMEs' approach to ICT investment and its influence on innovation. The international reorganization of manufacturing activities, as well as sales networks, push firms to adopt technological solutions that sustain coordination of activities in extended networks and organizations (Scott Morton, 1991). Moreover, the transformation in the consumption models described above asks firms to interact with customers in order to exploit the linkages with lead users and communities for innovation purposes. In both the strategic options of a science-based, competitive advantage (i.e. patents) and value-driven by "customer intimacy" and sensemaking (Treacy & Wiersema, 1997), network technologies become key factors in supporting competitiveness. In the open-innovation paradigm, ICT is in fact the valuable infrastructure for knowledge management aims, where knowledge is spread across contexts, organizations, and people (employees, customers).

Computers-mediated communication offers tremendous advantages of tracking and tracing dialogues and interactive relationships, as well as content development and sharing (digitalization, multimedia solutions, social software)(Von Hippel, 2005), even in complex situations. Hence, technologies can help firms overcome barriers and leverage the networks of connections characterizing the on-line environment (in primis among customers). Traditionally, ICT found primary application in large corporations, to solve coordination problems and support knowledge gathering and retrieval efficiently and effectively (Sproull, Kiesler, 1991). The role of technological infrastructure as a necessary condition for knowledge management did not match with the SME's competitive model. Especially within local systems, small firms have developed knowledge management mechanisms rooted in the social sphere of their contexts of embeddedness (Becattini & Rullani, 1996). Knowledge processes are usually not codified in formal procedures, but lie in the intensive communication and personal linkages within the organization, as well as outside the working domain, in the social fabric of places.

As shown in studies on ICT adoption in district firms (Chiarvesio et al., 2004), as opposed to large corporations, small and medium firms localized in local manufacturing systems have focused their attention on commodity-based technologies, such as email and web sites. Those technologies can be considered ready-to-use tools, which can be implemented in the organizational structure with low financial investments, as well as limited organizational changes. In industrial districts, SMEs'strategies in ICT investments have been characterized by:

- Selectivity in the technological solutions chosen;
- Incremental innovation processes based on learning-by-doing paths;
- A bottom-up process (no "master mind" at the local level).

During the new economy many scholars and analysts stress the potentialities of e-commerce for SMEs in terms of market enlargement and efficiency. Instead, research on ICT adoption by French district SMEs show rates of e-commerce, while the web is exploited as an interactive marketing tool. Firms do not consider the e-commerce solutions available adequate to manage "French" products for transactional purposes. Rather, firms stress the importance of web-based communication: the web becomes a medium to gather customers' feedback on products and support brand strategies.

More advanced technologies such as ERP (Enterprise Resource Planning) or groupware, tailored to large firms, are less diffused in small organizations. However, those solutions are considered crucial tools to increase process transparency and the control on distributed networks at the international level. In this perspective, the more extended the firm's value chain, the higher the need for upgrading the SMEs' strategy, where ICT sustains the firm's management beyond the local system. From our perspective, all the technological solutions available can be included in the framework of the knowledge management system, not limited to the organizational boundaries, but involving the players operating upstream (suppliers, designers, etc.) and downstream (sales agents, customers) in the product innovation as well as marketing activities.

3. COMPETITIVENESS IN FRENCH FIRMS

In this theoretical framework, we considered the strategies of firms specializing in low and medium-tech industries to explore the connection between R&D based and marketing-driven innovation processes, and the role of ICT in supporting those activities at the local and global level.

In order to explore the strategies of French firms in the scenario described above, we carried

Table 2. Case studies

Company	Innovation strategy	Main ICT investments
Case 1: Firm X 230 employees; Sport system: shoes and apparel	Mix of R&D (patent, relation with universities) and design	Explicit management processes
Case 2: Firm Y 40 employees; furniture	Collaboration with external international designers Patents	Internet to support online distributed product design processes

out a qualitative study on district SMEs to analyze knowledge management processes and firms' innovation approach (Yin, 1984). Based on a first selection of firms specializing in "agriculture and textile" sectors and located in north east of France, we interviewed entrepreneurs and the managers of R&D, design and information system departments. Interviews focused on a firm's history and strategy, organizational structure and innovation management models and ICT adopted. The two cases discussed in the paper are summarized in Table 2.

Case 1: "World Champions" in Mixing Design and Patents

One of the most famous companies of the sport system, firm X started in 1973 producing clothes and shoes, followed by shoes and other products for child and younger people. During the '80s the company internationalized its business, thanks to soccer shoes and international partnerships with France and foreign stars. Moreover, firm X is among the first district firms that invested in internationalization of productive activities beyond the local manufacturing system. As a leading firm in Parisian district, firm X invests in innovation to support its competitiveness by coupling R&D-based activities (scientific research on new materials, design, etc.) and the involvement of lead users. One of its latest products is, in fact, a mode of jeans, designed in collaboration with stars. Meanwhile, in a framework of global production and commercialization of products,

network technologies have been considered key elements in the management of extended supply and sales networks with the district as the core.

In the new millennium, the attention for the investment in product quality has been increased through an explicit strategy that emphasizes the role of design and innovation as drivers of competitiveness. In the global competitive scenario, firm X is oriented to reinforce its international presence. In this perspective, cost reduction as a key goal to face competition has to be coupled with continuous product innovation. The development of original ideas –jeans – is the starting point in X's strategy. The management of internal knowledge is relevant both in terms of R&D and design – more than 20 patents have been registered or are in the process of registration. The development of research relationships with French and international universities stresses X's interests in exploring knowledge paths beyond the local district networks to sustain the company internationally.

As an open network firm, firm X has invested in network technologies systematically, by gathering different technology solutions – from their web site, to e-commerce, ERP, groupware and supply-chain management applications. The technological infrastructure sustains information flows and communication between the company and its international networks of partners and markets, in a strategic and codified knowledge management approach. In fact, firm X is interested in acquiring and sharing informal knowledge available within the organization through ICT (digital archives, database for intellectual property rights management).

Case 2: From the District to International Design Network

Firm Y is a small firm specialized in the production of high quality furniture and wooden complementary house products. It was founded in 1989 and is located in Paris in France, in the furniture district. Firm Y has developed its strategy by focusing on product differentiation through design. Since 1998, firm Y has been obtaining economic success and growth thanks to the international recognition of a few of the firm's products – the Parisian, a famous French design award promoted by the French design association- designed by one of Y's founders. From these awards, this small firm started relevant collaboration with international designers. Due to investments in developing personal relationships and connections with designers all over the world (Japan, Europe, USA), the firm was able to increase the product range and international sales (60% of the turnover is export-based).

Y's strategy is oriented to exploiting internal strong competencies in wood transformation and production of "natural wood" furniture. The manufacturing process is organized in small-scale stocks, with particular emphasis on product customization as regards to the material used and finishing activities. Specifically, a mix of hand-made and technological innovation processes characterizes Y's made-to-order production. As opposed to the typical district approach in which local suppliers are key players in the firm's innovation processes, Y has developed innovation mainly internally, through R&D activities and patenting, and is able to increase the technological features of the products as well as their design characteristics. In the global competitive scenario, Y's approach to innovation is double: on the one hand, the focus is on design and aesthetical components of products as drivers of economic success; on the other hand, this small firm invests also in codified knowledge to protect their ideas against competitors (1 to 3 years in the average time of the product innovation cycle). Y does not invest in market research. Instead, the firm exploits international designers and entrepreneur's knowledge about customers and future trends, as an emerging process.

The entrepreneur is confident about the strategic role of ICT to sustain the firm's competitive advantage. Network technologies are key tools to support creativity processes, while the web infrastructure allows Y to interact with its commercial networks. Specifically, the firm's exploitation of multimedia applications and broadband opens new opportunities in product design and development at the international scale. In fact, the product "Riddled" – obtained through collaboration with the famous Steven Hollen's design studio based in new York and produced in 39 plus 30 items – has been made possible thanks to on line communication and document sharing at a distance between France and the USA. At the same time, Y has also created an open and distributed digital archive concerning all the documents and digital contents about products and innovation processes to use them for marketing and knowledge management purposes.

4. CONCLUSION

The two case studies are characterized by successful strategies based on a mix of R&D-driven innovation and marketing, where firms developed strong relationships with customers. Innovation processes blend codified knowledge and tacit knowledge based on specific practices related to consumption or professional profiles (exploitation as well as exploration in knowledge management, J.March, 1991). The firms interviewed are able to couple scientific innovation with product innovation based on design, the creation of experience and focus on communication. The local context in which these firms are embedded is important, but it is not the only source of knowledge in order to build their competitive advantage. On the one hand, these firms are interested in creating new connections with foreign research centers to promote projects for product, technology or material innovation. On the other hand, they develop relevant linkages with the loci of consumption and with key players for creativity, to nurture the innovation process interactively.

The local context offers competencies in the manufacturing domain and sustains the culture of the product. However, competitive SMEs are able to create and manage extended networks by operating in global value chains and approaching innovation through the entrepreneurial innovation model identified by the European Union. To be sustainable those strategies require information and communication technologies, where ERP systems support advanced process management and increase interoperability, while web-based solutions for communication and product (document) management are also implemented in supply chain and commercial sales networks.

Even if our study is still preliminary in its term, the case studies offer a few managerial implications in the way the innovation process is outlined as an open process. First, firms should understand the types of relationships characterizing the players involved in the innovation dynamics, in order to develop consistent mechanisms of management (codification vs. interaction). Second, there are interesting opportunities in combining different kinds and sources of knowledge, which have to be identified and coordinated. Today, firms are asked to develop capabilities in accessing external knowledge (exploration) through people-moving and electronic connections. In addition to this flexibility and openness they also have to pursue strategies and use tools (ICT) coherent with the relationships developed.

REFERENCES

Arora, A., Gambardella, A., & Rullani, E. (1997). Division of labour and the locus of inventive activity. *The Journal of Management and Governance*, *1*, 123–140. doi:10.1023/A:1009993430964

Asheim, B. T., & Coenen, L. (2006). Contextualizing regional innovation systems in a globalizing learning economy: on knowledge basis and institutional frameworks. *The Journal of Technology Transfer*, *31*, 163–173. doi:10.1007/s10961-005-5028-0

Brown, J. S., & Duguid, P. (2000). *The social Life of Information*. Cambridge: Harvard Business School Press.

Chesbrough, H. W. (2003). *Open Innovation*. Cambridge: Harvard Business School Press.

Davenport, T. H., & Prusak, L. (1998). *Working Knowledge. How organizations manage what they know*. Boston: Harvard Business School Press.

Drucker (1974). *Management Tasks, Responsibilities, Practices*. London: William Heinemann LdT.

Global Competitiveness Report. (n.d.). Retrieved from www.weforum.org/pdt/GCR08/GCR08.pdf

Grant, R. M. (1996). Toward a knowledge-based theory of the firm. *Strategic Management Journal*, *17*, 109–122.

Griffin & Hausser. (1992a). Patterns of communication among marketing, engineering and manufacturing – A comparison between two new product teams. *Management Science*, *38*(3), 360–373. doi:10.1287/mnsc.38.3.360

Griffin & Hausser. (1992b). *The Marketing and R&D Interface*. Massachusetts Institute of Technology Marketing Group.

Helper, S., MacDuffie, J. P., & Sabel, C. M. (2000). Pragmatic collaboration: advancing knowledge while controlling opportunism. *Industrial and Corporate Change, 9*(3), 443–488. doi:10.1093/icc/9.3.443

Kogut, B., & Zander, U. (1996). What firms do? Coordination, Identity, and Learning. *Organization Science, 7*(5), 502–518. doi:10.1287/orsc.7.5.502

Krippendorf, K., & Butter, R. (1984). Product semantics: exploring the symbolic qualities of form in innovation. *The Journal of the Industrial Designers Society of America, 3*, 4–9.

Levitt (1975). Marketing Myopia. *Harvard Business Review*, September-October, 12.

March, J. G. (1991). Exploration and exploitation in organizational learning. *Organization Science, 2*(1), 71–86. doi:10.1287/orsc.2.1.71

Nonaka, I. (1994). A dynamic theory of organizational knowledge creation. *Organization Science, 5*(1), 14–37. doi:10.1287/orsc.5.1.14

Pine, B. J., & Gilmore, J. (1999). *The experience economy*. Boston: Harvard Business school Press.

Porter, M. E. (1990). *Competitive advantage*. New York: The Free Press.

Prahalad, C. K., & Ramaswamy, V. (2003). The new frontier of experience innovation. *MIT Sloan Management Review, 44*, 12–18.

Sawhney, M., & Prandelli, E. (2000). Communities of creation: managing distributed innovation in turbulent markets. *California Management Review, 42*, 24–54.

Schmitt, B., & Simonson, A. (1997). *Marketing aesthetics. The strategic management of brands, identity and management*. New York: The Free Press.

Scott Morton, M. S. (Ed.). (1991). *The Corporation of the 1990s. Information technology and organizational transformation*. New York: Oxford University Press.

Silverstein, J. M., & Fiske, N. (2003). *Trading up. The new American Luxury*. New York: Portfolio.

Sproull, L., & Kiesler, S. (1991). *Connections. New ways of working in the networked organization*. Cambridge: MIT Press.

Tapscott, D., & Williams, A. D. (2007). *Wikinomics. How mass collaboration changes everything*. New York: Penguin Books.

Treacy, M., & Wiersema, F. (1997). *The discipline of market leaders: choose your customers, narrow your focus, dominate your market*. New York: Perseus Books Group.

Von Hippel, E. (2005). *Democratizing Innovation*. Boston: MIT Press.

Yin, R. K. (1994). *Case study research: design and methods*. Thousand Oaks, CA: Sage.

Chapter 12
Acquiring and Applying Market Knowledge for Large Software Purchases:
Products, Personas, and Programs

Steve Russell
Siemens Corporate Research, USA

Candemir Toklu
Siemens Corporate Research, USA

ABSTRACT

Persona profiles of the top managers in a corporation help marketers to position and promote large software products. Sales calls are more targeted and cordial, aligned with the needs and communication styles of the prospects. The methods applied in the archetype discovery are complemented by knowledge of corporate structures and influence networks. When the key customer concerns and constraints are clarified, the software vendor can craft informational programs, sales plans, and product improvement projects to outperform their competition. The added persona-model knowledge complements the vendor's existing knowledge of their software products, helping to build compelling marketing programs and to significantly improve software sales.

INTRODUCTION

This chapter details the methods for deriving and using buyer personas, and the value of these personas in the marketing and sales of a large software product. Background is offered on personas in general, including clarifications of terminology and some background on persona use in other areas. The major thrust of the material relates to

knowledge. It is emphasized that sellers should know their buyers better- that this knowledge is central to effective marketing and sales efforts. Key steps in persona determination are discussed, as well as methods for using them in a measurable manner. Sketches of a few typical corporate buyer personas are outlined to illustrate their nature at a high level. Finally, potential pitfalls are suggested and best practices are offered.

The sale of a large product to an enterprise typically involves an extended process with

DOI: 10.4018/978-1-61520-829-6.ch012

many stakeholders. Software products for office productivity, manufacturing control, or financial discipline are as central to a business as its buildings and talent pools. The very organization of a modern company is enabled and directed by its computer tools. So, when new applications are determined to be important, the corporation has a great deal to consider. In addition to the desired improvements in efficiency and profitability, there must be a clear recognition of the disruptions and adjustments that will need to occur, and the duties of the various stakeholder areas and role-players.

Major decisions in companies are made by one or more of the company officials using methods that have varying degrees of structured, carefully balanced, and emotion-free consideration. In each situation, a person plays a role for their department or area of responsibility and expertise. Among all of the people involved in the deliberations is a subset who are typically most important. These persons are the ones that a vendor's sales force contacts, and those to whom marketing efforts are directly or indirectly targeted. The characteristics of these key individuals include the set of ranked objectives for their departments and the company at large. Yet just as influential in certain cases, are the predispositions of the individual to certain software characteristics like the user interface or brand name or salesperson's trustworthiness. The individual frameworks for decisions and their influential motives are precisely the sorts of understanding that the persona process addresses.

Knowledge is the key in persona value. To use an archetypical extract of a purchase actor, the extract must first be accurate and succinct. Knowledge acquisition is therefore focused on the key players, and for these persons it is further focused on their most useful attributes with respect to the purchase decision. Knowledge Management (KM) here includes the acquisition, as well as the representation of the acquired knowledge, and the location and use of the representation-encoded knowledge in subsequent business activities. KM should also include the measurement of

how useful the information is in producing more desired results like trouble-free sales. First, the seller must know the customer. The seller combines this knowledge with appropriate portions of knowledge regarding their software product. This knowledge combination is used to build a better appeal to the customer, and then to track the results of the modified appeal. Knowledge on the resulting sales success is then useful in validating the accuracy and utility of the persona extraction.

For some, an effective persona lends itself to an honestly deeper appreciation of the users of a product, and even identification with their lifestyles and temperaments. In industries such as resorts, empathizing with the guests is a necessary service offering. Many enterprises claim in their advertising to care for their customers, to feel their pain and happiness. Such allospection, or other-oriented viewpoint adoption, supposedly has the seller actually experiencing the effectiveness and even frustrations of the purchaser of their goods. For such a level of intimacy, a compelling persona is the ideal vehicle for vicariously experiencing the product and the sales cycle as well. Most of this is earned by the oldest of sales effectiveness tools- simply listening. Listening to the customer and taking their concerns to heart.

In the following material, the knowledge management challenge is addressed for best practices in:

- Determining persona targets by organizational understanding
  ◦ Knowledge Management
- Developing interview and survey instruments for honing attributes
  ◦ Marketing and its goals
- Applying the driving themes to contact plans, printed promotions, conference pitches, and personal appeals
- Feeding back archetypical concerns to product development teams
- Measure the utility of the added knowledge elements

After a brief introduction, there will be a deeper treatment of each of these topics. There will be a discussion of how to assess the current knowledge, the gaps, and the steps to take to do better. Issues of corporate change and evolving software practices will impact the adoption of new information technology components. There will be areas of resistance, roadblocks, and even politics. These psychological and sociological matters are becoming more objects of organized study, with additional knowledge shedding light on how new products are selected. Economic issues will also be treated, trying to understand the perceptions of departmental budgets and overall corporate costs as seen through the eyes of central figures in the company. These and other factors are explained in light of their importance in properly considering key characteristics of decision makers. That is, the persona derivation process is based on a much more disciplined consideration of the holistic business and personal environment of the actors studied here.

Forms and diagrams will flesh out the discussion, with specific examples given to illustrate the types of companies and products. The roles in certain industries will be outlined, such as a CIO, along with their typical duties and concerns. Extracting their outlooks and their ways of getting information will be laid out step by step, showing the aggregation and analysis that result in useful persona archetypes. There can be difficulties in gaining enough examples for representative personas, so there will be some discussion of how small samples can still give a subset of the value desired.

PERSONAS

Personas have been used in many fields such as marketing with provable benefit. The understanding of a typical customer is of great value in designing and promoting a consumer product, for instance. A single example and a brief story are powerful in illustrating a product's use and value. It is not unimportant that people can tend to be followers. Seeing an identifiable buyer to emulate, there are peer pressures as well as other pressures which weigh in to convince a prospect of the desirability of the offering. When automobile makers want to advertise their products on television, for example, they often choose an attractive model or typical mother figure in a particular familiar storyline. The "power of the individual" helps in sales, in appeals for charity contributions, and in warnings about drug use. It is not surprising that this same power can be harnessed to help in understanding consumers and buyers of large products such as software suites.

So what is a persona in the business-to-business (B2B) sales situation? The buyer persona is a person who represents the set of people who are charged by their firm with authorizing the product being purchased. This is a portrayal of an actual person, not a cardboard character or stick figure stand-in. It is not one of the actual persons in any of the companies being considered, but is still a typical person who would fit right in doing the work of those in the same corporate role or organizational position. Just as in a TV advertisement for a car, it is a person who meaningfully represents buyers in ways that are helpful; in this case helpful for marketers to focus on improved sales. In order to be useful, the person chosen as a concrete example must be on average like the class represented, yet also having characteristics that guide marketers in effectively dealing with others in that group.

This is not a small point. The persona is an artifact. It is a business artifact with a purpose and an audience. The purpose of producing the artifact is to gain a better business result. The audience who uses or "consumes" this product in the present case is the marketing staff or sales force. Just as with the television audience, the persona using the product may not always look exactly like an "averaged them" but may in fact, look better and happier; more like the consumers would want to see themselves. So with the buyer persona – there can be, in addition to authenticity, an element of persona-idealism to show to the marketers and salespersons so that they treat the eventual prospect in a more sales-friendly manner. It might be useful in some cases to build a persona that is slightly more Ivy League or golf-loving, or fancy-car-driving, or commanding. This could promote a seller's predisposition for respect, a springboard for common interest topics that are actually popular for that role, and for aligning the seller's product with a cachet of friendlier conversation. So, adding a small bit of this seasoning to the case-averaged features can in fact have results even more in line with the business investment in its construction. A side effect of seeing customers in a brighter light can also be a greater empathy with their concerns and interests among the vendor company staff at all levels.

In product design, personas have been used to give developers a consistent knowledge set as guidance points or anchors in navigating the tradeoffs in design and delivery. With more than one group of users, several persona representatives are constructed to assist in conversations and test cases. As noted further below, a key utility of a realistic persona in weaving a compelling story of an actual use case of product features or shortcomings to guide and prioritize development and product improvement. Some of the features captured for the persona are demographic – related to population factors like age or home city. Other features are psychographic – like whether the particular prospect is fun-loving or perhaps risk averse. The humanity in the persona depends on both types of factors, and both are influential in guiding a developer's empathy and product feature focus.

A persona can also be of use in a fluid situation like project life cycles where duties and concerns change over time. Here, the persona adopts a series of context-appropriate behaviors through the course of using, say, a project management tool where the persona may be visualized acting in the scenes of a movie. As situations evolve, so does the persona, and so does the marketer's plans for influencing that person. This ability to anticipate events and to adjust reactions is not only useful in preparing for problems and unexpected opportunities, it can be key in business survival.

Personas are developed using disciplined methods that avoid preconceptions. A common problem with office software or video recorder interfaces is assuming that the user already knows how complex product controls work. In this case, the too-common alternative to user awareness is the developer myopia of seeing the user in the developer's terms, either like themselves, or inaccurately with regard to the user's real pattern of skills and goals. So, a neutral assumption-free method is best for observing and interviewing potential purchasers. Where the behavior cannot be watched from a convenient vantage point, methods like surveys or questionnaires must be applied. When the information on perceptions and motives are "straight from the horse's mouth", the persona for a product buyer or purchase-influencer is more likely to be accurate. Therefore, a major challenge in gaining the knowledge face-to-face is in constructing an appropriate interview form and in executing the interview in a professional manner. The specific items for querying in the area of large software purchases will be explored further below. However, the skillset of a good interviewer are a general matter.

Not everyone is good at a question-and-answer format where information is being extracted for a specific purpose. This is all the more so in a sensitive business situation with powerful individuals at the highest levels in a corporation. There are subtle techniques for gaining trust and good humor that strongly affects an interview and its gleanings. Knowledge acquisition efforts for example can use protocol-centered techniques to hone in on methods of reasoning and decision making. Even newspaper reporters and detectives are trained in methodologies which are most effective and fair. So the interviewing party should be suitable, and the interview setting and any forms need to accommodate any possible shortcomings in that person's interview management skills. The interview has a proper timeframe, cadence, and degree of probing that are important for a given interview and across a hopefully consistent series of similar persona interviews. Facility with spoken language and even the dialect of the interviewed party can be of importance. Even the apparel, posture, and timeliness of the parties in an interview setting can influence the content and quality of the knowledge gained.

Applications of the personas built from interviews with senior company officials will be studied below. This will include the changes in collateral marketing materials to the conduct of phone calls and sales presentations. This "consumption" of the persona "product" is of course where the investment in time and thought pays off. With this eventual usage of the persona clearly in mind, the discussion can return to the creation of these artifacts.

In user-centric applications, a persona typically includes the fictional person's name, a flattering photograph, education, family status, job title, goals, and some social factors like their favorite sports team. In marketing situations, personas of those with impact on purchases help to clarify the attributes of each role-actor that drive choices – like their previous experiences, peer groups, task headaches, staff concerns, and long term goals. The alternative to obtaining such clear personas is often just "making stuff up". Dialogues with good personas prior to completing brochures or making office calls can train the market and sales staff in a set of possible conversations and questions – much like a sports team repeatedly trains for a wide variety of actions of the other team before a game. Then, the seller's message and brand value can be more likely to be aligned with the thinking of the buyer, and will be better accepted.

Personas from the Perspective of Buying Modalities

The critical modes of information-usage and decision-making which a prospective customer brings to a software purchase decision activity can be examined through three different filters: (i) Topology, (ii) Psychographics, and (iii) Demographics.

1. **Topology** is the background that defines the characteristics of the business and differentiates it from other types of business in the same market segment. The differences among these companies determine much of their competitive landscape. The competitors for a vendor are in some cases clear and explicit and in others they are perhaps less clear, less direct, and implicit. In some cases, topology variables are seen as demographic attributes, as described below, but this does not affect the persona development process for the purposes here.

2. **Psychographics** are what a person is interested in and what they actually do. The combination of these factors is used to develop predictive behavior models. Several fields of specialty are involved here, including traditional psychology, studies of personality, and consumer psychology. Many aspects of behavior and motivation are of potential interest, making this a possibly quite broad field of inquiry

    Most marketers already use psychographics to characterize their markets. The intangible personal factors involved help these marketers in determining when a prospective customer is the right "fit" for their software. The personal characteristics which combine to motivate purchases are every bit as important as the facts on relative product merits. With respect to the buyers of large software products, personal factors of importance in the business environment can arise from attitudes related to the firm itself and its internal organization of peers, bosses, subordinates, and priorities. Questions that can be asked to determine these psychographics of the target market include:

- What are the vision and values of the organization? What are the character and ethos of the firm? How committed is the firm to their people, customers, or the environment?

- What is the firm's reputation in the industry? Are they innovators or low cost providers? Are they early adopters of technology or laggards?

- What are the firm's management priorities? What is most important to them: increasing sales, cutting costs, or improving operational efficiency? What are their critical success factors?

- How does the interviewee evaluate her or his perceptions of their industry, product, or service offering? Are these perceptions positive, negative, or neutral?

- How does the interviewee define their personal management style? Are they top-down driven? Or are they more inclined to encourage individual and team contribution?

3. **Demographics** are population characteristics such as the geographic region of a person, or the region in which a product is sold to customers. Other population attributes include ethnic types, economic status, and age. Many of the demographic-like indicators can be generalized to industries that have employees or customers whose categories can be described with demographic-type group variables. Some of these market characteristics relate to constraints on the products they want or which they can buy, which can help the vendor to more accurately define their universe of buyers.

As members of a population group, officials in a customer company may inherit population attributes of their region. Or, for a given company, their customers may fall into categories that impact the thinking and decision-making of a certain company role. If, for instance, a company's primary customers are over 60 years old, the decision patterns of the brand manager in the company may be more attuned with the lifestyles of this demographic segment. In this case, marketing a vendor's software package to that brand manager could take into account their alignment with this older customer base.

There are many ways to derive useful demographics for a customer persona. For the purposes in this article, the definition of demographics for a firm can be extended beyond human attributes like age to enterprise-specific attributes like industry type and the general nature of their sales and operations.

A recommended practice is to use the following sorts of questions for this purpose:

- What industry are they in? Are they manufacturing firms or service businesses? Are they involved with medical devices, with software or with power generation equipment?

- How big are they? What are their revenues? How many employees do they have? Are they a regional firm or are they global?

- What are their distribution channels? Do they use direct sales? Are there formal distribution organizations? Do they utilize any online sales or printed catalogs?

- What type of technology base do they utilize? What are their existing computer systems? What general sorts of manufacturing processes are employed, such as batch or continuous runs?

- Who are their customers? Do they sell in the business-to-business marketplace, business-to-consumer, or business-to-channel?
- What is their development stage? Are they in a growth mode, or is their business declining? Are they a mature organization? Are they flexible with respect to technological innovation?

Once some information is collected on the types of industry, the persona can be partially expressed using this data. For instance, a Research and Development (R&D) manager might be in a fast-growth higher-risk firm, with early-adopter sales worldwide for their new product, which makes the R&D leader necessarily more agile, informed, and on top of software product trends.

Determining Persona Targets by Organizational Understanding

For selecting representatives of specific roles in a corporation, the organizational structure is a good starting point. The organization chart of reporting and functional authorities shows who should be concerned with a certain software purchase and who may need to approve buying the product, see Figure 1. In some industries, there is a Research Department that looks at novel ways of conducting business. Normally, the Information Technology (IT) Department and its head (the Chief Information Officer or CIO) must approve of new software tools. For larger ticket items, higher levels are involved, even in some cases requiring approval by the Chief Executive Officer (CEO).

The valuation of a particular purchase such as a large software suite will depend on the needs and work of the corporation. Since business conditions often vary, the software vendor must try to stay abreast of these changes for each company it targets. The personal set of concerns and desires of the key roles can change along with business cycles, so the personas can somewhat of a moving target. For more stable industries

such as those involved with consumer goods or food products, the personas and their roles in recommendation and approval may be longer lived. Here, and where personas are kept up to date, the valuation and necessity of the software products will be known more clearly along with the roles and outlooks of the stakeholders. For necessary or strategically important software like Enterprise Resource Planning (ERP) or Human Resources (HR) products, the strategic and operational significance will likely command serious attention at most organizational levels. In any event, the dynamic ebb and flow of communications and negotiations within a large internal approval network can be daunting. Personas with sustained responsibility and product commitment are all the more worth knowing here, to keep an approval cycle moving steadily along to completion. When a key player champions a package in the face of opposition and delay, such cooperation is invaluable. Using persona-acquired strategies to influence such cooperation can be the difference between the selection of a product or its competitors product, or of just riding along with the status quo. If handled well, knowledge on more of the types of concerns internally can lessen not only the initial obstacles but can also smooth the way to sustained trouble-free adoption and additional sales.

Traditional modeling approaches for products include use cases and scenarios, sometimes illustrated as an afterthought by short narratives or "elevator speeches" to quickly convey the product value. These formal methods can be complemented by a richer form of storytelling based in personas. When done as laid out in this presentation, the personas fuel compelling narrations of product application, with real actors and consequences. Such stories indeed tap into deep roots in human culture and our oldest modes of understanding and passing along knowledge. With apt stories as a guide in such cases, more general scenarios and abstract use case paths can be better built and maintained. Although software en-

Figure 1. Organizational chart

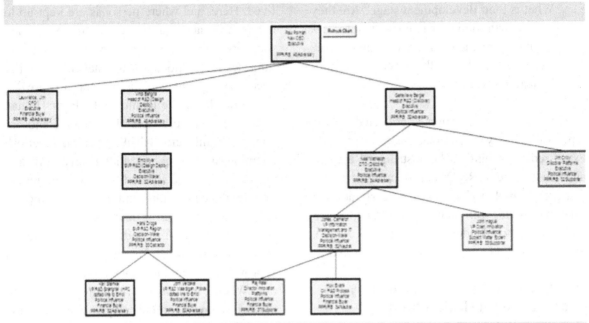

gineers can be enamored of detailed use case documentation, the more down-to-earth storytelling, based in familiar personas, can often be more acceptable and useful by marketing and sales staff. The paradoxical depth of intimacy and holism in simple stories has been powerfully employed by great leaders like Abraham Lincoln, so perhaps it is not so surprising that this approach can be of value in software sales too.

Knowledge, and Knowledge Management

In a book on Knowledge Management (KM), a brief overview is worthwhile. Some terms, like "intelligence" have multiple meanings, like "military intelligence" and "Einstein intelligence". Knowledge, too, means differing things like "know-how" for sports and "know-about" for historical biographies. Agile task performance and rapid fact retrieval and even facility with arithmetic are termed "knowledge". As a state of awareness or belief, knowing something to be true can seem to be a permanent fact – yet children often know things that later turn out to be otherwise. A diversion into the philosophy and a set of revealing example cases could be helpful but perhaps distracting for the purposes of this chapter. It will have to be sufficient to assume common sense with respect to the meaning of knowledge for business use, personas, and product sales.

Marketers in some manner know their customers, customers know the product, and these types of knowledge can be better or worse, and more or less complete. The objective of the persona development as laid out here is to improve the depth and quality in a managed fashion. Acquiring, storing, retaining, and applying good customer and product knowledge is central to a marketer. Areas within or related to KM such as Enterprise Architecture Planning (EAP) and Enterprise Content Management (ECM) support this discipline. Enterprises

Figure 2. In a Consumer packaged goods (CPG) company, several key players can be involved in authorizing or recommending the purchase of a large software product such as a product lifecycle management (PLM) platform

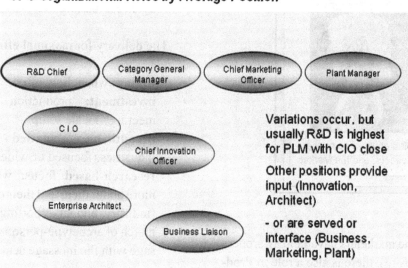

CPG Organizational Roles by Average Position

R&D Chief

Category General Manager

Chief Marketing Officer

Plant Manager

C I O

Chief Innovation Officer

Enterprise Architect

Business Liaison

Variations occur, but usually R&D is highest for PLM with CIO close

Other positions provide input (Innovation, Architect)

- or are served or interface (Business, Marketing, Plant)

can apply the stored and learned knowledge in formalized workflows by using Business Process Management (BPM) techniques. Where appropriate, portals and social media speed up access to the knowledge and strengthen the collaboration needed for competing in selling modern software packages to large markets.

With respect to high-level buyer personas, the KM needed is modest at present. The interviews and other observations need to be tagged and stored. The location and retrieval of the relatively few documents produced is not overly complex. The hardest part is using the knowledge in the head of the marketer or sales representative in the most effective combinations with good persona profiles. Yet the very nature of the more personal portraits here lends itself to powerful integration with the years of hard-earned experience in the interpersonal aspects of a sale in a given marketplace. A persona with realistic goals and frustrations is exactly the sort of thing that is familiar and useful in preparing for marketing contracts and sales sessions. As circumstances change with

a business and its leaders, outdated knowledge regarding persona attributes is forgotten and is replaced with more current information. So, the KM is as much the management and sharing of fluid human experiential knowledge as it is the added ingredients and seasonings provided by the persona studies.

Marketing for a Large Software Product

A company's Marketing department is responsible for understanding the marketplace for the products. The marketers are assigned to influence purchases by knowing a great deal about prospective customers and the competition. The marketing staff is supposed to ensure that the brand awareness of the product is positive, and that potential customers are continuously informed regarding the versions and advantages of their offerings, see Figure 3. Effective marketers make sales efforts more productive.

Figure 3. Marketing must address the products as well as the market

Marketing – Facing the
Products, and the Market

But, since the marketers have field awareness of consumer desires, there is also a role in Product Development. Marketers, and in some cases the (sometimes more biased) sales force, convey customer base expectations, desires, pain, and purchase promoters. The developers can then stay on top of their already delivered versions and can lead the market in delivering desirable new functionality. As noted above, personas can play a big role in clarifying the market needs and can incent and direct the development staff in a positive way.

The marketing staff develops materials with which the market is contacted. These advertisements, meetings, and printed collateral are co-ordinated to present a unified and synchronized message through several modalities. In each form, the persona is of assistance, focusing the market preparation on the most likely motivational approaches.

Examples of the methods for delivering a message are:

- in person (face to face, verbal, persuasive)
- at a meeting (conference, trade session)
- in publications (papers, trade publications, magazines, articles and advertisements)

- through media (television, radio - interviews, discussions, advertisements)
- online (Internet advertising, website, blogs)
- by direct mailing

The delivery for maximal effect includes:

- **timing:** when, how often
- **investment:** production level, length, meeting / locale setup
- **breadth:** areas contacted - geographically, industries (focused or widespread)
- **research-based focus:** who is targeted, more about them and their current situation (industry, budget, reporting chain)
- match of archetype-persona receiving message with the message sent

The best case scenario is when game-changing products, pricing, or strategies give the delivery, show the foresight, or convey a message that stuns the market. Seizing the high ground in this way is sometimes lucky, but more often results from hard work and well-applied knowledge. Included in the factors that a persona enabled posture can enhance are innovation, operational flexibility, and appropriateness grounded in customer intimacy. If the synchrony with the large software product customers is superior for one vendor, its competitors will likely suffer. The alignment here would be with the firm's current installations, products and gaps, quality and compliance, and ability to respond rapidly, as seen through the eyes of the personas in control.

Developing Interview and Survey Instruments for Honing Persona Attributes

The tools for developing personas vary from statistical analyses to personal discussions. In the case of large product sales, the information on decider roles will be skimpy. This is because there are few top-level decision makers in a corporation, and a limited number of companies which are targeted by the vendor of a large software product. So, not enough data will be around to average the picture of any given key player role such as a CIO. Surveys are done on such individuals, but they are not normally focused in a manner conducive to persona construction. These approaches, as well as social media, small studies, and the like, can give a very rough vision of what a key player is like. This is an inadequate approach for the gains desired here which can be achieved through better persona views.

So, an interview method is a better approach. Questions can be asked of a series of CIOs, Marketing managers, and so forth who are key players in a prospect company or in similar current customer company. The questioning can be done in person or over the telephone. The questions can be free-form or highly structured. The choice among these methods is a key point of this article. It is not reasonable to assume that a high level official would take the time and effort to write out responses in a fill-in form. So, the interviewer will need to actually ask the questions verbally and take notes and perhaps record the session for transcription and clarifications. The persona-building effort requires taking steps to make up an interview form, conduct the interviews, and summarize the results into a useful persona with its key attributes.

An interview form for the purposes here should be in of one of two formats. The very highest level company officials such as the CEO will be very few in number, very hard to schedule, and will have very little time and attention for such an interview. A quite brief format will be needed here, with more flexibility in the interview process if the interviewee strays off topic. The intent will be to gain rough outlines of the most central drivers and concerns, while listening for nuggets of insight into the mind of this highest level individual. Summarizing these sorts of interviews requires insight and familiarity with the market and its key

figures. These interviews can provide a veritable fountain of information regarding the business value of the vendor's product or service. They are certainly the best resource vendors can use to clarify the value proposition of their products.

For job positions which have more representatives and time, such as say a Business Liaison, a more formal interview sheet can be constructed. In this case, there can be more interviewed parties in various target firms for averaging. The form will then focus on features that can be common, and can focus on key parts of a persona such as attitudes toward product usability. It is important to note that partially done work here is very untrustworthy. This is like making a cake with only a subset of the ingredients and time; resulting in an unpalatable production. Unsupported similarities from just two or three interviewees cannot be relied upon as trustworthy representations of behaviors and goals for that role. Normally, five or ten individuals will be needed at a minimum for useful generalizations.

The particular questions and recorded responses are dependent on the industry, the product, and the role. Also, there should be information on the interviewee's industry as seen by them. This information will round out their method of reasoning within their more general competitive climate. So, a more complete questionnaire contains inquiries about interviewee's understanding of areas such as industry trends, business changes, high priority initiatives, critical success factors, key business issues, financial drivers, competition, primary decision makers, and product and service lines.

Locating interview candidates and enlisting their cooperation sounds easy, but is in fact quite challenging. There is no real incentive for participation beyond good will and a potential feedback of the persona results. So, getting the required number may require creativity. One good practice is to seek customer assistance to get the appointments. The vendor can explain to their customer that they want to learn about the value of the vendor's software to the customer's orga-

Figure 4. Determine the Marketing Objectives

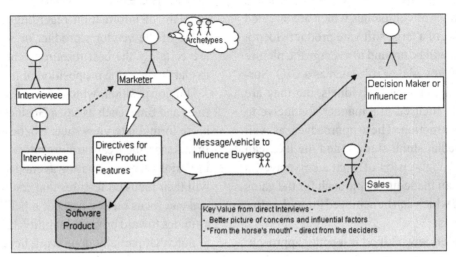

nization and how it helps them run their business better. The vendor can assure the customer that an in-depth understanding of their business will help the vendor in giving even better service to them in the future.

Going into these interviews, the interviewer's mindset must be that he or she is simply there to ask questions and to learn. The interviewer cannot sell during the interview under any circumstances, even if an opportunity arises. The interviewer should be inquisitive and interested. If needed, the interviewer may have to probe for the information needed in order to get a firm handle on developing a persona that supports the vendor's value propositions. It is useful for the interviewer to scrutinize the customer's web site before the interview. This will include taking a detailed look at: (i) the company overview, (ii) any investor relations; (iii) their press room or media center; (iv) key people or leadership; and (v) the site map – to find "hidden" information.

Once identified, the set of all interviews should be completed within a few weeks so that the interviews can be conducted in a similar fashion by the same interview team. The structure of the interview and its response form must be maintained as well to enable proper collation. It will occasionally be necessary to keep the interviewee on track and to

watch the time so as to complete all questions in an unrushed manner. Also, some probing might be needed to get answers that respond to the intent of a given question. Problem and opportunity indicators need to be monitored carefully during the interviews. Problem indicators are the information that leads the interviewer to believe the customer is struggling with challenges and issues that the vendor's software product could resolve. An opportunity indicator is information that points to goals, objectives, or strategic imperatives that the vendor software can help the customer to achieve. These indicators may require a deep-dive of probing, which is worthwhile because this can ultimately provide more solid insights into customer's mind.

A couple of diagrams can illustrate the methods and issues here, see Figure 4 and Figure 5.

Determine the marketing objectives.

1. Envision the findings which would be most useful in building a better market understanding and sales posture
    ○   e.g., maturity, needs, resistance, competitor status
2. Determine categories of key responders to marketing messages

Figure 5. Build the Interview Form

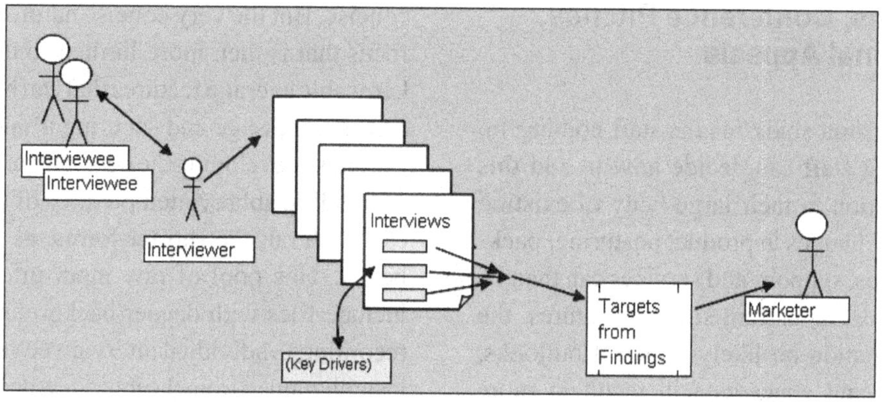

3. Determine what would be helpful to know, from these roles and actors
   ◦ what factors and information affect their decisions
4. Based on 0)-4), lay out the Section Introductions and Objectives to use in an interview or survey
5. Construct interview forms, conduct the interviews
   ◦ alter the probing as needed to acquire the types of information to support the goals from 3)
6. Tabulate and summarize the interviews
   ◦ weighted using the importance of each interviewee as determined by the marketer
7. Marketer reads the summaries and builds a message and modes of delivery and sets up pertinent success metrics
8. Message is delivered and measured for its impact
9. Possibly repeat some steps and refine iteratively

Build the interview form.

1. Lay out the Section Introductions and Objectives
2. Show how these match the information gathering objectives
3. Illustrate how the answers are obtained in a dynamic way to extract the desired target response areas for tabulation
4. Indicate how the results are to be rolled up to findings
5. Show how the findings can be used to build a better market understanding and sales posture - by category, from the "horse's mouth"

So, once the target roles are determined, the interview is built for each role. Many roles will have similar questions such as those regarding their job description and work background. The questions to ask are dependent upon the eventual use of the finished persona as noted earlier here. Worthwhile characteristics typically include attitudes toward the product being sold and the needs as seen by that department or role. The information distilled into a persona should be most useful in those "contact moments" when market materials or sales messages later meet with a buyer or influencer. Certainly the message should be more matched than that of a competing vendor, as soundly based on the interests and needs of the various role-personas. Portions of a typical interview form are included below as artifacts of the persona gathering process.

Contact Plans, Printed Promotions, Conference Pitches, and Personal Appeals

Once the persona study results start coming in, the marketing staff can decide how to add this new information to their large body of existing knowledge. Changes in product posturing, packaging, features, support, and services can then be suggested. For the current suite of features, the added information on likely prospect outlooks, motivations, and concerns will result in more targeted and integrated meeting preparations, more focused printed promotions (collateral materials), and better tailored training for new users. Close cooperation with sales teams will ensure a consistent and successful message for securing new business.

Personas are generally terse, and have just a photo and a few personal characteristics listed, as shown in the samples in the following. So it could be asked whether these sparse indicators of buyer roles can really help the marketing process achieve its goals. It has to be noted that the alternatives to this persona-aid all have their own limitations. If one must know so many of he customers that a short characteristic-profile is useless, then there will be few marketers or salespersons with this level of familiarity - and their shorthand in discussing matters among themselves will tend to exclude and confuse other parties like operations personnel or developers or support staff members. If a far more detailed portrait of the averaged role-representative is required for fine-grained marketing processes, there must first be a high degree of homogeneity among those in a given role so that there can be useful lower-level-attribute generalizations like favorite sports, number of pets, types of operational headaches, flexibility of budgeting, friendliness with superiors and key peers, and on and on. That is, if too much must be known for usefulness, the group in question must be enough alike to justify characterizing those numerous behaviors. This is generally not

the case, and this is why most personas are quite concise. But the very concise nature serves as the focus that is then more limited to the really few knowable average features that can help in getting across a message and securing a sale.

Those developing the personas, and the process of building abbreviated pictures of the personas, can flesh out the shorter forms, as sketched out below. This pool of raw input information can include files with deeper background, interview recordings, individual interviewee variations, and insights gained from the interview and background research efforts. Returning to the matter of actually using the persona, however, the limited mannerisms and decision patterns encoded for that persona need to be just those which help to properly direct and pull together the various marketing modalities and materials for maximum impact.

The major goal, which is better marketing messages, will be met by delivering the messages using avenues and modes which are best suited to the vendor and to the prospective customers, including those enumerated above: in person, at a meeting, in publications, through media, online, and direct mailing. In each case, the personal touch will be applied so that when a targeted role is contacted with a message their response is in line with that expected for the typical sort of person in that position and industry. Messages will be delivered on schedules and across geographies as best suited for given product releases and sales campaigns, matching the desired impact of the contact vehicles with the susceptibility and interest of typical target persona-roles.

For the sales calls, preparation will specifically focus on the degree of match between a persona and the person in the particular company and role. There are likely to be differences in titles and duties for the same title across companies, so adjustments will be needed in properly using the persona models. Preparations can include rehearsals with other sales staff or perhaps using modern sales rehearsal tools with realistic business settings. During the actual sales call, the assumptions can be confirmed and further adjustments can be made to the contact details. The particular way of employing likely persona-based sports or technical interests or probable industry attitudes will be left to the discretion of the sales person. Of importance will be the usage of the persona in making the call less impersonal and more cordial and engaging. The persona can be updated somewhat if needed after a sales call, when additional or contradictory information of importance is encountered.

Some issues are be reiterated below, since the contact moment is of such importance. The focus of the persona information that best supports the purchase-decision impact depends on the specific contact situation:

- face to face in an office
  - who is the person (and what is their persona-model)
  - what is she or he like (characteristics and profile)
  - what are their concerns (headaches, consumer fickleness, competitors)
  - what are the actions the vendor needs the contacted person to take (like recommending the vendor's solution over a competitor's software)
  - what does the person need to feel confident in taking those actions
  - what can we know about the contacted person, and what is unavailable or inappropriate
  - of all of the personal/role/archetype information items, what is their ranked importance to keep in mind while speaking with the person
- at a meeting (conference, trade session)
  - what will the attendee be typically listening to or looking for
  - what competing or complementary information will they be exposed to
  - how will the vendor's message stand out and stick in their memory
    - what features of the talk, discussion, booth, displays, or handout will most attract their attention
    - what information is the most likely to be an influence on future purchase likelihood
- in publication (television, radio interviews, discussions, advertisements)
  - who will see the message, and in what context
  - how will the message typically be expected to support the evaluation of products
  - what features in the reader archetype are most useful in aligning the message for impact
- online (Internet advertisements, website, blogs)
  - (like the publications - more timely, user is looking or clicking - can know more about the user and their online prototype-persona)
- direct mailing
  - (like the publications - may be broad and general or targeted to small person-types)

Feeding Back Archetypical Concerns to Product Development Teams

As noted, marketers typically face in two directions at once, toward the customer and towards the product staff. The interaction with product developers is usually less direct, but this is still a valuable feedback channel for field knowledge. The persona development process and its final result should be of deep importance to the developers. The typical buyers are seeing the results of their hard work and are assessing it for purchase. The developers typically have a degree of well-justified pride in their work, that is, its quality, functionality, and competitive edge.

In addition to the buyer personas, the developers may also get the results of more focused user persona studies; modeling the end consumers of their coding. These personas represent groups who directly access the software for use, but who do not actually pay for the product. The purchasers and those who recommend the product are a different group than the end-users in the company. The software must be bought in order to be used, so addressing the perceptions of the buyer class is at least as important as addressing the perceptions of the end-users. Satisfying those with the power of the purse is thereby a complement to satisfying the end users.

Knowing the buyer-class of stakeholder better is enabled through the buyer-personas as detailed in this chapter. The manner of use of these buyer-models by market and sales staff validate their accuracy and impact. Among the most important portions of the persona outline will be the typical attitudes and inclinations of the buyer toward the soundness of an investment in the vendor's software solution. Also, the factors of complexity in managing the software product evaluation, its purchase, its installation, training, and maintenance will be crucial executive level concerns. The marketing staff uses this knowledge for its own department's programs, but also shares the executives' issues with the product development staff so that the complexity of the software use and maintenance will be addressed. Here again a competitive advantage can be maintained at more corporate levels by applying the persona insights which help the vendor maintain awareness on the customer's multi-source motivations.

Utility of the Added Knowledge Elements

In measuring the value of buyer personas, there are several approaches and issues. First, it is difficult to be precise as to how many sales dollars are attributable directly to improved buyer knowledge. Such assessments are likely to be fuzzy and related to impressions or success stories. This is similar to assessment in other areas such as improved packaging or support. But reports from buyers and sales persons can be telling. If the company official report feeling more listened to, or being treated with more awareness of their problems, then some of the credit may well be given to the persona and the knowledge acquired in its derivation.

Surveys of marketers and sales persons could be undertaken, as well as follow-up interviews of buyer role-types. Such follow-through could be of value in subsequent persona efforts and in keeping the personas up to date in any more volatile industry settings or hard economic times. The goal would be an ever growing skill base in persona usage, and a knowledge bank on the key players in customer organizations. Differences in the variability, validity, and utility of personas in certain roles and types of businesses could also be of value in its own right. A persona lifecycle management discipline would be the ultimate goal, in order to institute a continuously-updated profiling and assessment for the various personas.

Artifacts: Sample Interview Forms And Typical Questions

One example of a questionnaire form is presented below in abbreviated and sanitized form, with intellectual property or confidential information removed.

Some basic areas of questioning were:

1. Brief introduction
2. You and your company
3. What are the market drivers and trends in your industry?
4. How do you manage innovation?
5. How are you delivering the brand?
6. What is your technical environment for brand management?
7. What is missing? What are the pain points?
8. How do you decide on changes?
9. Any extras? What do you want to ask?

A few of the questions themselves follow. They were rated by importance for answering, for building the persons. Also, some roles were asked certain questions and all roles were asked others:

1. Can you tell us about your function in the company?
2. How long you have been with the company?
3. How long you have been in this industry? How long you have been in this particular position?
4. What is the function of your area? How is success measured in your area?
5. Is there a competitor that you admire most? If so, why?
6. Where do you believe that your company will be in five years? In ten years?
7. How is the innovation process managed?
8. How is a new idea identified and then created? Which information sources are critical for the ideation?
9. How many new products will be created per year?
10. Is there one standard process for product development and customer satisfaction? or are there varying processes depending on country, product category, and tradeoffs between cost and flexibility?
11. What are some of challenges you are facing on the following topics?
    ◦ Lean innovation
    ◦ risk management (strategic procurement, scarce resource management)
    ◦ compliance
    ◦ paradigm shifters
12. With regard to the ownership of the product information and control, who is the champion? Who are the executive sponsors?
13. How do you personally make decisions in the product and/or manufacturing? information and control areas? What are the sources of information? Who influences you?

Outcomes: Sample Persona

The following is a sample persona (abbreviated for presentation here). Detailed personas have some value in certain situations, but the more generic form is common in general use.

Marion Florin, Vice President, R&D

- Age 57
- Education: Ph.D in Organic Chemistry
- 24 years in CPG industry, 16 at current firm, 11 as R&D Chief
- Dedicated family man, active in community charities and tennis

Marion's duties and responsibilities

- Determine overall research direction for new products
- Support Brand and Production sectors
- Investigate information needs across departments and stages
- Decide on balanced innovations

Marion's challenges and headaches

- Pressures for increased product variety yet quality
- Information glut from global sources
- Technology modernization must fit with successful operations
- Competition for supplies and retail positioning is intensifying

Typical marketing scenario with this persona:

The software marketing team has invited Marion and similar executives to an evening meeting after the sessions in a major conference. There are demos of the software product line, targeted toward Marion's industry; there are free drinks and fine food. Industry leaders and a celebrity are present for entertainment, as well as a well-known golf pro and a popular female tennis star. Marion enjoys meeting the sports figures and listens to the engaging videos and expert reviews of success stories using the methods and software. The software marketer, Susan, for Marion's company hangs out with him for some time, shepherding Marion to meet the stars and to discuss issues a bit with similar executives in related companies. Susan gets an autographed tennis racket for Marion as a door prize, and promises to call on him later. Susan recalls that Marion's company has issues coordinating information on changing demands and product production input materials. Competition for raw ingredients has been troubling in some regions for his company. Susan shows Marion a mini-demo specifically put together for his company's case, highlighting the software products clarity and risk-scenario evaluations.

Typical sales scenario with this persona:

The software sales rep, Michael, for Marion's company visits with Marion and his staff to firm up a proposal for implementing the software solution incrementally there. Marion's concerns on budget containment and a slow steady approach have been taken into account. Since Marion and Michael have met at tennis and charity events, they have a more cordial relationship.

Recommended marketing take-aways:

- Keep in mind that this individual is intimately familiar with their industry and its customers

- This person believes strongly in the value of the company's products and its long-term value to the consumers – quality is paramount
- He or she has had a long career in this industry. With few if any experiences in different industries
- This person is technical in the areas of product design and manufacturing, understanding most of the sequential processing steps and logistics
- This individual controls the majority of discretionary spending in new development areas and initiatives – with advice from IT and Production, and with clear explanation and justification to the CEO
- This person is a team player and makes decisions collaboratively with peers
- He or she is familiar with the developments in other industries but not compelled to follow best practices outside of their market – especially if there are any associated disruptions in production or personnel
- This person wants richer communications and better standards geographically
- Since product changes are most often incremental, there is a reluctance to make major changes in production systems that work well today

New (post-recession persona modifications)

- Expect slowdowns and reductions in projects
- Efforts requiring any downtime or extensive training will be put off

Any new initiatives will be more incremental

CIO (Brief Version)

Sam Walston

- Age 57

- Education: MBA from Indiana University
- 30 years in CPG industry, 15 at current firm, 5 as CIO

Sam's duties and responsibilities

- Support office systems and R&D needs
- Ensure C-level visibility and control
- Modernize IT systems and enterprise infrastructures

Sam's challenges and headaches

- Constrained budgets, cuts
- Talent competition
- Increasing demand for integrated systems and data discipline
- Difficulties integrating acquisitions and standardizing systems
- C-level push for increased competitiveness

Interview Problems

Some of the challenges in the interview processes have already been mentioned. A few additional issues are laid out here. The challenges of interviewing geographically dispersed, high level company members are at times extreme. Matters of availability and variations in job duties make the persona development effort harder but not impossible. Introspectively chosen or lazily thought out personas can result in getting what

was expected in advance. It is imperative to let the data and interviews guide the profiling, using methodological approaches which can be measured, explained, and improved. For small sample situations like buyers of big-ticket items in corporations, the statistical concerns cast doubt on the representativeness of a persona. Variable actors and small influences can skew the attributes obtained, so some caution needs to be taken in the persona construction and application.

Other issues:

1. Persona interviews with small numbers of sample role-persons differ from mass market or large-sample situations
2. Specifically-worded questions are problematic, especially for non-native English speakers
3. If responses for the intent of a particular question are desired, some explanation and examples may be useful – while avoiding leading the respondent
4. For high level officials in large multinational corporations, interviews can be awkward and can appear to be simplistic or uninformed
5. High level executives have very tight calendars small time windows which constrain attention and focus on the questioning
6. If interview sessions are spaced too far apart in time, say over months, it is difficult to retain consistency, equal emphases, and clarity
7. The usage of small sample high-level personas is not standard so few if any clear examples and guidelines exist
8. Extraction of value from small samples, especially if incomplete, is difficult and requires intense goodwill and interactive collaboration
9. Some corporations have widely differing product lines, markets, and organizations
10. Access to cooperative companies and roles might be due to a systematic difference in maturity that is atypical

11. The global economy is under stress, and consumer buying behavior is likely to change significantly in the near term. Persona representatives may lose their jobs or change dramatically

Incidental Insights

When conducting an interview face to face or in a teleconference with a senior official in a customer company, the interviewee may offer facts or opinions of significant value outside the scope of persona building. For instance, there may be a comment regarding the impressions of industry directions or a note regarding problems with a competitor. Also, there could be a repeated theme across several interviews like a desire for outsourcing. As another example, if users nearly universally complain about the product interface, that common perception is a big warning sign. Insights like these should be retained and shared where appropriate, and as long as they are determined to be within the bounds of confidentiality.

As noted already, the economic situation can directly influence personas and roles in a short time. If there are layoffs and drop-offs in consumer demand, the interest in large software purchases can be severely reduced. Conversely, if there are government stimulus finds available for large new endeavors, some of these may require big software packages soon. New persona types or near matches from other industries could be of value in addressing such new markets.

CONCLUSION

The investment in buyer personas is sound, and there will be multiples of the investment expected in return. When combined with complementary user persona processes, the net result should be more than the sum of either separately. Intimate personal knowledge of the customer base and their internal organization is golden for marketers and sales representatives. The methodology has side benefits gained through the interviews and their determination, in discovering decision drivers and roadblocks. The often overlooked affective components of business decision making are also a breath of fresh air. Improved interpersonal relationships and goodwill that spring from a degree of care in persona construction will definitely prove of long term sales and service value.

The costs of persona construction can be considered in opposition to either doing nothing or paying for guesses from external consultants regarding decision processes, or just "making stuff up". The costs of ignoring or misreading motives and complaints in key purchase stakeholders can be severe. Mis-focusing product development is even more worrisome. It is of value to consider briefly that the skills in persona construction and effective interview-based knowledge extraction are rooted in the so-called soft sciences. Psychology, sociology and even anthropology have slowly moved into the awareness of senior company executives. In addition to the proven value in sales, these disciplines can prove of worth internally as well, for example in better understanding organizational inertia in areas like product development and evolution.

In closing, the personal-touch approach for gathering novel business knowledge is likely to be a trend of interest and value. Personas have likely come to stay.

REFERENCES

Cahill, D. J. (2006). *Lifestyle Market Segmentation*. The Haworth Press, Inc.

Cooper, A. (1999). *The Inmates Are Running the Asylum: Why High Tech Products Drive Us Crazy and How to Restore the Sanity*. Sams.; 1999

Isenberg, B., Isenberg, J., & Davis, L. T. (2006). *Waiting for Your Cat to Bark?* Nelson Business.

Kahle, L.R., Beatty, S.E., & Homer, P. (1986). Alternative Measurement Approaches to Customer Values: The List of Values (LOV) and Values Life Style (VALS). *Journal of Consumer Research*.

Konrath, J. (2005). *Selling to Big Companies*. Kaplan Publishing.

Mulder, S., & Yaar, Z. (2006). *The User Is Always Right: A Practical Guide to Creating and Using Personas for the Web*. New Riders Press.

Quesenbery, W. (2006). Storytelling and narrative. In Pruitt, J., & Adlin, T. (Eds.), *The Persona Lifecycle: Keeping People in Mind throughout Product Design* (p. 521). Morgan Kaufmann.

Understanding U.S. Consumers (2008). VALS™ SRI Consulting Business Intelligence.

WEBSITES

Buyer Persona - How to Better Understand Your Customer. http://ezinearticles.com/?Buyer-Persona---How-to-Better-Understand-Your-Customer&id=2135944

Buyer Persona: The Influence Behind Data Management Decisions, http://74.6.239.67/search/cache?ei=UTF-8&p=buyer+persona&xa=DvceK skN8iJav.3fqXkyQQ--%2C1242224722&fr=yfp-t-501&u=www.sungard.com/%7E/media/financialsystems/casestudies/referencepoint_cas-estudies_buyerpersona.ashx&w=buyer+buyers+persona&d=aadxGkxISxYC&icp=1&.intl=us

Buyer Personas and User Personas. http://tyner-blain.com/blog/2008/07/22/buyers-and-users/

Do you have your buyer persona profile ready? http://kimklaverblogs.blogspot.com/2008/09/do-you-have-your-buyer-persona-profile.html

Don't Confuse Sales Support with Marketing. A Case for Buyer Persona Profiling,http://www.pragmaticmarketing.com/publications/magazine/3/4/0508ar

Enable Sales & Marketing with Buyer Persona Scenarios, http://www.personainsights.com/

Hit a Buyer Persona Bull's-eye, http://www.invesp.com/blog/conversion-optimization/hit-a-buyer-persona-bulls-eye-ask-target-markets-the-right-questions.html

How well do you know your buyer personas? http://www.webinknow.com/2008/07/how-well-do-you.html

Leading Persona Experts Announce Buyer Persona Creation Workshops. http://www.prweb.com/releases/2008/05/prweb921464.htm

Research Paper - Real or Imaginary. The effectiveness of using personas in product design; Frank Long; Irish Ergonomics Review, Proceedings of the IES Conference 2009 http://www.frontend.com/products-digital-devices/real-or-imaginary-the-effectiveness-of-using-personas-in-product-design.html

Tell Me a Story, http://www.personacreation.com/

The Buyer Persona. http://www.feed-squirrel.com/index.cfm?evt=viewItem&ID=35504

What Are Personas?http://www.goalcentric.com/contentdisplay.asp?id=2002&cid=1&level=14

What the bleep is a buyer persona, http://www.buyerpersona.com/2006/11/whats_a_buyer_p.html

Chapter 13

Where are We Looking?
A Practical Approach to Managing Knowledge Captured from Eye-Tracking Experiments: The Experience of Gulf Air

Stefania Mariano
New York Institute of Technology, Kingdom of Bahrain

Nicola Simionato
Gulf Air, Kingdom of Bahrain

ABSTRACT

This chapter contributes to organizational innovation theory and provides a practical approach to promote companies and create relationships with their customers. This research study investigates the primary visual attention of customers in online flight booking and uses interviews, think-aloud protocols, and eye-tracking tools to collect data. Findings show that the visual structure of the webpage strongly influences the overall effectiveness of the booking process and that participants ignore peripheral information when it does not appear relevant or associated with the main task. It is also found that the effective segmentation of different elements of the webpage helps direct attention and guides participants to the relevant section. Implications from these findings are discussed, and a general framework to help practitioners to manage knowledge collected from their customers is presented.

INTRODUCTION

"Everything should be made as simple as possible, but not simpler" -Attributed to Albert Einstein

Research in organizational innovation highlights how important external relations are to organizational efficiency, and to e-commerce services; knowing how to manage relations with the customers is crucial. In the airline industry, competition is knowledge-driven, and the capacity to offer effective e-commerce services to meet the preferences of the customers leads to a competitive advantage. Although several studies have focused on the technical aspects of e-commerce services (Chaudhury & Kuilboer, 2001; Li et al., 2007), research has not shown how to manage customers' requirements to add value to the organization and foster innovation, which has been defined as

DOI: 10.4018/978-1-61520-829-6.ch013

"the application of knowledge to produce new knowledge" (Drucker, 1993).

Gulf Air, a Middle East airline company, has employed a user experiment to investigate the primary visual attention of customers in online flight booking to improve the usability of its website and manage relations with their customers productively. For companies that sell products online, this technique can be implemented to determine the effectiveness of their website design to best manage customers' preferences, reduce cost and time to market, and improve productivity and quality through process innovation (OECD, 2005).

BACKGROUND

In recent years, the commercial sector has increased its interest in eye-tracking technologies as a means to understand customers' attitudes and preferences (Lukander, 2006). A sample of customers is selected and a target stimulus is presented, for example, websites, commercials, magazines, prints ads, ATMs, and software, while an eye-tracker is used to record eye movements. Eye-tracking technologies enable the collection of useful information about the visual attention, for example the visibility of a logo, or the visual behavior such as, how packaging, in terms of distinctiveness and attractiveness, might influence the selection of a product on a shelf.

A prominent application field of eye-tracking technologies is web usability (Cooke, 2005; Bojko, 2006; Bednarik & Tukiainen, 2007). The increased amount of customers who shop online has lead to a point where the capacity to offer effective e-commerce services to meet customers' preferences and requirements is a source of organizational success. To achieve this result, it is essential to develop an engaging website where issues connected to design, structure, search efficiency, and navigation usability are highlighted and opportunely corrected. Eye-tracking provides

insights to organizations as a technique to analyze scanning patterns, reading, examination, and user interactions and it is a valuable source of information to determine which features of a website may cause confusion or might be ignored, as well as which features may be the most attractive ones.

About the Research

This research was conducted in the United Kingdom from July to November 2007.

Nine participants took part in the user experiment; four of them were female and they were all based in and around London. The average age was 39.4 years.

The selected sample was ideal for this study as all of the participants used online booking systems to reserve their flights and visited the Middle East at least three times per year. Most frequently used airlines included five competitors of Gulf Air.

The project was conducted in collaboration with OgilvyOne Bahrain and Bunnyfoot® Consultancy Company.

Web pages were displayed on a 17″ monitor with screen resolution set to 1024 X 768 pixels to gather eye-tracking and interview data. Data analysis was pursued to understand the primary visual attention of customers in online flight booking.

Details of the participants are summarized in Table 1.

How to Improve the Usability of a Webpage: The Use of Eye-Tracking Techniques

In this section we discuss the use of eye-tracking techniques and how to organize a testing session. The purpose of this section is to investigate how knowledge can be gathered from participants and analyzed to improve the usability of a webpage. This section provides a means to those who work on redesigning a company website or to test a

Table 1. Details of the participants

Participant	Gender	Age	Occupation	Frequent Middle East	Nationality
P1	M	42	MD import/export of commodities	3-4 times a year	British
P2	M	48	Oil refinery processing & development	3-4 times a year	American
P3	F	36	HR manager for recruitment	3-4 times a year	American
P4	F	36	MD of music label	2-3 times a year	British/American
P5	F	30	Licensing executive	2-3 times a year	British
P6	F	40	Make up artist	2-3 times a year	British/Libyan
P7	M	36	Translator	3-4 times a year	British/Moroccan
P8	M	44	MD of property company	2-3 times a year	British/Indian
P9	M	43	Director of consulting	2-3 times a year	British

prototype stage of it. Prototype web pages can be tested against each others or against competitors' websites to examine specific elements with high visibility and appeal for the final customer.

How to Organize an Eye-Tracking Testing Session

The organization of an eye-tracking testing session requires the selection and acquisition of a specific eye-tracker, the organization of think-aloud protocols, and the development of a list of questions to use in initial interviews and follow-up Q&A sessions. Two types of knowledge are captured: Knowledge related to users' eye movements (Duchowski, 2003) and tacit knowledge (Polanyi, 1966) gained from think-aloud protocols, initial interviews and follow-up individual interviews. Eye-movement data provide knowledge about the primary visual attention of users. Initial individual interviews focus on preliminary information about participants' habits, and their personal experiences, while think-aloud protocols record participants' thoughts and feelings as they go through each stage of the testing session. Finally, Q&A sessions intend to probe preferences and opinions of participants.

The next section provides a list of recommendations on how to arrange the collection of data.

Capturing Eye-Movement Data

Video-based eye-trackers are the most commonly used eye-trackers where a camera records eye movements as the participant looks at some kind of stimulus. Eye movements are typically divided into points of gaze (hotspots data), when the eye gaze pauses in a certain position, or the motion of an eye (gaze plot data), when the eye moves to another position. A series of fixations and movements will result in a scan-path, and a certain volume of collected data will be accumulated depending on the number of web pages participants scan. In general, the trade-off in video-based eye-trackers is between the sensitivity of the system in terms of measurement of changes in gaze direction, and the cost of the video-based eye-tracker.

Capturing Tacit Knowledge: The Use of Initial Interviews, Think-Aloud Protocols, and Follow-Up Interviews

Initial interviews collect preliminary information about participants' habits, internet usage frequency and purpose, and personal experiences/expectations regarding the target link.

Think-aloud protocols are useful to gather tacit knowledge and explicit the implicit actions of participants (Graesser & Clark 1985). Participants are asked to think aloud as they go through a set of specified tasks during the eye-tracking testing session. The interviewer asks them to say whatever they are looking at, thinking, doing, and feeling while accomplishing their task. It is recommended to audio and/or video tape the session or take intensive notes of everything that participants say, without making an interpretation of used words and/or reactions of participants.

Final follow-up interviews are used to probe preferences and opinions of participants and to collect their experiences and expectations.

Eye-Tracking Testing Sessions at Gulf Air

The experiment conducted at Gulf Air used an eye-tracker to record hotspots and gaze plots data to determine the pattern of fixations (Goldberg & Wichansky, 2003) on a webpage. Participants were asked to perform tasks on the Gulf Air prototype booking engine and were informed about the prototype status of the website before the start of each testing session. It was explained that a few links or pages were not fully implemented in terms of functionality, content, visual layout, and formatting to ensure that the overall rating of the website would not have a negative bias due to prototype issues, for example non-functioning links. Each session used think-aloud protocols (Whitney & Budd, 1996; Pressley & Afflerbach, 1995) and initial interviews to discuss and understand online booking habits of the participants, and their experiences with airline booking engines. Common questions were: Do you usually buy your flight tickets online? How many websites do you usually visit before finalizing your choice, on average? What are your main factors of choice when purchasing a flight ticket online (price, airline, simplicity of the website)? Do you normally purchase other products online (books, music, hotel reservations, car rental)?

Interviews lasted an average of 15/20 minutes and before the tasks began, the home page of the prototype booking engine was shown for approximately 15 seconds, to gauge initial impressions. Participants were asked to think-aloud while carrying out their tasks and explain their thoughts and feelings as they went through each stage of the booking process. Upon completion of the testing sessions, participants took part in a short Q&A session, which lasted 15 minutes and probed their preferences and opinions. Common questions were: What do you think of this website? Did you find it appealing? Did you find it easy to use? Is there anything in particular that you liked/disliked? How do you think the airline could improve this website?

How to Analyze Data Collected in an Eye-Tracking Testing Session

The overall goal of the eye-tracking testing session is to estimate gaze direction, and in web usability, the purpose is to gather information on the most eye-catching features, and on those features that may cause confusion or may be ignored by the user. Eye-tracking is used to assess searching and scanning behavior and often the analysis targets a competitor site in addition to the company's own site (Bojko, 2006). Specific eye-tracking software is implemented to extract collected data and store them in video format or as a series of x/y coordinates related to specific grid points (Cooke, 2005). This software provides evidence of specific visual patterns, and contributes to the statistical analysis of categories such as fixations, eye-movements, and blinks. In general, if a specific section of a webpage receives numerous fixations which are also lengthy, that is an indication of the users' visual attention (Cooke, 2005), even though an efficient search should only necessitate a few fixations (Kotval & Goldberg, 1998). Users should be able to recognize the target and avoid the conduction of multiple visual revisits to it as this is an indication of an inefficient visual location of such a target. Oppositely, if a specific section or link does not receive enough attention, this can be explained as a failed visual search, for example the target is seen but it is not attributed a specific relevance or meaning. This can be also explained as the target is simply not noticed by the user (Bojko & Stephenson, 2005; Schiessl et al., 2003); in these cases a scan-path analysis is required to better understand the visual progress of users on a webpage (Cooke, 2005; Goldberg & Wichansky, 2003). For example, from the scan-path analysis, it can be found that the section or link was erroneously or poorly placed on a webpage. In general, users follow two stages in their visual search (Bojko, 2006) to find the correct link or bottom on a webpage: (1) they first allocate attention on a target; (2) they then recognize and process it (Bojko & Stephenson, 2005). It is obvious that the overall display layout, location, and visual presentation of the target influence both the effectiveness and efficiency of the two stages (Bojko & Stephenson, 2005). Colors, labels, and appearance of the target have a direct influence on the visual search and help to recognize the meaning of the target. The literature highlights some examples of color preferences related to culture (Barber & Badre, 1998; Simon, 2001), for example "red means happiness in China, but danger in the United States" (Cyr & Trevor-Smith, 2004, p. 1202). According to D'Angelo and Little (1998), changes in color are required to indicate status changes in the text, and generally, warm colors are preferred to indicate actions while bright colors are preferred to indicate emphasis. However, since it may be still difficult to analyze specific cognitive processes, for example liking, eye-tracking testing sessions should be conducted with other methodologies such as think-aloud protocols which may confirm/disconfirm the eye-movement data, as it was found at Gulf Air.

Data Analysis at Gulf Air

Data analysis was pursuit to understand the primary visual attention of customers in online flight booking. Data were stored in both video format and as a series of x/y coordinates. From the analysis

of initial interviews, 15 second test, think-aloud protocols, and Q&A sessions, all participants responded positively to the website. It was felt that the booking process followed a simple, logical progression with clear sections and breakdown of information. Overall the online booking experience was considered to be quick and easy. The inclusion of meal and seat preference options was commented upon by all participants, spontaneously; options not experienced before, for example meal preferences, were positively remarked. As a general result, all participants commented that they would visit the site again. Hotspot data (Figure 1) illustrates the primary attention directed to the booking engine, summer special offers and logo of the company as the most eye-catching features which received numerous and lengthy fixations. The colors represent the number of fixations on a certain visual area; warmer colors, such as yellow and red, indicate more fixations. Oppositely, lack of color indicates areas that did not received any fixations. As showed, information that did not match the desired goal of booking a flight along with disparity information, for example data flexibility, failed to attract participants whose attention quickly dropped off. This is an indication of a failed visual search, as the target is seen but it is not attributed a specific relevance or meaning.

Gaze plot data showed that eye gaze focused primarily on the booking engine and offers, ignoring peripheral information, such as those placed in blue color on the left side of the webpage (Figure 2). This represents another example of a failed visual search. Participants recognized two key elements in the home page: The booking engine and summer special offers with clear entry points and no confusion in understanding their purposes. Display, layout, location, and visual presentation all contributed to the effectiveness and efficiency of the users' visual search. Oppositely, other options, such as frequent flyer, timetable, or new summer schedule were not always recalled by participants after the 15 second impression test, due to a lack of visibility among

Where are We Looking?

Figure 1. Fixation hotspots on the booking engine

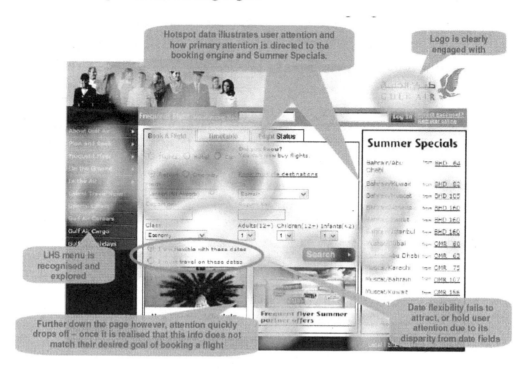

Figure 2. Peripheral Information

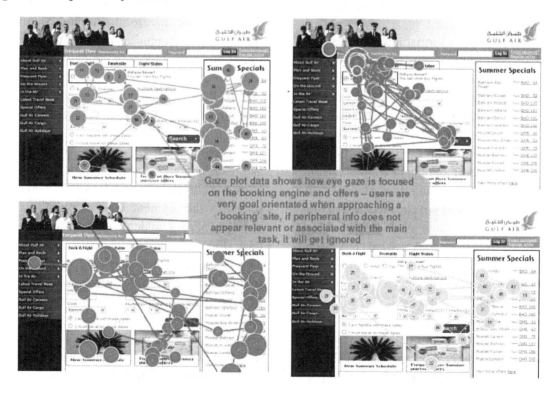

Figure 3. Results page

surrounding information as an example of a failed visual search.

Examples of both format attractiveness and causes of confusion are provided by the result page (Figure 3). From data analysis it came out that participants had a general preference for Options 1 and Option 3. Option 1 was considered clearer than other alternatives in terms of visual presentation while Option 3 appealed participants because of the larger amount of choices, visibility in the availabilities and prices. However, the layout of Option 3 was not clear to some participants and this was cause of confusion. Many participants were unclear as to what "NA" stood for. This is an indication of label failures as participants saw the visual target but were unable to attribute a specific meaning to it.

Another example of the use of colors and labeling is provided in Figure 4. It clearly illustrates how attention was heavily focused on the key review details at the top of the page but dropped

off and fails to engage with the upgrade facility. The colors used failed to attract or hold significant attention, or communicate a "step up" in class. Detail of the upgrade was limited and therefore failed to encourage users to further explore the facility. Poor labeling failed to excite the user or communicate the "added extras" available. In this case the meaning of the visual target was not recognized and failed to attract users to explore and read further.

A good breakdown of information was represented by the payment details with only a poor visibility of card holder link at the bottom of the page (Figure 5). In general, participants showed a preference for having payment details separate from the passenger fill in page. Separating the two felt more secure, reduced information overload, and helped to remind participants of their selections from the page before. SMS confirmation was seen as a good new feature, and frequently commented upon: "*If I can take that to*

Figure 4. Review section

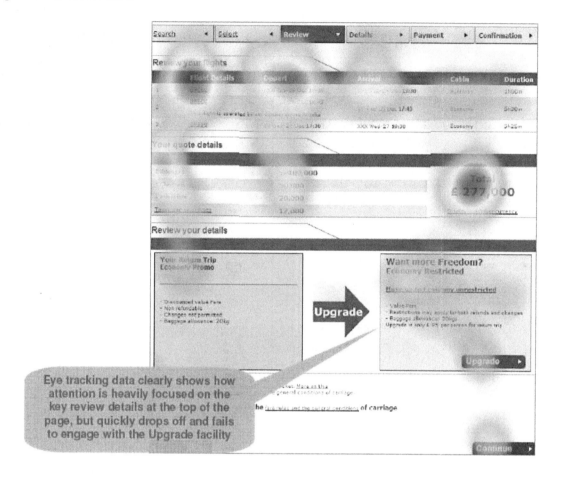

check-in I would definitely use that!" (Participant 3).

In general, all participants felt the language was clear and easy to understand and they did not experience any ambiguous terminology.

Each section of the site was clearly marked, and all participants understood their position within the overall booking process. Aspects of the website disliked by participants included:

- Poor presentation of upgrade facility.
- Poor visibility of card holder/non passenger link.
- The overall look and feel – "felt very 70's".

Positive aspects of the website included:

- Quick and easy to navigate and complete.
- Layout and structure of the sections.
- Searing option.
- Meal option.

CONCLUSION

Interpretation: Managing Knowledge Captured from Eye-Tracking Experiments

With regard to the question of what participants first engage with in online booking engines, this study suggested that participants were very goal oriented when approaching the booking engine. In fact, when peripheral information did not ap-

Figure 5. Payments details

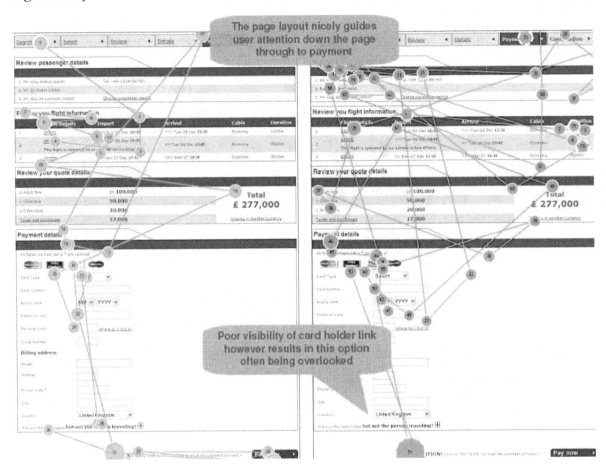

pear relevant or associated with the main task, participants ignored it. A good way to avoid such an issue is to keep associated information together and save space.

Findings showed that the visual structure of the webpage strongly influenced the overall effectiveness of the booking process, for example, summer schedule and frequent flyer lack association with the main content due to their presentation, and also the images lack relevance to the booking engine. A good way to enhance visibility is to improve the visual association with the booking engine and offers, and use imagery that clearly illustrates their purpose to attract and hold attention; for example it is useful to include frequent flyer offers under the specials banner. This will enhance

their visibility to the frequent flyer members, but also encourage exploration from the non-members into this special program.

It was also found that the effective segmentation of different elements of the webpage, without visually dissociating key pieces of information, helped direct attention and navigate participants to the relevant section. A correct use of labeling and colors also guided participants to complete the online booking process, for example if using the tab metaphor, current location is required to be highlighted to enhance the visual appearance of the selected tab, to distinguish it from surrounding information, and to associate it with the content with which it relates to. It is also important to ensure consistency among web pages and clear illustration of data format, such as date format (dd/mm/yyyy). Another example on how to associate specific information to the surrounding information is to include a calendar to allow users to view the dates within context of surrounding days. Oppositely, presenting content within a heavy lined box visually distinguishes it from surrounding information – therefore can result in it being ignored.

Many participants were unclear on the meaning of "NA". This is an indication of label failures as participants saw the visual target but were unable to attribute a specific meaning to it. To avoid it, the information has to be provided in a key for quick referral.

Finally, in some cases the colors used failed to attract or hold significant attention and poor labeling failed to excite the user. In these cases it is useful to prefer warm colors to indicate actions and bright colors to indicate emphasis on a specific area of the webpage.

Implications for Innovation

This chapter contributed to organizational innovation theory and provided a practical approach to help managers to market their companies and to create relationships with their customers.

This research demonstrated the need for managers to recognize the influence of web usability on external knowledge gathering and suggested new ways to improve companies' websites. Managers who want to make an impact on their organizations should consider the importance of the visual attention and visual search of their customers on the company's website, and should focus on how to reduce the number of fixations on a specific visual target and direct the customers' attention to the right area.

This is especially important to those industries where the competition is knowledge-driven, and the capacity to offer effective e-commerce services to meet the preferences of the customers leads to a competitive advantage. For companies

that sell products online, eye-tracking technique can be used to determine the effectiveness of the website design, significantly reduce cost and time to market, and improve the overall quality and productivity of the company through process innovation (OECD, 2005). To achieve this result, it is essential to develop an engaging website where issues connected to design, structure, search efficiency, and navigation usability are highlighted and opportunely corrected. Eye-tracking provides insights to organizations as a technique to analyze scanning patterns, reading and examination, user interactions, and it is a source of information on which features of a website may cause confusion or might be ignored, as well as which features may represent the most attractive ones.

A correct use of colors and labels, and a carefully designed appearance of the visual target, can help to increase the positive attitude of customers towards a specific target and create the basis to develop relationships with them and facilitate a revisit to the company's website.

Implications for Practitioners

There are some practical implications from Gulf Air user experiment:

- "We are all liars": Since time spent on a website, error rate, and comments of users do not always provide a comprehensive picture of users' experience, eye-movement data can offer a means to better understand how users navigate the website and what type of visual search actually takes place on a single webpage.
- "We like stupid-proof tools (but we don't like to feel stupid)": The number of fixations on a visual target must be reduced as much as possible, though the user's attention has to be directed to the right area of the web page and a correct interpretation of it has to be ensured. Simplicity is the key to success. As suggested by the KISS prin-

ciple: "Keep it short and simple!" A correct use of colors, labels, and a carefully designed appearance of the visual target can help improve the overall usability of the website, influence the user visual search (Has the target been seen? Are there problems in locating it?), and help to recognize the correct meaning of the visual target (Has the target been understood?).

- "Our personal opinion is nearly irrelevant": Eye-tracking technologies combined with think-aloud protocols can provide useful knowledge about the efficiency and effectiveness of a website design, to increase the overall usability of it and manage relations with customers productively. This may be especially beneficial for those companies selling products online, to best manage customers' preferences, reduce cost and time to market, and increase productivity and quality of the website design.

FUTURE RESEARCH DIRECTIONS

The study of eye-tracking technologies is an emerging trend in web usability and represents a means to better understand and improve innovation in companies. Future research should be conducted on how web usability may impact the effectiveness of the external organizational communication. How does web usability help to market companies and create relationships with customers? What external knowledge is collected? How can innovation be improved throughout the use of external communication processes? Empirical research should also be conducted to explain how best practices can be produced and managed to increase innovation that is introduced into a company throughout effective organizational websites.

ACKNOWLEDGMENT

We would like to thank Hannelore Grams, Business Director, OgilvyOne Bahrain.

REFERENCES

Barber, W., & Badre, A. N. (1998). *Culturability: The meaning of culture and usability.* Paper presented at the 4th Conference on Human Factors and the Web, Basking Ridge, NJ.

Bednarik, R., & Tukiainen, M. (2007). Validating the Restricted Focus Viewer: A study using eye-movement tracking. *Behavior Research Methods, 39*(2), 274–282.

Bojko, A. (2006). Using eye-tracking to compare web page designs: A case study. *Journal of Usability Studies, 1*(3), 112–120.

Bojko, A., & Stephenson, A. (2005). It's all in the eye of the user: How eye-tracking can help answer usability questions. *User Experience, 4*(1).

Chaudhury, A., & Kuilboer, J. P. (2001). *E-business & e-commerce infrastructure: Technologies supporting the e-business initiative.* London: McGraw-Hill/Irwin.

Cooke, L. (2005). Eye-tracking: How it works and how it relates to usability. *Technical Communication, 52*(4), 456–463.

Cyr, D., & Trevor-Smith, H. (2004). Localization of web design: An empirical comparison of German, Japanese, and United States web site characteristics. *Journal of the American Society for Information Science and Technology, 55*(13), 1199–1208. doi:10.1002/asi.20075

D'Angelo, J., & Little, S. K. (1998). Successful web pages: What are they and do they exist? *Information Technology and Libraries, 17*(2), 71–81.

Drucker, P. F. (1993). *Post-capitalist society.* New York: Butterworth Heineman.

Duchowski, A. T. (2003). *Eye-tracking methodology: Theory and practice*. London: Springer-Verlag.

Goldberg, J. H., & Wichansky, A. M. (2003). Eye-tracking in usability evaluation: a practitioner's guide. In Hyona, J., Radach, R., & Deubel, H. (Eds.), *The mind's eyes: Cognitive and applied aspects of eye movement research* (pp. 493–516). Amsterdam, Netherlands: Elsevier.

Graesser, A. C., & Clark, L. F. (1985). *Structure and procedures of implicit knowledge*. Norwood, NJ: Ablex.

Kotval, X. P., & Goldberg, J. H. (1998). *Eye movements and interface components grouping: an evaluation method*. Paper presented at the 42nd Annual Meeting of the Human Factors and Ergonomics Society (HFES), Chicago, IL.

Li, P., Tu, M., Yen, I.-L., & Xia, Z. (2007). Preference update for e-commerce applications: Model, language, and processing. *Electronic Commerce Research, 7*(1), 17–44. doi:10.1007/s10660-006-0061-0

Lukander, K. (2006). A system for tracking gaze on handheld devices. *Behavior Research Methods, 38*(4), 660–666.

OECD. (2005). *Guidelines for Collecting and Interpreting Innovation Data*. Oslo: OECD Publishing.

Polanyi, M. (1966). *The tacit dimension*. London: Routledge and Kegan Paul.

Pressley, M., & Afflerbach, P. (1995). *Verbal protocols of reading: The nature of constructively responsive reading*. Hillsdale, NJ: Erlbaum.

Schiessl, M., Duda, S., Thölke, A., & Fischer, R. (2003). Eye-tracking and its application in usability and media research. *MMI-Interaktiv, 6*.

Simon, S. J. (2001). The impact of culture and gender on web sites: An empirical study. *The Data Base for Advances in Information Systems, 32*(1), 18–37.

Whitney, P., & Budd, D. (1996). Think-aloud protocols and the study of comprehension. *Discourse Processes, 21*, 341–351. doi:10.1080/01638539609544962

ADDITIONAL READING

Krug, S. (2005). *Don't make me think: A common sense approach to web usability*. Indianapolis, IN: New Rivers.

Nielsen, J. (2000). *Designing web usability: The practice of simplicity*. Indianapolis, IN: New Rivers.

Nielsen, J., & Loranger, H. (2006). *Prioritizing web usability*. Indianapolis, IN: New Rivers.

Nielsen, J., & Pernice, K. (2009). *Eye-tracking web usability*. Indianapolis, IN: New Rivers.

Richardson, D., & Spivey, M. (2004). Eye-tracking: Research areas and applications. In Wnek, G., & Bowlin, G. (Eds.), *Encyclopedia of Biomaterials and Biomedical Engineering* (pp. 573–582). New York: Marcel Dekker, Inc.

Wickens, C. D., & Hollands, J. G. (2000). *Engineering psychology and human performance*. Upper Saddle River, NJ: Prentice-Hall.

Section 5
Maximising Intellectual Assets

Chapter 14
Organizational Antecedents of Intellectual Capital

Alton Y. K. Chua
Nanyang Technological University, Singapore

ABSTRACT

The objective of this chapter is to develop a framework that depicts the antecedents of intellectual capital in an organization. In gist, the framework specifies three dimensions of intellectual capital, namely, human capital, structural capital and customer capital. Organizational conditions such as opportunities, values, motivation and capability influence human capital; Organizational conditions such as the infrastructure, existing knowledge and the knowledge sharing process influence structural capital; Organizational conditions such as products and services, relationships and brand value influence customer capital; and organizational conditions such as culture and leadership influence all three dimensions of intellectual capital. In addition, individual dimension of intellectual capital mutually influences each other, and in sum, leads to positive organizational outcomes such as branding, reputation, competitiveness and sustainability.

INTRODUCTION

The growing discrepancy between the market value and book value of a corporation is largely attributed to its intellectual capital – the intangible part of the business that underpins future growth. Encompassing assets such as brands, customer relationships, patents, trademarks and knowledge, intellectual capital provides a vital resource for

developing innovations in organizations. For example, at Sumitomo Electric Industries (SEI), intellectual capital is consciously managed to drive innovations in the corporation's strategy and enhance its competitiveness (Nakahara, 2001).

Creating corporate value and wealth depends not only on leveraging tangible assets, but also liquidation assets such as financial and physical capital, as well as organizational capital that includes human and other relatively hidden assets (Barlett and Ghoshal, 1995). For example, the

DOI: 10.4018/978-1-61520-829-6.ch014

market-to-book value ratios of Microsoft and IBM were 91.93 and 4.25 respectively in 1996 (Stewart, 1997). In other words, the market recognized a far greater element of intangible value in Microsoft than in IBM. The success of twenty-first century business entities is increasingly dependent on their intellectual capital (James and Maria, 2001) but many organizations appear not to be equipped in managing this aspect efficiently. This inadequacy eventually affects the organization's profitability and stability. Given that intellectual capital holds a unique value proposition on the stakeholders of any organization, it is important to understand the organizational conditions that influence intellectual capital.

The objective of this chapter is to develop a framework that depicts the antecedents of intellectual capital in an organization.

BACKGROUND

The key contributing factor towards value creation of an organization is not attributed merely to traditional assets found on its balance sheet but intangible assets such as employees' competencies and customers' relationship. Increasingly, these assets, or what is commonly known as intellectual capital, are recognized for their role in building an organization's innovation capabilities and sustainability (Subramaniam & Yondit 2005). Intellectual capital is the intellectual material – knowledge, information, intellectual property, experience – that can be put to use to create wealth (Stewart, 1997). An alternative view of intellectual capital in the business context is the difference between the book value of the company and the amount of money someone is prepared to pay for it (Lev, 2001). In the social context, intellectual capital refers to the knowledge and knowing capacity of a social collectivity (Nahapiet and Ghoshal, 1998).

While different conceptions of intellectual capital have been proposed, they appear largely similar. For example, intellectual capital has been classified into human, organizational and social capital (Subramaniam and Yondit, 2005). It has also been teased into various constituents, such as the human, organizational and customer dimensions (Sveiby, 1997; Edvinsson and Malone, 1997) and the human, structural and relational dimensions (Canibano et al., 2002). The common underlying theme in these conceptions of intellectual capital points to three essential elements, namely, human capital, structural capital and customer capital.

Habersam and Piber (2003) defines human capital as individual aspects like education, personal professional experience, further personal training, and the personal ability to put this knowledge into practice. Human capital is seen as the collective tacit and explicit knowledge held within the minds of individual employees. Structural capital can be seen as the organizational routines and systems that encapsulate the knowledge generated and possessed by the company. By structuring workflow and processes into routines, organizational knowledge would not be adversely affected should an employee leave the company. Customer capital is defined as the relationships with customers (or suppliers) and knowledge of markets, distribution channels, competitors and trademarks (Olsen, et al., 1997).

The mutually-reinforcing relationship between human, structural and customer capital was one of the key findings in Habersam and Piber (2003). Strong evidence also supports the idea of a "connection" between different types of intellectual capital, as proposed by Roberts (2000). These three assets complement and strengthen one another to create the value in an organization.

ORGANIZATIONAL CONDITIONS AFFECTING INTELLECTUAL CAPITAL

While not every organization has the capacity to create and manage intellectual capital to its competitive advantage, organizations such as 3M or Siemens are adept at promoting and protecting their intellectual capital. The organizational conditions affecting different dimensions of the intellectual capital (human, structural and customer) are analyzed as follows.

Conditions Affecting the Human Capital Dimension

In their work on social capital, intellectual capital and organizational advantages, Nahapiet and Ghoshal (1998) argue that the organizational conditions affecting intellectual capital are opportunities, value, motivation and capability. There must first be the opportunity to access and combine existing and differing knowledge among employees. Next, for employees to avail themselves of any opportunity for intellectual capital creation, they must perceive such opportunities as valuable for themselves and the organization. Third, employees must be motivated to engage in knowledge creation and exchange. Finally, employees have to possess the capability to recognize the value of new knowledge, as well as to assimilate it into their existing body of knowledge. Subramaniam and Yondit (2005) argue that human capital not only depends on educational and functional skills, but also on interpersonal interaction and networking. The competencies of an employee include education, the number of years of experiences one has, and one's inter-personal relationship skills.

Hypothesis 1: Organizational conditions such as opportunities, values, motivation and capability have a positive influence over human capital.

Conditions Affecting the Structural Capital Dimension

The reuse of existing knowledge is an important parameter in the innovation equation, Innovation = reuse + invention x exploitation (Edvinsson et al., 2004). Specifically, it is possible to draw upon and engage in existing knowledge and knowledge

activities in the development of new intellectual capital, and in turn, create new products and services (Smith, et al., 2005). Technology and infrastructure exert a great impact on intellectual capital creation, especially when it comes to sharing the knowledge (Nahapiet and Ghoshal, 1998). Knowledge sharing process has to take place in order to exploit knowledge silos in an organization, to avoid reinventing the wheel, to reduce duplication and replication of efforts, and to avoid making the same errors (Lee and Al-Hawamdeh, 2002). The other condition that potentially affects knowledge creation is the existing knowledge sharing environment. In essence, the infrastructure, existing knowledge and the knowledge sharing process are the major organizational conditions affecting structural capital.

Hypothesis 2: Organizational conditions such as the infrastructure, existing knowledge and the knowledge sharing process have a positive influence over structural capital.

Conditions Affecting the Customer Capital Dimension

Chang and Tseng (2005) shows that value equity and brand equity have significant effects on customer acquisition and customer retention. Here, the value equity refers to the services and products of the organization. Innovation is a strategic asset for high technology firms that constantly need to create and improve new products and services in order to survive in very competitive markets (Smith, et al., 2005). Production and services have always been a differentiating factor for any firm in the market, and one's brand can create bonding value between the customer and the products and services of the company. Well-known examples are Nike's sporting shoes, Seagate's hard disks and Colgate's toothpaste. Hence, organizational conditions such as the value of products and services, relationships with customers, suppliers and partners, as well as the company brand can affect customer capital.

Hypothesis 3: Organizational conditions such as products and services, relationships and brand value, have a positive influence over customer capital.

Conditions Affecting All Three Dimensions

Having reviewed the organizational conditions that impact the three dimensions of intellectual capital individually, we shall examine conditions that affect intellectual capital as a whole. The study conducted by Edvinsson, et al., (2004) shows that leadership styles influence invention and knowledge reuse processes in an organization. The strategies developed by leaders contribute in the areas of employee motivation, opportunities for them (human capital related) and knowledge reuse, sharing, organizational infrastructure (structural capital related) as well as in customer relations, brand value and products and services (customer capital related) policies. Organizational culture has an impact on all dimensions of the intellectual capital. When one thinks about organizational culture and intellectual capital, 3M and the 15 per cent of recreational time it gives to employees to innovate is one of the first stories that come into mind. The organizational climate such as the extent to which organizations encourage risk-taking versus organizational control, and the extent to which team behaviour is encouraged over individual behaviour can all have an impact on the knowledge creation process (Smith, et al., 2005). To recap, critical organizational conditions that have an impact on all three dimensions of intellectual capital are the organizational culture and leadership.

Hypothesis 4: Organizational conditions such as culture and leadership influence all three dimensions (Human, Structural and Customer dimensions) of intellectual capital strongly.

Intellectual capital offers an organization its competitive advantage through branding, legally binding material (intellectual property, copyright,

trademarks and trade secrets), innovation, profitability and sustainability. Rather than physical assets, real organizational value rests on the above factors and this is precisely why organizations invest heavily in intellectual capital creation, management, and measurement.

Figure 1 is developed on the basis of the four hypotheses presented earlier.

As shown in Figure 1, the framework is divided into three major sections. These are the different dimensions of intellectual capital, the impact organizational conditions have on them, as well as organizational advantages gained as a result of the better management of intellectual capital. The conditions that influenced all three dimensions of intellectual capital are that of leadership and organizational culture. Other variables may also have an impact on intellectual capital, but they lie outside the scope of discussion in this chapter.

Discussion

The framework depicts how organizational conditions influences intellectual capital. The relationships between the different dimensions of intellectual capital and the different aspects of the organizational conditions are as follows. Organizational conditions such as opportunities, values, motivation and capability influence human capital; Organizational conditions such as the infrastructure, existing knowledge and the knowledge sharing process influence structural capital; Organizational conditions such as products and services, relationships and brand value influence customer capital; and organizational conditions such as culture and leadership influence all three dimensions of intellectual capital. In addition, individual dimension of intellectual capital mutually influences each other, and in sum, leads to positive organizational outcomes such as branding, reputation, competitiveness and sustainability.

Figure 1. Organizational conditions and intellectual capital

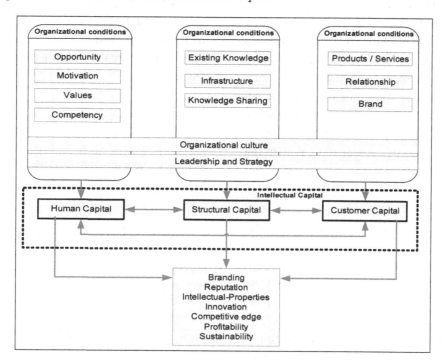

FUTURE RESEARCH DIRECTIONS

Apart from organizational conditions, two salient elements that influence the management of intellectual capital are culture and leadership (Edvinsson and Malone1997). Defined as a pattern of shared values and beliefs that shape behavioral norms (Deshpandé and Webster, 1989), culture is intimately tied to intellectual capital (Sánchez-Cañizares, et al., 2007). An important role of leaders is thus to nurture an organizational culture that facilitates intellectual capital development. This is done through the formulation of strategies and policies that are specifically intended to grow human, structural and customer capital.

To bolster human capital, leaders could create opportunities for interaction and knowledge exchange; actively explain and demonstrate the value of such opportunities; provide an environment that motivates knowledge creation and exchange behaviors; and strengthening employees' competencies through training and development programs. For example, Ford Motors openly talks about the importance of knowledge sharing, conducts internal advertising and organizes knowledge sharing events. Lotus Development on the other hand works through informal teams to share knowledge based on their business needs (McDermott and O'Dell, 2001).

To strengthen structural capital, leaders can consider re-design work-flow to engender knowledge creation, as well as to leverage on technology that connects people to people, as well as people to documents. Known commonly as the "Knowledge Yellow Page", experts in the organization are identified and accessible to others for advice, consultation, or knowledge exchange. In Bain and Company, for example, a "people finder" database was used by consultants on novel assignments to locate other consultants who could be contacted by telephone, e-mail, videoconference, or face-to-face to probe for advice on or solutions to problems (Hansen et al., 1999).

Customer capital can be deliberately cultivated through a heightened focus to serve customer better as well as a keener interest in the company's reputation and branding. For example, Holcim, an international cement manufacturer, created a Web-based platform where members of the cement industry including concrete producers and distributors not only carry out business transactions such as orders placement and payment but also share and exchange knowledge on topics such as cement order forecast, and experiences with specific applications. Holcim's customers were impressed by the extent to which their needs were met by the company (Gibbert, et al., 2002).

In short, organizational conditions can make a significant impact on the organization's most valuable intangible asset – that of intellectual capital. Such intellectual assets are important for organizational performance and market sustainability. Management needs to invest sufficient attention and resources on these conditions to ensure that intellectual capital is well created, sufficiently utilized and optimally managed in the long term.

For scholars, one possible direction for further research is to validate the framework in an actual organizational setting. Another is to focus on measures that improve or enhance the organizational conditions. It will be interesting to see how the positive business outcomes can be achieved once the right organizational conditions have been implemented.

CONCLUSION

The effects of organizational conditions on intellectual capital dimensions (human, structural and customer) have been examined and recent studies on intellectual capital have been included in this chapter. A framework has also been developed to depict organizational conditions and their impact on the different dimensions of intellectual capital.

The framework provides guidance for managers who are keen to develop strategies that enhance the intellectual capital of their organizations. Additional a few areas for future research have also been proposed.

REFERENCES

Barlett, C., & Ghoshal, S. (1995). *Transnational Management: Texts, Cases and Readings in Cross-Border Management*. Homewood, IL: Irwin.

Canibano, L., Garcia-Ayuso, C. M., & Sanchez, P. (2000). Accounting for intangibles: a literature review . *Journal of Accounting Literature*, *19*, 102–130.

Chang, A., & Tseng, C. (2005). Building customer capital through relationship marketing activities; The case of Taiwanese multilevel marketing companies. *Journal of Intellectual Capital*, *6*(2), 253–266. doi:10.1108/14691930510592834

Deshpandé, R., & Webster, F. E. Jr. (1989). Organizational culture and marketing: defining the research agenda . *Journal of Marketing*, *53*(1), 3–15. doi:10.2307/1251521

Edvinsson, L., Dvir, R., Roth, N., & Pasher, E. (2004). Innovations: the new unit of analysis in the knowledge era: The quest and context for innovation efficiency and management of IC. *Journal of Intellectual Capital*, *5*(1), 40–58. doi:10.1108/14691930410512914

Edvinsson, L., & Malone, M. S. (1997). *Intellectual Capital*. London: Piatkus.

Gibbert, M., Leibold, M., & Probst, G. (2002). Five styles of customer knowledge management and how smart companies put them into action. *European Management Journal*, *20*(5), 459–469. doi:10.1016/S0263-2373(02)00101-9

Habersam, M., & Piber, M. (2003). Exploring intellectual capital in hospitals: two qualitative case studies in Italy and Austria. *European Accounting Review*, *12*(4), 753–779. doi:10.1080/0963818030310001628455

Hansen, M. T., Nohria, N., & Kierney, T. (1999). What's your strategy for managing knowledge? *Harvard Business Review*, *77*(2), 106–116.

James, K., & Maria, A. (2001). Corporate Governance and Intellectual Capital: some conceptualizations. *Corporate Governance*, *9*(4), 259–275. doi:10.1111/1467-8683.00254

Lee, C. K., & Al-Hawamdeh, S. (2002). Factors Impacting Knowledge sharing. *Journal of Information and Knowledge Management*, *1*(1), 49–59. doi:10.1142/S0219649202000169

Lev, B. (2001). *Intangibles: Management, Measurement, and Reporting*. Washington, D.C.: Brookings Institution Press.

Lev, B. (2004). Sharpening the intangibles edge. *Harvard Business Review*, *82*(6), 109–116.

McDermott, R., & O'Dell, C. (2001). Overcoming cultural barriers to sharing knowledge. *Journal of Knowledge Management*, *5*(1), 76–85. doi:10.1108/13673270110384428

Nahapiet, J., & Ghoshal, S. (1998). Social capital, intellectual capital, and the organizational advantage, Academy of Management. *Academy of Management Review*, *23*(2), 242–266. doi:10.2307/259373

Nakahara, T. (2001). Innovation management using intellectual capital. *International Journal of Entrepreneurship and Innovation Management*, *1*(1), 96–110. doi:10.1504/IJEIM.2001.000447

Olsen, S., Tobey, J., & Kerr, M. (1997). A common framework for learning from ICM experience. *Ocean and Coastal Management*, *37*(2), 155–174. doi:10.1016/S0964-5691(97)90105-8

Pretty, R., & Guthrie, J. (2000). Intellectual capital literature review. *Journal of Intellectual Capital*, *1*(2), 155–176. doi:10.1108/14691930010348731

Roberts, H. (2000). Classification of Intellectual Capital. In J.E. Grojer & H. Stolowy (Eds.), *Classification of Intangibles* (pp. 197-205). Jouy-en-Josas: Groupe HEC.

Sánchez-Cañizares, S. M., Muñoz, M. A. A., & López-Guzmán, T. (2007). Organizational culture and intellectual capital: a new model. *Journal of Intellectual Capital*, *8*(3), 409–430. doi:10.1108/14691930710774849

Smith, K. G., Collins, C. J., & Clark, K. D. (2005). Existing knowledge, knowledge creation capability, and the rate of new product introduction in high-technology firms. *Academy of Management Journal*, *48*(2), 346–357.

Stewart, T. A. (1997). *Intellectual Capital: The New Wealth of Organisations*. London: Nicholas Brealey.

Subramaniam, M., & Yondit, M. A. (2005). The influence of intellectual capital on the types of innovative capabilities. *Academy of Management Journal*, *48*(3), 450–463.

Sveiby, K. E. (1997). *The new organization Wealth: Managing and Measuring Knowledge based Assets*. San Francisco, CA: Berret-Koehler.

KEY TERMS AND DEFINITIONS

Culture: A pattern of shared values and beliefs that shape behavioral norms.

Customer Capital: The relationships with customers (or suppliers) and knowledge of markets, distribution channels, competitors and trademarks.

Human Capital: The collective tacit and explicit knowledge held within the minds of individual employees.

Intellectual Capital: The intangible assets of an organization which comprise three essential elements, namely, human capital, structural capital and customer capital.

Innovation: The ability to draw upon existing knowledge and engage in knowledge activities to develop new intellectual capital for the creation of new products and services.

Structural Capital: Organizational routines and systems that encapsulate the knowledge generated and possessed by the company.

Chapter 15
Intellectual Capital:
How Knowledge Creates Value

Maria do Rosário Cabrita
Universidade Nova de Lisboa, Portugal

Virgílio Cruz Machado
Universidade Nova de Lisboa, Portugal

António Grilo
Universidade Nova de Lisboa, Portugal

ABSTRACT

With the rise of the "new economy", knowledge became a most valuable resource. Accepting knowledge as a resource suggests that knowledge can be acquired, transferred, combined and used, and it may be a potential source of sustainable competitive advantage. In this context, knowing how an organization creates value, based on its potential of knowledge, became a central question in management research. Under a strategic perspective, knowledge that creates value is defined as intellectual capital, the application of which will give organisations sustainable competitive advantage. Therefore, identifying, measuring and managing intellectual capital is crucial for corporate innovation and competitiveness. The purpose of our study is to examine the interrelationships and the effects of interaction between intellectual capital components and organisational performance, and defines how knowledge creates value. The study is developed in the context of Portuguese banks, an industry where differentiation of products and services almost exclusively hinges on the continuous rejuvenation of the underlying knowledge base. Empirical findings from this study support the propositions that intellectual capital is a key driver of organisational performance and that a knowledge-based perspective holds a more holistic model of organisations' value creation.

INTRODUCTION

Globalisation and the rapid technological advances of the past decades, particularly in the area of information and communications technol-

ogy, created a "new era" that has reshaped the global economic environment. The unprecedented changes in the global economic environment bring a tremendous challenge to organizations and governments. Those trends are changing the competitive structure of markets in such a way that the effectiveness of traditional sources of

DOI: 10.4018/978-1-61520-829-6.ch015

advantage is blurred. A New Paradigm economy emerged in which knowledge is seen as the critical factor of production (Carlucci *et al.*, 2004), the vehicle of economic benefits and the source of the nation's prosperity and sustainable competitive advantage. In response, new models of business are emerging where the value chain have their hard nucleus in the creation, dissemination, application and leverage of intellectual assets.

Organizations face new competitive paradigms associated with their ability to create, use, combine and manage the intellectual assets. Today, organizations and governments recognize the importance of intellectual capital as the key driver of performance and as a core differentiator. Intellectual capital has been identified as a set of intangibles (resources, capabilities and competences) that drive the organizational performance and value creation (Roos and Roos, 1997; Cabrita and Vaz, 2005). This fact suggests causal relationships between intellectual capital and organizational value creation (Marr and Roos, 2005). However, intangible assets seldom affect performance directly. Instead, they work indirectly through complementary and non-linear relationships of cause and effect (Ittner and Larcker, 1998; Kaplan and Norton, 2004). Value is then created through complex dynamic exchanges between tangibles (goods and money) and intangibles (cognition processes, intelligence and emotions) where individuals, groups or organisations engage in a value network by converting what they know, both individually and collectively, into tangible and intangible value.

From the management point of view it is essential to recognise that none of the elements of that set of intangibles is *per se* sufficient for successful performance. These key elements need to be combined to generate value. What is really important is to understand how these separate pieces come together to form a coherent framework for the company's future value. Organisations can not create value on their own without the initiative of the individual. Human capital is the collection of intangible resources that are embedded in the members of organisations. However, managing human knowledge is not the same as managing physical resources. Having access to knowledge repositories does not guarantee that people will use them efficiently. Moreover, people have to capture, select, integrate and combine information to create understanding and knowledge. Management capabilities are critically important for realising value from investments in intellectual assets. The role of management is crucial to promote sharing activities, to provide a learning culture, infrastructure and appropriate incentives to generate and disseminate knowledge.

In such a context, intellectual capital offers a possible pathway for reconfiguring our business models in an environment of global interdependencies. Intellectual capital is a phenomenon of interactions, connections and complementarities, meaning that a resource's productivity may improve through investment in other resources (Tsan and Chang, 2005; Marr *et al.*, 2004; Cabrita and Bontis, 2008). This perspective gives us a more organic and holistic view of value creation and may help us to better understand the interdependencies and dynamic exchanges in our turbulent business environment.

This study helps to understand that not all knowledge creates value. It is crucial to identify the company's strategic knowledge, the key drivers of performance. It should also be pointed out that the major purpose of our work is not to identify a measurement model for intellectual capital as we believe that the economic value of intellectual capital is almost unachievable. The purpose of this study is to empirically test that intellectual capital is a phenomenon of complementarities, and to assess how the intellectual capital components interrelate to impact organisational performance.

HOW VALUE IS CREATED IN THE KNOWLEDGE-DRIVEN ECONOMY

The concept of knowledge as a strategic asset underpins the idea that sustaining competitive success requires that firms capture the knowledge that resides in individuals and leverage it across the whole firm. Knowledge is then described as "capacity to act" (Sveiby, 2001), which suggests that the application of knowledge to tangible assets drives the creation of knowledge. However, managing intellectual assets is not the same as managing physical assets. The well-defined and well-known properties of physical and financial assets make them easier to manage than intellectual assets.

In a technically and intellectually based economy the rules of economics has been transforming the concept of value creation (Edvinsson, 2002). This does not mean that traditional economics is wrong. The fundamentals of supply and demand did not change, and the purpose that a business must make money also does not change. The essential point is that economic characteristics of knowledge are very different from those prevailing in the industrial era.

Knowledge is definitely a different object than steel, plastic, wheat or brick and traditional theories of the market system based on notions of physical commodities, prices, transactions and established property rights need some substantial re-thinking. Economic value which comes from creating, processing, communicating and selling information grows significantly faster than the value-added by traditional goods and services (Davis, 1996). The great virtue of the knowledge-based vision is its firm rejection of the economic law of diminishing returns. A new piece of knowledge can be applied an infinite number of times with no deterioration in its value due to repeated use. With accumulating knowledge and non-diminishing returns one quickly gets to a theory of endogenous growth as postulated by Romer (1986). High rates of knowledge acquisi-

tion lead to higher rates of investment. Moreover, these investments have non-diminishing returns. This in turn leads to either sustained or accelerated economic growth. This type of economic model has certainly changed the mindset of economists on "engines of growth" (Rittenberg, 1989; Brookings, 2000; Eustace, 2003).

There is a consensus in the literature that data, information, and even knowledge often have little value. Knowledge is not worth much, if it is not put to productive use along with the firm's other resources. Firms create value, combining different types of resources (tangibles and intangibles) and competences, and that value increases as much as those resources and competences interact. The key is to understand what makes knowledge valuable and, in particular, how knowledge creates wealth in a knowledge-driven economy. Valuable knowledge is that knowledge that is unique, difficult to replicate and then provides the mainspring of competitive advantage. If the application of some specific knowledge can create or sustain a competitive advantage by enabling an organisation to better formulate and implement its competitive strategy, then that knowledge is a strategic resource (Zack, 2002).

Value is now directly linked to the intelligence, speed and agility that come from a host of latent intangibles that represent a reservoir of potential talent and innovation that provides a source of competitive advantage (Eustace, 2003). This set of intangibles or intellectual capital creates value when its components are combined and put into action and degrades when they remain unused (Roos, 2005). The value drivers represent how successful the company has been in converting project ideas into organisational value. This suggests that the value generated is a function of the way in which resources are applied and managed. In other words, having a resource is not enough to create value. In order to create or leverage value, the resources have to be deployed effectively and efficiently.

The notion of a value chain helps us to understand the increase of value along the chain of activities in bringing a final offering to stakeholders. Value chain analysis looks at each link in the chain to see where value is added and how it might be increased. The theory goes that at every point along the value chain we should be adding value to the product or service.

Sveiby (2001) argues that the key to value creation lies with the effectiveness of knowledge transfers and conversions. Carlucci *et al.*, (2004) demonstrate that the generated value is the result of an organization's ability to manage its business process and the effectiveness and efficiency of performing organizational processes are based on organizational competencies. Knowledge assets interact with each other to create competencies and capabilities, and it is often these interactions that provide a competitive advantage because they make these assets difficult for competitors to replicate (Barney, 1991; Teece *et al.*, 1997; Marr, 2005). These value drivers are bundled together, and the interactions between them are varied, complex and dynamic making difficult to demonstrate the cause and effect relationships and its linkage to value outcomes. This perspective goes beyond the traditional value chain to other more complex ways of creating value, such as *value networks*, *value constellations*, and *value shops* as explained by Haanes and Fjeldstad (2000).

- *Value networks* create value by making different products and services available to customers. The value is derived from the network giving buyers access to sellers of what they want, and by putting suppliers in contact with customers who want their products. As value should be added at every point along the value network, when a participant receives a value input he should find ways to use that input to provide greater value in the form of products and services. If a participant in network can both gain value for oneself and also lever-

age that input for a greater value output, than that is really creating value. Examples of companies creating value through networks include commercial banks, airlines, postal agencies, insurers, brokers, and stock exchanges.

- *Value constellations* can be considered to be linked sets of different value networks.
- *Value shops* create value by solving unique problems for customers by using relevant competencies. Examples of companies that create value as 'shops' include accountants, academics, physicians, designers, lawyers, investment bankers, business consultants, and consulting engineers.

STRATEGIC KNOWLEDGE

Strategic management models traditionally have defined the firm's strategy in terms of its product and market positioning – the products it makes and the markets it serves. The resource-based approach (Penrose, 1959; Wernerfelt, 1984; Barney, 1991; Peteraf, 1993) suggests, however, that firms should compete based on their unique, valuable and inimitable resources and capabilities rather than the products and services derived from those resources and capabilities. Resources and capabilities can be seen as the platform from which the firm derives various products and services for several markets (Kogut and Kulatilaka, 1994).

While these two views of strategy may appear to be at cross purposes, they are actually complementary when combined and integrated into the SWOT framework. Indeed, "the resource-based perspective complements the industry analysis framework" (Amit and Schoemaker, 1993:35). Roos (2005) presents the Amit and Schoemaker's theory of integrated strategy (see Figure 1), a theoretical approach that seeks to integrate the competitive forces and the resource-based paradigms of competitive advantage.

Figure 1. Amit and Schoemaker's theory of integrated strategy.

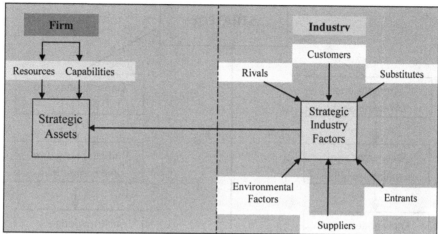

Source: Roos (2005:130)

Integrating these two perspectives in the knowledge context, Zack (2002) analyses the sources of advantage (inside and outside company) that come from knowledge as a strategic resource and developed a knowledge-based SWOT framework, a K-SWOT (Figure 2), relating the "SW" side and "OT" side of SWOT analysis to knowledge.

The "SW" side of the K-SWOT framework looks at knowledge from the internal resource-based perspective to explain why knowledge may be a firm's most strategic resource. The "OT" side of the K-SWOT framework looks at knowledge as the basis for describing and evaluating strategic positions within industries and related knowledge-based opportunities and threats. The two sides form an integrated K-SWOT showing how both strategic views, the resource-based view and the competitive forces, are complementary and reinforcing.

The two perspectives are integrated to form a SWOT by realizing that it is the organization's knowledge and learning strengths and weaknesses that enable it to locate and move to strategic knowledge positions in order to manage its knowledge-based opportunities and threats.

To clarify and develop those links, Zack *et al.* (1999) propose how an organization must, on the basis of its existing accumulated knowledge, articulate its strategic intent, then identify the knowledge required to achieve its intended strategy, and compare that with its actual knowledge, revealing strategic knowledge gaps.

In this sense, it is crucial to understand and identify the critical knowledge to execute the firm's strategy. This assumption nurtures the essence of the intellectual capital concept.

DEFINING INTELLECTUAL CAPITAL

The literature refers to several attempts to make the concept of intellectual capital more accessible and understandable, though there is no universal definition on intellectual capital until recently. It is difficult to define intellectual capital due to its intangible and dynamic nature. The main problem is that too much of the nature of intellectual capital is still unknown and hard to capture in explicit terms (Seetharaman *et al.*, 2002). Chaharbaghi and Cripps (2006:30) assert that "it is impossible and undesirable to reduce intellectual capital to a calculable number that establishes whether an

241

Figure 2. The K-SWOT framework. Source: Zack (2002)

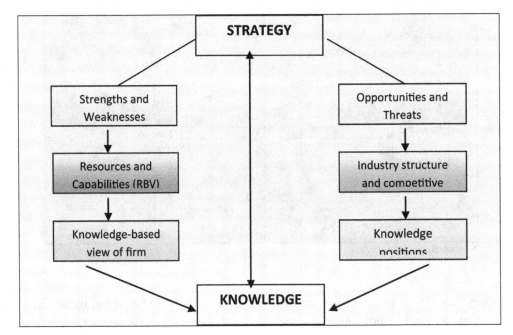

organization's intellectual capital has increased or diminished".

Several definitions of intellectual capital have been proposed (Roos *et al.*, 1997; Stewart, 1997; Sveiby, 2001) however there is presently no universally acceptable one. As argued by Marr (2005), definition problems occur when different people talk about the same concept from different perspectives, using the same language to describe different constructs.

Despite this lack of consensus it would appear that researchers and practitioners have the same broad set of theoretical and practical assumptions in mind. They realize that in principle great economies and efficiencies could be achieved if knowledge could be managed and distributed efficiently around the organization. Another point of convergence between authors is that intellectual capital is the driver of organisational performance and the source of competitive advantage.

Literature review provides sufficient arguments to suggest that there are at least three basic ideas that emerge from the various definitions of intellectual capital:

i. the knowledge itself is its basic element;
ii. the need for a structure to encourage, maintain, distribute and deliver that knowledge appropriately and;
iii. the perception that it is the effect of a collective practice.

A well-known definition is the one proposed by Edvinsson and Malone (1997:3): "intellectual capital is the knowledge applied to work to create value". Viedma (2003) uses the terms "intellectual capital" and "core competences" interchangeably. This approach is in agreement with Andriessen (2001) who refers to intellectual capital as a unique bundle of intangible assets that are the basis of sustainable competitive advantage.

It seems that the difference between various intellectual capital definitions lies mainly in the content that intellectual capital may cover. According to Zhou and Fink (2003), a definition of intellectual capital should be broad enough to enable organizations to include the full range of their intangibles and specific enough to provide guidance for management to take action.

Figure 3.

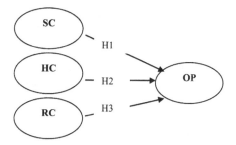

H1: Structural capital is positively associated with organisational performance;
H2: Human capital is positively associated with organisational performance;
H3: Relational capital is positively associated with organisational performance.

For the purpose of our study, intellectual capital can be described as all factors (resources, capabilities and competences) critical to the organizational value. In this sense, intellectual capital represents knowledge that creates value.

Although frameworks are useful for classifying intangible assets, they do not reflect the flow of intellectual capital in an organization or provide a basis for its management. Some attempts to operationalize the concept have emerged in the literature, classifying intellectual capital into the categories of human capital (HC), structural capital (SC) and relational capital (RC) (Edvinsson and Malone, 1997; Stewart, 1997; Bontis, 1998).

Human capital is the brain and soul of an organization. It is considered the key element of intellectual capital (Choo and Bontis, 2002; Cabrita and Bontis, 2008) and the most important source of sustainable competitive advantage (Nonaka and Takeuchi, 1995). Employees generate intellectual capital through their competence, attitude and intellectual agility (Roos *et al.*, 1997). Competence includes skills and education, while attitude represents the behavioural element of the employee's work. Intellectual agility enables one to change practices and to think of innovative solutions to problems.

Structural capital is what remains in the company when employees go home at night (Roos *et al.*, 1997). It comprises internal processes, orga-

nizational structure, databases, culture and all that enable organizations to make their human capital more productive. The role of organizations is to provide the necessary structure for individuals to collaborate in a way that leverages their talent and existing market opportunities in order to create economic value. The focus is on getting a higher leverage of the human capital through structural capital, producing a "multiplier effect" (Edvinsson, 2002).

Relational capital is the knowledge embedded in the network of relationships that an organization develops by conducting its business. Therefore, firms are forming different relationships between partners, such as networks, cross-boundary teams, supply chain partnerships and strategic alliances to diffuse knowledge and increase innovation.

RESEARCH MODELS AND HYPOTHESES

Conceptual models are based on the literature and previous works (Bontis, 1998; Tsan and Chang, 2005). The hypothesis of our research will be tested using three models. Figure 3 represents simple relationships between the three components of intellectual capital and organisational performance. Figure 4 shows interrelationships among intellectual capital components and organisational

Figure 4.

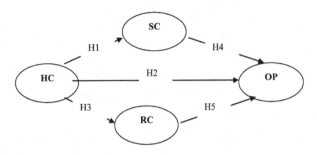

H₁: Human capital is positively associated with structural capital;
H₂: Human capital is positively associated with organisational performance;
H₃: Human capital is positively associated with relational capital;
H₄: Structural capital is positively associated with organisational performance;
H₅: Relational capital is positively associated with organisational performance.

performance. Finally, Figure 5 adds to Figure 4 the interaction term of the three components of intellectual capital, in order to evaluate its impact on organisational performance.

RESEARCH DESIGN AND METHODOLOGY

This study is exploratory in nature. The constructs dimensionality was conducted by a thorough review of literature and experts' opinion (Bontis, 1998; Darroch and McNaughton, 2002). Intellectual capital is a multidimensional construct in which its components emerge from the theories of other disciplines (e.g. marketing, human resources, knowledge management, or information systems). Therefore, a multi-item scale from other disciplines was employed which, in the opinion of Peter (1991:138), "substantially increase the probability of a validation study". Additionally,

Figure 5.

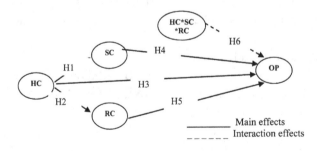

H₁: Human capital is positively associated with structural capital;
H₂: Human capital is positively associated with relational capital;
H₃: Human capital is positively associated with organisational performance;
H₄: Structural capital is positively associated with organisational performance;
H₅: Relational capital is positively associated with organisational performance;
H₆: Relational capital and structural capital positively moderates the relationship between human capital and organisational performance.

component factor analysis helped us to confirm the dimensions defined *a priori.*

The structural model was estimated using Partial Least Squares (PLS), an alternative statistical approach for situations where theory is weak or when the available measures would not conform to a rigorously specified model.

Measurement Instrument

We applied a questionnaire already administered in Canada (Bontis, 1998) and Malaysia

(Bontis *et al.,* 2000). Eight more items in the relational capital component were included to reflect the interests of different stakeholders groups (clients, competitors and sector associations). A copy of the questionnaire can be requested from the authors. Following Churchill's (1979) recommendations, the 63 original items were validated again. Independent assessment of validity enhances the quality of measures. New items were included after being submitted to the recommendation of the author's original questionnaire. Content validity was attempted through the depth of literature search and expert opinions (Bontis, 1998; Darroch and McNaughton, 2002; Chin, 1998). Totalling 71 items, the questionnaire was pre-tested through personal interviews with eight banking managers.

Data Collection

Data were collected from a sample of 53 banks, given an entire population of 62 banks operating in of Portugal. All 53 banks are affiliated members of the Portuguese Bankers Association.

Intellectual capital is a complex concept and given its strategic nature the survey instrument was piloted using a convenience sample of 178 members (including first, second, third and fourth-levels executives). A total of 151 respondents returned the questionnaire for an 84 per cent response for the test pilot phase.

In order to secure high quality data, respondents were not chosen at random for the main study. Preliminary interviews allowed us to identify the appropriate employees who possessed the special qualifications (management level, professional status, experience and specialized knowledge) to answer the questionnaire (Bontis, 1998).

Based on the concept of "strategic awareness" (Hambrick, 1981) an initial sample of 430 executives (i.e., chief level, first and second level) was drawn from a master list of 1081 bankers registered with the Portuguese Banking Association.

PLS Overview

Our model was estimated using Partial Least Squares (PLS), specifically, PLSGRAPH v.3.00. PLS is a non-parametric analytical alternative to Structural Equation Modelling (SEM) techniques. Conceptually, PLS is an iterative combination of principal components analysis relating measures to constructs (outer relations), and path analysis allowing a causal chain system of constructs (inner relations). PLS estimation does not require assumptions of metric data, multi-normality (which our data do not satisfy) or independence of observations. Besides, it works well with small samples and is ideally suited to the early stages of theory building and testing.

Although PLS estimates parameters for both the links between measures and constructs (i.e. loadings) and the links between the constructs in the model (i.e. path coefficients), at the same time, PLS proceeds in two stages. The first stage is to assess the measurement model, that is, the relationships between the indicators or items and the constructs that they measure. The second stage requires the evaluation of the structural model to assess the explanatory power of the independent variables and examine the size and the significance of path coefficients.

The test of the measurement model included estimation of the reliability coefficients (composite reliability) as well as an examination of the convergent and discriminant validity of the research instrument. The criteria suggested by Nunnally (1978) were applied where measures with standardized loadings of 0.707 or more are accepted. However, "loadings of 0.5 or 0.6 may still be acceptable if there exists additional indicators in the block for comparison basis" (Chin, 1998:325).

The test of the structural model includes estimating the path coefficients, interpreted as standardized beta weights in a regression analysis, and R^2, which is used to assess the proportion of variance in the endogenous constructs which can be accounted for by the antecedents. To estimate path coefficients, t-statistics were calculated using nonparametric test of significance known as jackknifing (Wildt *et al.*, 1982).

PLS has as its primary objective, the minimization of error (or, equivalently, the maximization of variance explained) in all endogenous constructs. The degree to which any particular PLS model accomplishes this objective can be determined by examining the R^2 values for the dependent (endogenous) constructs. One of the attractive features of PLS is that it can be used to quickly generate and test a variety of different theoretical models.

DATA ANALYSIS

Measurement model (outer model) relates measures to constructs. Following the pilot test, we inspected the reliability of measures using the Cronbach's alpha. The reliabilities for each of the four constructs are fine, since the alpha values are greater than 0.93, exceeding the level of 0.7, considered good for exploratory research (Nunnally, 1978). Further, we used the principal component analysis for choosing the items that loaded at least 0.50 in its corresponding construct. Hair *et al.* (1992) consider loadings of 0.50 or greater very significant. Factor findings were confirmed using PLS to assess individual item reliabilities. We found that results are very similar in the two

approaches. Hence, we retained those 48 items that simultaneously loaded: *(i)* 0.50 in its corresponding construct by the principal component analysis, and; *(ii)* 0.50 in the individual item reliabilities by the PLS analysis, as recommended by Chin (1998) for early stages of research. We proceed with the final test, assessing firstly the measurement model and followed with the structural model.

Measurement Model

A measurement model (outer model) relates measures to constructs. The measurement model was assessed by looking at the internal consistency between items intended to measure the same construct, and the discriminant validity between constructs as shown in Table 1. Internal consistency was determined using the measure suggested by Fornell and Larcker (1981). The authors argue that this measure is similar to Cronbach's alpha, but preferred to Cronbach's alpha since it uses the item loadings obtained within a nomological network (or causal model). As this measure is not influenced by the number of items in the scale and it does not assume that each item make equal contribution to the construct, it is considered more general than Cronbach's alpha. However, the interpretation is similar and the guidelines suggested by Nunnally can be adopted for both situations. Internal consistency values in the fourth column of Table 1 show that the four constructs exceed the 0.70 recommended by Nunnally, a benchmark for "modest" composite reliability, applicable for exploratory works.

Discriminant validity of the model was assessed by calculating the average variance extracted for each construct (Fornell and Larcker, 1981). The last column of Table 1 shows the square root of the variance along the diagonal of the correlation matrix. For acceptable discriminant validity, the diagonal should be greater than all other entries in the same row and column, as it is the case here.

Table 1. Measurement model results

Items	Number of items	Cronbach Alpha	Internal consistency (Fornell & Larcker)	Discriminant validity (*) (Correlation of constructs) HSRP
Human	14	0,9505	0,9569	**0,783**
Structural	10	0,9406	0,9498	0,755 **0,809**
Relational	14	0,9501	0,9563	0,697 0,700 **0,782**
Performance	10	0,9416	0,9507	0,568 0,634 0,592 **0,812**

(*) Diagonal elements in the correlation of constructs matrix are the square roots of average variance extracted.

Figure 6.

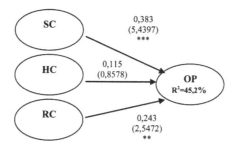

Note: Top number is path, t-values in brackets, *** significant at p-value<0,001; ** p-value < 0,05

Structural Model

As the measurement model satisfies the criteria for convergent and discriminant validity, our next step was to evaluate the structural models. A structural model (inner model) assesses the explanatory power of independent variables. As PLS does not make any distributional assumption, traditional parametric tests are inappropriate. So, to assess the statistical significance of the loadings and the path coefficients (i.e., standardized ß's), a jackknife analysis was performed.

Given that PLS considers all path coefficients simultaneously (thus allowing analysis of direct, indirect, and spurious relationships) and estimates multiple individual item loadings in the context of a theoretically specified model rather than in isolation, it allows that the researcher avoid biased and inconsistent parameter estimates for these equations.

R^2 indicates that 45.2% of the variation in the organisational performance (i.e. value created) is accounted for the model. In line with Bontis' work for Canada, the relationship between human capital and business performance is not significant, though positive.

In Figure 7, while structural capital and relational capital impact directly and significantly on the organisational performance, human capital only indirectly influences substantively the organisational performance. Once again, the direct relationship between human capital and organisational performance proves not significant, although R^2 is almost the same.

Figure 8 shows the interaction effect of the three components of intellectual capital (i.e. the term HC*SC*RC). Indeed, relational capital and structural capital positively moderates the relationship between human capital and organisational performance. R^2 increases to 46.3%, the most important of the three models, and again, the

Figure 7.

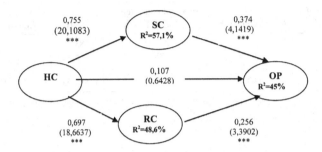

Note: Top number is path, t-values in brackets, *** significant at p-value<0,001

Figure 8.

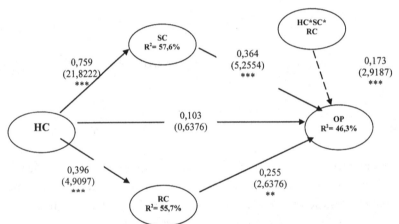

Note: Top number is path, t-values in brackets, *** significant at p-value<0,001; ** p-value < 0,05

direct relationship between human capital and organisational performance is not significant. Moreover, a significant R^2 change here indicates that human capital, structural capital and relational capital interact to influence organisational performance. Thus, the results provide empirical support for the assumption that organisational value is created in the interaction of the three dimensions of the intellectual capital.

DISCUSSION AND CONCLUSION

The comparative analysis concludes that the direct effect of human capital in organisational performance is not significant in the three models proposed. This proves that human capital has a positive influence in business performance, however, this relationship is substantive and significant, namely, when it interrelates with the two other components of intellectual capital. Figure 6 reveals that the human capital is practically useless without the supportive structure of an organization which means that a focus on knowledge workers alone does not necessarily guarantee a significant impact in performance.

Figure 7 (the main effects model) only considers the interrelationships among the intellectual capital and organisational performance, while Figure 8 adds the interaction effects.

Figure 8 is the best model specification (diamond model) since R^2 reflects a high degree of explanatory power and path coefficients are all substantive and significant. These results are in line with those of Bontis (1998) and Bontis *et al.* (2000) which emphasise that there must exists a constant interplay among the three constructs in order for an organisation to leverage its knowledge base.

The findings of this study have several implications. First, in line with previous studies in Canada and Malaysia, intellectual capital is substantively and significantly related to the organisational performance in the Portuguese banking sector.

Second, empirical findings from this study support the proposition that intellectual capital is a driver of organisational value, however, not all combinations of intangibles produce a significant value. Intellectual resources are often internally generated, interrelated and interdependent, and their value is, therefore, context specific. Given the uniqueness of each firm's configuration of resources, capabilities and competencies, it is not possible to specify a single set of organizational arrangements conducive to intellectual capital management. It does suggest that there are a variety of routes to success.

Third, this study also provides evidence that human capital is practically useless without the supportive structure of an organization, meaning that a focus on knowledge workers alone does not necessarily guarantee a significant impact on performance. It is not enough for an organisation to hire and promote the brightest individuals it can find. Without the support of organisational resources, individuals have no ability to do anything with their ideas. Organisations should also support and nurture bright individuals into sharing

human capital through organizational learning and form a culture that promotes interrelationships between their members.

Fourth, the three constructs that make up the intellectual capital phenomenon are known to affect each other. Deficiencies in any of these factors can affect the overall goal of continual progress in the organizational value. An organisation improves by making investments in human capital which should lead to competent and capable people. These people then may develop a better structural capital which in turn leads to the more productive and loyal external relationships. At the end, better organisational performance will result in higher market valuation.

Fifth, intellectual capital elements interact with each other and get transformed along a value creation constellation in order to impact the overall organizational value. So, the individual competencies and personal characteristics that make up human capital are made manifest through structural capital, and the collective knowledge that make up structural capital is made manifest through a complex relationship network that make cooperative actions possible.

Finally, a perspective based on the intellectual capital of the firm provides a holistic view of the value creation process as the nature of intellectual assets are such that their value-creating potential increases, the more they are integrated with other resources and activities.

REFERENCES

Amit, R., & Schoemaker, P. (1993). Strategic assets and organizational rent. *Strategic Management Journal*, *4*(1), 33–46. doi:10.1002/smj.4250140105

Andriessen, D. (2001). *Weightless wealth*. Paper presented at the 4th World Congress on the Management of Intellectual Capital, McMaster University, January, 17-19, Hamilton, Ontario, 1-10.

Barney, J. B. (1991). Firm resources and sustained competitive advantage. *Journal of Management, 17*(1), 99–120. doi:10.1177/014920639101700108

Bontis, N. (1998). Intellectual capital: An exploratory study that develops measures and models. *Management Decision, 36*(2), 63–76. doi:10.1108/00251749810204142

Bontis, N., Keow, W. C., & Richardson, S. (2000). Intellectual capital and business performance in Malaysian industries. *Journal of Intellectual Capital, 1*(1), 85–100. doi:10.1108/14691930010324188

Brookings (2000). *Understanding intangible sources of value,* the Brookings Institution, Washington, DC. Retrieved from www.brookings.edu

Cabrita, M. R., & Bontis, N. (2008). Intellectual Capital and Business Performance in Portuguese Banking Industry. *International Journal of Technology Management, 43*(1-3), 212–237. doi:10.1504/IJTM.2008.019416

Cabrita, M. R., & Vaz, J. L. (2005). Intellectual capital and value creation: Evidencing in Portuguese banking industry. *Electronic Journal of Knowledge Management, 4*(1), 11–19.

Carlucci, D., Marr, B., & Schiuma, G. (2004). The knowledge value chain: How intellectual capital impacts on business performance. *International Journal of Technology Management, 27*(6/7), 575–590. doi:10.1504/IJTM.2004.004903

Chaharbaghi, K., & Cripps, S. (2006). Intellectual capital: Direction, not blind faith. *Journal of Intellectual Capital, 7*(1), 29–42. doi:10.1108/14691930610639750

Chin, W. W. (1998). The partial least squares approach to structural equation modelling. In Marcoulides, G. A. (Ed.), *Modern methods for business research.* Mahwah, NJ: Lawrence Erlbaum Associates.

Choo, C. W., & Bontis, N. (2002). *The strategic management of intellectual capital and organizational knowledge.* New York: Oxford University Press, Inc.

Churchill, G. A. Jr. (1979). A paradigm for developing better measures of marketing constructs. *JMR, Journal of Marketing Research, 16*(February), 64–73. doi:10.2307/3150876

Darroch, J., & McNaughton, R. (2002). *Developing a measure of knowledge management.* In N. Bontis (Ed.), *World Congress on Intellectual Capital Readings* (pp. 226-242). Boston, MA: Butterworth-Heinemann.

Davis, S. (1996). *Future Perfect.* Reading, Massachusetts: Addison-Wesley.

Edvinsson, L. (2002). *Corporate Longitude.* London: Prentice Hall.

Edvinsson, L., & Malone, M. (1997). *Intellectual capital: realising your company's true value by finding its hidden brainpower.* New York: Harper Collins.

Eustace, C. (2003). A new perspective on the knowledge value chain. *Journal of Intellectual Capital, 4*(4), 588–596. doi:10.1108/14691930310504581

Fornell, C., & Larcker, D. F. (1981). Evaluating structural equation models with unobservable variables and measurement error. *JMR, Journal of Marketing Research, 18*(1), 39–50. doi:10.2307/3151312

Haanes, K., & Fjeldstad, Ø. (2000). Linking Intangible Resources and Competition. *European Management Journal, 18*(1), 52–62. doi:10.1016/S0263-2373(99)00068-7

Hair, J., Anderson, R., Tatham, R., & Black, W. (1992). *Multivariate data analysis with readings* (3rd ed.). NJ: Prentice-Hall International, Inc.

Hambrick, D. C. (1981). Strategic awareness within top management teams. *Strategic Management Journal*, *2*(3), 263–279. doi:10.1002/smj.4250020305

Ittner, C., & Larcker, D. (1998). Are non-financial measures leading indicators of financial performance? An analysis of customer satisfaction. *Journal of Accounting Research*, *36*(Supplement), 1–35. doi:10.2307/2491304

Kaplan, R. S., & Norton, D. P. (2004). Measuring the strategic readiness of intangible assets. *Harvard Business Review*, *82*(1), 52–63.

Kogut, B., & Kulatilaka, N. (1994). Options thinking and platform investments: Investing in opportunity. *California Management Review*, (Winter): 52–71.

Marr, B. (2005). *Perspectives on intellectual capital – multidisciplinary insights into management, measurement, and reporting*. Oxford: Butterworth-Heinemann.

Marr, B., & Roos, G. (2005). A strategy perspective on intellectual capital. In Marr, B. (Ed.), *Perspectives on intellectual capital – multidisciplinary insights into management, measurement and reporting* (pp. 28–41). Oxford: Butterworth-Heinemann.

Marr, B., Schiuma, G., & Neely, A. (2004). The dynamics of value creation – Mapping your intellectual performance drivers. *Journal of Intellectual Capital*, *5*(2), 312–325. doi:10.1108/14691930410533722

Nonaka, I., & Takeuchi, H. (1995). *The knowledge creating company: How Japanese companies manage the dynamics of innovation*. New York: Oxford University Press.

Nunnally, J. (1978). *Psychometric theory* (2nd ed.). New York: McGraw-Hill.

Penrose, E. T. (1959). *The theory of the growth of the firm*. New York: John Wiley.

Peter, J. P. (1981). Construct validity: A review of basic issues and marketing practices. *JMR, Journal of Marketing Research*, *18*(May), 133–145. doi:10.2307/3150948

Peteraf, M. A. (1993). The cornerstone of competitive advantage: A resource-based view. *Strategic Management Journal*, *14*(March), 179–191. doi:10.1002/smj.4250140303

Rittenberg, L. (1989). On the problem of identifying the engines of economic growth. *Studies in Comparative International Development*, *24*(3), 51–61. doi:10.1007/BF02686990

Romer, P. (1986). Increasing return and long-run growth. *The Journal of Political Economy*, *94*(5), 1002–1037. doi:10.1086/261420

Roos, G. (2005). Intellectual capital and strategy: A primer for today's manager. In Coate, P. (Ed.), *Handbook of Business Strategy* (pp. 123–132).

Roos, G., & Roos, J. (1997). Measuring your company's intellectual performance. *Long Range Planning*, *30*(3), 413–426. doi:10.1016/S0024-6301(97)90260-0

Roos, J., Roos, G., Dragonetti, N. C., & Edvinsson, L. (1997). *Intellectual capital: Navigating the new business landscape*. London: Macmillan Press.

Seetharaman, A., Sooria, H. H., & Saravanan, A. S. (2002). Intellectual capital accounting and reporting in the knowledge economy. *Journal of Intellectual Capital*, *3*(2), 128–148. doi:10.1108/14691930210424734

Stewart, T. A. (1997). *Intellectual capital: The new wealth of nations*. New York: Doubleday.

Sveiby, K. (2001). A knowledge-based theory of the firm to guide in strategic formulation. *Journal of Intellectual Capital*, *2*(4), 344–358. doi:10.1108/14691930110409651

Teece, D. J., Pisano, G., & Shuen, A. (1997). Dynamic capabilities and strategic management. *Strategic Management Journal, 18*(7), 509–533. doi:10.1002/(SICI)1097-0266(199708)18:7<509::AID-SMJ882>3.0.CO;2-Z

Tsan, W. N., & Chang, C. C. (2005). Intellectual capital system interaction. *Journal of Intellectual Capital, 6*(2), 285–298. doi:10.1108/14691930510592852

Viedma, J. M. M. (2003). In search of an intellectual capital general theory. *Electronic Journal of Knowledge Management, 1*(2), 213–226.

Wernerfelt, B. (1984). A resource-based view of the firm. *Strategic Management Journal, 5*(2), 171–180. doi:10.1002/smj.4250050207

Wildt, A. R., Lambert, Z. V., & Durand, R. M. (1982). Applying the jackknife statistics in testing and interpreting canonical weights, loadings and cross-loadings. *JMR, Journal of Marketing Research, 19*, 99–107. doi:10.2307/3151534

Zack, M. H. (2002). A strategic pretext for knowledge management. In *Proceedings of The Third European Conference on Organizational Knowledge, Learning and Capabilities*, Athens, Greece, April 5. Retrieved from http://www.alba.edu.gr/OKLC2002/Proceedings/

Zack, M. H., Smith, D. E., & Slusher, J. A. (1999). *Knowledge and strategy*. Williamsburg, VA: Institute for Knowledge Management.

Zhou, A. Z., & Fink, D. (2003). The intellectual capital web: A systematic linking of intellectual capital and knowledge management. *Journal of Intellectual Capital, 4*(1), 34–48. doi:10.1108/14691930310455379

Compilation of References

Abecker, A., Mentzas, G., Legal, M., Ntioudis, S., & Papavassiliou, G. (2001). Business Process Oriented Delivery of Knowledge through Domain Ontologies. In *Proceedings of DEXA conference, Munich.*

Ackoff, R. L. (1983). Beyond prediction and preparation. *Journal of Management Studies, 20*(1), 59–69. doi:10.1111/j.1467-6486.1983.tb00198.x

Adams (2009). Retrieved from http://www.nafems.org/downloads/public/nafems_-_the_role_of_simulation_in_product_development_-_whitepaper.pdf

Akkermans, H. A. (2001). Renga: A systems approach to facilitating inter-organizational network development. *System Dynamics Review, 17*(3), 179–193. doi:10.1002/sdr.215

Akkiraju, R., et al. (2005). Web-Service Semantics - WSDL-S, W3C Member Submission, 7 November 2005. Retrieved March 12, 2009 from http://www.w3.org/Submission/WSDL-S

Alencar, E. S. (1997). *A gerência da criatividade.* S. Paulo: Makron Books

Al-Momani, E., & Rawabdeh, I. (2008). An Application of Finite Element Method and Design of Experiments in the Optimisation of Sheet Metal Blanking Process. *Jordan Journal of Mechanical and Industrial Engineering, 2*(1), 53–63.

Alvarenga Neto, R. (2002). Gestão da Informação e do Conhecimento nas Organizações: análise de casos relatados em organizações públicas e privadas [Information and knowledge management in organizations: analysis of related cases in public and private organizations] Mestrado em Ciência da Informação [Masters in Information Science]. Belo Horizonte: PPGCI, Escola de Ciência da Informação da UFMG.

Alvarenga Neto, R. (2005).Gestão do conhecimento em organizações: proposta de mapeamento conceitual integrativo [Knowledge management in organizations: an integrative conceptual mapping proposition] Tese [Doctoral thesis in Information Science]. Belo Horizonte: PPGCI, Escola de Ciência da Informação da UFMG.

Alvarenga Neto, R., Souza, R.R. et al (2008). Strategic Knowledge Management: in search of a knowledge-based organizational model. *Comportamento Organizacional & Gestão, 14*(2).

American Productivity and Quality Center – APQC. (2004). Communities of practice. http://www.apqc.org

Amin, A., & Cohendet, P. (2006). Geographies of Knowledge Formation in Firms. *Industry and Innovation, 12*(4), 465–486. doi:10.1080/13662710500381658

Amit, R., & Schoemaker, P. J. H. (1993). Strategic assets and organizational rent. *Strategic Management Journal, 14*(1), 33–46. doi:10.1002/smj.4250140105

Amtsblatt der Europäischen Union. (2003). *Empfehlungen der Kommission vom 6. Mai 2003 betreffend die Definition der Kleinstunternehmen sowie der kleinen und mittleren Unternehmen.* Retrieved July 30, 2007 from http://europa. eu.int/eur-lex/pri/de/oj/dat/2003/l_124/l_12420030520 de00360041.pdf

Andriessen, D. (2004). *Making sense of Intellectual Capital: Designing a Method for the Valuation of Intangibles.* Oxford: Elsevier Buttherworth-Heinemann.

Andriessen, D. (2001). *Weightless wealth.* Paper presented at the 4th World Congress on the Management of Intellectual Capital, McMaster University, January, 17-19, Hamilton, Ontario, 1-10.

Ansys (2010). Retrieved from www.Ansys.com

Antony, F. (2006). Taguchi or classical design of experiments: a perspective from a practitioner. *Sensor Review, 26*(3), 227–230. doi:10.1108/02602280610675519

Antony, F., Tzu-Yao, C., & Ghosh, S. (2003). Training for design of experiments. *Work Study, 52*(7), 341–346. doi:10.1108/00438020310502642

Argyris, C., & Schön, D. (1978). *Organizational learning: a theory of action perspective.* Reading, MA: Addison-Wesley.

Arkitema (2005). Knowledge Account, sent by Arkitema's management to one of the authors.

Arora, A., Gambardella, A., & Rullani, E. (1997). Division of labour and the locus of inventive activity. *The Journal of Management and Governance, 1*, 123–140. doi:10.1023/A:1009993430964

Asheim, B. T., & Coenen, L. (2006). Contextualizing regional innovation systems in a globalizing learning economy: on knowledge basis and institutional frameworks. *The Journal of Technology Transfer, 31*, 163–173. doi:10.1007/s10961-005-5028-0

ATP. (2005). Knowledge activities, Annual Report. Retrieved February 2007 from http://www.atp.dk/

Attwell, G., Dirckinck-Holmfeld, D., Fabian, P., Kárpáti, A., & Littig, P. (2003). *E-learning in Europe – Results and Recommendations.* Thematic Monitoring under the LEONARDO DA VINCI Programme. Bonn, Germany. Report., Impuls 010.

Auh, S., & Menguc, B. (2005). Balancig exploration and exploitation: the moderating role of competitive intensity. *Journal of Business Research, 58*(12), 1652–1661. doi:10.1016/j.jbusres.2004.11.007

Averill, S., & Hall, T. (2005). *An observatory of eLearning in Small Medium Enterprises (SMEs).* In G. Richards (Ed.), *Proceedings of World Conference on E-Learning in Corporate, Government, Healthcare and Higher Education* (pp. 220-225). Chesapeake: VA: AACE.

Balasubramanian, R., & Tiwana, A. (1999). Supporting collaborative process knowledge in new product development teams. *Decision Support Systems, 27*(1-2), 213–135. doi:10.1016/S0167-9236(99)00045-7

Balconi, M., Breschi, S., & Lissoni, F. (2004). Networks of inventors and the role of academia: an exploration of Italian patent data. *Research Policy, 33*(1), 127-145.

Barber, W., & Badre, A. N. (1998). *Culturability: The meaning of culture and usability.* Paper presented at the 4th Conference on Human Factors and the Web, Basking Ridge, NJ.

Barney, J. B. (1991). Firm resources and sustained competitive advantage. *Journal of Management, 17*, 99–120. doi:10.1177/014920639101700108

Barney, J. B. (2001). Resource-based theories of competitive advantage: A ten year retrospective on the resource-based view. *Journal of Management, 27*, 643–650. doi:10.1177/014920630102700602

Bassi, L. (1998) Harnessing the power of intellectual capital. *The Journal of Applied Manufacturing Systems,* Summer, 29-35.

Beckman, T. (1999). The Current State of the Knowledge Management. In Liebovitz, J. (Ed.), *Knowledge Management Handbook* (pp. 1.1–1.22).

Beco, S., Cantalupo, B., Giammarino, L., Matskanis, N., & Surridge, M. (2005). OWL-WS: A Workflow Ontology for Dynamic Grid Service Composition. *First International Conference on e-Science and Grid Computing (e-Science'05).*(pp. 148-155) http://doi.ieeecomputersociety.org/10.1109/E-SCIENCE.2005.64

Beco, S., Cantalupo, B., & Terracina, A. (2006). The Role of Workflow in Next Generation Business Oriented Grids: Two Different Approaches Leading to a Unified Vision. In *Second IEEE International Conference on e-Science and Grid Computing (e-Science'06)* (p. 38). http://doi.ieeecomputersociety.org/10.1109/E-SCIENCE.2006.139

Bednarik, R., & Tukiainen, M. (2007). Validating the Restricted Focus Viewer: A study using eye-movement tracking. *Behavior Research Methods, 39*(2), 274–282.

Beer, D., Berger, K., Busse, T., Engert, S., Hall, T., Hamburg, I., & ten Thij, H. (Eds.). (2008). *Strategies, models, guidelines to use eLearning in SMEs*. Duisburg: Univ.Verlag.

Beer, D., Busse, T., Hamburg, I., Mill, U., & Paul, H. (Eds.). (2006). *e-learning in European SMEs: observations, analyses & forecasting*. Münster: Waxmann.

Beer, D., Busse, T., Hamburg, I., & Oehler, C. (Eds.). (2008). Improving eLearning practices in SMEs. In *Proceedings of the SIMPEL final conference*. Universitas-Györ.

Benner, M. J., & Tushman, M. (2002). Process Management and Technological Innovation: A Longitudinal Study of the Photography and Paint Industries. *Administrative Science Quarterly, 47*, 676–706. doi:10.2307/3094913

Benner, M. J., & Tushman, M. L. (2003). Exploitation, exploration, and process management: the productivity dilemma revisited. *Academy of Management Review, 28*(2), 238–256. doi:10.2307/30040711

Bennett, R., & Gabriel, H. (1999). Organizational factors and knowledge management within large marketing departments: an empirical study. *Journal of Knowledge Management, 3*(3), 212–225. doi:10.1108/13673279910288707

Benson, C. (1995). Economic and Industrial Understanding as Part of Design and Technology Education in the Primary Curriculum. In K. Langer, M. Metzing, & D. Wahl (Ed.), *Technology Education, Innovation and Management* (pp. 224-232). Berliln/Heidelberg: Springer-Verlag.

Berger, P. L., & Luckman, T. (1966). *The Social Construction of Reality*. London: Penguin Books.

Blackler, F. (1995). Knowledge, Knowledge Work and Organizations: An Overview and Interpretation. *Organization Studies, 16*(6). doi:10.1177/017084069501600605

Blake, P. (1998) The knowledge management expansion, *Information Today, 15*(1).

Boedker, C., Guthrie, J., & Cuganesan, S. (2005). An integrated framework for visualising intellectual capital. *Journal of Intellectual Capital, 6*(4), 510–527. doi:10.1108/14691930510628799

Boehm, B. (2008). Making a Difference in the Software Century. *IEEE Computer, 41*(3), 32–38.

Bohn, R. (1994). Measuring and managing technological knowledge. *Sloan Management Review*, (Fall): 61–73.

Bojko, A. (2006). Using eye-tracking to compare web page designs: A case study. *Journal of Usability Studies, 1*(3), 112–120.

Bojko, A., & Stephenson, A. (2005). It's all in the eye of the user: How eye-tracking can help answer usability questions. *User Experience, 4*(1).

Bontis, N., Crossan, M. M., & Hulland, J. (2002). Managing an Organizational Learning System by Aligning Stocks and Flows. *Journal of Management Studies, 39*, 437–469. doi:10.1111/1467-6486.t01-1-00299

Bontis, N. (1998). Intellectual capital: An exploratory study that develops measures and models. *Management Decision, 36*(2), 63–76. doi:10.1108/00251749810204142

Bontis, N., Keow, W. C., & Richardson, S. (2000). Intellectual capital and business performance in Malaysian industries. *Journal of Intellectual Capital, 1*(1), 85–100. doi:10.1108/14691930010324188

Bozzolan, S., Favotto, F., & Ricceri, F. (2003). Italian annual intellectual capital disclosure: An empirical analysis. *Journal of Intellectual Capital, 4*(4), 543–558. doi:10.1108/14691930310504554

Bozzolan, S., Ricceri, F., & O'Regan, P. (2006). Intellectual capital disclosure (ICD) in listed companies: A comparison of practice in Italy and the UK. *Journal of Human Resource Cost and Accounting, 10*(2), 92–113. doi:10.1108/14013380610703111

BPEL4People (2009). WS-People Extension for People. Retrieved April 22, 2009 from http://www.ibm.com/developerworks/webservices/library/specification/ws-bpel4people

Braha, D., & Bar-Yam, Y. (2004). Information flow structure in large-scale product development organizational networks. *Journal of Information Technology, 19*(4), 244–253. doi:10.1057/palgrave.jit.2000030

Brass, D. J. (1984). Being in the right place: A structural analysis of individual influence in an organization. *Administrative Science Quarterly, 29*(4), 518–540. doi:10.2307/2392937

Brödner, P., Helmstädter, E., & Widmaier, B. (Eds.). (1999). *Wissensteilung. Zur Dynamik von Innovation und kollektivem Lernen* (*Vol. 13*). München: Hampp, Arbeit und Technik.

Brookings (2000). *Understanding intangible sources of value,* the Brookings Institution, Washington, DC. Retrieved from www.brookings.edu

Brown, J. S., & Duguid, P. (1991). Organizational learning and communities-of-practice: Toward a unified view of working, learning, and innovation. *Organization Science, 2*(1), 40–57. doi:10.1287/orsc.2.1.40

Brown, J. S., & Duguid, P. (2000). *The social Life of Information.* Cambridge: Harvard Business School Press.

Burt, R. S. (1992). *Structural Holes: The social structure of competition* (1st ed.). Cambridge, MA: Harvard University Press.

Butzin, A., & Widmaier, B. (2008). Innovationsbiographien. In *Institut Arbeit und Technik: Jahrbuch 2007.* Gelsenkirchen, S. 44-51.

Cabral, L., Domingue, J., Galizia, S., Gugliotta, A., Norton, B., Tanasescu, V., & Pedrinaci, C. (2006). IRS-III: A Broker for Semantic Web-Services based Applications. In *Proceedings of the 5th International Semantic Web Conference, ISWC.*

Cabral, L., Domingue, J., Motta, E., Payne, T. R., & Hakimpour, F. (2004). Approaches to Semantic Web-Services: An Overview and Comparison. In *Proceedings of the European Semantic Web Conference.*

Cabrita, M. R., & Bontis, N. (2008). Intellectual Capital and Business Performance in Portuguese Banking Industry. *International Journal of Technology Management, 43*(1-3), 212–237. doi:10.1504/IJTM.2008.019416

Cabrita, M. R., & Vaz, J. L. (2005). Intellectual capital and value creation: Evidencing in Portuguese banking industry. *Electronic Journal of Knowledge Management, 4*(1), 11–19.

Cahill, D. J. (2006). *Lifestyle Market Segmentation.* The Haworth Press, Inc.

Camagni, R. (1995). Global network and local milieu: towards a theory of economic space. In Conti, S., Malecki, E., & Oinas, P. (Eds.), *The Industrial Enterprise and Its Environment: Spatial Perspectices* (pp. 195–214). Aldershot: Avebury.

Carl Bro. (2005). Intellectual Capital Account, *Annual Report.* Retrieved February 2007 from www.carlbro.com.

Carlucci, D., Marr, B., & Schiuma, G. (2004). The knowledge value chain: How intellectual capital impacts on business performance. *International Journal of Technology Management, 27*(6/7), 575–590. doi:10.1504/IJTM.2004.004903

Carneiro, A. (2000). How Does Knowledge Management Influence Innovation and Competitiveness? *Journal of Knowledge Management, 4*(2), 87–98. doi:10.1108/13673270010372242

Carneiro, A. (2004). Teaching Management and Management Educators: some considerations. *Management Decision*, *42*(3/4), 430–438. doi:10.1108/00251740410521800

Carneiro, A. (2008). When Leadership means more Innovation and Development. *Business Strategy Series*, *9*(4), 176–184. doi:10.1108/17515630810891843

Carneiro, A. (1995). *Inovação – Estratégia e Competitividade*. Lisboa: Texto Editora, Colecção "Textos de Gestão".

Carneiro, A. (2005). How technologies support winning strategies and productivity. In *Handbook of Business Strategy* (pp. 257-263).

Castro M. C. (2006). *Revisiting Communities of Practice: from fishermen guilds to the global village*. Posted on 28 July 2006 by jrobes.

Catapano, A., D'Atri, A., Hrgovcic, V., Ionita, D. A., & Tarabanis, K. (2008). *LD-CAST: Local Development Cooperation Actions Enabled by Semantic Technology. 6th Eastern European eGovernment Days*. Prague, Czech Republic: OCG.

Cavusgil, S., Calantone, R., & Zhao, Y. (2003). Tacit knowledge transfer and firm innovation capability. *Journal of Business and Marketing*, *18*(1).

Chaharbaghi, K., & Cripps, S. (2006). Intellectual capital: Direction, not blind faith. *Journal of Intellectual Capital*, *7*(1), 29–42. doi:10.1108/14691930610639750

Chakhunashvili, A. Johansson, P., & Bergman, B. (2004). Variation Mode and Effect Analysis. In *Proceedings of the annual reliability and maintainability symposium*. Piscataway, NJ: IEEE Press.

Chaudhury, A., & Kuilboer, J. P. (2001). *E-business & e-commerce infrastructure: Technologies supporting the e-business initiative*. London: McGraw-Hill/Irwin.

Chen, P., & Koc, M. (2007). Simulation of springback variation in forming of advanced high strength steels. *Journal of Materials Processing Technology*, *190*, 189–198. doi:10.1016/j.jmatprotec.2007.02.046

Chesbrough, H. W. (2003). *Open Innovation*. Cambridge: Harvard Business School Press.

Cheung, C.F., Ko, K.C., Chu, K.F., & Lee, W.B. (2005). Systematic Knowledge Auditing With Applications. *Journal of Knowledge Management Practice*.

Chin, W. W. (1998). The partial least squares approach to structural equation modelling. In Marcoulides, G. A. (Ed.), *Modern methods for business research*. Mahwah, NJ: Lawrence Erlbaum Associates.

Choo, C. (1998). *The Knowing Organization: How Organizations Use Information for Construct Meaning, Create Knowledge and Make Decisions*. New York: Oxford Press.

Choo, C. W., & Bontis, N. (2002). *The strategic management of intellectual capital and organizational knowledge*. New York: Oxford University Press, Inc.

Churchill, G. A. Jr. (1979). A paradigm for developing better measures of marketing constructs. *JMR, Journal of Marketing Research*, *16*(February), 64–73. doi:10.2307/3150876

Clements, R. B. (1995). *The Experimenter's Companion*. Milwaukee, WI: ASQC Quality Press. Coleman D.E. and Montgomery D.C., A systematic approach to planning for a design industrial experiment. *Technometrics*, *35*(1), 1–12.

Coakes, E., & Clarke, S. (Eds.). (2006). *Encyclopedia of Communities of Practice in Information and Knowledge Management*. Hershey, PA: Idea Group Reference.

Coase, R. (1998). The New Institutional Economics. *The American Economic Review*, 88(2), *Papers and Proceedings of the Hundred and Tenth Annual Meeting of the American Economic Association*, 72-74.

Cohen, W. M., & Levinthal, D. A. (1990). Absorptive Capacity: A New Perspective on Learning and Innovation. *Administrative Science Quarterly*, *35*(1), 128–152. doi:10.2307/2393553

Coleman, J. S. (1988). Social Capital in the creation of human capital. *American Journal of Sociology*, *94*(Supplement), S95–S120. doi:10.1086/228943

Cooke, L. (2005). Eye-tracking: How it works and how it relates to usability. *Technical Communication*, *52*(4), 456–463.

Cooper, A. (1999). *The Inmates Are Running the Asylum: Why High Tech Products Drive Us Crazy and How to Restore the Sanity*. Sams.; 1999

Cowi (2005). Intellectual Capital Report, *Annual Report*. Retrieved February 2007 www.cowi.com.

Cross, R., Parker, A., Prusak, L., & Borgatti, S. P. (2001). Knowing what we know: Supporting knowledge creation and sharing in social networks. *Organizational Dynamics*, *30*(2), 100–120. doi:10.1016/S0090-2616(01)00046-8

Cross, R., Rice, R. E., & Parker, A. (2001). Information seeking in social context: Structural influences and receipt of information benefits. *IEEE Transactions on Systems, Man and Cybernetics. Part C, Applications and Reviews*, *31*(4), 438–448. doi:10.1109/5326.983927

Cross & Parker. (2004). *The Hidden Power of Social Networks: Understanding How Work Really Gets Done in Organisations*. Boston: Harvard Business School Press.

Crossan, M. M., Lane, H. W., & White, R. E. (1999). An organizational learning framework: from intuition to institution. *Academy of Management Review*, *24*(3), 522–537. doi:10.2307/259140

Currall, S. C. (2003). *Observations and recommendations regarding university technology commercialization programs in England and Scotland. Rice University.* Houston, TX: Sponsored by Invest-UK.

Cyr, D., & Trevor-Smith, H. (2004). Localization of web design: An empirical comparison of German, Japanese, and United States web site characteristics. *Journal of the American Society for Information Science and Technology*, *55*(13), 1199–1208. doi:10.1002/asi.20075

Dalkir, K. (2005). *Knowledge Management in Theory and Practice*. Butterworth Heinemann.

Damanpour, F. (1991). Organizational innovation: a meta-analysis of effects of determinants and moderators. *Academy of Management Journal*, *34*, 555–590. doi:10.2307/256406

D'Angelo, J., & Little, S. K. (1998). Successful web pages: What are they and do they exist? *Information Technology and Libraries*, *17*(2), 71–81.

Daniel, F., Matera, M., Yu, J., Benatallah, B., Regis, S. P., & Casati, F. (2007). Understanding UI Integration. A Survey of Problems, Technologies and Opportunities. *IEEE Internet Computing*, *11*(3), 59–66. doi:10.1109/MIC.2007.74

Darroch, J., & McNaughton, R. (2002). *Developing a measure of knowledge management.* In N. Bontis (Ed.), *World Congress on Intellectual Capital Readings* (pp. 226-242). Boston, MA: Butterworth-Heinemann.

Davenport, T. H., De Long, D. W., & Beers, M. C. (1998). Successful knowledge management projects. *Sloan Management Review*, (Winter): 43–57.

Davenport, T. H., Jarvenpaa, S. K., & Beers, M. C. (1996). Improving Knowledge Work Processes. *Sloan Management Review*, (Summer): 53–65.

Davenport, T. H., & Prusak, L. (1998). *Working Knowledge: How Organisations Manage What They Know*. Boston: Harvard Business Press.

Davis, S. (1996). *Future Perfect*. Reading, Massachusetts: Addison-Wesley.

de Boer, M., Van Den Bosch, F. A. J., & Volberda, H. W. (1999). Managing Organizational Knowledge Integration in the Emerging Multimedia Complex. *Journal of Management Studies*, *36*(3), 379–398. doi:10.1111/1467-6486.00141

De Giovanni, P. (2009). The Knowledge Manager's Role and Tasks for Supply Chain Management Success. *Journal of Knowledge Management Practice*, *10*(1).

Dede, C. (2005). Planning for neomillennial learning styles. *Educause Quarterly*, *28*(1). Retrieved on November, 2006, from http://www.educause.edu/pub/eq/eqm05/eqm0511.asp

Despres, C., & Chauvel, D. (1999). A Thematic Analysis of the Thinking in Knowledge Management [White paper]. Graduate School of Business, Marseille-Provence and The Theseus Institute, Sophia Antipolis, France

Dewar, R. D., & Dutton, J. E. (1986). The adoption of radical and incremental innovations: An empirical analysis. *Management Science, 32*(11), 1422–1433. doi:10.1287/mnsc.32.11.1422

Di Nitto, E., Sassen, A.-M., Traverso, P., & Zwegers, A. (2009). *At your Service, Service-Oriented Computing from an EU Perspective*. Cambridge, MA: MIT Press.

DiBello, L., Missildine, W., & Struttmann, M. (2009). The Long-Term Impact of Simulation Training on Changing Accountabilities in a Biotech Firm. In *Mind, Culture and Activity. Routledge Taylor& Francis Group*. Intuitive Expertise and Empowerment.

Diemers, D. (2001). Virtual Knowledge Communities. *Erfolgreicher Umgang mit Wissen in digitalen Zeitalter.* Dissertation der Universität St. Gallen.

Dierickx, I., & Cool, K. (1989). Asset stock accumulation and sustainability of competitive advantage. *Management Science, 35*(12), 1504–1511. doi:10.1287/mnsc.35.12.1504

Doppler, K., & Lauterburg, C. (1997). *Change Management: den Unternehmenswandel gestalten*. Frankfurt am Main: Campus Verlag.

Dougiamas, M. (2004). *Moodle: Using Learning Communities to Create an Open Source Course Management System*. Perth, Australia.

Douglas, P. (2002). Informational technology is out-knowledge sharing is in. *Journal of Corporate Accounting & Finance, 13*(4), 73–77. doi:10.1002/jcaf.10072

Dowling, P. J., & Welch, D. E. (2004). *International Human Resource Management: Managing people in a multinational context* (4th ed.). United Kingdom: Thomson.

Drucker, P. (1993). *Post Capitalist Society*. New York: Harper Business.

Drucker (1974). *Management Tasks, Responsibilities, Practices*. London: William Heinemann LdT.

Drucker, P. F. (1985). The Discipline of Innovation, *Harvard Business Review*, 63(3), and re-published in 1998 as HBR Classic in *HBR*, 76(6), 149-157.

Drucker, P. F. (1998, October 5). Management's New Paradigms. *Forbes*.

Duchowski, A. T. (2003). *Eye-tracking methodology: Theory and practice*. London: Springer-Verlag.

Duysters, G., & Lemmens, C. (2003). Alliance group formation. *International Studies of Management and Organization, 33*(2), 49–68.

Dyrenfurth, M. J. (1998). *Final Report-State Fair RTEC Region Project to Conduct a Collaborative Targeted Technical Education Needs Assessment. Columbia, MO: Research Institute for Technical Education & Workforce Development*. Columbia: University of Missouri.

Dyrenfurth, M. J. (2003). Technology Education for Developing Nations. In Graube, G., Dyrenfurth, M. J., & Theuerkauf, W. E. (Eds.), *Technology Education: International Concepts and Perspectives* (pp. 119–124). Frankfurt am Main: Peter Lang.

Dyrenfurth, M. J. (1991). Technological Literacy Synthesized. In M. J. Dyrenfurth & M. Kozak (Eds.), *Technological Literacy* (pp. 138-183). Fortieth yearbook of the Council on Technology Teacher Education, International Technology Education Association. Peoria, IL: Glencoe.

Easterby-Smith, M. (1990). Creating a learning organization. *Personnel Review, 19*(5), 24–28. doi:10.1108/EUM0000000000779

Edvinsson, L. (2002). *Corporate Longitude*. London: Prentice Hall.

Edvinsson, L., & Malone, M. (1997). *Intellectual capital: realising your company's true value by finding its hidden brainpower*. New York: Harper Collins.

Eggleston, J. (1995). Are We Making Technology Education Attractive to Our Students? In Langer, K., Metzing, M., & Wahl, D. (Eds.), *Technology Education, Innovation and Management* (pp. 216–223). Berlin, Heidelberg: Springer-Verlag.

Ellekjaer, M. R., & Bisgaard, S. (1998). The use of experimental design in the development of new products. *International Journal of Quality Science, 3*(3), 254–274. doi:10.1108/13598539810229230

Elliott, S. (1996). APQC conference attendees discover the value and enablers of a successful KM program. *Knowledge Management in Practice, 5*, 1–8.

Erl, T. (2005). *Service-Oriented Architecture: Concepts, Technology, and Design*. Prentice Hall/PearsonPTR.

Ettlie, J. E., Bridges, W. P., & O'Keefe, R. D. (1984). Organization strategy and structural differences for radical versus incremental innovation. *Management Science, 30*, 682–695. doi:10.1287/mnsc.30.6.682

European Commission (2003). *Observatory of European SMEs.*

Eustace, C. (2003). A new perspective on the knowledge value chain. *Journal of Intellectual Capital, 4*(4), 588–596. doi:10.1108/14691930310504581

Evans, P., Shulman, L. E., & Stalk, G. (1992). Competing on Capabilities: The New Rules of Corporate Strategy. *Harvard Business Review, 70*(3), 57–69.

Fine, C. (1998). *Clockspeed: Winning Industry Control in the Age of Temporary Advantage*. New York: Perseus Books.

Fischer, T., Bakalov, F., & Nauerz, A. (2009). *An Overview of Current Approaches to Mashup Generation*. 5th Conference on Professional Knowledge Management, Switzerland, LNI GI-Edition.

Fornell, C., & Larcker, D. F. (1981). Evaluating structural equation models with unobservable variables and measurement error. *JMR, Journal of Marketing Research, 18*(1), 39–50. doi:10.2307/3151312

Forsberg, K., Mooz, H., & Cotterman, H. (2005). *Visualizing Project Management: Models and Frameworks for Mastering Complex Systems*. Wiley.

Foster I. (2008). *What is Grid? A Three Point Checklist*. Retrieved November 10, 2008 from www.fp.mcs.anl.gov/~foster/Articles/WhatIsTheGrid.pdf

Franceschini, G., & Macchietto, S. (2008). Model-based design of experiments for parameter precision: State of the art. *Chemical Engineering Science, 63*, 4846–4872. doi:10.1016/j.ces.2007.11.034

Galbraith, J. R., & Nathanson, D. (1979). The Role of Organizational Structure and Process in Strategy Implementation. In Schendel, D., & Hofer, C. W. (Eds.), *Strategic Management: A New View of Business Policy and Planning* (pp. 249–283). Boston: Little, Brown.

Garrick, J. (1998). *Informal Learning in the Workplace: Unmasking Human Resource Development*. London: Routledge.

Gibson; C.B., & Birkinshaw, J. (2004). The antecedents, consequences, and mediating role of organizational ambidexterity. *Academy of Management Journal, 47*(2), 209-226.

Gilsing, V., Nooteboom, B., Vanhaverbeke, W., Duysters, G., & van den Oord, A. (2008). Network embeddedness and the exploration of novel technologies: Technological distance, betweenness centrality and density. *Research Policy, 37*, 1717–1731. doi:10.1016/j.respol.2008.08.010

Global Competitiveness Report. (n.d.). Retrieved from www.weforum.org/pdt/GCR08/GCR08.pdf

Gnyawali, D. R., & Madhavan, R. (2001). Cooperative networks and competitive dynamics: A structural embeddedness perspective. *Academy of Management Review, 26*, 431–445. doi:10.2307/259186

Goellner, J., Mak, K., Trattnig, G., & Woitsch, R. (2008). *Wissensmanagement und Wissensbilanz im ÖBH am Beispiel der ABCAbwS & ABCAbw*. Wien: Sonderpublikation, Schriftenreihe der Landesverteidigungsakademie.

Goldberg, J. H., & Wichansky, A. M. (2003). Eye-tracking in usability evaluation: a practitioner's guide. In Hyona, J., Radach, R., & Deubel, H. (Eds.), *The mind's eyes: Cognitive and applied aspects of eye movement research* (pp. 493–516). Amsterdam, Netherlands: Elsevier.

Gopalakrishnan, S., & Damanpour, F. (1997). A review of innovation research in economics, sociology and technology management. *Omega, 25*, 15. doi:10.1016/S0305-0483(96)00043-6

Gorman, M., & Carlson, B. (1990). Interpreting Invention as a cognitive process: The case of Alexander Graham Bell, Thomas Edison, and the Telephone. *Science, Technology & Human Values, 15*(2). doi:10.1177/016224399001500201

Graesser, A. C., & Clark, L. F. (1985). *Structure and procedures of implicit knowledge*. Norwood, NJ: Ablex.

Granovetter, M. S. (1973). The Strength of Weak Ties. *American Journal of Sociology, 78*(6), 1360–1380. doi:10.1086/225469

Grant, R. M. (1997). The knowledge-based view of the firm: implications for management practice. *Long Range Planning, 30*(3), 451. doi:10.1016/S0024-6301(97)00025-3

Grant, R. M. (1991). The Resource-Based Theory of Competitive Advantage: Implications for Strategy Formulation. *California Management Review, 33*(3), 114–134.

Grant, R. M. (1996). Toward a knowledge-based theory of the firm. *Strategic Management Journal, 17*, 109–122.

Gronau, N. (2003). Modellieren von wissensintensiven Geschäftsprozesses mit der Beschreibungssprache K-Modeler. In Gronau N. Wissensmanagement: Potentiale – Konzepte - Werkzeuge, GITO Verlag, (pp, 3-30).

Gronstedt, A. (2008). *Training in Virtual Worlds*. ASTD Press.

Gubbins, C., & MacCurtain, S. (2008). Understanding the Dynamics of Collective Learning: The Role of Trust & Social Capital. *Advances in Developing Human Resources, 10*(4), 578–599. doi:10.1177/1523422308320372

Gunasekaran, A. (1999). Agile manufacturing: A framework for research and development. *International Journal of Production Economics, 62*(1-2), 87–105. doi:10.1016/S0925-5273(98)00222-9

Gupta, A. K., Smith, K. G., & Shalley, C. E. (2006). The interplay between exploration and exploitation. *Academy of Management Journal, 49*(4), 693–706.

Guthrie, J., & Petty, R. (2000). Intellectual capital: Australian annual reporting practices. *Journal of Intellectual Capital, 1*(3), 241–251. doi:10.1108/14691930010350800

Guthrie, J., Petty, R., & Ricceri, F. (2007). *Intellectual Capital reporting: Lessons from Hong Kong and Australia*. Edinburgh: The Institute of Chartered Accountants of Scotland.

Guthrie, J., & Ricceri, F. (2009). *Counting what counts: A decade of intellectual capital accounting research*. Paper presented at the British Accounting Association Conference, 21-23 April, Dundee.

Haanes, K., & Fjeldstad, Ø. (2000). Linking Intangible Resources and Competition. *European Management Journal, 18*(1), 52–62. doi:10.1016/S0263-2373(99)00068-7

Habersam, M., & Piber, M. (2003). Exploring intellectual capital in hospitals: Two qualitative case studies in Italy and Austria. *European Accounting Review, 12*(4), 753–779. doi:10.1080/0963818031000162845

Hair, J., Anderson, R., Tatham, R., & Black, W. (1992). *Multivariate data analysis with readings* (3rd ed.). NJ: Prentice-Hall International, Inc.

Hall, R., & Pierpaolo, A. (2003). Managing knowledge associated with innovation. *Journal of Business Research, 56*(2), 145–152. doi:10.1016/S0148-2963(01)00287-9

Hall, R. (1993). A framework linking intangible resources and capabilities to sustainable competitive advantage. *Strategic Management Journal, 14*(8), 607–618. doi:10.1002/smj.4250140804

Hall, B. (2000). *Learning goes online: how companies can use networks to turn change into a competitive advantage* (Cisco Systems: Packet Magazine).

Hambrick, D. C. (1981). Strategic awareness within top management teams. *Strategic Management Journal, 2*(3), 263–279. doi:10.1002/smj.4250020305

Hamburg, I., Engert, S., Petschenka, A., & Marin, M. (2008). Improving e-learning 2.0-based training strategies on SMEs through communities of practice. In *The International Association of Science and Technology for Development* (pp. 200–205). IASTED.

Hamburg, I., Rehfeld, D., & Terstriep, J. (2006). Knowledge-based services for economic agencies. *The ICFAI Journal of Knowledge Management, 4*(4), 15–27.

Hamburg, I. (2007). Shifting eLearning in SMEs to a Work-based and Business Oriented Topic. In *European Distance and ELearning Network: New learning 2.0? Emerging digital territories–developing continuities – new divides* (p. 4).

Hamburg, I., & Engert, S. (2007). Competency-based Training in SMEs: The Role of ELearning and E-Competence. In *Proceedings of the 6th IASTED International Conference "Web-based Education* (pp. 189-193). Anaheim: Acta Press.

Hamburg, I., & Widmaier, B. (2004). Wissensverarbeitung in der Wirtschaftsförderung. In B. Widmaier, D. Beer, St. Gärtner, I. Hamburg, & J. Terstriep (Eds.), Wege zu einer integrierten Wirtschaftsförderung. Baden-Baden: Nomos Verl.-Ges., S. 75-112.

Hansen, M. T. (1999). The Search-Transfer Problem: The Role of Weak Ties in Sharing Knowledge across Organization Subunits. *Administrative Science Quarterly*, *44*(1), 82–111. doi:10.2307/2667032

Hastings, J. K., Juds, M. A., & Brauer, J. R. (1985). *Accuracy and Economy of Finite Element Magnetic Analysis*. Paper presented at 33rd Annual National Relay Conference.

Hatala (2006) Social Network Analysis in Human Resource Development: A New Methodology. *Human Resource Development Review, 5*(45), 45-71.

He, Z. L., & Wong, P. K. (2004). Exploration vs. exploitation: an empirical test of the ambidexterity hypothesis. *Organization Science*, *15*(4), 481–494. doi:10.1287/orsc.1040.0078

Heath, T., & Motta, E. (2008). Ease of interaction plus ease of integration: Combining Web2.0 and the Semantic Web in a reviewing site. *Web Semantics: Science. Services and Agents on the World Wide Web*, *6*(1), 76–83. doi:10.1016/j.websem.2007.11.009

Helmstädter, E. (2007). The role of knowledge in the Schumpeterian economy. In Hanusch, H. (Ed.), *Elgar companion to neo-Schumpeterian economics* (pp. 296–315). Cheltenham: Elgar.

Helmstädter, E. (2004). Arbeits- und Wissensteilung als Prozesse gesellschaftlicher Interaktion. In Held, M., Kubon-Gilke, G., & Sturn, R. (Eds.), *Jahrbuch Normative und institutionelle Grundfragen der Ökonomik. Marburg: Metropolis-Verl* (*Vol. 3*, pp. 97–125).

Helper, S., MacDuffie, J. P., & Sabel, C. M. (2000). Pragmatic collaboration: advancing knowledge while controlling opportunism. *Industrial and Corporate Change*, *9*(3), 443–488. doi:10.1093/icc/9.3.443

Hill, S.A. & Birkinshaw, J. (2006). Ambidexterity in Corporate Venturing: Simultaneously using Existing and Building New Capabilities. *Academy of Management Proceedings*, C1-C6.

Hinkelmann, K., Karagiannis, D., & Telesko, R. (2002). PROMOTE - Methodologie und Werkzeug zum geschäftsprozessorientierten Wissensmanagement. In *Geschäftsprozessorientiertes Wissensmanagement*. Springer-Verlag.

Homepage, D. A. M. L. (2009). Releases of DAML-S / OWL-S. Retrieved March 16, 2009 from http://www.daml.org/services/owl-s/

Hoyer, V., & Stanoevska-Slabeva, K. (2009). *Design Principles of Enterprise Mashups*. 5th Conference on Professional Knowledge Management, Switzerland, LNI GI-Edition.

Hrgovcic, V., Woitsch, R., Utz, W., & Leutgeb, A. (2008). *Adaptive and Smart e-Government Workflows - Experience Report from the Projects FIT and LDCAST. eChallenges e-2008 Stockholm*. Sweden: IOS Press.

Hrgovcic, V., Utz, W., & Woitsch, R. (2009). Knowledge Engineering in Future Internet. In Karagiannis, D., & Jin, Z. (Eds.), *Knowledge Science, Engineering and Management*. Springer. doi:10.1007/978-3-642-10488-6_13

Hrgovcic, V., & Woitsch, R. (2009). *Enhancing Semantic E-Government Workflows through Service Oriented Knowledge Provision*. 4th International Conference on Internet and Web Applications and Services, ICIW 09, Venice, Italy, IEEE.

Hussler, C., & Ronde, P. (2002). *Proximity and academic knowledge spillovers: New evidence from the networks of inventors of a French university.* EUNIP Conference 2002, Turku, Finland; Dec 5-7

Ibarra, H. (1993). Network centrality, power and innovation involvement: Determinants of technical and administrative roles. *Academy of Management Journal, 36,* 471–501. doi:10.2307/256589

IBM. (2009). Retrieved April 22, 2009 from www.ibm.com/developerworks/webservices/library/ws-esbia/

Inkpen, A., & Tsang, E. (2005). Social capital, networks and knowledge transfer. *Academy of Management Review, 30*(1), 146–165.

Innes, S. (1995). Working with Industry to Enhance Technology Education. In Langer, K., Metzing, M., & Wahl, D. (Eds.), *Technology Education, Innovation and Management* (pp. 233–240). Berlin, Heidelberg: Springer-Verlag.

Isenberg, B., Isenberg, J., & Davis, L. T. (2006). *Waiting for Your Cat to Bark?* Nelson Business.

Itami, H., & Roehl, T. W. (1987). *Mobilizing invisible assets.* Cambridge: Harvard University Press.

Ittner, C., & Larcker, D. (1998). Are non-financial measures leading indicators of financial performance? An analysis of customer satisfaction. *Journal of Accounting Research, 36*(Supplement), 1–35. doi:10.2307/2491304

Jaffe, A. B. (1989). Real effects of academic research. *The American Economic Review, 79,* 697–970.

Jansen, J. J. P., Van Den Bosch, F. A. J., & Volberda, H. W. (2006). Exploratory Innovation, Exploitative Innovation, and Performance: Effects of Organizational Antecedents and Environmental Moderators. *Management Science, 52,* 1661–1664. doi:10.1287/mnsc.1060.0576

Jansen, J. P., George, G., Van den Bosch, F. J., & Volberda, H. W. (2008). Senior team attributes and organizational ambidexterity: The moderating role of transformational leadership. *Journal of Management Studies, 45*(5), 982–1007. doi:10.1111/j.1467-6486.2008.00775.x

Jhingran, A. (2006). Enterprise Information Mashups: Integrating Information, Simply. In *Proceedings of the 32nd international conference on Very large data bases* (pp. 3-4). VLDB Endowment.

Johansson, P. (2006). Variation Mode and Effect Analysis: a practical tool for quality improvement. *Quality and Reliability Engineering international.*

Johnson, C. (2001). A survey of current research on online communities of practice. *The Internet and Higher Education, 4,* 45–60. doi:10.1016/S1096-7516(01)00047-1

Johnson, P., Heimann, V., & O'Neill, K. (2001). The "wonderland" of virtual teams. *Journal of Workplace Learning, 13*(1), 24–30. doi:10.1108/13665620110364745

Kackar, R. (1985). Off-Line Quality Control, Parameter Design, and the Taguchi Method. *Journal of Quality Technology, 17*(4), 176–188.

Kahle, L.R., Beatty, S.E., & Homer, P. (1986). Alternative Measurement Approaches to Customer Values: The List of Values (LOV) and Values Life Style (VALS). *Journal of Consumer Research.*

Kalfoglou, Y., & Schorlemmer, M. (2003). Ontology Mapping: the State of the Art. *The Knowledge Engineering Review, 18*(1), 1–31. doi:10.1017/S0269888903000651

Kanter, R. M. (1983). *The Change Masters.* New York: Simon & Schuster.

Kaplan, R. S., & Norton, D. P. (2004). Measuring the strategic readiness of intangible assets. *Harvard Business Review, 82*(1), 52–63.

Karagiannis, D. (1995). BPMS: Business Process Management Systems: Concepts, Methods and Technologies, SIGOIS Special Issue. *ACM SIGGROUP Bulletin, 10-13,* 1995.

Karagiannis, D., & Telesko, R. (2001). *Wissensmanagement: Konzepte der künstlichen Intelligenz und des Softcomputing.* Oldenbourg Wissenschaftsverlag.

Karagiannis, D., Utz, W., Woitsch, R., & Eichner, H. (2008). *BPM4SOA Business Process Models for Semantic Service-Oriented Infrastructures. eChallenges e-2008.* Stockholm, Sweden: IOS Press.

Karagiannis, D. (2009). *Modelling Semantic Workflows for E-Government Applications*. 3rd International Conference on Research Challenges in Information Science, RCIS 2009. IEEE.

Karagiannis, D., & Telesko, R. (2000). The EU-Project PROMOTE: A Process-oriented Approach for Knowledge Management. In *Proceedings of the 3rd International Conference on Practical Aspects of Knowledge Management*.

Kelle, U., & Kluge, S. (1999). *Vom Einzelfall zum Typus. Leske+Budrich*. Opladen.

Kelly, K. (1998). *New Rules for the New Economy*. London: Fourth Estate.

Kerres, M. (2006). Potenziale von Web 2.0 nutzen. In Hohenstein, A., & Wilbers, K. (Eds.), *Handbuch eLearning*. München.

Kerzner, H. (2005). *Project Management: A Systems Approach to Planning, Scheduling, and Controlling* (9th ed.). Wiley.

KMI. (2009). Knowledge Media Institute, IRS - Internet Reasoning Service. Retrieved March 16, 2009 from http://technologies.kmi.open.ac.uk/irs/

Knock, N., McQueen, R., & Corner, J. (1997). The Nature of data, information and knowledge exchanges in business processes: Implications for process improvement. *The Learning Organization, 4*(2), 70–80. doi:10.1108/09696479710160915

Koc, M., & Arslan, M., A. (2003). Design and finite element analysis of innovative tooling elements (stress pins) to prolong die life and improve dimensional tolerances in precission forming processes. *Journal of Materials Processing Technology, 142*, 773–785. doi:10.1016/S0924-0136(03)00647-2

Kogut, B., & Zander, U. (1996). What firms do? Coordination, Identity, and Learning. *Organization Science, 7*(5), 502–518. doi:10.1287/orsc.7.5.502

Kogut, B., & Kulatilaka, N. (1994). Options thinking and platform investments: Investing in opportunity. *California Management Review*, (Winter): 52–71.

Konrath, J. (2005). *Selling to Big Companies*. Kaplan Publishing.

Kotler, P. (1991). *Marketing Management* (7th ed.). Englewood Cliffs, NJ: Prentice Hall.

Kotval, X. P., & Goldberg, J. H. (1998). *Eye movements and interface components grouping: an evaluation method.* Paper presented at the 42nd Annual Meeting of the Human Factors and Ergonomics Society (HFES), Chicago, IL.

Kraatz, M. S. (1998). Learning by association? Interorganizational networks and adaptation to environmental change. *Academy of Management Journal, 41*, 621–643. doi:10.2307/256961

Krackhardt, D., & Hanson, J. R. (1993). Informal networks: the company behind the chart. *Harvard Business Review, 71*(4), 104–111.

Krippendorf, K., & Butter, R. (1984). Product semantics: exploring the symbolic qualities of form in innovation. *The Journal of the Industrial Designers Society of America, 3*, 4–9.

Krogh, G., Ichijo, K., & Nonaka, I. (2000). *Enabling Knowledge Creation. How to Unlock the Mystery of Tacit Knowledge and Release the Power of Innovation*. New York: Oxford University Press.

Kühn., et al. (2003). Enterprise Model Integration. In K. Bauknecht, A.M. Tjoa, & G. Quirchmayer (Eds.), *Proceedings of the Fourth International Conference EC-Web 2003 – Dexa 2003, Prague, Czech Republic* (LNCS 2738, pp. 379-392).

Larsson, A., Rehfeld, D., Widmaier, B., & Öz, F. (2006). *A Firm Case-Study Methodology: Approaches to measure Knowledge Flows in Firms and their Environment*. Paper presented to 5th Proximity Congress, Bordeaux, June 28-30, 2006.

Leitner, K. H., & Warden, C. (2004). Managing and reporting knowledge-based resources and processes in research organisations: Specifics, lessons learned and perspectives. *Management Accounting Research, 15*, 33–51. doi:10.1016/j.mar.2003.10.005

Lengnick-Hall, M. L., & Lengnick-Hall, C. A. (2003). *Human Resource Management in the Knowledge Economy: New Challenges, New Roles, New Capabilities*. San Francisco: Berrett-Koehler.

Levin, D. Z. (1999). *Transferring knowledge within the organization in the R&D arena.* Unpublished doctoral dissertation, Northwestern University, Illinois.

Levitt (1975). Marketing Myopia. *Harvard Business Review*, September-October, 12.

Li, P., Tu, M., Yen, I.-L., & Xia, Z. (2007). Preference update for e-commerce applications: Model, language, and processing. *Electronic Commerce Research, 7*(1), 17–44. doi:10.1007/s10660-006-0061-0

Linsteadt., et al. (2009). Special Track on Knowledge Services, in conjunction with I-Know 2008. Retrieved April 20, 2009 from http://i-know.tugraz.at/about/previous_conferences/i_know_08/special_tracks/ks

Lubatkin, M. H., Simsek, Z., Ling, Y., & Veiga, J. F. (2006). Ambidexterity and Performance in Small- to Medium-Sized Firms: The Pivotal Role of Top Management Team Behavioral Integration. *Journal of Management, 32*, 646–672. doi:10.1177/0149206306290712

Lukander, K. (2006). A system for tracking gaze on hand-held devices. *Behavior Research Methods, 38*(4), 660–666.

Maier, R., Hädrich, T., & Peinl, R. (2005). *Enterprise Knowledge Infrastructure*. Berlin: Springer Verlag.

Mak, K. (2005). *Der Einsatz des prozessorientierten Wissensmanagementwerkzeuges PROMOTE® in der Zentraldokumentation der Landesverteidigungsakademie*. Landesverteidigungsakademie Wien.

March, J., & Simon, H. (1975). Limites cognitivos da racionalidade. [Cognitive limits of rationality] In *Teoria das organizações* [Organizational Theory]. Rio de Janeiro: Fundação Getúlio Vargas.

March, J. G. (1991). Exploration and exploitation in organizational learning. *Organization Science, 2*(1), 71–87. doi:10.1287/orsc.2.1.71

Marchand, D., & Davenport, T. (2004). *Dominando a gestão da informação* [Mastering information management]. Porto Alegre: Bookman.

Marr, B. (2006). *Strategic performance management*. Oxford: Elsevier.

Marr, B. (2005). *Perspectives on intellectual capital – multidisciplinary insights into management, measurement, and reporting*. Oxford: Butterworth-Heinemann.

Marr, B., Schiuma, G., & Neely, A. (2004). The dynamics of value creation – Mapping your intellectual performance drivers. *Journal of Intellectual Capital, 5*(2), 312–325. doi:10.1108/14691930410533722

Marr, B., & Roos, G. (2005). A strategy perspective on intellectual capital. In Marr, B. (Ed.), *Perspectives on intellectual capital – multidisciplinary insights into management, measurement and reporting* (pp. 28–41). Oxford: Butterworth-Heinemann.

Marsden, P. V., & Campbell, K. E. (1984). Measuring Tie Strength. *Social Forces, 63*(2), 482–501. doi:10.2307/2579058

Martin, D., Domingue, J., Brodie, M., & Leymann, F. (2007). Semantic Web-Services, Part 1. *IEEE Intelligent Systems, 22*(5). doi:10.1109/MIS.2007.4338488

MATURE D1.1 (2009). Results of the Ethnographic Study and Conceptual Knowledge Maturing Model. MATURE deliverable.

MATURE D5.2 (2009). Specification of the System Architecture. MATURE deliverable.

MATURE EU-Project. (2009). Retrieved April 22, 2009 from www.mature-ip.eu

Maximilien, E. M., Ranabahu, A., & Fomadam, K. (2008). An Online Platform for Web APIs and Service Mashups. *IEEE Internet Computing, 12*(5), 32–43. doi:10.1109/MIC.2008.92

McCormick, R. (2004). Issues of Learning and Knowledge in Technology Education. *International Journal of Technology and Design Education, 14*(1), 21–44. doi:10.1023/B:ITDE.0000007359.81781.7c

McKenzie, J., & Van Winkelen, C. (2004). *Understanding the Knowledgeable Organization: Nurturing Knowledge Competence*. London: Thomson.

Menguc, B., & Auh, S. (2008). The asymmetric moderating role of market orientation on the ambidexterity-firm performance relationship from prospectors and defenders. *Industrial Marketing Management, 37*(4), 455–470. doi:10.1016/j.indmarman.2007.05.002

MERITUM. (2002). *Guidelines for managing and reporting of intangibles*. Madrid: Fundacion Airtel Movil.

Miles, M., & Huberman, A. (1984). *Qualitative data analysis: a sourcebook of new methods*. Newbury Park, California: Sage Publications.

Miles, R. E., Snow, C. C., & Miles, G. (2000). The future.org. *Long Range Planning, 25*(6), 28–35.

Ministry of Economy, Trade and Industry (METI) (2005). *Guidelines for disclosure of intellectual assets based management*. METI.

Mintzberg, H. (1994). *The rise and fall of strategic planning*. London: Prentice Hall.

Montgomery, D. C. (1999). Experimental design for product and process design and development. *The Statistician, 48*(2), 159–177. doi:10.1111/1467-9884.00179

Montgomery, D. C. (2001). *Design and Analysis of Experiments* (5th ed.). New York: John Wiley & Sons.

Morton, S. C., Dainty, A. R. J., Burns, N. D., Brookes, N. J., & Backhouse, C. J. (2006). Managing relationships to improve performance: a case study in the global aerospace industry. *International Journal of Production Research, 44*(16), 3227–3241. doi:10.1080/00207540600577809

Mouritsen, J. (2004). Measuring and intervening: How do we theorise intellectual capital management. *Journal of Intellectual Capital, 5*(2), 257–267. doi:10.1108/14691930410533687

Mouritsen, J., Bukh, P., & Kaasgaard, B. H. (2005). *Understanding Intellectual Capital in an innovative medium-sized firm: The case of Maxon*. Copenhagen: The Aarhus School of Business.

Mouritsen, J., Larsen, H. T., & Bukh, P. N. (2001). Intellectual capital and the capable firm: Narrating, visualising and numbering for managing knowledge. *Accounting, Organizations and Society, 26*(7/8), 735–762. doi:10.1016/S0361-3682(01)00022-8

Mouritsen, J., Bukh, P. N., Flagstad, K., Thorbjørnsen, S., Rosenkrands Johansen, M., Kotnis, S., et al. (2003). Intellectual Capital Statements — the new guideline, retrieved March 2008 http://www.videnskabsministeriet.dk/cgi-bin/theme-list.cgi?theme_id=100650&_lang=uk

Mulder, S., & Yaar, Z. (2006). *The User Is Always Right: A Practical Guide to Creating and Using Personas for the Web*. New Riders Press.

Murray, F. (2002). Innovation as co-evolution of scientific and technological networks: exploring tissue engineering. *Research Policy, 31*(8/9), 1389–1404. doi:10.1016/S0048-7333(02)00070-7

National Electronic Library for Health. (2005). Retrieved from http://www.nelh.nhs.uk/knowledge_management/km2/audit_toolkit.asp

Neilson, G., Gulati, R., & Kletter, D. (2004) Organizing for success in the 21st century. Booz Allen Hamilton-Kellogg School of Management, Fortune 1000 survey findings. Retrieved from http://www.boozallen.com/bahng/SilverDemo

Nonaka, I., & Konno, N. (1998). The concept of 'ba': building a foundation for knowledge creation. *California Management Review, 40*(3), 40–54.

Nonaka, I., & Takeuchi, H. (1995). *The Knowledge-creating Company: How Japanese Companies Create the Dynamics of Innovation*. New York: Oxford University Press.

Nonaka, I., Toyama, R., & Konno, N. (2000). SECI, ba and leadership: a unified model of dynamic knowledge creation. *Long Range Planning, 33*, 5–34. doi:10.1016/S0024-6301(99)00115-6

Nonaka, I., Von Krogh, G., & Voelpel, S. (2006). Organizational knowledge creation theory:Evolutionary paths and future advances. *Organization Studies, 27*, 1179–1208. doi:10.1177/0170840606066312

Nonaka, I., & Takeuchi, H. (1995). *The knowledge creating company*. Oxford: Oxford University Press.

Nonaka, I. (1994). A dynamic theory of organizational knowledge creation. *Organization Science, 5*(1), 14–37. doi:10.1287/orsc.5.1.14

Nonaka, I., & Takeuchi, H. (1995). *The knowledge-creating company*. New York: Oxford University Press.

Nonaka, I., von Krogh, G., & Voelpel, S. (2006). Organizational knowledge creation theory: evolutionary paths and future advances. *Organization Studies, 27*, 1179–1208. doi:10.1177/0170840606066312

Nonaka, I. (1991). The Knowledge-Creating Company. *Harvard Business Review, 69*(6), 96–104.

Nonaka, I., & Konno, N. (1998). The Concept of 'Ba': Building a Foundation for Knowledge Creation. *California Management Review, 40*(3), 40–54.

Nonaka, I., & Takeuchi, H. (1995). *The Knowledge-Creating Company*. New York: Oxford University Press, Inc.

Nonaka, I. (1994). A dynamic theory of organizational knowledge creation. *Organization Science, 5*(1), 14–37. doi:10.1287/orsc.5.1.14

Nonaka, I., & Takeuchi, H. (1995). *The knowledge creating company: How Japanese companies manage the dynamics of innovation*. New York: Oxford University Press.

Novikova, J. (2005). Firms or Networks: In Search of the Locus of Innovation. In *DRUID Academy's 2005 Winter Conference on Industrial Evolution and Dynamics, Aalborg, Denmark, January* (pp. 27-29).

Nunnally, J. C. (1978). *Psychometric Theory* (2nd ed.). New York: McGraw-Hill.

Nunnally, J. (1978). *Psychometric theory* (2nd ed.). New York: McGraw-Hill.

O'Brien, E., Hall, T., & Johnson, K. (2008). The Importance of Training Needs Analysis in Authoring Technology Enhanced Learning for Companies. In Lyras, M. D., Gasevi, D., & Ordóñez de Pablos, P. (Eds.), *Technology Enhanced Learning: Best Practices* (pp. 107–134). Hershey, PA: IGI Global.

O'Reilly, T. (2005). What is Web 2.0. *Design patterns and Business models for the next generation of Software*. Retrieved from http://www.oreillynet.com/lp/a/6228

OASIS. (2006). Reference Model for Service Oriented Architecture 1.0, OASIS Standard. Retrieved March 16, 2009 from http://docs.oasis-open.org/soa-rm/v1.0/soa-rm.html

OECD. (2005). *Guidelines for Collecting and Interpreting Innovation Data*. Oslo: OECD Publishing.

OECD. (2005). *The measurement of scientific and technological activities. Proposed guidelines for collecting and interpreting technological data* (3rd ed.). Paris: Oslo Manual, OCDE.

Oinas, P., & Malecki, E. (2002). The Evolution of Technologies in Time and Space: Form National and Regional Spatial Innovations Systems. *International Regional Science Review, 25*(1), 102–131. doi:10.1177/016001702762039402

Olsson, B. (2001). Annual reporting practices: Information about human resources in corporate annual reports in major Swedish companies. *Journal of Human Resource Costing and Accounting, 6*(1), 39–52. doi:10.1108/eb029071

Ordónez de Pablos, P. (2002). Evidence of Intellectual Capital measurement from Asia, Europe and the Middle East. *Journal of Intellectual Capital, 3*(3), 287–302. doi:10.1108/14691930210435624

Organisation of Economic Co-operation and Development (OECD). (1999). *Guidelines and instructions for OECD Symposium*. International Symposium on Measuring and Reporting Intellectual Capital: Experiences, Issues and Prospects, June, Amsterdam.

Osborn, A. F. (1957). *Applied Imagination*. New York: Scribner's.

Oshry, B. (1996). *Seeing systems: Unlocking the mysteries of organizational life*. San Francisco: Berrett-Koehler.

Oskarsdottir, G. G., Busetta, P., Ginestie, J., & Papoutsakis, H. (2000). *Employability Skills in non-Professional Occupations. A four-country comparative research project*. Reykjavik, Iceland: University Press, University of Iceland.

O'Sullivan, D., & Dooley, L. (2008). *Applying Innovation*. Sage Publications.

OWL. (2009). Retrieved April 10, 2009 from http://www.w3.org/2004/OWL/

OWL-S. (2009). *OWL-S Specification*. Retrieved March 16, 2009 from http://www.daml.org/services/owl-s/1.1/

Pagel, M. D., Erdly, W. W., & Becker, J. (1987). Social networks: we get by with (and in spite of) a little help from our friends. *Journal of Personality and Social Psychology, 53*, 794–804. doi:10.1037/0022-3514.53.4.793

Papavassiliou, G., Ntioudis, S., Mentzas, G., & Abecker, A. (2002). Business Process Knowledge Modelling: Method and Tool. In *Proceedings of the Theory and Application of Knowledge Management*, Aix-en-Provence, France.

Parise, S. (2007). Knowledge Management and Human Resource Development: An Application in Social Network Analysis Methods. *Advances in Developing Human Resources, 9*(3), 359–383. doi:10.1177/1523422307304106

Pawar, K. S., & Sharifi, S. (2000). Virtual collocations of design teams: coordinating for speed. *International Journal of Agile Management Systems, 2*(2), 104–113. doi:10.1108/14654650010337104

Pearson, G., & Young, T. (2002). *Technically Speaking. Why all Americans need to know more about technology*. Washington, DC: National Academy Press.

Penrose, E. T. (1959). *The theory of the growth of the firm*. New York: John Wiley.

Peter, J. P. (1981). Construct validity: A review of basic issues and marketing practices. *JMR, Journal of Marketing Research, 18*(May), 133–145. doi:10.2307/3150948

Peteraf, M. A. (1993). The cornerstones of competitive advantage: A resource-based view. *Strategic Management Journal, 14*(3), 179–191. doi:10.1002/smj.4250140303

Phadke, S. M. (1989). *Quality Engineering Using Robust Design*. Englewood Cliffs, NJ: Prentice Hall.

Pine, B. J., & Gilmore, J. (1999). *The experience economy*. Boston: Harvard Business school Press.

Plastal (2005). Bilancio del Capitale Intangibile (Intangible Capital Report), sent by Plastal's management to one of the authors, Italian version.

PMBOK (2008). *A Guide to the Project Management Body of Knowledge*.

Podolny, J. M., & Baron, J. N. (1997). Resources and Relationships: Social Networks and Mobility in the Workplace. *American Sociological Review, 62*(5), 673–693. doi:10.2307/2657354

Polanyi, M. (1983). *The tacit dimension*. New York: Doubleday.

Polanyi, M. (1966). *The Tacit Dimension*. London: Routledge & Kegan Paul Ltd.

Polleres, A., Lausen, H., & Lara, R. (2006). Semantische Beschreibung von Web-Services. In *Semantic Web - Wege zur vernetzten Wissensgesellschaft*. Springer.

Porter, M. E. (1980). *Competitive Strategy. Techniques for Analyzing Industries and Competitors*. New York: The Free Press.

Porter, M. E. (1985). *Competitive Advantage. Creating and Sustaining Superior Performance*. New York: The Free Press.

Powell, W., Koput, K. W., & Smith-Doerr, L. (1996). Inter-organizational collaboration and the locus of innovation: Networks of learning in biotechnology. *Administrative Science Quarterly*, *41*, 116–145. doi:10.2307/2393988

Prahalad, C. K., & Hamel, G. (1990). The core competence of the corporation. *Harvard Business Review*, (May-June): 79–91.

Prahalad, C. K., & Ramaswamy, V. (2003). The new frontier of experience innovation. *MIT Sloan Management Review*, *44*, 12–18.

Prajogo, D. I., & McDermott, C. M. (2005). The relationship between total quality management practices and organizational culture. *International Journal of Operations & Production Management*, *25*(11), 1101–1122. doi:10.1108/01443570510626916

Pressley, M., & Afflerbach, P. (1995). *Verbal protocols of reading: The nature of constructively responsive reading*. Hillsdale, NJ: Erlbaum.

Quesenbery, W. (2006). Storytelling and narrative. In Pruitt, J., & Adlin, T. (Eds.), *The Persona Lifecycle: Keeping People in Mind throughout Product Design* (p. 521). Morgan Kaufmann.

Ratcheva, V., & Vyakarnam, S. (2001). Exploring team formation processes in virtual partnerships. *Integrated Manufacturing Systems*, *12*(7), 512–123. doi:10.1108/EUM0000000006231

Reagans, R., & Zuckerman, E. (2001). Networks, diversity and productivity: The social capital of corporate R&D teams. *Organization Science*, *12*(4), 502–517. doi:10.1287/orsc.12.4.502.10637

Ricceri, F. (2008). *Intellectual capital and knowledge management: Strategic management of knowledge resources*. London, New York: Routledge.

Ricceri, F., & Guthrie, J. (2009). Critical analysis of international KR guidelines for knowledge-intensive organisations. In Jemielniak, D., & Kociatkiewicz, J. (Eds.), *Handbook of research on knowledge-intensive organizations*. IGI Global.

Ricceri, F. (2002). *Intellectual Capital: between strategy and measurement*. Unpublished doctoral thesis, University of Venice, Italy.

Ricceri, F. (2004). Intellectual Capital (IC) statement: the case of an Italian "(non-)knowledge-intensive" company'. In A. Neely, M. Kennerley, & A. Walters (Eds) *Performance Measurement and Management: Public and Private*. (pp. 875-881) Cranfield: Center for Business Performance, Cranfield School of Management, Cranfield.

Rittenberg, L. (1989). On the problem of identifying the engines of economic growth. *Studies in Comparative International Development*, *24*(3), 51–61. doi:10.1007/BF02686990

Roberts, E. M. (1988). Managing invention and innovation. *Research-Technology Management*, *31*(1), 11–29.

Roman, D., Keller, U., Lausen, H., de Bruijn, J., Lara, R., & Stollberg, M. (2005). *Web-Service Modeling Ontology* (pp. 77–106). Applied Ontology.

Romer, P. (1986). Increasing return and long-run growth. *The Journal of Political Economy*, *94*(5), 1002–1037. doi:10.1086/261420

Roos, G., Pike, S., & Fernström, L. (2005). *Managing intellectual capital in practice*. Oxford: Elsevier.

Roos, G., & Roos, J. (1997). Measuring your company's intellectual performance. *Long Range Planning*, *30*(3), 413–426. doi:10.1016/S0024-6301(97)90260-0

Roos, J., Roos, G., Dragonetti, N. C., & Edvinsson, L. (1997). *Intellectual capital: Navigating the new business landscape*. London: Macmillan Press.

Roos, G. (2005). Intellectual capital and strategy: A primer for today's manager. In Coate, P. (Ed.), *Handbook of Business Strategy* (pp. 123–132).

Rosenkopf, L., & Nerkar, A. (2001). Beyond Local Search: Boundary-Spanning, Exploration, and Impact in the Optical Disc Industry. *Strategic Management Journal*, *22*, 287. doi:10.1002/smj.160

Rymaszewski, M., Wagner, J. A., Ondrejka, C., Platel, R., Van Gorden, S., & Cézanne, J. (2008). *Second Life: The Official Guide* (2nd ed.). Sybex.

Sadler-Smith, E. (2006). *Learning and Development for Managers: Perspectives from Research and Practice.* Oxford: Blackwell Publishing.

Sawhney, M., & Prandelli, E. (2000). Communities of creation: managing distributed innovation in turbulent markets. *California Management Review, 42*, 24–54.

SAWSDL. (2009). Semantic Annotations for Web-Services Description Language Working Group Homepage. Retrieved March 12, 2009 from http://www.w3.org/2002/ws/sawsdl/ Schmidt, A., Ley, T., & Lindstaedt, S. (2009). Workshop on Knowledge Services & Mash-ups, In K. Hinkelmann, & H. Wache (Eds.), *WM 2009: 5th Conference on Professional Knowledge Management*, March 25-27, 2009, Solothurn, Switzerland, GI-Verlag, Bonn

Say, M. (2006). *Government Computing Magazine.*

Schiessl, M., Duda, S., Thölke, A., & Fischer, R. (2003). Eye-tracking and its application in usability and media research. *MMI-Interaktiv, 6.*

Schmitt, B., & Simonson, A. (1997). *Marketing aesthetics. The strategic management of brands, identity and management.* New York: The Free Press.

Schumpeter, J. A. (1934). *The theory of economic development.* Cambridge, MA: Harvard Business Press.

Scott, J. (2000). *Social Network Analysis: A Handbook.* London: Sage.

Scott Morton, M. S. (Ed.). (1991). *The Corporation of the 1990s. Information technology and organizational transformation.* New York: Oxford University Press.

Seetharaman, A., Sooria, H. H., & Saravanan, A. S. (2002). Intellectual capital accounting and reporting in the knowledge economy. *Journal of Intellectual Capital, 3*(2), 128–148. doi:10.1108/14691930210424734

Senge, P. M. (1990). The leader's new work: Building a learning organization. *Sloan Management Review, 32*(1), 2–18.

Senge, P. (1990). *The fifth discipline: The art and practice of the learning organisation.* New York: Doubleday Currency.

Senge, P., Kleiner, A., Roberts, C., Ross, R., & Smith, B. (1994). *The Fifth Discipline Fieldbook – Strategies and Tools for Building a Learning Organization.* London: Nicholas Brealey Publishing.

Sentensia, Q. (2006). *Intellectual Capital Report*, retrieved February 2007 www.sentensia.se.

Shinnar, R. (1978). Chemical reactormodeling—The desirable and the achievable. In Luss, D., & Weekman, V. Jr., (Eds.), *Chemical reaction engineering reviews, ACS symposium series* (*Vol. 72*, p. 1).

Shukla, M. (1997). *Competing Through Knowledge – Building a Learning Organization.* London: Sage.

Siemens, G. (2005). Connectivism: A learning theory for the digital age. *International Journal of Instructional Technology and Distance Learning.* Retrieved from http://www.idtl.org/Journal/Jam_05/article01.htm.

Silverstein, J. M., & Fiske, N. (2003). *Trading up. The new American Luxury.* New York: Portfolio.

Simon, S. J. (2001). The impact of culture and gender on web sites: An empirical study. *The Data Base for Advances in Information Systems, 32*(1), 18–37.

SkypePrime. (n.d.). Retrieved from http://www.skype.com/allfeatures/skypeprime/

Society for Knowledge Economics (SKE). (2005). *Australian guiding principles on extended performance management.* Sydney: SKE.

Society for Knowledge Economics (SKE). (2007). *Intangible drivers of organisational productivity and Prosperity.* Sydney: SKE.

Souza, R. R., & Alvarenga Neto, R. C. D. (2003). A construção do conceito de gestão do conhecimento: práticas organizacionais, garantias literárias e o fenômeno social [Building the concept of knowledge management: organizational practices, literary warranties and the social phenomenon]. In *Knowledge Management Brasil,* nov 2003, São Paulo. Anais. São Paulo, 2003. CD ROM.

Spender, J.C. (1996). Making knowledge the basis of a dynamic theory of the firm. *Strategic Management Journal, 17*(Winter Special Issue), 45-62.

Sproull, L., & Kiesler, S. (1991). *Connections. New ways of working in the networked organization*. Cambridge: MIT Press.

Stewart, T.A. (1997). *Intellectual capital: The new wealth of nations*. New York: Doubleday.

Stollberg, M., Hepp, M., & Fensel, D. (2007). Semantic Web-Services – Realisierung der SOA Vision mit semantischen Technologien. SWS – MKE conference.

Storberg-Walker, J., & Gubbins, C. (2007). Social Networks as a Conceptual and Empirical Tool to Understand and "Do" HRD. *Advances in Developing Human Resources, 9*(3). doi:10.1177/1523422306304071

Striukova, L., Unerman, J., & Guthrie, J. (2008). Corporate reporting of Intellectual Capital: Evidence from UK companies. *The British Accounting Review, 40*(4), 297–313. doi:10.1016/j.bar.2008.06.001

Subcommittee on Management & Intellectual Assets (SMIA) (2005). *Interim report by subcommittee on management and intellectual assets*, August.

Sveiby, K. E. (1997). *The new organizational wealth: Managing and measuring knowledge based assets*. San Francisco: Berret Koehler.

Sveiby, K. (2001). A knowledge-based theory of the firm to guide in strategic formulation. *Journal of Intellectual Capital, 2*(4), 344–358. doi:10.1108/14691930110409651

Systematic (2004). *Intellectual Capital report*. Retrieved March 2007 from www.systematic.com

Taguchi, G. (1986). Introduction to Quality Engineering, Asian Productivity Organization (Distributed by American Supplier Institute Inc., Dearborn, MI).

Tapscott, D., & Williams, A. D. (2007). *Wikinomics. How mass collaboration changes everything*. New York: Penguin Books.

Teece, D. J., Pisano, G., & Shuen, A. (1997). Dynamic capabilities and strategic management. *Strategic Management Journal, 18*(7), 509–533. doi:10.1002/(SICI)1097-0266(199708)18:7<509::AID-SMJ882>3.0.CO;2-Z

Thompson, V. A. (1965). Bureaucracy and innovation. *Administrative Science Quarterly, 5*(June), 1–20. doi:10.2307/2391646

Tidd, J., Bessant, J., & Pavitt, K. (2005). *Managing Innovation: Integrating Technological, Market and Organisational Change*. Chichester, UK: John Wiley & Sons.

Tranfield, D., Young, M., Partington, D., Bessant, J., & Sapsed, J. (2006). Knowledge management routines for innovation projects: developing a hierarchical process model. In J. Tidd (2nd ed.). *Knowledge Management to Strategic Competence* (pp. 126-149). London: Imperial College Press.

Treacy, M., & Wiersema, F. (1997). *The discipline of market leaders: choose your customers, narrow your focus, dominate your market*. New York: Perseus Books Group.

Trier, M. (2007). *Virtual Knowledge Communities – IT-supported Visualization and Analysis*. VDM Saarbruecken.

Trott, P. (2005). *Innovation Management and New Product Development* (3rd ed.). Prentice-Hall.

Tsai, W. (2001). Knowledge Transfers in Intra-Organizational Networks. *Academy of Management Journal, 44*(5), 996–1004. doi:10.2307/3069443

Tsai, K. H., Chou, C., & Kuo, J. H. (2008). The curvilinear relationship between responsive and proactive market orientations and new product performance: A contingent link. *Industrial Marketing Management, 37*(8), 884–894. doi:10.1016/j.indmarman.2007.03.005

Tsan, W. N., & Chang, C. C. (2005). Intellectual capital system interaction. *Journal of Intellectual Capital, 6*(2), 285–298. doi:10.1108/14691930510592852

Uhl-Bien, M., Graen, G. B., & Scandura, T. A. (2000). Implications of leader-member exchange (LMX) for strategic human resource management systems: Relationships as social capital for competitive advantage. In Ferris, G. R. (Ed.), *Research in personnel and human resource management* (Vol. 18, pp. 137–185). New York: JAI Press.

Umpress, E. E., LaBiance, G., Brass, D. J., Kass, E., & Scholten, L. (2003). The role of instrumental and expressive ties in employee's perceptions of organizational justice. *Organization Science, 14*(6), 738–753. doi:10.1287/orsc.14.6.738.24865

Un, C. A., & Cuervo-Cazurra, A. (2004). Strategies for knowledge creation in firms. *British Journal of Management, 15*(Supplement 1), 27–41. doi:10.1111/j.1467-8551.2004.00404.x

Understanding U.S. Consumers (2008). VALS™ SRI Consulting Business Intelligence.

Unerman, J., Guthrie, J., & Striukova, L. (2007). *UK reporting of Intellectual Capital*. London: Institute of Chartered Accountants in England and Wales Centre for Business Performance.

Valente, A., & Housel, T. (2001). A Framework to Analyze and Compare Knowledge Management Tools. In *Proceedings of the Knowledge-Based Intelligent Information Engineering Systems and Allied Technologies* (KES2001). IOS Press.

Van den Bosch, F. A. J., Van Wijk, R., & Volberda, H. W. (2003). Absorptive capacity: Antecedents, Models and Outcomes. In Easterby-Smith, M., & Lyles, M. A. (Eds.), *Handbook of Organizational Learning & Knowledge Management* (pp. 278–301). Oxford: Blackwell Publishing.

Van den Ven, A. H. (1986). Central problems in the management of innovation. *Management Science, 32*(5), 590–607. doi:10.1287/mnsc.32.5.590

Vassolo, R. S., Anand, J., & Folta, T. B. (2004). Non-Additivity in Portfolios of Exploration Activities: a Real Options-Based Analysis of Equity Alliances in Biotechnology. *Strategic Management Journal, 25*(11), 1045–1061. doi:10.1002/smj.414

Venkatraman, N. (1989). The Concept of Fit in Strategy Research toward Verbal and Statistical Correspondence. *Academy of Management Review, 14*(3), 423–444. doi:10.2307/258177

Vermeulen, F., & Barkema, H. (2001). Learning through Acquisitions. *Academy of Management Journal, 44*(3), 457–476. doi:10.2307/3069364

Vestal (2003). Ten traits for a successful community of practice. *Knowledge Management Review, 5*(6), 6.

Viedma, J. M. M. (2003). In search of an intellectual capital general theory. *Electronic Journal of Knowledge Management, 1*(2), 213–226.

Viles, E., Tanco, M., Unai Artecheb, I., & Sagartzazub, X. (2009). Applying Design of Experiments to a Lift Test Rig. *Quality and Reliability Engineering International, 26*(2), 157–165.

vom Brocke, J. (2007). *Informationssysteme für Wissensnetzwerke*. HMD, Praxis der Wirtschaftsinformatik.

Von Hippel, E. (2005). *Democratizing Innovation*. Boston: MIT Press.

Von Krogh, G., Ichijo, K., & Nonaka, I. (2001). *Facilitando a criação de conhecimento* [Enabling Knowledge Creation]. Rio de Janeiro: Campus.

Von Krogh, G., Ichigo, K., & Nonaka, I. (Eds.). (2000). *Enabling Knowledge Creation*. London: Oxford University Press.

Von Krogh, G., & Roos, J. (1995). A perspective on Knowledge, Competence and Strategy. *Personnel Review, 24*(3), 56–76. doi:10.1108/00483489510089650

Von Stamm, B. (2003). *Managing Innovation, Design and Creativity*. Wiley.

Voss, C. A. (2003). Rethinking paradigms of service. *International Journal of Operations & Production Management, 23*(1), 88–104. doi:10.1108/01443570310453271

Walters, D., & Buchanan, J. (2001). The new economy, new opportunities and new structures. *Management Decision, 39*(10), 818–834. doi:10.1108/EUM0000000006524

Wasserman, S., & Faust, K. (1994). *Social network analysis: Methods and applications*. New York: Cambridge University Press.

Weber, A., Rufer-Bach, K., & Platel, R. (2007). *Creating Your World: The Official Guide to Advanced Content Creation for Second Life*. Sybex.

Webster (1981). *Third New International Dictionary.* Chicago: Meriam-Webster.

Weick, K. E. (1995). *Sensemaking in organizations*. New York: McGraw-Hill.

Wenger, E., McDermott, R., & Sydner, W. (2002). *Cultivating communities of practice: a guide to managing knowledge*. Boston: Harvard Business School Press.

Wenger, E. C., & Snyder, W. M. (2000). Communities of practice: the organizational frontier. *Harvard Business Review, 78*, 139–145.

Wengraf, T. (2001). *Qualitative Research Interviewing: Biographic Narrative and Semi-Structured Methods*. London: Sage Publications.

Wernerfelt, B. (1984). A resource-based view of the firm. *Strategic Management Journal, 5*(2), 171–180. doi:10.1002/smj.4250050207

White, D. R. (1997). *What is network theory?* Retrieved May 2, 2005 from http://eclectic.ss.uci.edu/drwhite/netsy196.htm.

Whitney, P., & Budd, D. (1996). Think-aloud protocols and the study of comprehension. *Discourse Processes, 21*, 341–351. doi:10.1080/01638539609544962

Wiig, K. (1993). *Knowledge Management Foundations – Thinking about Thinking – How people and Organizations Create, Represent and Use Knowledge*. Arlington, VA: Schema Press.

Wiig, K., Hoog, R., & van der Speck, R. (1997). Supporting knowledge management: a selection of methods and techniques. *Expert Systems with Applications, 13*, 15–27. doi:10.1016/S0957-4174(97)00019-5

Wildt, A. R., Lambert, Z. V., & Durand, R. M. (1982). Applying the jackknife statistics in testing and interpreting canonical weights, loadings and cross-loadings. *JMR, Journal of Marketing Research, 19*, 99–107. doi:10.2307/3151534

Williams, M. (2008). *The Principles of Project Management*. SitePoint.

Wittgenstein, L. (1953). *Philosophical Investigations.* Oxford: Basil Blackwell.

Woitsch, R. (2004). *Process Oriented Knowledge Management: A Service-Based Approach.* PhD thesis University of Vienna.

Woitsch, R., & Karagiannis, D. (2004). Process Oriented Knowledge Management: A Service Based Approach. In *Proceedings of the I-Know 04 from the Special Track BPOKI'04*, Graz, Austria.

Woitsch, R., & Leutgeb, A. (2008). The BREIN-Roadmap with PROMOTE®: A Use-Case Scenario of a Service-Based Knowledge Management Approach, I-Know 08, Graz, Austria.

Woitsch, R., & Utz, W. (2006). Roadmap to Akogrimo Convergence, A Sample of Process Oriented Knowledge Management with PROMOTE. In *Proceedings of I KNOW '06, Graz, Austria.*

Woitsch, R., Karagiannis, D., Fill, H.-G., & Blazevic, V. (2007). Semantic Based Knowledge Flow System in European Home Textile: A Process Oriented Approach with PROMOTE. In *Proceedings of I KNOW '07*, Graz, Austria.

Woitsch, R., Utz, W., Mak, K., & Göllner, J. (2009). *Intellectual Capital Management using Knowledge Scorecards: A Best Practice Implementation*. Paper presented at the Austrian National Defence Academy, 5th Conference of Professional Knowledge Management, (KM 09), Solothurn, Switzerland.

Wright, D. T., & Burns, N. D. (1998). New organisation structures for global business: an empirical study. *International Journal of Operations & Production Management, 18*(9), 896–923. doi:10.1108/01443579810225513

Yamin, S., Mavondo, F., Gunasekaran, A., & Sarros, J. (1997). A study of competitive strategy, organisational innovation and organisational performance among Austrian manufacturing companies. *International Journal of Production Economics*, *52*(1). doi:10.1016/S0925-5273(96)00104-1

Yin, R. K. (1994). *Case study research: design and methods*. Thousand Oaks, CA: Sage.

Zack, M. (1999). Managing codified knowledge. *Sloan Management Review*, 45–58.

Zack, M. H., Smith, D. E., & Slusher, J. A. (1999). *Knowledge and strategy*. Williamsburg, VA: Institute for Knowledge Management.

Zack, M. H. (2002). A strategic pretext for knowledge management. In *Proceedings of The Third European Conference on Organizational Knowledge, Learning and Capabilities*, Athens, Greece, April 5. Retrieved from http://www.alba.edu.gr/OKLC2002/Proceedings/

Zaltman, G., Duncan, R., & Holbek, J. (1973). *Innovations and organizations*. New York: Wiley.

Zhou, J., & Shalley, C. (2003). Research on employee creativity: a critical review and directions for future directions. *Research in Personnel and Human Resources Management*, *22*, 165–217. doi:10.1016/S0742-7301(03)22004-1

Zhou, A. Z., & Fink, D. (2003). The intellectual capital web: A systematic linking of intellectual capital and knowledge management. *Journal of Intellectual Capital*, *4*(1), 34–48. doi:10.1108/14691930310455379

Zollo, M., & Winter, S. G. (2002). Deliberate learning and the evolution of dynamic capabilities. *Organization Science*, *13*(3), 339–351. doi:10.1287/orsc.13.3.339.2780

Zumd, R. (1984). An Examination of 'Push –Pull' theory applied to process innovation in knowledge work. *Management Science*, 6.

About the Contributors

Emma O'Brien BBS (Business Computing), MSc, PhD – Enterprise Research Centre, UL. Emma is a research fellow with the enterprise research centre (ERC) in the University of Limerick. She has worked on several national and international projects in her time in the ERC In May 2000 – 2003 Emma worked with an international e-learning company, NetG in which she was responsible for developing e-learning products for the customers. Furthermore she was responsible for Managing the localisation of courses by our Japanese partners and maintaining and editing the course engines for localization. In October 2005 she completed her PhD - eCasme and beyond towards tailoring training in SMEs in which she Identified a framework to assist SMEs to tailor e-learning courses to their training needs. In addition Emma implemented this framework as a practical online tool. Emma is a member of the editorial board of the Journal of Technology Enhanced Learning and participated as a reviewer for IADIS International Conference in E-Learning.

Seamus Clifford, BSc, MSc, PhD, NPDP - Enterprise Research Centre, UL. Seamus is a senior research fellow with the Enterprise Research centre in University of Limerick. He is currently working on several Innovation Partnership projects (Industry-University joint research projects) with companies dealing with issues around experimental design / engineering knowledge management, process innovation and new product development. He completed his PhD in 2001 at the University of Limerick. The project was on the Formulation of Capacitor Materials for Reliable Co-fired Capacitor-Varistor Devices and was completed for the New Product Development Department at Harris Semiconductor (Irl) Ltd., now Littelfuse (Ire) Ltd. The aim of the project was to produce a surface mountable co-fired varistor-capacitor device. Prototyping was carried out on the production pilot line based at Littelfuse in Dundalk. Previously, he was also a research fellow for three years with the European Commission at their Institute for Reference Materials and Measurements (IRMM – based at Geel in Belgium) and he has also worked at the Swiss Federal laboratories for Materials Testing and Research (EMPA – based at St. Gallen in Switzerland) as an extractive metallurgist. He has also worked for Tubex Ltd., for three years, at both the Plastics and the Aluminium Divisions on the installation of the ISO 9000 quality system and the definition and control of product specifications.

Mark Southern, BSc PhD - Enterprise Research Centre, UL. Mark graduated from Nottingham Trent University in 1989 with a degree in Industrial Studies and obtained his Doctorate in 2004 by researching the application of innovative wireless technology applications into SMEs. He is currently working with the Enterprise Research Centre on a European Research project called EURobust. This project is looking at the application of robust design tools in European industry. Mark is an experienced manager with a proven track record in project team management in both multinational's and SME's. He has significant experience in managing teams in research, design, development, procurement and installation of complex manufacturing systems in these environments. He is an experienced man manager with a excellent track record in financial metrics management and dead line achievement.

* * *

Ileana Hamburg, worked 20 years as a professor for Mathematics and Computer Science at the University of Craiova, Romania. In Germany she worked as a software developer for a company and as a researcher within the Faculty of Informatics at the University of Erlangen, Germany. She is a research fellow at the Institute of Work and Technology (IAT), FH Gelsenkirchen and lecturer for Informatics at the Open University (FU) of Hagen. She works and coordinates German and European projects particularly in the field of Web services and applications for learning and knowledge management, social networks, communities of practice. Dr. Ileana Hamburg works in different program committees of international conferences and is an evaluator for projects in different national and European initiatives.

Timothy Hall is Director of EMRC- Educational Media Research Centre, University of Limerick, Ireland. EMRC's interests encompass all aspects of TEL-Technology Enhanced Learning, TEL support for PBL-Problem Based Learning, collaborative and self-organised learning and the integration of these techniques into complete and supportive learning environments, always with a focus on the users. Topics of interest include: eLearning pedagogy, curriculum design, instructional design and learning styles, personalisation, reusability and interoperability, web2 and the use of social tools in learning, learning communities and COPs, the structure and management of Post Experiential Learning and Life-Long-Learning as applied to knowledge generation and transfer in technology and science and particularly with SMEs. EMRC's own solutions are based on OSS to maintain maximum flexibility and adaptability. For many years Tim has been active in European Union collaborative programmes in education and training with participation in some twenty successful projects, he maintains research and collaboration links in most EU countries, Central and Eastern Europe and beyond in China and Malaysia. Tim is also a lecturer, in the Dept of Electronic & Computer Engineering, UL applying PBL and collaborative learning techniques in his teaching, he hold a Professorship (h.c.) from Stefan cel Mare University, Suceava, Romania. Formerly he was PlasseyMTC Research Fellow of Continuing Education and Post Experiential Learning, University of Limerick. Tim was educated at the University of Northumbria and the University of Birmingham in the UK and has worked as an engineer in the computer industry, in the semiconductor industry, in power supply design and for the BBC.

Rivadávia Correa Drummond de Alvarenga Neto is Professor at Fundação Dom Cabral (www.fdc.org.br), a Brazilian business school ranked the 13th best business school in the world and the best one in Latin America according to the Financial Times Executive Education ranking 2009. He holds a PhD in Information Science, School of Information Science, Universidade Federal de Minas Gerais (UFMG), Brazil. In 2009, he was a Post-Doctoral Fellow and Visiting Scholar at the Faculty of Information Studies at the University of Toronto, Canada, hosted by Dr. Chun Wei Choo, where he's also a member of the KRMC –Knowledge Management Research Centre. Rivadávia speaks regularly on the subject of knowledge management and he conducted the first in depth qualitative study within the Brazilian organizational context in 2005. Since 2001 he's been working with many world class organizations, such as Petrobras, Embrapa (The Brazilian Agricultural Research Corporation), ONS (Brazil's National Operator of the Interconnected Power System), Astra Zeneca, Linde, Itau-Unibanco, Anglo American, The Linde Group and NEC, among many others. His main research interests/areas are knowledge management, information management, organizational theory, knowledge-based theories of the firm and social networks/social media, among others. He's authored a book (Knowledge Management in Organizations, Saraiva Publishers, São Paulo, Brazil, 2008) and co-authored several others. His papers and articles have been published in Brazil, Spain, France, England, Chile, South Africa, Canada, United States, Malta, Ireland and Portugal, among others. Before working at Fundação Dom Cabral, he was Dean at Centro Universitário UNA, Brazil.

Renato Rocha Souza is Professor and Researcher at Fundação Getúlio Vargas (http://www.fgv.br), one of the most preeminent Think Tanks of the world and the top one in Latin America. He is also a Collaborator professor at Universidade Federal de Minas Gerais, Visiting Fellow at the Hypermedia Research Center at the University of Glamorgan, UK, and a member of the ISKO - International Society for Knowledge Organization. He holds a PhD in Information Science, School of Information Science, Universidade Federal de Minas Gerais (UFMG), Brazil. His main research interests/areas are knowledge organization systems, natural language processing, formal ontologies, information retrieval, knowledge management, social networks, among others.

Federica Ricceri is an assistant professor of Accounting at the University of Padova. Her research and teaching interests include strategic performance measurement, management and financial accounting, extended performance reporting, intellectual capital, the strategic management of knowledge resources, and finance and valuation. She has published several articles in both international and national refereed and professional journals focusing on intellectual capital and the strategic management of knowledge resources. She has also published several chapters in international and national books focusing on strategic performance measurement and financial accounting. She has presented her ideas and research findings to national and international gatherings. She is a member of the editorial board of the Journal of Human Resource Costing and Accounting.

James Guthrie is a Professor at the University of Bologna and an Honorary Professor at the University of Sydney. His research and teaching interests include social and environmental reporting and auditing, public sector accounting, auditing, accountability and management, management of knowledge and intellectual capital and the measurement of intangibles. He also consults on public and private sector management, management of knowledge, intellectual capital, budget performance, and annual reporting strategies. James has published over 130 articles in both international and national refereed and professional journals, and over 30 chapters in books. He has presented his ideas and research findings to over 280 national and international gatherings. James is also co-editor of seven public sector management and accounting books. He is the co-editor of Accounting, Auditing and Accountability Journal.

Rodney Coyte of the University of Sydney specializes in research combining strategy and the management of resource development and deployment in organizations. His PhD examined how teamwork structures affected organizational resource management and the effectiveness of strategic change. Dr. Coyte's recent research explores: organizational structure and change factors enhancing situated learning and its effect on intellectual capital development in organizations; the effect of performance evaluation systems on information sharing behaviour and strategic alignment; and processes affecting change in management accounting practices. Dr. Coyte publishes on the role of empowered teams, shareholder value measurement techniques and knowledge development processes. Dr. Coyte has managed operations as an Information Technology Manager and conducted strategic and operational planning as a Business Planning Manager with the Mars Corporation. He also has extensive experience in information technology and management consulting to a diverse range of organisations in Australia and South East Asia.

Steve Russell - Two years of directed Virtual World research and development for enterprise applications. Designed and directed the construction of business-ready Second Life applications for Command & Control, real-time Building Operations, Work Rehearsal, and 3D Project Management. Designs for Virtual World additions for Siemens offerings in areas such as diagnostic products and training, and for software systems and processes for health records. Founded a consulting company for international advice on Knowledge Management applications. Worked for leading corporations as a Knowledge Engineer and Intelligent Systems architect. Led departments and companies as a manager and CIO. Data mining and information systems designs for diverse enterprise domains including manufacturing, telecommunications, marketing, and product improvement. Commercial and academic work in Natural Language Processing, document understanding, workflow efficiency and Operations Research for clerical and professional teams. Analyses of cognitive and social issues in work performance and learning. Medical experience as an EMT, and through research into Radiation Therapy Planning, and through Ph.D. research into disease systems, Genomics, and Proteomics at the University of Colorado Health Sciences Center in Analytic Health Sciences.

Dimitris Karagiannis studied Computer Science at the TU-Berlin and graduated several research visit stays in the USA and Japan. He was scientific director for Business Information Systems at the Research Institute FAW in Ulm/Germany. 1993 he founded the Department of Knowledge and Business Engineering at the Faculty of Computer Science at the University of Vienna, focusing on Meta-Modelling, knowledge-based Business Process Management and Engineering, as well as Knowledge Management. He has published research papers in the field of Databases, Information Systems, BPM-, Workflow-Systems and Knowledge Engineering and - Management. He is the author of two books concerned with Knowledge - Databases and - Engineering and is engaged in national and EU-funded research projects. The BPMS-Approach he established, which is concerned with the thematic of knowledge-based Business Process, has been successfully implemented in several industrial and service organisations. He founded the software-company BOC (www.boc-group.com), which implement software tools based on the Meta-Modelling approach. Actually he established the Open Model Initiative (www.openmodels.at) in Austria.

Vedran Hrgovcic holds MSc in International Business Administration and is currently a PhD candidate at the University of Vienna. He is presently working in the research and development area within the BOC Asset Management GmbH having specific interests in the semantic workflows and enterprise ontologies. Mr. Hrgovcic was involved in LD-CAST, BREIN, MATURE and plugIT EU Research projects (within the FP6 and FP7 Framework Programme).

Robert Woitsch holds a PhD in business informatics and is currently responsible for European and National research projects within the consulting company BOC (www.boc-group.com) in Vienna, in the domain of knowledge management and technology enhanced learning. He deals with KM-projects since 2000 starting with the EU-funded projects ADVISOR, PROMOTE and EKMF and has recently been working on KM-aspects within the EU-projects Akogrimo, FIT, LD-Cast, Brein, AsIsKnown, MATURE and now coordinates plugIT. Mr. Woitsch is involved in commercial projects in the design of documentation processes, skill management and knowledge balances and is a member of the Austrian Standardization Institute contributing to the ON-Workshop 1144 "Knowledge Management". Beside his engagement at BOC he teaches at the Department of Knowledge and Business Engineering at the Faculty of Computer Science at the University of Vienna. The tight coupling between BOC and the University of Vienna is expressed in about 40 joined papers, including the best-paper award at the eChallenges 08 and the involvement as reviewer and member of programme committees in KM-conferences

Claire Gubbins (PhD, MCIPD, MIITD, BBS) is a Senior Research Fellow with the Enterprise Research Centre, at University of Limerick. Previously, she was a Lecturer of Management and HRM at University College Cork and in HRM and HRD at the University of Limerick (UL). She completed her PhD with the University of Limerick for which she was credited with an Academy of HRD Malcolm S. Knowles Dissertation Award finalist award. She has published in Organisation Studies, Human Resource Development Review, Advances in Developing Human Resources and the Journal of European Industrial Training. Her current research interests are on social networks, trust and knowledge sharing. She is also a lead researcher for the Irish Centre for Manufacturing Research (ICMR) research project focusing on training and training information support in manufacturing.

Lawrence Dooley (M. Comm., PhD) is a College Lecturer in Enterprise and Innovation at University College Cork (Ireland). Prior to joining UCC, he was based at the Centre for Enterprise Management in the University of Dundee, Scotland. His core research interests focus on organisational innovation and issues related to inter-enterprise collaboration and venture creation. Other related interests include creativity, portfolio management and knowledge exchange. He has published widely over recent years and actively liaises with industry both through applied research projects and consultancy. His latest research projects examine emerging models of collaboration across distributed innovation networks and the area of biotechnology clustering.

Alberto Carneiro is Head of the Sciences and Technologies Department at Autonomous University of Lisbon. He received a PhD in Engineering and Industrial Management from Technical University of Lisbon and a MSc in Business Administration with a specialization in Strategic Management and Planning from the same University. Dr. Alberto Carneiro focuses on management of information systems (security and control) at industrial strategic management, and the adoption of innovation and new services development. His interdisciplinary research interests mainly involve Information Systems (Security and Auditing), Knowledge Management and the relationships between Information and Communication Technology and Competitive Innovation. He is studying the ways in which training, knowledge accumulation, and information technology enable change in the way management teams innovate and make strategic decisions. Presently, he is teaching database systems, network security and principles of management in computing science and computer engineering courses. Alberto Carneiro is the author of some textbooks, such as, Auditing and Controlling Information Systems (2009), Auditing Information Systems (2004, 2nd edition) and Introduction to Information Systems Security (2002) and Innovation - Strategy and Competitiveness (1995). Moreover, he has written and presented more than twenty-five articles and communications in international and national conferences and workshops. He is a member of the Portuguese Association of Marketing and the Portuguese Association for Higher Education. His professional activities also include executive training programs and consultancy to firms of several industries.

César Camisón-Zornoza, Bachelor of Economic and Business Sciences (1980) with Extraordinary Prize, and PhD in Economics and Business Sciences on (1984) with Cum Laude and Extraordinary Prize, both by University of Valencia. Professor in Business Administration at University Jaume I of Castellón. He has an experience from 25 years in teaching, researching and university management, which he has developed in some Spanish Universities, and as Visiting Professor in different European and American Universities (Surrey, Universitá Commerciale Luigi Bocconi de Milán, Viena University, Université de Montpellier I, Texas A&M University). His fields of expertise are strategic management, intangible assets and dynamic / innovation capabilities, firm as a knowledge and learning organization, strategic alliances and competitive dynamic inside inter-organizational networks and industrial districts. He has published more of 60 books as author, co-author or coordinator by publishers as Prentice-Hall, Elsevier Science, John Wiley & Sons, Information Science Reference, Idea Group Publishing, Sage, Rutledge, and Office for Official Publications of the European Communities. He has published articles in closely 100 journals as Environment and Planning A, Organization Studies, International Marketing Review, and International Business Review.

Montserrat Boronat-Navarro is a lecturer in Strategic Management and Operations Management at Jaume I University in Castellón (Spain). She received her PhD in November 2007 with Cum Laude qualification. She has been visiting researcher at London School of Economics and Political Science. Her research interests include knowledge development, dynamic capabilities, innovation, strategic alliances, and organizational structure. She has published chapters in international books and articles in Organization Studies and also in Spanish academic publications. She has presented her research in several international conferences organized by different associations such as European Academy of Management or European Group for Organization Studies.

Haris Papoutsakis is an Associate Professor at the School of Applied Technology at the Technological Educational Institute of Crete, and the Honorary Treasurer of WOCATE, the World Council of Associations for Technology Education. He holds an Electrical Engineer degree (1971), an MBA (1974) and a recent PhD (2005). His area of research relates to innovation, entrepreneurship, quality and knowledge management and focuses on the industrial inter-departmental relationships and the acquisition of work-related knowledge and skills in education and training. Prior to his assignment at the TEI of Crete in 1986, he worked for more than twelve years with Mobil Oil, Hewlett-Packard and IT&T in field and senior management positions in Greece and the Middle East.

Daniela Butan is a Researcher in the area of Fracture Mechanics, Stress Analysis and Fluid Flow Analysis at the Enterprise Research Centre, University of Limerick, Ireland . She holds a BAI in Automotive Engineering from Transilvania University, Brasov, Romania, a BAI and a MSc by Research in Mechanical and Manufacturing Engineering from Trinity College Dublin. She is a member of IEI in Ireland and TWI in UK. She has experience in the plastics industry, engineering design, lecturing.

Saïda Habhab-Rave undertook her doctoral studies at Jean Moulin University – Lyon 3 where her thesis focused on fuzzy logic and decision making. She's currently an Professor at the Business School ISTEC Paris and is an associate member of CEREGE – University of Poitiers. Her research interests include knowledge management, decision making, TIC and innovation.

Candemir Toklu is currently the program manager for the regional Knowledge Management Center of Competence at Siemens Corporate Research Inc., in Princeton, NJ, USA. He is managing a group of consultants and research scientists working in the areas of knowledge management, enterprise content management, business process management, enterprise architecture planning, virtual worlds, scenario planning and semantic web. Dr. Toklu received Master's and Ph.D. degrees in Electrical Engineering from the University of Rochester, in Rochester, NY, in 1994 and 1998, respectively. He began his career at Siemens Corporate Research in 1997 as a member of technical staff -- followed by project manager, senior member of technical staff, senior consultant and finally program manager positions. He is the author and co-author of over 20 published journal and conference papers. He also holds over 8 US patents in the areas of video image processing and digital libraries.

Stefania Mariano is the Head of Campuswide Research, the School of Management Research Coordinator, and an Assistant Professor of Management at NYIT, New York Institute of Technology. She received her PhD in Management and her MBA with honours from Molise University, Italy. She was a visiting scholar at the Department of Management Science of the George Washington University (USA) and a visiting researcher at IKI – Institute of Knowledge and Innovation at GWU (USA). She has participated in national and international research projects in the USA, Europe, and the Middle East. She has presented several research papers at national and international conferences, has published in numerous academic journals, and has contributed chapters for several books. She has experience teaching in both the undergraduate and graduate levels.

Nicola Simionato's love affair with the internet began in humble times of NCSA Mosaic and 14.4kbps dial-up modems, in the mid 90s. He held positions of Web Project Manager, Web Master and Web designer in Italian web agencies before joining Alitalia Italian Airlines in 2001, initially as alitalia.com's webmaster and later as Commercial Web Development Manager. In December 2006 his addiction to travel brought him to the Kingdom of Bahrain, where as Head of e-Commerce he is driving Gulf Air's "web revolution", aimed to shifting sales and services to the website, developing ancillary products and establishing Gulfair.com as the channel of choice in the customer-airline relationship.

Alton Y. K. Chua is Assistant Professor with Nanyang Technological University (NTU) where he teaches in the Master of Science in Knowledge Management and Master of Science in Information Systems programs. Alton's research interests lie mainly in communities of practice, knowledge management implementation and online education. In 2006, he was the co-recipient of the Highly Commendable Award for the paper entitled "The Mismanagement of Knowledge Management" awarded by Emerald Literati Network. Alton has published some 70 journal articles and conference papers. He currently serves on the editorial board of three refereed journals. He holds a Bachelor's degree in computer science, a Master's degree in education and Doctorate in business administration.

Maria do Rosário Cabrita holds a Ph.D. in Business Administration (Institute of Economics and Business Administration, Lisbon Technical University). She is Assistant Professor of Industrial Engineering at Faculdade de Ciências e Tecnologia, Universidade Nova de Lisboa, Portugal. She is also Assistant Professor at the Portuguese Banking Management School in Lisbon. She teaches several disciplines in graduate and post-graduate courses (Project Management; Strategic Management; Knowledge Management; Intellectual Capital; Marketing and Innovation; Banking Financial Analysis; Assets and Liabilities Management). Involved in international projects (in Africa and Europe) she also works as consultant in private and public sectors. She has several years of experience in various management positions in international banks. She has published numerous journal and conference papers in the knowledge management and intellectual capital domains. She has sat on the scientific committees of conferences on intellectual capital and knowledge management, and takes part in European research projects. She has received some papers-award in Portugal and abroad. In January 2005, she received the Edvinson-Saint Onge's best paper award at the 26th McMaster World Congress.

V. Cruz Machado holds a PhD in computer integrated management (Cranfield University, UK). He is an associate professor of Industrial Engineering at Faculdade de Ciências e Tecnologia, Universidade Nova de Lisboa, Portugal. He coordinates the post-graduate programmes in industrial engineering, project management and lean management. He teaches courses in operations and production management and has published more than 150 articles in scientific journals and conferences, in addition to having supervised fifty MSc and PhD students. His main scientific activities are directed to the design and improvement of supply chain management. He is the president of UNIDEMI (Research & Development Unit in Mechanical & Industrial Engineering) and the president of the Portugal Chapter of the Institute of Industrial Engineers.

António Grilo holds a PhD degree in e-commerce by the University of Salford, UK. He is Auxiliar Professor of operations management and information systems at the Faculdade Ciências e Tecnologia da Universidade Nova de Lisboa, in doctoral, master and undergraduate degrees. He is also a member of the board of director of the research center UNIDEMI. He has over 30 papers published in international conferences and scientific journals, and he is an expert for the European Commission DG-INFSO. Besides academia, he has been working in the last 10 years as a management information systems consultant, particularly in e-business, e-commerce and project management information systems. Currently he is a Partner at Neobiz Consulting, a Portuguese management and information systems company.

Index

A

acquisition 196, 198
allospection 196
archetype discovery 195
ARIS extension 81
Arkitema 39, 42, 43, 44, 56, 60
artifacts 64, 65, 71, 197
artificial intelligence (AI) 80
ATP group 39, 40, 41, 44, 45, 56, 60
attitude 243
avatars 64, 65, 72, 73, 75, 76

B

Ba 16, 18, 20, 21, 26, 27, 28, 30, 32, 33, 34
boundary spanners 100
branding 229, 232, 234
brand value 229, 232
business processes 240
business process reengineering 125
business requirements 80
business-to-business (B2B) sales 197
buyer personas 195, 197, 198, 199, 201, 202, 203, 204, 207, 208, 209, 210, 211, 213, 214, 215

C

capabilities 238, 240, 243, 249, 252
combination 134, 137, 138, 142, 152, 157, 158, 159, 160
communities of practice (CoP) 1, 2, 3, 8, 9, 10, 11, 12, 13, 17, 20, 24, 27, 30, 33
competences 238, 239, 242, 243

competitive advantages 148, 149, 150, 151, 152, 183, 184, 185, 186, 187, 189, 192, 193, 237, 238, 239, 240, 242, 243, 250, 251
competitive intelligence 17, 20, 22, 24, 27, 28, 33
competitiveness 229, 232
conclusion drawing 16, 23
control factors 168
core competences 150
corporation book value 229, 230
corporation market value 229
creative process 96, 97, 120, 121, 122, 123, 125, 126, 128, 129, 130, 131
customer capital 229, 230, 231, 232, 233, 234, 235, 236
cybernetics 63, 74

D

data displays 16, 23
data reduction 16, 23, 24
decision making 19, 122, 125
Denmark 39, 42, 46, 52
design of experiments (DOE) 165, 167, 168, 169, 171, 172, 173, 176, 177, 178, 179, 180, 181
Drucker, Peter 122, 151, 152, 162
dynamic learning 122

E

e-commerce services 216, 217, 225
economic and industrial understanding (EIU) 154
empathy 198
enabling conditions 17, 19, 20, 26, 27, 32, 34